ASTRONOMY MADE SIMPLE

NEW REVISED EDITION

ASTRONOMY
MADE SIMPLE

NEW REVISED EDITION

By MEIR H. DEGANI, Sc.D.

SCIENCE DEPARTMENT, STATE UNIVERSITY OF NEW YORK
MARITIME COLLEGE

A Made Simple Book
Doubleday
NEW YORK   LONDON   TORONTO   SYDNEY   AUCKLAND

A Made Simple Book
Published by Doubleday, a division of
Bantam Doubleday Dell Publishing Group, Inc.,
666 Fifth Avenue, New York, New York 10103.

Made Simple and **Doubleday** are trademarks of Doubleday,
a division of Bantam Doubleday Dell Publishing Group, Inc.

Library of Congress Cataloging in Publication Data
Degani, Meir H.
Astronomy made simple.
(Made simple books)
Includes index.
1. Astronomy.   I. Title.
QB44.2.D43 1976   520
ISBN: 0-385-08854-X
Library of Congress Catalog Card Number 76-2836

CONTENTS

Contents

ASTRONOMY MADE SIMPLE

NEW REVISED EDITION

A BRIEF HISTORY OF ASTRONOMY

The history of astronomy may be conveniently divided into three periods: the geocentric, the galactic, and the universal. The first had its beginnings in ancient history, and came to a close in the sixteenth century. The second extends from the seventeenth through the nineteenth centuries. And the third began and continues in the present century.

0.1 THE GEOCENTRIC PERIOD

Early astronomers believed the earth to be in the center of the universe; and assumed that the sun, moon, and stars revolved about that stationary earth. Their interest, hardly scientific in our sense of the term, was mainly in practical matters, in the real and supposed relation of celestial events to those on the earth; in searching the skies for clues to good and evil omens.

Even so, remarkable discoveries were made then. The calendar was developed with great accuracy. The apparent path of the sun among the stars—the ecliptic—was carefully defined. The complete cycle of solar and lunar eclipses was determined. And as early as the second century B.C., the motion of the earth's axis was well understood.

The great figure of Nicolaus Copernicus (1473–1543) is closely associated with the end of the primitive geocentric period in the sixteenth century.

0.2 THE GALACTIC PERIOD

Modern astronomy can be said to have begun in this period. Copernicus demonstrated that the earth, far from being the center of the universe, was merely one of the planets revolving about the central sun.

Hardly unique, the earth was found to be a quite ordinary planet, going through ordinary motions in an ordinary way.

Indeed the central sun itself was realized to be merely one star among the multitudes in the heavens, one among billions of similar stars in every direction about us—some larger, some smaller, some heavier, some lighter than our sun.

In this period the approach became increasingly scientific, motivated largely by the desire to know, to understand the basic laws governing the motion of heavenly bodies, to explain what the eye saw.

Progress from the sixteenth through the nineteenth centuries resulted from the effective combination of extended observation, improved instruments, and the work of scientific genius.

Observation. Great quantities of data of fundamental importance were painstakingly gathered by careful observers, chief among whom is the great name of Tycho Brahe (1546–1601).

Instruments. The introduction of the telescope in 1610 by Galileo Galilei (1564–1642) was, of course, a milestone in the development of the science of astronomy; as was the later invention and introduction of the spectroscope. The two instruments complement one another: the telescope permits us to see the stars more clearly; the spectroscope analyzes stellar light, furnishing us with much information about the stars.

Genius. Like every science, astronomy requires for its advancement the labors of great minds that are able to apply to the observed data insight, imagination, intuition, as well as great learning. Such minds were Johannes Kepler (1571–1630) and Sir Isaac

Newton (1642–1727): Kepler by the discovery of the laws of planetary motion and Newton by the discovery of the Universal Law of Gravitation.

0.3 THE UNIVERSAL PERIOD

Now it became apparent that the galaxy of stars to which our sun belongs is merely one of many galaxies—some larger, some smaller than ours. To these much of the astronomical research of the last half century has been devoted, in an effort to achieve a "complete" picture of the universe. To aid this research ever greater optical telescopes, as well as gigantic radio telescopes, have been constructed.

The great theoretical genius associated most closely with this period in the public mind (although he was primarily a physicist and mathematician) is the late Dr. Albert Einstein (1879–1955). Cosmology and astrophysics depend more and more on his theory of relativity.

This is the astronomic period in which we live. And it is far from concluded.

CHAPTER 1

THE UNIVERSE

PART I: THE COMPONENTS

1.1 INTRODUCTION AND DEFINITIONS

For as long as man has been conscious of himself and the universe he inhabits, he has regarded the sky with awe and wonder—a source of constant and compelling fascination. Awe and wonder generate study and science; man seeking ceaselessly to conquer ignorance and solve mysteries, thus developing finally into the science of astronomy.

Astronomy is the science of the positions, motions, constitutions, histories, and destinies of celestial bodies. In the course of its development as a science, it has already discovered many of the basic laws governing those bodies. But it is the nature of scientific investigation that its work is never done—and here, as elsewhere, immense labors remain to be performed.

1.2 WHY STUDY ASTRONOMY?

We study astronomy because the intelligent, inquiring mind must ask questions and seek answers; must know "Why?" and discover "How?" And from the beginning, whenever man has looked up, there was the sky—always confronting him with seemingly imponderable problems, always challenging him to solve its mysteries.

On one level, man has stated his reaction in magic and mythology, and this has been expressed in the world's art, literature, and religions. On another level, he has attempted to explain the celestial phenomena perceived by his senses in scientific terms—and these explanations are the subject matter of the science of astronomy.

1.3 THE COMPONENTS

The earth we live on is a planet—one of a number of planets that revolve about the sun. The unassisted eye is capable of detecting the sun, several planets, one satellite (our moon), several thousands of stars, shooting stars (meteors), and once in a great while a comet.

These celestial bodies are the components

that constitute the universe, in much the same way that homes, churches, hospitals, and parks are components of a community.

To the best of our knowledge, **the universe consists of stars** (billions and billions of these), nebulae, planets, planetoids, satellites, comets, etc.

1.4 STARS

Stars are large globes of intensely heated gas, shining by their own light. At their surface, they reach temperatures of thousands of degrees; in their interior, temperatures are much higher.

At these temperatures, matter cannot exist either in solid or in liquid form. The gases constituting the stars are much thicker than those on the earth usually are. The extremely high values of their density are due to enormous pressures which prevail in their interior.

Stars move about in space, although their motion is not immediately perceptible. No change in their relative position can be detected in a year. Even in a thousand years, the stars will seem not to have moved substantially. Their pattern now is almost exactly that of a thousand years ago. This seeming fixedness is due to the vast distance separating us from them. At these distances it will take many thousands of years for the stellar pattern to undergo a noticeable change: This **apparent** constancy of position accounts for the popular name "fixed stars."

1.5 NEBULAE

A Nebula is a vast cloud composed of dust and gas. The gases which compose it are extremely thin and of low temperature. Nebulae do not shine by their own light, but are made visible by the light of neighboring stars. When they are so visible, they appear to the unaided eye not unlike a fuzzy star. Their actual size and structure, however, can be determined only with the aid of a telescope. Other nebulae are dark and obscure the stars beyond them.

1.6 PLANETS

The planets that revolve around our sun are large, solid, nearly spherical masses. The best known to us is, of course, our own earth. All of them are relatively cool and are made visible by reflected sunlight; several can be seen at one time or another by the unaided eye. Three planets, however, can be seen only with the aid of a telescope. At first glance, planets look very much like the multitude of stars that glitter in the sky; but an observer can identify a planet by one or more of the following characteristics:

A. Planets shine with a **steady light**, while stars do not. The light reaching our eyes from

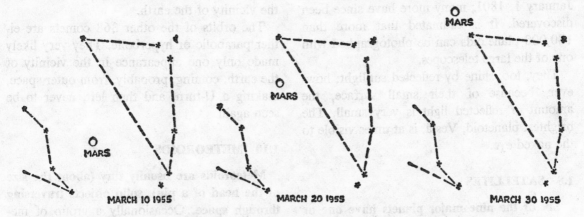

FIG. 1.6. Views of the same part of the sky on three different dates, March 10, March 20, and March 30, 1955. Note that the stars maintain the same relative position. The planet (Mars) has wandered considerably in that time.

stars seems to change rapidly in both color and brightness. These changes in color and brightness cause the **twinkling** of the stars.

B. Planets **wander** in the heavens: A planet which at one time was close to one star may later be observed close to another star. Stars, on the other hand, seem to keep the same positions relative to one another. See Fig. 1.6. The very word "planet" is derived from a Greek word meaning "wanderer."

C. Planets, when observed through telescopes, appear as **small disks** of light. The greater the magnification, the larger will be the diameter of the disk. Stars, even with the largest telescope, appear only as points of light. Even in the 200-inch telescope, they appear as mere points, having no measurable diameter.

D. Planets may be found **only in a narrow strip** in the sky. Their motions are limited to the boundaries of this strip. Stars, of course, may be found in any part of the sky.

1.7 PLANETOIDS

Planetoids are small, irregularly shaped solid bodies revolving, like the major planets, about the sun, and differing from planets primarily in size. They are also known either as asteroids or as minor planets. The largest planetoid, Ceres, has a diameter of 600 miles; but many of them have a diameter of only two miles. The first planetoid was discovered on January 1, 1801; many more have since been discovered. It is estimated that more than 100,000 planetoids can be photographed with one of the large telescopes.

They, too, shine by reflected sunlight; however, because of their small surface, the amount of reflected light is very small. The brightest planetoid, Vesta, is at times visible to the naked eye.

1.8 SATELLITES

Six of the nine major planets have one or more moons revolving round them. These are called satellites. The earth has only one moon (satellite), while the planet Jupiter, for example, has fourteen. To date, thirty-four satellites have been discovered, the last as recently as 1975.

1.9 COMETS

Comets are celestial bodies of unique form and large size which appear from time to time. A typical comet consists of a luminous sphere, or head, connected to a long, tenuous cylinder, or tail. The head may seem as large as the sun; the tail describes an arc in the sky.

To the naked-eye observer a comet appears as motionless as the moon. Actually it moves at speeds of hundreds of miles per second. The exact speed can be determined from its changing position relative to the fixed stars.

There are 625 comets with reliably determined orbits known to date. Several new ones are discovered each year.

The vast majority are too faint to be visible to the naked eye. Fairly great comets are rather rare; these appear, on the average, once or twice in a lifetime.

Of the 625 or so known comets, more than 257 are known to move in "closed orbits"—that is, in more or less elongated, cigar-shaped paths. The fact that the orbit is "closed," has no beginning or end, is of great importance. Comets moving in them go round the same path continuously; many of them have been observed several times during their returns to the vicinity of the earth.

The orbits of the other 368 comets are either parabolic or hyperbolic. They very likely made only one appearance in the vicinity of the earth, coming, probably, from outer space, making a U-turn, and then left, never to be seen again.

1.10 METEOROIDS

Meteoroids are usually tiny (about the size of the head of a pin), solid objects traversing through space. Occasionally a group of meteoroids is attracted to the earth and becomes entangled in its atmosphere. The heat resulting from this encounter consumes the object; the dust resulting from this cremation falls to the earth. Hundreds of tons of meteoric dust descend each year. On rare occasions large meteoroids manage to reach the earth before they are consumed. **The light phenomenon which results from the entry of the meteoroid into the earth's atmosphere is called meteor, or "shooting star,"** the glow of which may persist several seconds.

PART II: THE DESIGN

1.11 INTRODUCTION

The universe is composed of stars, nebulae, planets, comets, and other celestial bodies. Here, the components are assembled to form the design of the universe.

The planets, planetoids, satellites, comets, and meteorites revolve about a single star: the star we call the sun. Together they form the Solar System. The sun, and billions of other stars, form the community of stars known either as Our Galaxy, or the Milky Way Galaxy. The universe contains many such stellar communities, or galaxies.

Stellar distance is of an order of magnitude entirely different from that of planetary distance: the former is enormously greater than the latter.

Distances between galaxies are still greater than distances between stars. In attempting to comprehend such extraordinary distances it is essential to use a scale. The plan of the universe on such a scale is given later in this section.

1.12 THE SUN

Although it may not seem so, the sun is just an ordinary star, similar to numerous other stars that we see in the sky.

The sun appears large to us because it is, relatively speaking, near to us. All other stars appear as small points of light in the sky because they are far away. See Figs. 1.12a and 1.12b. Our interest in this star (the sun) derives from the fact that the earth receives from it both heat and light—energy of funda-

FIG. 1.12a. The sun is just an ordinary star. All the other stars look tiny, as they are so remote that we see them only as mere points of light.

FIG. 1.12b. Other objects, too, appear smaller with increasing distance. Note the apparent size of the distant tree.

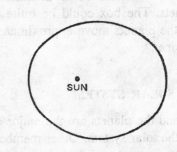

FIG. 1.12c. The oval curve suggests the circumference of the whole universe. The dot represents the location of the sun.

mental importance in maintaining life. The oval curve in Figure 1.12c represents the universe and the dot the position of the sun within the universe. (Note that Fig. 1.12c, as well as Figs. 1.14, 1.16, and 1.17, are symbolic representations and not figures drawn to scale.)

1.13 PLANETS

There are nine planets revolving about the sun: Mercury, Venus, Earth, Mars, Jupiter, Saturn, Uranus, Neptune, and Pluto. Mercury is closest to the sun, and at a somewhat greater distance is Venus; then, the earth; and the farthest known planet from the sun is Pluto.

The earth is 93 million miles from the sun. **This distance is often referred to as an Astronomical Unit.** Mercury is only four tenths the earth's distance from the sun. Pluto, the most distant planet, is forty times the earth's distance. The distance of Pluto can be stated as forty times 93 million miles, or simply as forty astronomical units.

A reducing scale may help to visualize these distances. The scale that is commonly used represents the sun-earth distance as one foot long:

93 million miles equal 1 foot; or,

1 astronomical unit equals 1 foot.

On this scale, Mercury is four tenths of a foot; Venus is seven tenths; and the earth is one foot away from the sun. The farthest planet is forty feet from the sun. A circular box of forty-foot radius could accommodate all the planets. The box could be quite shallow, as all the planets move approximately in the same plane.

1.14 THE SOLAR SYSTEM

The sun and the planets are the major components of the solar system. Other members of this system are:

1. the host of smaller planets known as planetoids or asteroids

2. the several moons, known as satellites, that revolve about six of these planets;
3. comets that appear from time to time;
4. the vast number of meteoroids.

The circle around the dot in Figure 1.14 represents the entire solar system.

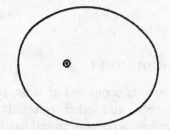

Fig. 1.14. The oval curve suggests the circumference of the whole universe. The dot and the small circle represent the sun and the solar system, respectively.

1.15 THE STARS

Distances to stars are immensely greater than distances to planets. Even the star nearest our own sun is at a distance of 270,000 astronomical units. Using the scale (one foot equals one astronomical unit, or 93 million miles), the star closest to our sun would be at a distance of fifty miles.

The two units should be carefully noted. Distances between planets are stated in **feet,** while those between stars are stated in **miles.** A mental picture might help to visualize this distinction. The sun, and all the planets, could be accommodated in a circular house of forty foot radius. The closest star, by our scale, would be in a house fifty miles away. Other stars, by our scale, are at scale distances of thousands and hundreds of thousands of miles from the sun.

1.16 OUR GALAXY

These stars form a large community called our galaxy or the Milky Way galaxy. It is estimated that the number of stars in our galaxy is close to a hundred billion—otherwise stated as 100×10^9, or a hundred thousand million.

The outer surface of the galaxy is often compared either to a grindstone or to a lens.

A top view of the galaxy would reveal its circular shape as well as the spiral design formed by the stars. A side view would suggest its similarity to a lens, namely, that it is thick in the center, and thins out toward the edges.

Again using the one foot scale, the diameter of the circle would be close to a million miles, while the maximum thickness is only about one sixth of the diameter.

Our galaxy is represented in Figure 1.16.

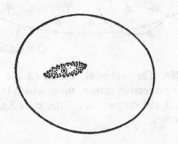

FIG. 1.16. The oval curve represents the circumference of the universe. Our galaxy is indicated inside the oval. The dot and the circle represent the sun and the solar system, respectively.

1.17 OTHER GALAXIES

Ours is not the only galaxy in the universe: many have been discovered in recent years, strikingly similar to our own. The scale distances between them are from ten to twenty million miles. A highly simplified picture of the universe is shown in Figure 1.17.

1.18 SUMMARY

The universe, then, consists of billions of galaxies, as galaxies consist of billions of stars. One of these, the sun, is the star around which our earth moves, as do the other planets of our solar system.

1.19 OUTLINE OF THE UNIVERSE IN TERMS OF ACTUAL DISTANCES

The distance to the sun is 93 million miles; the distance to our nearest star, Alpha-Cen-

FIG. 1.17. The "complete" universe consists of many galaxies. One, containing the sun, is known as our galaxy, the galaxy, or the Milky Way galaxy.

tauri, is 25,000,000,000,000 miles, or 25 million million miles. Distant stars are inconceivably more remote.

The mile unit is of no use in dealing with the distances of stars and galaxies—instead, astronomers use the unit "light-year": one light-year is the distance that a beam of light travels in one year. The distance covered by a beam of light in one second is 186,000 miles; hence:

One light-year=

$$186{,}000 \times 60 \left(\frac{\text{seconds}}{\text{minute}} \right) \times 60 \left(\frac{\text{minutes}}{\text{hour}} \right)$$

$$\times 24 \left(\frac{\text{hours}}{\text{day}} \right) \times 365\frac{1}{4} = 5{,}880{,}000{,}000{,}000 \text{ miles}$$

or 6 million million miles, approximately.

The star nearest the solar system is 4.3 light-years away. The diameter of our galaxy is about 100,000 light-years; its maximum thickness is 15,000 light-years. An average distance between galaxies would be approximately a million light-years.

The sun is only a minute fraction of a light-year from the earth. The distance to the sun may be stated as 8 light minutes.

Distances to heavenly bodies, when stated in terms of light, have an added meaning—for the sun, it implies that it takes a beam of sunlight 8 minutes to reach the earth.

So for the stars. A ray of light from Alpha-Centauri reaches the earth 4⅓ years after leaving the star.

The most distant object seen by the unaided eye is the Andromeda galaxy—2 million light-years away. The light entering the observer's eye has been en route for that time.

1.20 A BRIEF HISTORY OF THE UNIVERSE

The most tenable theory to date for the history of the universe is the one known as the "big bang theory." According to that theory, all the matter and all energy that is present in the universe was once concentrated in a small, enormously hot, preposterously dense ball.

Then 10, or more, thousand million years ago the ball exploded (big bang!), sending into space torrents of gas (primarily protons, neutrons, electrons, and some alpha particles), immersed in a vast ocean of radiation.

As time went on, concentration of matter formed in that turbulent gas—each concentration contracting in response to its own gravitational field, while moving outward in the ever-expanding universe.

These concentrations of gas (also known as nebulae) became galaxies when they fragmented into massive blobs to form protostars (masses of gas that in due course of time are destined to become stars).

Many of these protostars, while shrinking and flattening under influence of their own gravitational and centrifugal forces, became unstable, causing smaller masses of gas to break away and form protoplanets; and the protoplanets similarly produced protosatellites.

The protostars eventually became stars; the protoplanets and protosatellites, after proper cooling, condensing, and contracting, became planets and satellites.

To the best of our knowledge, the transition of our sun from a protostar to a star took place some 5 billion years ago. The planets and the satellites of the solar system were formed shortly thereafter.

1.21 WHAT DOES THE UNAIDED EYE SEE?

On a clear night far away from city lights, the naked eye can see

A. Some 2,000 to 3,000 stars in each hemisphere of the sky. Some of these are only a few

light-years away, others at distances of many hundreds of light-years.

NOTE: To the human eye, all of these stars appear equally distant and it is helpful to imagine that all these stars are attached to the inside of an imaginary large sphere called the celestial sphere. See Fig. 1.21a.

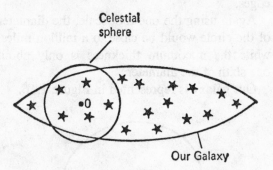

FIG. 1.21a. The celestial sphere is an imaginary spherical projection screen, upon which the observer, situated at the center, "sees" the stars and other celestial bodies.

B. Several planets traveling among the stars, each planet at its own characteristic velocity.

C. Meteors, five or ten every hour, each streaking across the sky and leaving a flash of light in its wake.

D. Comets, really bright ones—once or twice in a lifetime.

E. Nebulae—e.g., the great emission nebula in Orion.

F. The Milky Way. An irregular belt describing a complete circuit of light on the surface of the celestial sphere. The belt varies from 5° to 50° in width. The light is due to the combined radiation emitted by the billions of stars along the long dimension of our flattened galaxy (lines AB in Figure 1.21b). This band contrasts with the relative darkness (due to the paucity of stars) along the narrow dimension (lines AC) of the galaxy.

G. Other galaxies—e.g., the galaxy in Andromeda, that can be seen in northern latitudes and the two galaxies known as Magellanic Clouds in southern latitudes.

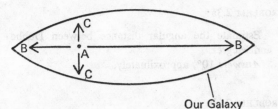

Our Galaxy

FIG. 1.21b. An observer at point A sees the merging light from billions of stars along lines AB. This forms the Milky Way. There are much fewer stars along lines AC, hence comparative darkness.

CHAPTER 2

STARS WITHOUT A TELESCOPE

PART I: THE BIG DIPPER

2.1 INTRODUCTION

Astronomy is one of the several sciences engaged in the study of nature. Much remains to be learned, and many important discoveries can still be made without the use of any equipment. The sky is the laboratory. The time is any fine, clear evening. The place is outdoors, preferably away from city lights, with an unobstructed view of the sky.

The brighter stars appear on the celestial sphere in groups known as constellations.

The names of forty-eight constellations are listed in a catalog published as long ago as A.D. 150.

The ancients either imagined that the groups formed pictures of gods, heroes, animals, etc., or they wanted to honor their gods, heroes, animals, etc., and named the constellations accordingly.

Modern astronomy recognizes eighty-eight constellations, each with its own clearly defined boundaries and each bearing the name originally given to it. The eighty-eight areas completely cover the celestial sphere.

NOTE: Celestial objects outside our own galaxy are also identified with the constellation in which they are seen. Hence the names "galaxy in Andromeda" or "galaxy in Ursa Major."

In this chapter, we shall pay particular attention to some thirty well-known constellations, such as Orion, the Big and Small Dippers, Cassiopeia, and so on, and we shall begin with the group that is probably easiest to identify—the Big Dipper. As its name implies, the stars form the outline of a dipper. It is important to become familiar with that group of stars as it is with reference to it that the locations of other constellations are most often determined. The Big Dipper can be seen every clear evening in most of the northern hemisphere. This section deals primarily with the stars of that constellation.

2.2 THE STARS OF THE BIG DIPPER

Seven bright stars form the pattern of the Dipper. The four forming the "bowl" are known as Dubhe, Merak, Phecda, and Megrez, all Arabic names: Dubhe means "bear," Merak "loin," Phecda and Megrez, "thigh" and "the root of the bear's tail," respectively.

The stars forming the "handle" of the Dipper are known as Alkaid, Mizar, and Alioth, also Arabic names, meaning "the chief," and "the apron"; the precise meaning of the name "Alioth" is still disputed.

Close to Mizar is the small star Alcor. The Arabs called these two stars "the Horse and the Rider." The star Alcor was used by them in a test for good eyesight. See Fig. 2.2

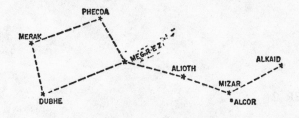

Fig. 2.2. The Big Dipper.

2.3   SCALE OF ANGULAR DISTANCES

Locations of stars are stated in terms of angles or arcs. The angular distance, measured in degrees, is the angle or arc, subtended by these stars at the vantage point of the observer.

FIG. 2.3a. The angular distance of the full moon is about half a degree.

It is of importance to be able to gauge small angles in the sky. The diameter of the full moon is about half a degree, otherwise stated more formally as: The angle, or arc, subtended at our eye by the diameter of the full moon is .5°. See Fig. 2.3a.

Another angular distance often used is the one between Dubhe and Merak—close to five degrees.

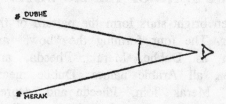

FIG. 2.3b. The angle subtended by Dubhe and Merak at the eye of a terrestial observer is close to 5°.

Ten moons could be placed side by side in the distance between these two stars. See Fig. 2.3b.

PROBLEM 2.3a:

Estimate the angular distance between Dubhe and Megrez.
Answer: 10°, approximately.

PROBLEM 2.3b:

Find the North Star, using the following data: (See Fig. 2.17.)
a. The North Star is on the extension of the line joining Dubhe and Merak.
b. It is 29° from Dubhe, and, of course, 34° from Merak.

2.4   LEGENDS

One of the early names given to this constellation was the "Great Bear" and the Arabic names meaning "thigh," "loin," etc., describe parts of the bear. See Fig. 2.4.

FIG. 2.4 The Great Bear. Note the position of the Big Dipper.

The reason for this is not known, as an observer can scarcely imagine the outline of a bear or any other animal in that constellation.

An ancient legend held that the Bear represented Callisto, a daughter of the King of Arcadia, beloved of Jupiter, who, in order to protect her, changed her into a Bear and transferred her to the skies.

Another legend held that the Great Spirit purposely put the Great Bear in the sky to act as a "calendar" for earthly bears. During the half year when the Great Bear is low in the sky, all earthly bears stay in their dens and keep warm. When the Bear is high in the sky, bears leave their dens, for summer has begun.

2.5   OTHER NAMES

The names Great Bear and Big Dipper are still in common use. The scientific name for the constellation is the Latin translation of

Great Bear—Ursa Major. In England, the constellation is known as the Plough, or the Wain (for wagon).

NOTE: To be accurate, the term Big Dipper should be used to refer to the seven bright stars and the term Great Bear or Ursa Major to refer to all the stars in the constellation. Often, however, these terms are used interchangeably.

2.6 APPARENT BRIGHTNESS OF STARS

The seven stars of the Big Dipper differ materially in apparent brightness. The brightest star is Alioth; the faintest, Megrez.

Technically this is stated in terms of apparent magnitude. Alioth has the smallest apparent magnitude (1.7); Megrez, the largest (3.4).

2.7 HIPPARCHUS' CLASSIFICATION OF STARS ACCORDING TO BRIGHTNESS

The ancient Greek astronomers classified the visible stars according to their apparent brightness, into six classes. This basic classification, in the main, is still valid. To Hipparchus, who lived on the island of Rhodes in the second century B.C., goes the credit for this classification. The twenty brightest stars known to him were arbitrarily designated as stars of the **first magnitude;** and the next fifty in order of apparent brightness were designated as stars of the **second magnitude;** and so on. The designation of **sixth magnitude** was given to several hundred stars barely visible to the normal human eye. See Fig. 2.7. Thus a completely arbitrary clas-

sification of stars, according to their brightness, was obtained. These magnitudes are, however, only *apparent* magnitudes. Some stars are actually bright, but appear faint because of their great distance.

2.8 DECIMAL DIVISION OF APPARENT MAGNITUDES

In the nineteenth century, the decimal division was introduced. In this classification, a star of magnitude 5.5 has an apparent brightness halfway between that of a star of magnitude 5.0 and that of a star of magnitude 6.0. Similarly, to state that the North Star (Polaris) has a magnitude of 2.1 signifies that its apparent brightness is only slightly less than the brightness of a star of magnitude 2.0. Increasingly, the decimal method of denoting magnitudes has been applied more extensively and made more precise.

2.9 RELATION BETWEEN APPARENT MAGNITUDE AND APPARENT BRIGHTNESS

There is a simple relationship between the apparent magnitude and apparent brightness.

This is based on a psychophysical law that states that if a stimulus, e.g., brightness, increases in a geometric progression, such as 1,2,4,8,16, etc., the sensation resulting from it increases in an arithmetic progression 1,2, 3,4,5, etc.

From that law it was determined empirically that magnitude 2 stars are 2.5 (more precisely, 2.512) times brighter than magnitude 3 stars. Similarly, magnitude 3 stars are 2.512 times brighter than magnitude 4 stars, and so on.

PROBLEM 2.9:

The star Dubhe in the constellation Ursa Major has an apparent magnitude of 2.0. An unknown star, X, had an apparent magnitude of 4.0. How much brighter is Dubhe than star X?

Solution: A decrease in one order of magnitude corresponds to an increase of 2.5 times in apparent

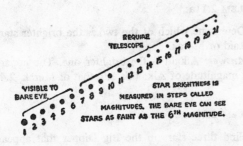

FIG. 2.7. The relationship between brightness and magnitude.

brightness. A decrease of two orders of magnitude is the same as an increase of $2.5 \times 2.5 = 6.25$ times in apparent brightness.

Answer: To the eye, Dubhe will appear more than six times brighter than the star X.

Stars down to magnitude 19 are visible with the 200-inch Mount Palomar telescope, and stars as dim as magnitude 24 can be photographed (long exposure) with that telescope. Even fainter stars can be photographed with the aid of image tubes (see Sec. 5.24).

2.10 ZERO AND NEGATIVE VALUES OF APPARENT MAGNITUDE

The twenty stars originally designated as first magnitude stars were subsequently regrouped. This was necessary because some of the stars were much brighter than others. The brighter stars of this group were designated as having magnitudes of .9, .8, .7, etc., through .0 to negative numbers. The star with the greatest apparent brightness at night is Sirius. Its apparent magnitude is −1.6. On the same scale, the apparent magnitude of our sun is 26.7.

2.11 DETERMINING APPARENT MAGNITUDES

The method of determining the magnitude of stars by observation is rather simple. With practice, fairly accurate results (an accuracy of .1 of a magnitude) can be obtained. The method was used extensively by the German astronomer Friedrich Argelander (1799–1875) and his associates in the preparation of the great star catalog, the "B.D. Catalog." (B.D. is the abbreviation of the German title of the catalog, *Bonner Durchmusterung*—"Bonn Catalog.") By this method, the observer compares the apparent brightness of a star with two or more neighboring stars of known magnitudes. Thus, a star that appears somewhat fainter than a neighboring star of 2.4 magnitude and somewhat brighter than another neighboring star of 2.6 magnitude, will be designated as having a magnitude of 2.5. In using this method it is advisable to make sure that:

A. The star to be measured and the known magnitude stars should be at about the same distance above the horizon.

B. The known magnitude stars should be as close as possible to the star to be measured.

C. One of the known magnitude stars should be somewhat brighter and the other somewhat fainter than the star to be measured.

The following table contains a list of stars of known apparent magnitude. These can be used for the determination of magnitude of many other stars.

Star	Constellation	Apparent Magnitude
Alpheratz	Andromeda	2.2
Schedar	Cassiopeia	2.5
Diphda	Cetus	2.2
Achernar	Eridanus	.6
Hamal	Aries	2.2
Acamar	Eridanus	3.1
Aldebaran	Taurus	1.1
Rigel	Orion	.3
Capella	Auriga	.2
Bellatrix	Orion	1.7
Canopus	Carina	− .9
Sirius	Canis Major	−1.6
Procyon	Canis Minor	.5
Pollux	Gemini	1.2
Regulus	Leo	1.3
Dubhe	Ursa Major	2.0
Acrux	Crux	1.1
Arcturus	Boötes	.2
Zubenelgenubi	Libra	2.9
Shaula	Scorpius	1.7
Nunki	Sagittarius	2.1
Markab	Pegasus	2.6

NOTE: On maps these figures are rounded off to the nearest integer.

PROBLEM 2.11a:

Determine which of the two is the brighter star, Alkaid or Merak.

Answer: Alkaid is the brighter one. The apparent magnitude of Alkaid is 1.9; that of Merak, 2.4.

PROBLEM 2.11b:

Find three stars in the Big Dipper that appear to be of equal brightness.

Answer: Mizar, Merak, and Phecda have almost

the same apparent brightness. Precisely, they are designated as being 2.4, 2.4, and 2.5 magnitude stars, respectively. Phecda is by a very slight degree fainter than the other two.

PROBLEM 2.11c:

Determine the apparent magnitude of the North Star (Polaris).

Answer: Polaris is but slightly brighter than Merak, and slightly fainter than Dubhe. It is usually designated as a 2.1 magnitude star.

Note again, this refers to **apparent** magnitudes. Actually, Polaris is much brighter than our sun—in fact, nearly 1,500 times brighter. The great distance accounts for its being only a magnitude 2.1 star. Stated in terms of time, it takes light, traveling at the speed of 186,000 miles per second, 8⅓ minutes to reach earth from the sun; and 400 years to reach earth from Polaris.

2.12 APPARENT DAILY MOTIONS OF STARS

It is common knowledge that the sun seems to rise in the east, describe an arc in the sky, and set in the west.

The stars, too, seem to move in arcs in the sky—also from the eastern to the western part of the horizon. A complete revolution takes 23 hours, 56 minutes and 4.09 seconds. This can very easily be approximately verified any clear evening with the aid of a good watch.

PROBLEM 2.12:

Object: To verify a complete revolution of a star. (This period is known as a "sidereal" day, or a "starday.")
Equipment: A good watch.
Procedure:
a. Note the time at which some bright star appears just above the eastern horizon.

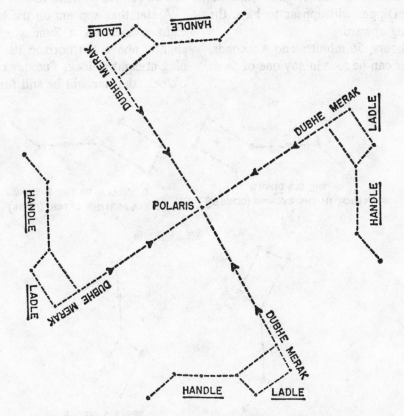

FIG. 2.12. In the course of approximately 24 hours, the Big Dipper completes one revolution in the sky. Only part of that circle can actually be observed, as sunlight makes it impossible to observe the stars during the daytime. This figure shows the Big Dipper at 6-hour intervals.

b. The next day repeat the procedure under (a).

Results: The experiment demonstrates that every star completes one apparent revolution in 23 hours, 56 minutes and 4 seconds.

The term "apparent" is often repeated here for good reason. The motion is really *only* apparent; it may even be considered an optical illusion. Actually it is the earth, spinning on its axis in the opposite direction, that causes the stars to seem to move as they do.

This daily rotation can also very effectively be observed by watching a constellation, such as Ursa Major.

If, when first observed, the constellation appears level with the bowl on the right:

Six hours later it will appear with the handle pointed downward;

Twelve hours after the original observation, the Big Dipper will appear with the open part of the bowl pointing downward;

Eighteen hours after the original observation, the Big Dipper will appear to have the handle pointing upward.

In any 23 hours, 56 minutes and 4 seconds, the Big Dipper can be seen in any one of those positions.

During part of that time, the sun will interfere with the observations. The faint starlight cannot be discerned in the bright sky of day.

2.13   THE APPARENT ANNUAL MOTION OF THE STARS

The fact that stars complete a revolution in less than twenty-four hours is of great importance. It signifies, of course, that the stars make more than one revolution in a 24-hour period.

The difference between 24 and the period of revolution is:

$$\begin{array}{r} 24 \text{ hours} \\ -23 \text{ hours, 56 minutes, 4 seconds} \\ \hline 3 \text{ minutes, 56 seconds.} \end{array}$$

Thus, the stars begin the next revolution in the remaining 3 minutes and 56 seconds. This can be verified by observation.

A star that appears on the horizon, say, at eight o'clock on a Sunday evening will be slightly **above** the horizon the following evening at eight o'clock. Tuesday evening at eight o'clock, the star will be still further above the

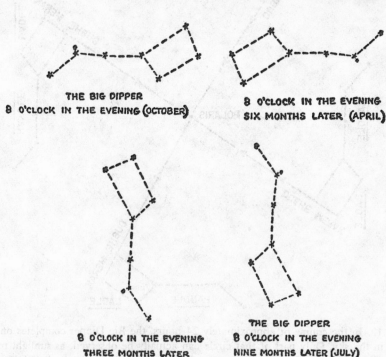

THE BIG DIPPER
8 O'CLOCK IN THE EVENING (OCTOBER)

8 O'CLOCK IN THE EVENING
SIX MONTHS LATER (APRIL)

8 O'CLOCK IN THE EVENING
THREE MONTHS LATER

THE BIG DIPPER
8 O'CLOCK IN THE EVENING
NINE MONTHS LATER (JULY)

FIG. 2.13.

horizon and a month later at eight o'clock in the evening, the star will be substantially above the horizon.

After three months, at eight o'clock in the evening, the star will be a quarter of a circle away from the eastern horizon. At the end of a year, the star will have completed an apparent circle.

This movement of a star is also an *apparent* movement. It is due to the **real** movement of the earth about the sun. The earth completes a revolution around the sun in 12 months.

This apparent annual movement of stars obtains for constellations as well.

Thus Ursa Major at eight o'clock in the eve-

ning in October is close to the horizon with the bowl opening upward.

Three months later at the same time in the evening, the handle will point downward.

In April at the same time of the evening, the Big Dipper will be high above the horizon and will appear with the bowl to the left.

In July at the same time of the evening, the Big Dipper will appear with the bowl at the bottom.

Thus in a period of 365¼ days, the Big Dipper completes 366¼ apparent revolutions: 365¼ of them are due to the rotation of the earth on its axis, and one is due to the revolution of the earth about the sun.

PART II: NORTH CIRCUMPOLAR STARS

2.14 INTRODUCTION

At any given latitude some stars appear to rise and set; **others, called circumpolar stars, are continuously above the horizon.** Circumpolar (=near the pole) stars can be seen every night of the year, weather permitting. They would be observable during the day as well were it not for the interference of the sun, whose bright light makes it impossible to discern the faint light of the stars.

2.15 LATITUDE AND NORTH CIRCUMPOLAR STARS

The number of north circumpolar stars varies with latitude, increasing with distance from the equator. To an observer at 20° N, the stars of the Big Dipper are not circumpolar—they rise and set and, part of the time, are below the horizon. To an observer at 40° N, however, the stars of the Big Dipper are circumpolar.

2.16 NORTH CIRCUMPOLAR CONSTELLATIONS

In addition to the Big Dipper (Ursa Major), four other well-known constellations are continuously in view in latitudes north of

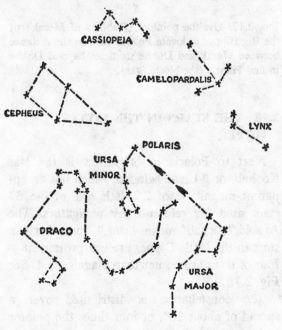

FIG. 2.16. North circumpolar constellations.

40°. These are the Little Dipper (Ursa Minor), Cassiopeia, the Dragon (Draco), and Cepheus. See Fig. 2.16.

2.17 THE LITTLE DIPPER

The best known and brightest star in this constellation is the North Star. It is easy to locate: The starting points are two stars in the bowl of the Big Dipper, Dubhe, and Merak, known as the Pointers. An extension of the line joining these two stars points to the North Star, which is also known by the names **Polaris** and **α (alpha)-Ursae Minoris**. The angular distance from Dubhe to Polaris is 6 times the pointer distance. See Fig. 2.17.

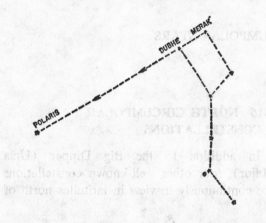

FIG. 2.17. Use the pointers (Dubhe and Merak) of the Big Dipper to locate Polaris. Extend the distance between Merak and Dubhe six times beyond Dubhe to find Polaris (the North Star).

2.18 THE STARS IN THE LITTLE DIPPER

Next to Polaris in brightness is the star Kochab, or β-Ursae Minoris, which has an apparent magnitude of 2.2 **It is one of the 57 stars used for reference by navigators.** The Arabic "kochab" means "star." The other five stars in the Little Dipper are less prominent— four of them are fainter than magnitude 4. See Fig. 2.18.

The constellation is distributed over a spread of about 20°, or four times the pointer distance.

FIG. 2.18. The stars of the Little Dipper.

2.19 LEGENDS

The Little Dipper is known also as the Little Bear or Ursa Minor and, as in the case of the Great Bear, the name is entirely inappropriate. See Fig. 2.19.

According to a remarkable American Indian legend about the Little Bear, an Indian hunting party had lost its way in the forest. In answer to their prayers, a little girl appeared to guide them safely to their homes. She proved to be the spirit of the North Star; and the hunters, after their death, were placed in heaven to be close to her, forever.

FIG. 2.19. The Little Bear.

2.20 THE NORTH STAR IN NAVIGATION

The North Star is often used to determine:

A. The north point on the horizon (geographic north).
B. The latitude of the observer.

Geographic north is located by dropping a vertical line from Polaris to the horizon. The point at which the vertical line touches the horizon circle is geographic north.

The determination of latitude is based on the formula:

Latitude of any place in the northern hemisphere=Altitude of North Star at same place.

Thus, to an observer at 40° N, the star Polaris has an altitude of 40°; to an observer at 60° N, it would have an altitude of 60°; and so on.

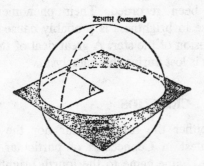

FIG. 2.20. The observer is at A. The altitude of the star is the angle between a line to the star and a line to the horizon. The angle is also denoted by A. When the star is close to the horizon the altitude is small; when the star is at zenith the angle is 90°.

The altitude of a star, measured in degrees, is the angle along a vertical circle between the horizon of the observer and the star. The angle A in Figure 2.20 represents the altitude of the star.

2.21 THE CELESTIAL POLES

The name Polaris derives from the fact that the pole of the earth, if extended, would intersect the sky very close to this star. **This extension of the earth's axis is known as the celestial axis.**

Theoretically, the celestial axis extends an infinite distance both up and down. "Up" in this case means beyond the earth's North Pole; "down," the earth's South Pole. The earth's axis is only a minute part of the celestial axis. **The points at which the celestial axis pierces the sky are known as North Celestial Pole and South Celestial Pole, respectively.**

The celestial poles are the intersections of the extended axis with the celestial sphere. See Fig. 2.21.

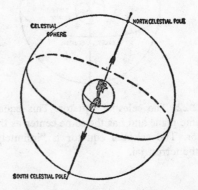

FIG. 2.21. The celestial axis is the extension of the earth's axis. The point where the northern part of the axis intersects the celestial sphere is the North Celestial Pole. The intersection of the southern extension of the axis with the celestial sphere is the South Celestial Pole. We discussed the celestial sphere in Section 1.20 and noted there that the celestial sphere is a figment of the imagination. No definite size can be ascribed to it. It may be assumed to have an "infinite" radius.

NOTE: Astronomy deals with two spheres: one is the earth; another, infinitely larger than the earth, is a "projection screen" upon which we see all the stars in the heavens.

It should be noted that we live on the *outside* of the real terrestrial sphere and *inside* the imaginary celestial sphere.

2.22 THE CELESTIAL EQUATOR

The points on the celestial sphere halfway between the north and the south celestial poles form the celestial equator.

Theoretically, the celestial equator is a circle of infinite radius, lying in the same plane as the earth's equator, the two circles having the same center.

Another way of visualizing the celestial equator is by imagining that the radius of the earth's equator is made increasingly large, until the circle coincides with the inner surface of the celestial sphere. See Fig. 2.22.

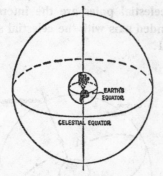

FIG. 2.22. The celestial equator. This equator is in the same plane and has the same center as the earth's equator. The celestial equator is "infinitely" larger than the terrestrial.

2.23 CASSIOPEIA AND CEPHEUS

An extension of the line through the pointers of the Big Dipper, beyond the North Star, leads to the constellations of Cepheus and Cassiopeia. Cepheus has the shape of a triangle built on a square; and Cassiopeia is somewhat similar to the letters M or W. See Fig. 2.23.

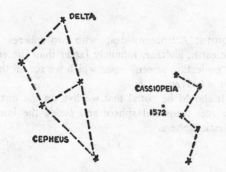

FIG. 2.23. The constellations Cepheus and Cassiopeia. Note that the latter appears either as a W or an M depending on whether she is below Polaris or above that star. The point marked 1572 is the location of Tycho Brahe's star.

2.24 TYCHO'S STAR

The constellation Cassiopeia made history in 1572. On November 11 of that year, a "new" star quite suddenly appeared in that constellation, bright enough at one time to be seen in daylight. The Danish astronomer, Tycho Brahe (1546–1601), made a careful study of that "new" star and recorded a detailed description of its adventures. The historic star has long since lost its tremendous brightness. It is still known as **Tycho's star.**

Tycho's star would now be classified as a Supernova. **Supernovae are stars that quite suddenly increase in brightness tremendously**—many million times their original brightness. This increase is followed by a gradual decline, at the end of which the star retains only a small fraction of its original pre-supernova brightness. Other supernovae have also been recorded. Their phenomenal increase in brightness is probably caused by an explosion of the star. A great deal of the star's mass is lost during this cataclysm.

2.25 CEPHEIDS

Neither the brightest star nor the second brightest in Cepheus is of particular importance. Fame came to the fourth brightest star in that constellation, δ (delta)-Cephei.

Many hundreds of stars are currently classified as "Cepheids." These are **variable-brightness** stars. δ (delta)-Cephei's maximum brightness is two and a half times greater than its minimum. Its apparent magnitude varies from a maximum 3.3 to a minimum 4.5 in highly regular periods of 5 days, 8 hours, 47 minutes, 39 seconds.

The probable reason for this variation in brightness is pulsation. The volume of such stars seems to increase and decrease periodically, producing changes in brightness.

Astronomy owes a special debt to these stars. The Cepheids are of enormous aid in estimating distances to the farthest points in the universe. Thus, distances to neighboring galaxies are determined with the aid of these variable brightness stars.

2.26 THE MILKY WAY

The Milky Way passes through Cassiopeia and Cepheus, appearing to the naked eye as a narrow band of hazy light. (The Milky Way was fully discussed in section 1.21.)

2.27 LEGENDS ABOUT CASSIOPEIA AND CEPHEUS

According to mythology, Cassiopeia was the beautiful but vain Queen of Ethiopia. Her husband was Cepheus, and their daughter, Andromeda. As punishment for her vanity, Cassiopeia was doomed to be transformed into a group of stars traveling eternally round the pole, watched over by her jealous husband, Cepheus.

2.28 THE CONSTELLATION DRAGON

The Latin name for "dragon" is "draco." This is a fairly long and curving constellation —part of it, halfway between the Big and Little Dippers; the rest coiling about the Little Dipper, ending in a group of four stars. These four stars mark the head of the Dragon. See Fig. 2.28.

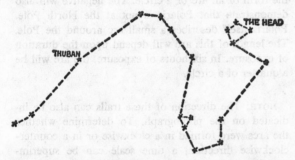

THE HEAD

THUBAN

FIG. 2.28. The constellation Dragon. Note the star Thuban in Draco; 5,000 years ago it was the North Star. The earth's axis was pointing to that star. In the year A.D. 22,000 it will again be the North Star.

Five thousand years ago Thuban or α (alpha)-Draconis was the North Star, because the North Celestial Pole was near it. At that time Thuban appeared as the only "stationary" star in the sky, all the other stars describing circles about it. Thuban was venerated by the Egyptians. At present, the North Celestial Pole is near Polaris.

The North Celestial Pole describes a complete circle once every 25,800 years. The motion of the North Celestial Pole, as well as that of the South Celestial Pole, is due to the fact that the axis of our earth precesses, i.e.,

describes a slender double cone, once every 25,800 years.

2.29 A MAP OF NORTH CIRCUMPOLAR CONSTELLATIONS

The constellations near the North Celestial Pole are indicated on Fig. 2.16.

Each star in a constellation is designated by a Greek letter.

GREEK ALPHABET (LOWER CASE)

α	alpha	ι	iota	ρ	rho
β	beta	κ	kappa	σ	sigma
γ	gamma	λ	lambda	τ	tau
δ	delta	μ	mu	υ	upsilon
ε	epsilon	ν	nu	φ	phi
ζ	zeta	ξ	xi	χ	chi
η	eta	o	omicron	ψ	psi
θ	theta	π	pi	ω	omega

2.30 NAMES OF STARS

Some sixty well-known stars are often called by proper names. Among these are Polaris (the North Star), Sirius (the brightest star in the sky), Kochab, and Regulus.

Generally, the stars are identified by Greek letters, used as prefixes to the constellation. The stars in the Big Dipper are known as α (alpha)-Ursae Majoris, β (beta)-Ursae Majoris, γ (gamma)-Ursae Majoris, and so on. (The genitive form of the constellation is used: The genitive of Ursa Major in Latin is Ursae Majoris.)

Usually the brightest star gets the α (alpha) prefix; the second brightest is denoted by β (beta); and so on.* The brightest star in the constellation Big Dog (Canis Major) is known as α (alpha)-Canis Majoris. The third brightest star in the constellation Twins (Gemini) is known as γ (gamma)-Geminorum. If the number of bright stars in a constellation exceeds the number of Greek letters, lower case Roman letters are also used. Should the number of stars surpass the num-

* There are exceptions to this. Thus the brightest star in the constellation Twins (Gemini) is designated β (beta)-Geminorum, while the second brightest star in that constellation is known as α (alpha)-Geminorum.

ber of letters in both alphabets, astronomers resort to Arabic numerals.

2.31 HOW TO USE A STELLAR MAP

Beginners in astronomy often have difficulty in using a map. It is not clear perhaps how the map should be held so as to correspond with the stars in the sky. The difficulty is probably due to the fact that the observer is on the **outer** surface of one sphere (the earth) observing the stars on the **inner** surface of another sphere (the celestial sphere).

To use this map properly, imagine that it has glue on its reverse side, like a postage stamp. The map is to be pasted to the **inner** surface of the celestial sphere. The "glue" will thus "stick" to the stars. Before attaching the map, it is necessary to align it properly: Make Polaris on the map cover Polaris in the sky; and the Big Dipper on the map cover the Big Dipper in the sky. The other stars on the map will then correctly represent the real stars.

2.32 APPARENT DAILY AND ANNUAL MOTION OF THE STARS

Every star and every constellation takes part in these apparent rotations, and it is a great pleasure to watch the stars move in their assigned orbits.

It is an even greater pleasure to photograph the trails of these stars. Rather good photographs can be obtained with relatively inexpensive equipment. The procedure for this follows:

Object: To obtain a star-trail photograph of the circumpolar region.

Equipment:
a. A good camera.
b. Fast plate or film.
c. Flashlight.

Procedure:
a. Point camera so as to bring Polaris to center of film.
b. Focus, carefully, on Polaris.
c. Open shutter to widest aperture compatible with a good definition of the stars.
d. Expose for several hours. Four to five hours is a reasonable time.
e. Dew may form on lens. Should this happen, it must be wiped off at intervals. Do not shift the camera while wiping the lens. Careful use of a dim flashlight may help. The flashlight should never be pointed into the lens.
f. Develop the negative.

Results: The developed negative will show the trails of the circumpolar stars. Each trail will be in the form of an arc of a circle. The negative will also demonstrate that Polaris is not at the North Pole. Polaris itself describes a small arc around the Pole. The length of this arc will depend upon the duration of exposure. In six hours of exposure, the arc will be a quarter of a circle.

NOTE: The direction of these trails can also be indicated on the photograph. To determine whether the arcs were formed in a clockwise or in a counterclockwise direction, a time scale can be superimposed on these trails. To accomplish this, the exposure is interrupted at fixed intervals. The first interval may be one hour; the next two intervals, half hours; the remainder of the time, at fifteen-minute intervals. From the different lengths of arc formed by the same star, the apparent rotation is easily deduced.

PART III: NON-CIRCUMPOLAR STARS

2.33 INTRODUCTION

The previous section dealt with the stars that can be seen in the northern hemisphere every night of the year—the north circumpolar stars of the north circumpolar constellations.

The present section deals with stars that are above the horizon at night only part of the year for observers in the middle latitudes. The rest of the year they are above the horizon during daytime and cannot be seen. But since stars, because of their annual apparent rotation, rise four minutes earlier each day, they

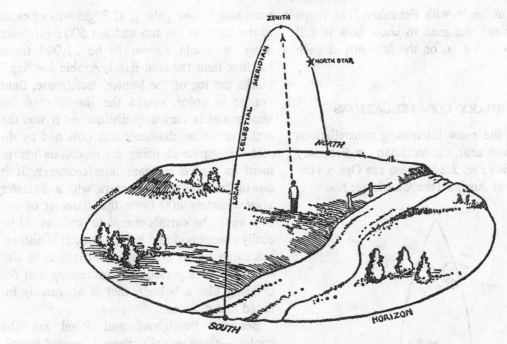

FIG. 2.33. The local celestial meridian is an imaginary circle in the sky. It goes through the north and south points on the horizon and the zenith. Observe the stars at about 8 P.M. near the middle of the month and in a year's time you will see the entire parade of stars pass this line.

will eventually be seen above the horizon during the nighttime hours.

The middle latitudes include most of the United States, Canada, and Europe.

Watching the stars may be compared to watching a parade. Over a period of twelve months, the complete parade of non-circumpolar stars can be observed. This parade repeats itself, year after year.

Becoming familiar with many of the bright stars is not difficult; nor is learning some of the well-known constellations. To accomplish this, you need not look for them all over the sky. An imaginary circle can be drawn across the sky and the constellations observed as they approach or cross the circle. The circle that can serve this purpose most conveniently is the **Local Celestial Meridian.** This circle goes through the zenith, and the north and south points on the observer's horizon. The **Zenith is the point in the sky directly above the observer.** Only half of this celestial meridian, of course, is above the horizon.

The best way to outline the local celestial meridian in the sky is by drawing an imaginary line through the following three points (Fig. 2.33):

A. North on the horizon. A simple magnetic compass will help here.
B. Zenith—the point in the sky directly above the observer.
C. The point marking south on the horizon. Use a magnetic compass.

Note that the local celestial meridian will also go through Polaris, the North Star.

The parade of stars is conveniently divided into twelve parts, one part for each month.

The constellations near the celestial meridian each month are described below. A description of the stars as they appear on one evening a month will serve our purpose. If you learn how the sky looks on one evening a month, or twelve evenings a year, you will be familiar with the nightly appearance of the sky. We can begin with any month and any hour. Let us begin with February. The maps of the sky are designed to show how it will look at about 8 P.M. on the fifteenth of each month.

2.34 FEBRUARY CONSTELLATIONS

Two of the most interesting constellations can be found near the meridian on February evenings. See Fig. 2.34. These are Orion (the Hunter) and Auriga (the Charioteer).

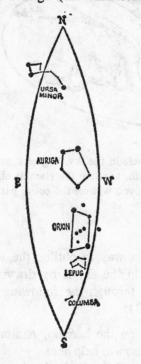

FIG. 2.34. February constellations. The constellations near the local celestial meridian at 8 P.M. about the middle of February. Follow instructions on how to use the map in Sec. 2.31. Only the more familiar constellations are indicated. Stars of the third magnitude and brighter are shown, as well as fourth-magnitude stars that are part of the design usually associated with the constellation. The size of the dot corresponds to the brightness of the star. The larger the dot, the brighter the star.

2.35 THE STARS IN ORION

Rigel and Betelgeuse are the two bright stars in this constellation. See Fig. 2.35. Rigel is the seventh brightest star in terms of apparent brightness. In reality, it is a most lumi-

nous star in our galaxy. If Rigel was as close to the earth as the sun and not 500 light-years away, it would appear to be 21,000 times brighter than the sun. Rigel, Arabic for "leg," marks the leg of the hunter. Betelgeuse, light orange in color, marks the shoulder of the hunter and is variously distinctive. It was the first star whose diameter was obtained by direct measurement using an ingenious instrument known as a beam interferometer. It is one of the largest known stars, with a diameter approximately 800 times the diameter of our own sun. The earth's complete orbit would be easily accommodated by this star. It is also remarkable for its continuous variations in size —its diameter periodically increasing and decreasing like a balloon that is alternately inflated and deflated.

Between Betelgeuse and Rigel are the triplets—three equally spaced second-magnitude stars—which outline the belt of Orion.

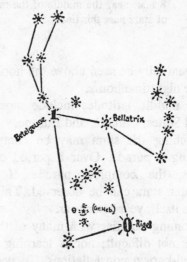

FIG. 2.35. Orion (the Hunter). The number indicates the magnitude. Stars up to and including the fourth magnitude are shown. When they form part of the design usually associated with the constellation, fifth-magnitude stars are included and indicated by a five-point symbol.

An object of great interest is located in the sword of Orion. There the naked eye observes a rather fuzzy star; closer study reveals this to be the Great Nebula of Orion, a vast mass of gas and dust in a continuous state of agitation, estimated to be 10,000 times the mass of the sun. The nebula is seen by the light of the star θ (theta)-Orionis, which lies near the center of this vast cloud. Theta-Orionis is actually a quadruple star, the four stars forming the shape of a trapezium.

2.36 LOCATING ORION IN THE SKY

Orion is about 90° from Polaris. The constellation can easily be located by facing south and looking upward about halfway between the horizon and zenith.

2.37 ORION IN LEGEND

There is much folklore concerning Orion. One of the legends states that Orion boasted that no animal could overcome him. He paid for this boast with his life. A scorpion sent by Jupiter killed him. The goddess Diana pitied Orion and transported him to heaven and placed him as far away from the Scorpion as possible—halfway across the sky from the Scorpion.

FIG. 2.37. Orion is shown holding a club in one hand and a lion's skin in the other. Rigel is in the leg of the Hunter. Betelgeuse, Arabic for "armpit," appears as shown. The sword is usually pictured as ending in the Great Nebula.

Orion is often pictured (see Fig. 2.37) as holding a club in one hand and a lion's skin in the other.

2.38 THE STARS IN AURIGA

This constellation is characterized by its clearly defined pentagon of stars. See Fig. 2.38.

Actually, only four of the stars belong to Auriga; the fifth star β (beta)-Tauri belongs to the constellation Taurus, the Bull. Capella, the brightest star in this pentagon, ranks fifth in apparent brightness among all the stars. The Charioteer is usually pictured holding a she-goat, the star Capella representing the heart of the goat. The little triangle of stars near Capella should also be noted. The three stars were known to the Arabs as the Kids.

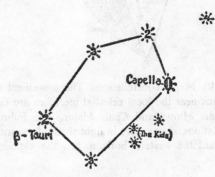

FIG. 2.38. Auriga (the Charioteer).

2.39 LOCATING AURIGA

Auriga is directly overhead, about halfway between Orion and the North Star. Its pentagonal shape, as well as the brightness of Capella (apparent magnitude .2), helps identify this group of stars.

2.40 MARCH CONSTELLATIONS

Three most interesting constellations can be found near the meridian in March. Gemini (the Twins), Canis Minor (the Little Dog), and Canis Major (the Big Dog) adorn the sky near the celestial meridian. Constellations that were here in February have moved on. Orion and Auriga are now to the west of the meridian. See Fig. 2.40.

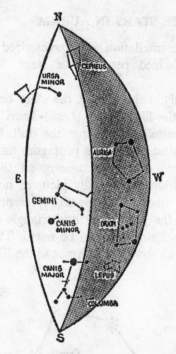

FIG. 2.40. March constellations. The prominent constellations near the local celestial meridian are Gemini, Canis Minor, and Canis Major. The February constellations, shown here in light shade, have moved on toward the western horizon. See the caption of FIG. 2.34.

2.41 THE STARS IN GEMINI

Castor and Pollux are the two bright stars in this constellation. See Fig. 2.41. They are commonly known as the twins. Pollux is a giant first-magnitude star; Castor is slightly dimmer.

In scientific terminology, Pollux, the brighter star, is known as β (beta)-Geminorum, and Castor as α (alpha)-Geminorum. This is one of the cases in which the rule that the brightest star is designated as the α star has not been followed.

In Greek mythology Castor and Pollux were the twin sons of Leda and Jupiter and the brothers of Helen of Troy. The Arabs affectionately referred to them as the Peacocks; to

the Hindus they are known as the Twin Deities.

And yet they are not twins. The two stars, though seemingly neighbors in the same part of the sky, are in reality widely separated. Castor is much farther from our earth than is Pollux.

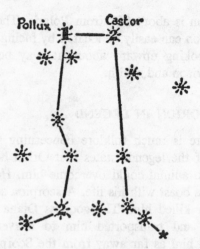

FIG. 2.41. Gemini (the Twins). Pollux' magnitude is 1.2 and Castor's is 1.6. Castor is actually a double star: the brighter component has an apparent magnitude of 2.0; the fainter component has an apparent magnitude of 2.9.

2.42 THE STARS IN CANIS MINOR

The bright star in the Little Dog constellation is Procyon. It has an apparent magnitude of .5, with a characteristic yellowish hue, rising half an hour before Sirius, the bright star of the Big Dog. The name Procyon is derived from two Greek words meaning "before the dog." See Fig. 2.42.

FIG. 2.42. Canis Minor (the Little Dog) is a very small constellation. Procyon, the eighth-brightest star, is one of the nearest stars to earth, only 11.2 light-years away.

2.43 THE STARS IN CANIS MAJOR

Here is the brightest star in the night sky: Sirius, with an apparent magnitude of −1.6. See Fig. 2.43. Its apparent brightness is due both to its intrinsic brightness—it is 27 times more luminous than our sun—and to its closeness to our solar system. It is 8.6 light-years away. Sirius is the closest star that can be seen from most parts of the United States. In the southern states, stars can be observed that are closer to the earth than Sirius.

As famous as it is, Sirius has a still more remarkable companion, the Pup: Sirius and the Pup together form a binary star. **(Two stars revolving around a common center of gravity are called a Binary Star.)** The Pup is only 1/10,000 as bright as Sirius. Its claim to fame is due to its unusually high density, caused by a large mass contained in a fairly small volume. The mass of the Pup is estimated to be 250,000 times the mass of the earth. Its diameter is a mere three times that of the earth. One cubic inch of the Pup's matter would weigh a ton!

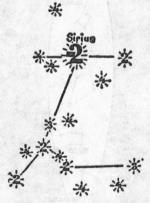

FIG. 2.43. Canis Major (the Big Dog).

2.44 LEGENDS ABOUT THE DOGS

Orion being the Hunter, it was natural to regard the Dogs as his property. Both the Big and the Little Dog follow closely on Orion's heels in the sky.

There is a touching legend about Icarius

and the faithfulness of his dog Mera. Mera stood by his master during his lifetime and after he was murdered. According to the legend, the gods rewarded Mera's faithfulness by placing him among the stars, and he became "Canis Minor."

2.45 LOCATING THE TWINS AND THE DOGS

The Twins cross the celestial meridian close to the zenith. Canis Major crosses close to the south point of the horizon; Canis Minor is about halfway between the Big Dog and the Twins.

Various aids are used to identify individual stars. It is helpful to know that Betelgeuse in Orion, Sirius in Canis Major, and Procyon in Canis Minor form an equilateral triangle. Each side in the triangle subtends an angle of 25°, or about five times the pointer distance.

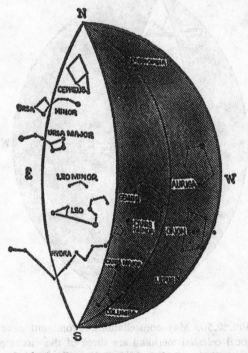

FIG. 2.46. April constellations. Leo, Leo Minor, and Hydra are among the prominent constellations near the local celestial meridian. The March constellations, shown in light shading, have moved to the west, and the February constellations (Auriga and Orion) are now close to the western horizon. See the caption of Fig. 2.34.

Another guiding line is often used to locate Sirius: an extension of the "belt stars" in Orion to the southeast points to Sirius.

2.46 APRIL CONSTELLATIONS

Leo (the Lion), Leo Minor (the Little Lion), and Hydra (the Sea Serpent) are near the meridian in April. The Twins and the Dogs are now west of the meridian. The Hunter and the Charioteer are close to the western horizon. See Fig. 2.46.

2.47 THE STARS IN LEO

The stars that belong to Leo, the larger of the two lions, form the design of a sickle followed by a triangle. See Fig. 2.47. In mythology, this constellation represented the lion

slain by Hercules as the first of his twelve chores. The bright star at the bottom of the sickle is Regulus, the Little King. This name

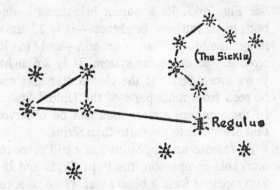

FIG. 2.47. Leo (the Lion). Regulus, with a magnitude of 1.3, is 71 light-years away from the sun. It is receding from earth at an approximate rate of 5,000 miles per hour. Regulus is nearly 100 times more luminous than the sun.

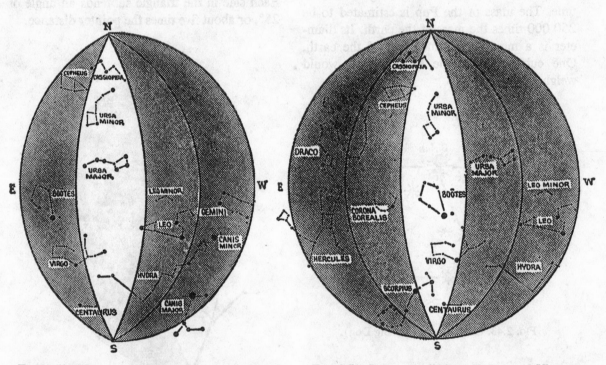

FIG. 2.50. May constellations. Prominent near the local celestial meridian are three of the circumpolar constellations: Ursa Minor, Ursa Major, and Cassiopeia. The April constellations, in light shading, are to the west of the meridian and the March constellations (Gemini, etc.) are well on their way toward the western horizon. To the east, in light shading, are Boötes, Virgo, and Centaurus. See the caption of Fig. 2.34.

FIG. 2.51. June constellations. Boötes and Virgo are prominent, close to the local celestial meridian. The April constellations (Leo, etc.) are well on their way toward the western horizon. Corona Borealis and Scorpius are in the lightly shaded segments and will be near the local celestial meridian in July. Hercules, in the heavily shaded segment near the eastern horizon, will be near the local celestial meridian in August. See the caption of Fig. 2.34.

was bestowed on the star by Copernicus. The star is also known by a variety of other names, such as the King, the Mighty, the Hero, and the Ruler.

Regulus is a white, first-magnitude star and is visible at middle latitudes for eight months of the year. It rises a little north of east at about 9 P.M. local time on New Year's Eve, and can be seen at night until the end of August.

2.48 LOCATING LEO

Regulus can easily be located by following the pointers in the Big Dipper, away from the North Star, through an angle of 35°, or seven times the distance between Dubhe and Merak, the pointer stars.

2.49 THE SEA SERPENT

This constellation stretches more than a quarter of a circle across the sky. The head of the serpent is near Canis Minor, its tail nearly 100° away, close to the constellation Libra. The stars in this constellation are faint: the brightest is a second-magnitude star named Alphard, which means "the solitary one." It is a red star located in the heart of the Serpent.

According to an old legend, the Sea Serpent was a rather peculiar creature. It had many heads and the ability to replace them. As one head was cut off, two new ones grew in its place.

2.50 MAY CONSTELLATIONS

High in the sky is Ursa Major (the Big Dipper). See Fig. 2.50. The pointers cross the meridian close to the zenith. The bowl of the Dipper is open downward and the handle stretches to the east. Ursa Major was described in detail in Sec. 2.2.

2.51 JUNE CONSTELLATIONS

Boötes (the Plowman) and Virgo (the Virgin) are the two constellations to be observed

this month. Each has one bright star to help identify it. See Fig. 2.51.

While Boötes is crossing the meridian near the zenith, Virgo is halfway between the zenith and the southern point of the horizon.

Close to the southern horizon, several stars belonging to the constellation Centaurus can also be seen. The brightest stars of this constellation are never above the horizon in middle latitudes. They can be seen in latitudes close to the equator and southward.

2.52 THE STARS IN BOÖTES

Of the eight clearly visible stars in Boötes, a (alpha)-Boötes, commonly known as Arcturus, is of particular interest. See Fig. 2.52. A bright reddish star, it is one of the few stars mentioned in the Bible. In 1933 the light coming from Arcturus—focused on a photoelectric cell—was used to open the Chicago World's Fair. At the time it was thought that Arcturus was 40 light-years from the earth, and hence a ray of light would have been on the road since 1893, the year of the previous World's Fair in Chicago. More recent computations indicate that Arcturus is actually 38 light-years away.

Arcturus is the fourth-brightest star visible in middle latitudes (app. mag. .2) and is the sixth-brightest star seen anywhere in the sky. It is also one of the fastest moving of the bright stars. Its speed is estimated to exceed 80 miles a second. Because of its distance, it

FIG. 2.52. Boötes (the Plowman or the Herdsman). Arcturus is about 80 times brighter than the sun. It is a giant star with a low temperature and a low density.

will take Arcturus more than eight hundred years to move half a degree on an arc across the sky. Eight hundred years from now Arcturus will be closer to the constellation Virgo by half a degree, a distance equal to the apparent diameter of the moon.

2.53 LOCATING BOÖTES

The handle of the Big Dipper is often used to help locate Arcturus, the bright star in Boötes. The arc described by the handle is extended about 30° (six times the pointer distance); the extended arc leads to Arcturus.

2.54 THE STARS IN VIRGO

The bright star in the constellation is Spica. See Fig. 2.54. It is a beautiful white star, rising a little to the southeast in March, and remaining visible, in middle latitudes, throughout the summer. Legend has it that Spica represents an ear of wheat, held in the hands of the Virgin, reminding the farmer that planting time has arrived.

Two important circles on the celestial sphere—the celestial equator and the ecliptic —intersect near Spica. **The Ecliptic is the apparent circle described by the sun on the celestial sphere.**

The point where the equator and ecliptic intersect is called the Autumnal Equinox. The sun is at that point on or about September 23.

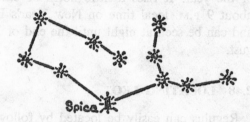

FIG. 2.54. Virgo (the Virgin). Spica, with an apparent magnitude of 1.2, is the bright star in this constellation. In ancient times Spica was known as the Star of Prosperity, and temples were built in its honor.

2.55 LOCATING VIRGO

The handle of the Big Dipper and Arcturus are often used as aids to locate Spica, the bright star in Virgo. The arc of the handle, when extended through Arcturus, points to Spica.

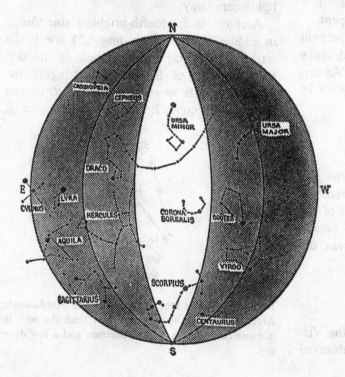

FIG. 2.56. July constellations. Corona Borealis and Scorpius are prominent near the local celestial meridian. The June stars, in light shading, have passed the meridian and are on their way to the western horizon. The August stars, in light shading, and the September stars, in heavy shading, are to the east of the line. See the caption of Fig. 2.34.

2.56 JULY CONSTELLATIONS

The constellations Scorpius (the Scorpion) and Corona Borealis (the Northern Crown) —see Fig. 2.56—cross the celestial meridian in the early evening in July. Corona Borealis is near the zenith, while Scorpius is near the southern horizon. The stars in Scorpius appear to form an outline of a scorpion and the stars in Corona Borealis suggest the outline of a crown.

2.57 THE STARS IN SCORPIUS

The bright star is Antares, one of the few bright and distinctive red stars. See Fig. 2.57. A giant of a star, its diameter is about 300 times larger than that of the sun.

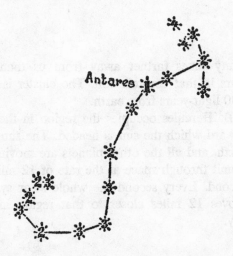

FIG. 2.57. Scorpius (the Scorpion). Scorpius is one of the twelve constellations of the Zodiac. The sun is in this constellation late in October and early in November. Antares, the bright star, has an apparent magnitude of 1.2.

2.58 THE STARS IN CORONA BOREALIS

The constellation is composed of seven stars in the form of a semicircle. See Fig. 2.58. Six of the seven principal stars are of fourth magnitude. The star in the middle is of the second magnitude and is known as the Pearl of the Crown.

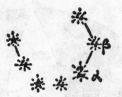

FIG. 2.58. Corona Borealis (the Northern Crown). The α (alpha) star is known as the Pearl of the Crown. Navigators call it Alphecca.

2.59 CORONA BOREALIS IN LEGEND

Legend has it that this crown once belonged to the beautiful Ariadne, wife of Theseus, who was one of the many Athenians destined to be a sacrifice to the Minotaur, the ferocious half man, half bull that inhabited a famous labyrinth near Crete. Theseus, with the aid of Ariadne, killed the monster. Ariadne supplied her lover with a sword and a spool of thread. Unwinding the thread, Theseus penetrated the labyrinth and accomplished his mission. Then, retracing his steps with the aid of the thread, he escaped. The story, however, has an unhappy ending. The marriage of Theseus and Ariadne did not last long. Theseus deserted his wife. The god Bacchus, to console Ariadne, presented her with the crown, which after her death was placed in the sky.

Again, this constellation is merely an effect of chance. No two of the seven stars are moving in the same direction or at the same speed. The two stars α (alpha)- and β (beta)- Coronae Borealis are moving in opposite directions and have nearly exchanged places in the past fifty thousand years. In another fifty thousand years the constellation will no longer bear a resemblance to a crown.

2.60 AUGUST CONSTELLATIONS

The constellation Hercules (the Kneeler)— see Fig. 2.60—is overhead. It follows in the footsteps of Boötes and Corona Borealis, which have already passed the meridian and are on their way to the western horizon.

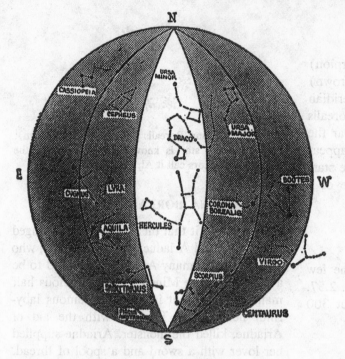

FIG. 2.60. August constellations. Hercules is near the local celestial meridian. The July constellations, in light shading, and the June constellations, in heavy shading, are in the western sky. The September constellations, in the light shading, and the October constellations, in the heavy shading, are to the east of the meridian. See the caption of Fig. 2.34.

2.61 THE STARS IN HERCULES

The interest in this constellation is not due to the brightness of its stars. There are no zero-, first-, or second-magnitude stars in this constellation. The several bright stars that seem to form the letter "H" are all of the third magnitude. See Fig. 2.61. There are, however, two major reasons for great interest in Hercules:

A. It contains one of the finest globular clusters. This is the cluster that is generally known by its number in the Messier catalog— M13. It is barely visible to the unaided eye on a clear, moonless night, appearing there as a hazy star of the fifth magnitude. Telescopic magnification reveals this hazy spot of light to be a closely packed cluster of stars. More than 50,000 individual stars in the cluster are bright enough to be observed with available telescopes. The stars close to the center of the cluster are too crowded to be counted separately. Estimates run to 500,000.

It should be noted that the cluster only appears to be in Hercules. In reality it is many, many times farther away from us than the stars in that constellation. The cluster is 34,-000 light-years from earth.

B. Hercules occupies the region in the sky toward which the sun is headed. The sun, the earth, and all the other planets are moving as a unit through space at the rate of 12 miles a second. Every second the whole solar system moves 12 miles closer to that region in the sky.

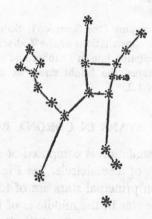

FIG. 2.61. Hercules (the Kneeler). The brightest stars in this constellation are of the third magnitude.

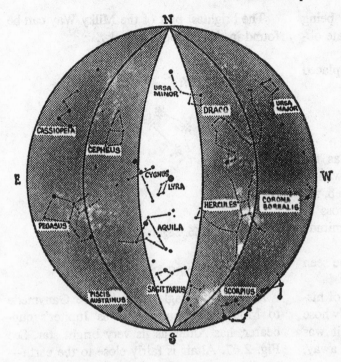

FIG. 2.62. September constellations. Cygnus, Lyra, Aquila, and Sagittarius crowd the local celestial meridian. Corona Borealis, in the heavily shaded zone, is near the western horizon. Pegasus, which is near the eastern horizon, will be discussed with the November constellations. See the caption of Fig. 2.34.

2.62 SEPTEMBER CONSTELLATIONS

The meridian is again crowded with wonderful constellations. See Fig. 2.62. Lyra (the Lyre) and Cygnus (the Swan) are close to the zenith. Sagittarius (the Archer) is close to south on the horizon. Aquila (the Eagle) is halfway between the Archer and the Lyre.

2.63 THE STARS IN LYRA

The bright star in the Lyre is Vega. See Fig. 2.63. It is a zero-magnitude star, the fourth-brightest of all the stars. Vega was once the earth's North Star and in 12,000 years it will again be the Pole Star. The axis on which our earth rotates describes a slender double cone once every 25,800 years. **This motion of the axis is known as precession** and is explained in detail in Sec. 13.7. The axis now points to *a* (alpha)-Ursae Minoris. In the year A.D. 14,000 it will again point to Vega.

Another star of interest in this constellation is β (beta)-Lyrae. This star changes its apparent magnitude every 12.9 days. The change in brightness ranges from 3.4 to 4.3 This variation can be observed by the naked eye by

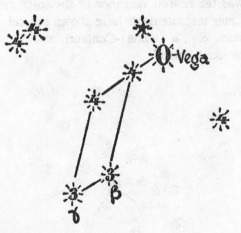

FIG. 2.63. Lyra (the Lyre). Vega, the bright star, has an apparent magnitude of .1. In 1850, Vega became the first star to be photographed.

comparing β (beta)-Lyrae with its neighbor γ (gamma)-Lyrae. At its brightest, β (beta) is almost as bright as γ (gamma), apparent magnitude 3.3; at its dimmest, it is considerably fainter.

2.64 LEGENDS ABOUT THE LYRE

The constellation Lyra symbolically represents the lyre which Apollo gave to Orpheus.

Orpheus was renowned in his day for being able to charm both animate and inanimate objects with his music.

After the death of Orpheus, Jupiter placed the magic lyre in the sky.

2.65 THE STARS IN CYGNUS

Cygnus (the Swan) is also known as the Northern Cross. See Fig. 2.65. The Swan is usually pictured as flying south with Deneb, the brightest star, marking the tail; the Cross as pointing northward with the 1.3 magnitude star, Deneb, marking the head.

The flimsy, whitish Milky Way can be seen is the background of this constellation.

Another star in Cygnus, 61 Cygni, is of historical importance. It was the first star whose distance was measured. At one time it was thought that 61 Cygni, 11.1 light-years away, was the nearest neighbor of the solar system. Later measurements have shown several other stars, e.g., α (alpha)-Centauri, and Sirius, to be much closer.

FIG. 2.65. Cygnus (the Swan). This constellation is also known as the Northern Cross. Stars whose magnitudes are as bright or brighter than the fourth magnitude are shown.

2.66 THE STARS IN SAGITTARIUS

Sagittarius (the Archer), see Fig. 2.66, has no very bright stars. A line from the sun extended through Sagittarius would point to the center of our galaxy.

The brightest part of the Milky Way can be found in this region of the sky.

FIG. 2.66. Sagittarius (the Archer).

2.67 THE STARS IN AQUILA

Aquila (the Eagle), which bore Ganymede to Mount Olympus to act as Jupiter's cup-bearer, has Altair as its very bright star. See Fig. 2.67. Altair is fairly close to the earth—its distance is a mere 14 light-years (or 80 trillion miles). Aquila attracted great attention in 1918 when for a brief time a very brilliant star that reached a maximum apparent magnitude of −1.4 appeared in that constellation, then waned rapidly in brilliance. It is now restored to the faint magnitude 12.

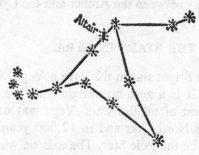

FIG. 2.67. Aquila (the Eagle)

2.68 OCTOBER CONSTELLATIONS

Cepheus, the circumpolar constellation, is now high in the sky. The celestial meridian divides it in half.

Piscis Austrinus (the Southern Fish) is the other constellation near the meridian that is of particular interest. It is also known as Piscis Australis. See Fig. 2.68.

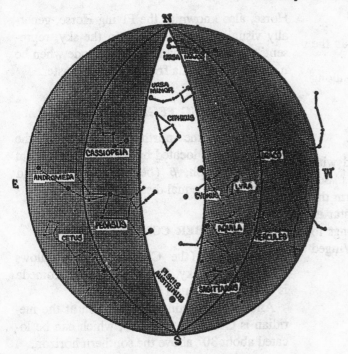

FIG. 2.68. October constellations. Cepheus and Piscis Austrinus are near the local celestial meridian. The lightly shaded zones indicate the September and November stars. The heavily shaded zones indicate the August and December stars. See the caption of Fig. 2.34.

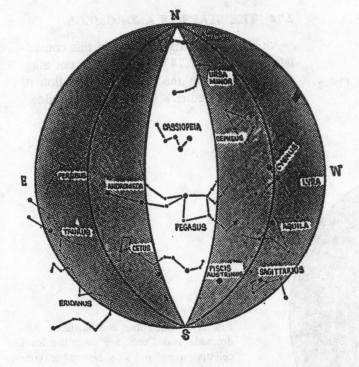

FIG. 2.70. November constellations. Cassiopeia and Pegasus are near the local celestial meridian. Near the western horizon, in the heavily shaded zone, are the September constellations. In the heavily shaded zone near the eastern horizon are Taurus and Perseus. See the caption of Fig. 2.34.

2.69 THE STARS IN PISCIS AUSTRINUS

Fomalhaut, a first-magnitude star, is the bright star not only in that constellation but also in this whole region of the sky. Fomalhaut was one of the four Royal Stars of astrology. (The other three were Regulus, Antares, and Aldebaran.) In ancient astrology Fomalhaut was considered to be indicative of power and eminence.

2.70 NOVEMBER CONSTELLATIONS

Cassiopeia is now high in the sky near the celestial meridian. See Fig. 2.70.

Pegasus (the Winged Horse) is also along the meridian.

2.71 THE STARS IN PEGASUS

This constellation is usually identified with the aid of the Great Square of Pegasus. See Fig. 2.71. Only three of the stars that form the square actually belong to Pegasus. The star at the northeastern corner, Alpheratz, belongs to the constellation Andromeda. The Winged

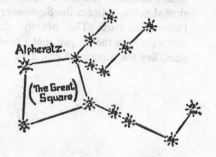

FIG. 2.71. Pegasus (the Winged Horse or the Flying Horse).

Horse, also known as the Flying Horse, generally visualized upside down in the sky, represents the horse on which Perseus rode when he rescued Andromeda from the Sea Monster.

2.72 LOCATING PEGASUS

Alpheratz, the northeastern star of the Square, can be located by drawing a line from Polaris to Caph, β (beta)-Cassiopeiae, and extending it an equal distance.

2.73 DECEMBER CONSTELLATIONS

Andromeda (the Chained Lady) follows Pegasus in the sky. See Fig 2.73. Andromeda is closer to the zenith than Pegasus.

Another interesting constellation at the meridian is Cetus (the Whale), which can be located about 30° above the southern horizon.

2.74 THE STARS IN ANDROMEDA

Alpheratz, the brightest star in this constellation (see Fig. 2.74), has an apparent magnitude of 2.1. In the Bayer classification of stars it is denoted as α (alpha)-Andromedae.

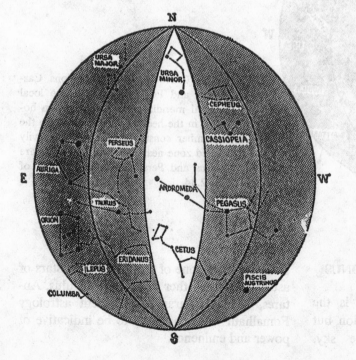

FIG. 2.73. December constellations. Andromeda and Cetus are near the local celestial meridian. The November constellations, in light shading, and the October constellations, in heavy shading, are in the western part of the sky. The January constellations, lightly shaded, and the February constellations, heavily shaded, are to the east of the meridian. See the caption of Fig. 2.34.

Of great interest in this part of the sky is an object denoted scientifically as M31, or as NGC224, located near *ν* (nu)-Andromedae. To the naked eye, it appears as a fuzzy star of about fifth magnitude; its true character can be realized only with the aid of a high-power telescope. M31 is a galaxy quite similar to our galaxy. It consists of billions of stars and is a bit larger than our galaxy. It is the farthest object in space that can be seen with the unaided eye. Light leaving the great galaxy in An-

dromeda reaches us after traveling through space for nearly 2,000,000 years.

2.75 ANDROMEDA IN LEGEND

Andromeda, the beautiful daughter of Cepheus and Cassiopeia, enraged the sea nymphs by her boastful vanity. To punish her, Neptune chained her to a rock at the seashore as prey to the sea monster then ravaging the coast. Perseus came to her rescue. Just as the monster was about to attack Andromeda, Perseus magically turned the monster into a stone, saving her.

2.76 JANUARY CONSTELLATIONS

Perseus (the Champion), Taurus (the Bull), and Eridanus (the River Po), are near the meridian this month. See Fig. 2.76. Perseus can be seen close to the zenith, Taurus to the southeast of it, and Eridanus stretches over a large portion of the southern sky. To the east of the meridian are Auriga, the Charioteer, and Orion, the Hunter. A new cycle of the procession of stars is about to begin.

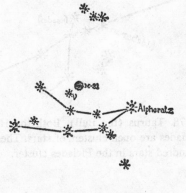

FIG. 2.74. Andromeda (the Chained Lady). Alpheratz marks the head of Andromeda.

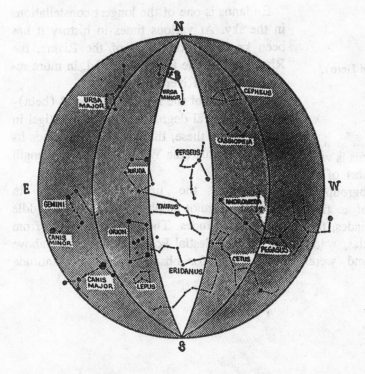

FIG. 2.76. January constellations. Perseus, Taurus, and Eridanus are close to the celestial meridian. Near the western horizon, in heavy shading, are the November constellations. Near the eastern horizon, also in heavy shading, are the March constellations. See the caption of Fig. 2.34.

2.77 THE STARS IN PERSEUS

There are no really bright stars in Perseus; however, the star β (beta)-Persei is of interest. See Fig. 2.77. It is an eclipsing star. β (beta)-Persei, also known as Algol (the Demon), consists actually of two stars of unequal brightness 11 million miles apart, revolving about their center of gravity. Their orbits are inclined 8° from the edgewise position relative to the earth. Every 2 days, 21 hours, the fainter star eclipses the brighter companion, and the apparent brightness of the combination is reduced to one third its normal value —i.e., from apparent magnitude 2.2 to apparent magnitude 3.5. The eclipse of the faint companion by the bright one causes only a minute diminution of brightness.

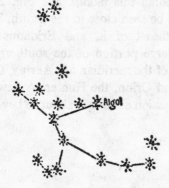

FIG. 2.77. Perseus (the Champion or the Hero).

2.78 THE STARS IN TAURUS

The beautiful constellation of Taurus is well known because the Pleiades form part of it. See Fig. 2.78. The Pleiades are a subgroup of seven stars arranged in a form of a tiny dipper. According to legend, the Pleiades, the seven daughters of the powerful Atlas, were pursued by Orion, the Hunter, and were changed into doves to escape him.

The other subgroup of Taurus is the Hyades. Sometimes the Hyades are pictured as outlining the head of the Bull, the Pleiades forming the shoulders.

The brilliant, red, first-magnitude star Aldebaran is invariably placed in the left eye of the Bull. Aldebaran means "the follower" in Arabic. It follows the Pleiades in the sky.

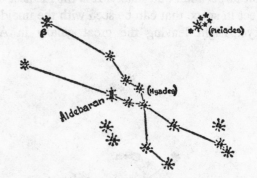

FIG. 2.78. Taurus (the Bull). Both the Hyades and the Pleiades are open clusters of stars. There are several hundred stars in the Pleiades cluster.

2.79 THE STARS IN ERIDANUS

Eridanus is one of the longest constellations in the sky. At various times in history it has been known as the King of the Rivers, the River Jordan, the River Nile, and, in more recent times, the River Po.

The source of the river is the star β (beta)-Eridani, several degrees northwest of Rigel in Orion. From these, the constellation winds its way past Cetus (the Whale) for a total length of 130°.

Achernar, the first-magnitude star in Eridanus, cannot be observed from the middle northern latitudes. The star is only 33° from the South Celestial Pole and never rises above the horizon for observers north of latitude 33° N.

PART IV: SOUTH CIRCUMPOLAR STARS

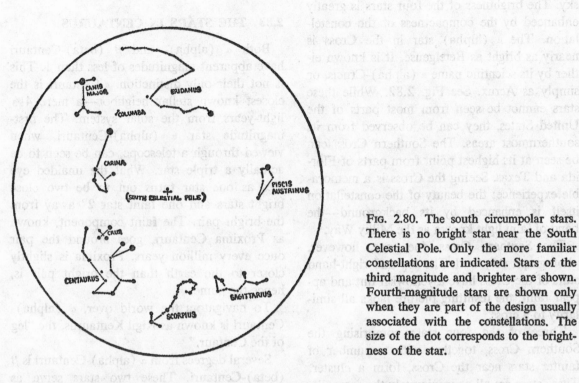

FIG. 2.80. The south circumpolar stars. There is no bright star near the South Celestial Pole. Only the more familiar constellations are indicated. Stars of the third magnitude and brighter are shown. Fourth-magnitude stars are shown only when they are part of the design usually associated with the constellations. The size of the dot corresponds to the brightness of the star.

2.80 INTRODUCTION

This section deals with the stars that are always **below** the horizon for observers at middle latitudes. These are termed **South Circumpolar Stars**, and can be seen from the earth's southern hemisphere, and observed ideally from Australia, South Africa, or South America. See Fig. 2.80.

Three beautiful constellations embellish the sky "down under." Carina (the Ship's Keel) is one of these constellations; Crux (the Southern Cross), an object of great interest to the people of the Antipodes, is another. The third constellation is Centaurus (the Centaur), twice represented in the list of the twenty brightest stars.

2.81 THE STARS IN CARINA

The *a* (alpha) star in Carina is Canopus, the second-brightest star in the sky. Its appar-

ent magnitude is —.9 as compared to —1.6 for the brightest star, Sirius. Canopus can be seen on winter evenings in the southern regions of the United States. It crosses the local celestial meridian about the same time as Sirius. See Fig. 2.81.

FIG. 2.81. Carina (the Ship's Keel). Some astronomers regard Carina as part of another constellation known as Argo.

2.82 THE STARS IN CRUX

The Southern Cross is generally considered to be the most beautiful constellation in the sky. The brightness of the four stars is greatly enhanced by the compactness of the constellation. The α (alpha) star in the Cross is nearly as bright as Betelgeuse. It is known either by its scientific name α (alpha)-Crucis, or simply as Acrux. See Fig. 2.82. While these stars cannot be seen from most parts of the United States, they can be observed from its southernmost areas. The Southern Cross can be seen at its highest point from parts of Florida and Texas. Seeing the Cross is a memorable experience: the beauty of the constellation itself is enhanced by its background—the band of faint light known as the Milky Way.

The Southern Cross does not, however, photograph very well. The top and right-hand stars of the Cross have a yellowish tint and appear faint; the resulting picture lacks all similarity to a cross.

Three of the four stars comprising the Southern Cross, together with a number of fainter stars near the Cross, form a cluster. These stars are all approximately the same distance from the solar system. They are moving away from us, describing parallel tracks, at an average speed of 15 miles per second. The stars are also similar in their physical characteristics: they are all very hot, among the hottest known.

It is most probable that the stars in the cluster had a common origin. According to this theory, they were all created from one "chunk" of matter in the remote past. In time, relatively small velocities with respect to each other caused them to separate and form their present pattern—a pattern of individual stars receding continuously along parallel lines from the solar system.

2.83 THE STARS IN CENTAURUS

Both α (alpha)- and β (beta)-Centauri have apparent magnitudes of less than 1. This is not their only distinction. α-Centauri is the closest known stellar neighbor—a mere 4⅓ light-years from the solar system. The first-magnitude star α (alpha)-Centauri, when viewed through a telescope, can be seen to be actually a triple star. What the unaided eye sees as one star turns out to be two close bright stars and one faint star 2° away from the bright pair. The faint component, known as Proxima Centauri, goes around the pair once every million years. Proxima is slightly closer to the earth than the bright pair is, hence the name.

To navigators the world over, α (alpha)-Centauri is known as Rigil Kentaurus, the "leg of the Centaur."

Several degrees from α (alpha)-Centauri is β (beta)-Centauri. These two stars serve as pointers in the southern hemisphere. A line

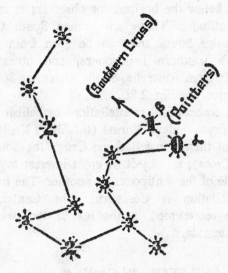

Fig. 2.83. Centaurus (the Centaur). When the line from α to β is extended, it points to the Southern Cross.

Fig. 2.82. Crux (the Southern Cross).

through α and β points to the northernmost star of the Southern Cross. See Fig. 2.83.

The closeness of β (beta)-Centauri to α is only apparent. The β star is nearly fifty times more distant than α star. The distance to β (beta)-Centauri is more than 190 light-years.

CHAPTER 3

ELEMENTS OF NAVIGATION

3.1 INTRODUCTION

Stars have addresses: The location of every star is specified by a pair of numbers which fit only that star. One of these numbers is known as the **Sidereal Hour Angle** of the star; the other, the **Declination of the Star.**

The units in both cases are units or angle i.e. degrees, minutes and seconds. Thus the star Vega has a sidereal hour angle of 81°15′, and a declination of 38°45′.

NOTE: These addresses change very slowly with time. Hence, to be very accurate, it is necessary to specify the date, known as epoch, when the star has the particular sidereal hour angle and declination. The slight changes in these numbers are due to the phenomenon known as "precession of the equinoxes," which in turn is due to precession of the earth's axis. Due to these phenomena, the vernal equinox, the point from which the sidereal hour angle is measured, moves continuously westward.

The sidereal hour angle and declination of stars and other heavenly bodies are listed in various catalogs and almanacs, among them the American Nautical Almanac, published annually by the United States Naval Observatory, to provide astronomical data for mariners.

The method of specifiying location on the celestial sphere for any epoch is similar to the method of specifying location on earth. In the stellar system, stars are located on the inner surface of the celestial sphere; in the case of the earth, cities, towns and mountains are located on its outer surface.

The numbers specifying location on the earth are known as Longitude and Latitude. The longitude and latitude of Washington, D.C., for example, are 77° W and 39° N, respectively.

Longitude and latitude on earth are determined with the aid of two sets of circles—**imaginary circles known as Meridians and Parallels of Latitude.**

Similar sets of circles are drawn on the celestial sphere, in reference to which they are often called **Hour Circles** and **Parallels of Declination.** An understanding of this system of circles, both on the earth's (terrestrial) sphere and on the celestial sphere, is essential.

3.2 PARALLELS OF LATITUDE

The points on the earth's surface, halfway between the North Pole and the South Pole, form the global equator. The equator thus divides the earth into two hemispheres, the northern and the southern. See Fig. 3.2a.

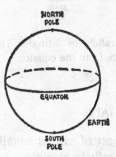

FIG. 3.2a. The equator divides the earth into two hemispheres.

Each hemisphere can be further subdivided by drawing circles parallel to the equator which are known as parallels of latitude and are designated by numbers in the northern hemisphere, beginning with zero at the equator and ending with 90° N at the North Pole. The parallels of latitude in the southern hemisphere are denoted by the suffix "S"; thus, the latitude of the South Pole is 90° S.

The parallels of latitude are used in stating any point's angular distance, in degrees, from the equator. See Fig. 3.2b. This distance is known as the latitude of that point—thus, Key West has a latitude of 25° N, Washington, D.C., 39° N, and Paris, France, 49° N. This can also be stated by saying that the angles subtended by these points and the equator at the center of the earth are 25, 39 and 49 degrees, respectively. The latitudes are stated to the nearest degree. When greater accuracy is desired, the angles are stated in terms of degrees, minutes and seconds of arc. For Washington, D.C., the more accurate latitude figure is 38 degrees, 53 minutes, and 51 seconds of arc, more compactly written as 38° 53' 51".

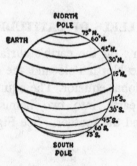

FIG. 3.2b. Parallels of latitude. They indicate the angular distance from the equator.

3.3 MERIDIANS

The other set of circles usually drawn on a globe are called meridians of longitude. Unlike the parallels of latitude, they are all of equal size, each circle passing through both the North and the South Poles. See Fig. 3.3.

Since the meridians are of equal size and are otherwise equal in importance, the map makers had to designate one of these as being the prime meridian, in reference to which all the others are marked. In 1884, it was decided, by international agreement, to designate the one passing through Greenwich, Eng-

land, as the prime meridian, which is also known as the zero meridian, i.e., longitude 0°. The meridians to the west are marked 1° W, 2° W, and so on, to 180° W. The meridians to the east are designated 1° E, 2° E, and so on, to 180° E. 180° E and 180° W are, therefore, the same longitude.

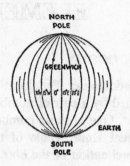

FIG. 3.3. Meridians. The zero meridian passes through Greenwich, England. These lines indicate longitude on the earth.

3.4 THE CELESTIAL SPHERE

This sphere has already been discussed. It has been shown that this sphere serves as a background upon which the stars are projected. The observer sees all the stars as if they were attached to the inside of a vast spherical surface. The celestial sphere is concentric with the terrestrial one, and is infinitely larger. No definite value is assigned to its radius, **as the sphere is merely imaginary.**

The two spheres not only have a common center, but also a common axis and a common equatorial plane.

The celestial axis extends indefinitely beyond the earth's North Pole and South Pole. **The points of its intersection with the celestial sphere are termed North Celestial Pole and South Celestial Pole.**

The celestial equator is an extension of the terrestrial one; both are in the same plane but the radius of the celestial equator, which divides the sphere into two halves, is infinitely larger. See Fig. 3.4.

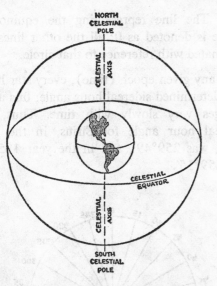

FIG. 3.4. The celestial sphere. We live on the *outside* of the terrestrial sphere. The stars appear to an observer as if attached to the *inside* surface of the celestial sphere.

The celestial axis is merely an extension of the earth's axis beyond the North and South Poles of the earth.

The celestial equator is an extension of the terrestrial equator.

3.5 PARALLELS OF DECLINATION

Each half of the celestial sphere can be further subdivided: one method is to draw circles parallel to the equator. **These circles are called Parallels of Declination.** In the northern hemisphere, they are designated by number, starting with zero for the celestial equator and ending with 90° N declination for the North Celestial Pole.

Similar numbers are given to the parallels of declination in the southern half of the celestial sphere. The designations here run from 0° at the equator to 90° S declination at the South Celestial Pole.

These parallels of declination on the celestial sphere serve a purpose similar to that of the parallels of latitude on the terrestrial sphere. They are used to state the angular distance between any object in the heavens and the equator; and this distance, in degrees of angle, is known as the declination of the object. See Fig. 3.5.

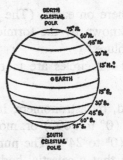

FIG. 3.5. Parallels of declination. These circles on the celestial sphere are similar to parallels of latitude on the terrestrial one except for the fact that they are to be visualized as drawn on the inside surface of the sphere.

Parallels of declination are used in stating the declination of a star on the celestial sphere, that is, the angular distance between a star and the celestial equator.

PROBLEM 3.5:

Using a star catalog or an almanac, find the declinations of the following stars: Rigel, Pollux, and Spica.

Answer: Rigel   8° S
Pollux 28° N
Spica 11° S

NOTE: Mariners often use the signs + and − instead of North and South. The above answers will then be stated as −8, +28, and −11, respectively.

3.6 HOUR CIRCLES

The earth's meridians of longitude also have counterparts on the larger sphere known as Hour Circles, which pass through the North and South Celestial Poles. They are all of equal size and importance. By international agreement, one of these was chosen as the prime hour circle.

The hour circle so designated is the one that goes through the First Point of Aries (the Greenwich of the sky). The First Point of Aries is a point on the celestial equator denoted by the symbol ♈. Our sun, in its apparent movement in the sky, crosses the equator at that point as it moves from the southern to the northern celestial hemisphere. When the sun is at that point, days are equal in length to nights everywhere on earth. (The prime hour circle is also known by the formidable name "equinoctial colure.")

The other hour circles are marked as follows:

A. Eastward, by astronomers, in either degrees of angle (0° to 360°) or, more often, in units of time (0ʰ to 24ʰ). The number of degrees or hours that a celestial body is east of the prime hour circle is known as the right ascension of that body.

B. Westward, by navigators, in degrees (0° to 360°). The angle that a celestial body is west of the prime hour circle is known as the sidereal hour angle.

The sidereal hour angle of any circle can easily be visualized in one of two ways:

1. Along the celestial equator. The circles divide the equator into arcs. The circle going through the point 15° west of zero is, then, designated as 15° west hour circle, the circle going through 30° west of zero in the 30° west circle, and so on. See Fig. 3.6a.

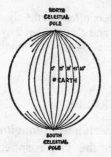

FIG. 3.6a. Hour circles. These are similar to meridians on the surface of the earth.

Hour circles are used to denote the angular distance of a heavenly body from the zero-hour-circle. These angular distances are similar to longitudes on the terrestrial sphere.

Note, though, that we are looking at the inside of the celestial sphere, and 15° is to the left of 0°.

2. From a vertical view. At the poles, a different view of the circles is obtained. Those at the North Pole, say, appear to be straight lines emanating from the Pole, and are, of course, vertical views of these circles. See Fig.

3.6b. The line representing the equinoctial colure is denoted as 0; all the other lines are designated with reference to that circle.

At any given epoch (time), every star has a well-determined sidereal hour angle; this angle changes very slowly with time. Thus, the sidereal hour angle for Sirius, in the year 1900, was 259°49′, and in the year 1950 it was 259°15′.

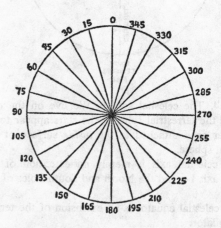

FIG. 3.6b. A vertical view of the hour circles. Looking directly up to the North Celestial Pole, the hour circles appear as straight lines emanating from that pole.

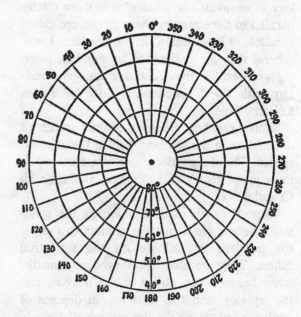

FIG. 3.6c. Polar chart to be used to plot three of the circumpolar constellations.

PROBLEM 3.6a:

Using a star catalog or an almanac, find the sidereal hour angle for the following stars: Betelgeuse, Dubhe, and Arcturus.

Answer: Betelgeuse 272
Dubhe 195
Arcturus 147

PROBLEM 3.6b:

Object: To plot the stars of Ursa Major, Ursa Minor, and Cassiopeia on a star chart.

Equipment:
a. A polar chart. See Fig. 3.6c.
b. A list of declinations and sidereal hour angles for the stars in the three constellations.
Results: Part of a circumpolar star chart.

LIST OF DECLINATIONS AND SIDEREAL HOUR ANGLES
FOR THE STARS IN PROBLEM 3.6B

	S.H.A.	*Declinations*
Ursa Major	195	62
	195	57
	184	54
	176	58
	167	57
	160	55
	154	50
Ursa Minor	137	74
	128	72
	114	76
	123	78
	105	82
	90	87
	330	89
Cassiopeia	359	59
	350	56
	346	60
	339	60
	332	63

3.7 EFFECT OF LATITUDE ON VIEW OF THE SKY

It has been stated that the view of the sky changes with the latitude of the observer. This change can easily be explained with the aid of the terrestrial and celestial spheres. Figure 3.7 describes the view as seen by an observer at 40° N (about the latitude of New York).

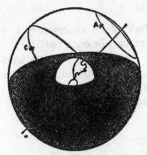

FIG. 3.7. Effect of latitude. The orbit of star A is completely above the horizon in this latitude. This star can be seen in the sky every night of the year. The orbit of star B is completely below the horizon in this latitude. It cannot be observed from this point on the earth. Star C is part of the year above the horizon at night, and during the rest of the year is below the horizon at night. The relative number of stars in each group varies with terrestrial latitude.

The heavily lined circle here represents the horizon as seen by that observer. The straight line is the axis about which the celestial sphere makes its apparent rotation, inclined 40° to the horizon. All the stars within 40° of the Pole are continuously above the horizon. For an observer at 30° N, all the stars within 30° of the Pole are classified as circumpolar; for an observer at 18° N all the stars within 18° of the Pole are circumpolar, and so on. This can also be stated in terms of declinations. For an observer at 40° N, all the stars having declinations between 50° and 90° N are continuously above the horizon. For an observer at 30° N, the same is true for stars having declinations between 60° and 90° N, while for an observer at 18° N this will be true for all the stars having declinations between 72° and 90° N.

PROBLEM 3.7a:

The geographical latitude of an observer is 43°. Which stars are north circumpolar in that latitude?
Solution: All the stars within 43° of the North Pole are north circumpolar at that latitude. The declinations of these stars are between the limits of 90° and (90−43=)47° N.
Answer: All stars having a declination larger than 47° N are north circumpolar.

PROBLEM 3.7b:

The latitude of an observatory is 47° N. How far south can stars be observed?

Solution: An observer can see stars as far beyond the equator as 90° minus his latitude. At this observatory, stars are visible which are (90−47=)43° south of the equator.

PROBLEM 3.7c:

At which latitude will Capella be a north circumpolar star? The declination of Capella is stated as +46 or 46° N.

Answer: At any geographical latitude north of 44° (say north of Portland, Maine) Capella is constantly above the horizon.

PROBLEM 3.7d:

An observatory is 25° N. Which stars can never be seen at that observatory?

Answer: All of the stars having declinations of 65° S. to 90° S.

PROBLEM 3.7e:

Which stars are north circumpolar at the equator?

Answer: There are no circumpolar stars at the equator. At any time of the year, an observer sees half of all the visible stars in the sky. Six months later, the other half of the sky is in view.

CHAPTER 4

VIEWING STARS WITH A SMALL TELESCOPE

4.1 INTRODUCTION

The telescope, of course, makes possible a far clearer view of the sky; and the excitement it contributes is immense. An entire new perspective unfolds: The very boundary of the sky is enlarged; the observer can reach farther into the universe. The Milky Way, until now a flimsy, thin, whitish background, becomes an almost infinite number of colorful stars, forming a multitude of geometric patterns.

A fuzzy small point of light, which had seemed a relatively unimportant object in the sky, is actually a galaxy consisting of billions of stars. The faintness of the light is due entirely to its vast distance from the observer.

The telescope may reveal that another undistinguished point of light is a **star cluster —a group of stars crowded together in a small volume in space.** There are many such clusters in our galaxy, many of them containing hundreds of thousands of stars. Those clusters that appear to have closely packed stars are in a spherical shape and are known as **Globular**

Clusters. Others, loosely assembled, are called **Open Clusters.**

Many objects that appear to be normal-variety stars are, in fact, double stars, the two usually very close to one another. The stars revolve continuously about a point in space— the point is the center of gravity of the double star. Two such close stars are known as a **Binary Star** or a **Binary System.**

When both stars of the pair can be seen through the telescope, the pair is known as a **Visual Binary.** Fifty thousand visual binaries are known, and many are yet to be discovered.

When the two stars are too close together for the telescope to resolve into two separate entities, the star is called a **Spectroscopic Binary,** as the existence of the pair is determined from a study of its spectrum.

Spectroscopic binaries, too, are very common. A study of the hundred brightest stars showed that twenty of them are such binaries.

When the orbit of revolution of the Spectroscopic Binary pair is edgewise to the earth, then the two stars alternately eclipse one another. Such a binary is known as an **Eclipsing Binary.** About 3,000 of these are known.

Another group of variable-light stars is known as **Cepheids.** These stars seem to pulsate, alternately increasing and decreasing in size. The brightness of the Cepheids changes with size, the Cepheid being brightest at maximum expansion velocity.

Some objects that look like fuzzy stars are in reality **Nebulae, that is, clouds of gases and dust**—their true nature revealed by telescopic observation.

There are two kinds of telescopes: **Refracting** and **Reflecting.** Both have an objective (facing the object viewed), and an eyepiece through which the observer looks.

The objective forms an image of the distant object; the eyepiece magnifies that image.

The refracting telescope uses a lens for an objective (the light going through the lens is refracted), while the reflecting telescope uses a mirror as an objective (the light is reflected by the mirror to form an image near the eyepiece).

Telescopes are rated according to the dimensions of the clear diameter of the objective—the aperture. The largest refractor in the world, at the Yerkes Observatory, Williams Bay, Wisconsin, has a 40-inch aperture. The largest reflector, near Tiflis, in the U.S.S.R., has a mirror 236 inches in diameter. For amateur work, a 3-inch refractor or a slightly larger reflector is ideal. Fairly good telescopes are now available at reasonable prices or may easily be constructed by the amateur hobbyist. (Instructions for building a refractor and a reflector will be found in the Appendix.)

4.2 SELECTED LIST OF OBSERVATIONS

Numerous interesting observations can be made with the aid of a small telescope. These include:

A. Double and multiple stars in all parts of the heaven.
B. Variable stars.
C. Star clusters.

D. Nebulae.
E. Galaxies.

Of particular interest are the Variable Stars, which change periodically in brightness. A great deal of further information is necessary to solve the mystery of their behavior. The giant telescopes are usually engaged in other projects and hence are seldom turned on these stars. Amateur astronomers are doing important work in providing information about them.

Variable stars, as well as objects in groups A, C, D, and E, of interest to amateur observers are indicated in the remainder of this chapter. First, we shall focus our attention on the north circumpolar constellations, then on those objects near the local meridian every month of the year.

The day should be about the middle of the month, the hour about eight or nine o'clock in the evening, local time.

4.3 NORTH CIRCUMPOLAR CONSTELLATIONS

A. **Ursa Major.** The star Mizar, at the middle of the handle, is a double star: the brighter component has an apparent magnitude of 2.1; the fainter star, 4.2. This was the first of the double stars to be discovered, in 1650. The angle they subtend at an observer is 15 seconds of arc. Subsequent spectroscopic research showed that the brighter star of this binary system is in itself a double, thus making Mizar a triple star. See Fig. 4.3a.

FIG. 4.3a. Ursa Major. The star Mizar is a double star. Its two components have apparent magnitudes of 2.1 and 4.2. Both are greenish white in color—a good double to watch with a low-power telescope.

The location of the Owl Nebula, M97, is also indicated.

Another object of interest in the Big Dipper is the Owl Nebula. It is a round large cloud known by catalog numbers M97 or NGC3587.

The first catalog of nebulae and star clusters was compiled by the French astronomer Charles Messier (1730–1817) in 1781. The list contains 103 objects, more than half of which are star clusters. (M97 means object 97 in the Messier catalog.)

The New General Catalog, containing a comprehensive list of nebulae and clusters, was published in 1888 in England, and supplementary lists were later added to it. Most nebulae and star clusters are commonly known by their number in that catalog. Thus, Messier 97 is object number 3587 in the New General Catalog.

B. **Ursa Minor.** Polaris, α (alpha)-Ursae Minoris, is a double star. The two companions differ greatly in apparent brightness. One of the stars in this binary system has an apparent magnitude of 2.0, while the value of the other star is 9.0. A 3-inch telescope and good atmospheric conditions are needed to see the faint companion, which is located below the bright one in November, and above it in May. See Fig. 4.3b.

C. **Cassiopeia.** Cassiopeia is rich in double stars, star clusters, and other objects for telescopic observation. The α (alpha) star in Cassiopeia as well as the η (eta), ι (iota), and σ (sigma) stars are doubles. The σ (sigma) star has a particularly beautiful color combination. One of the stars is very blue; the other is green. See Fig. 4.3c.

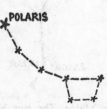

FIG. 4.3b. Ursa Minor. Polaris, the North Star, is a double. The bright companion is blue, and has an apparent magnitude of 2.0; the dim partner is also bluish, its magnitude a dim 9.0. A 3-inch telescope is needed to resolve this binary system.

FIG. 4.3c. Double stars in Cassiopeia. The α (alpha) star is a double that can be resolved with a 1-inch telescope. The bright companion is yellowish in color, having an apparent magnitude of 3.0; the dim companion is a 9.0 apparent magnitude star, bluish in hue.

The η (eta) star can also be resolved with a fairly small telescope.

One of the most beautiful star clusters (designated as number 7789 in the New General Catalog) is located in Cassiopeia. Its great beauty has been universally extolled.

D. **Cepheus.** δ (delta)-Cephei is a double star. The brighter component is the historically important Variable Star, which gave its name to the whole class of stars known as Cepheids.

The companion star to δ (delta)-Cephei is a 7.5 magnitude star. It is bluish in color and can be seen even with a 1-inch telescope. See Fig. 4.3d.

FIG. 4.3d. The δ (delta) star in Cepheus is a double star. The brighter companion varies in magnitude from 3.7 to 4.6; the dim partner is a 7.5 apparent magnitude star, blue in color.

4.4 FEBRUARY OBSERVATIONS

Near the celestial meridian at about eight or nine in the evening are the constellations of Orion and Auriga.

A. Orion. The most remarkable object in this constellation is, no doubt, the Great Nebula. It is invariably thought to be the most wonderful object in the sky; and it is barely visible to the unaided eye. Its real beauty, however, can only be appreciated with the aid of a telescope. The larger the telescope, the better. The Great Nebula in Orion is also known by its catalog numbers M42 or NGC 1976. It is greenish in color and fairly irregular in form.

Orion is rich in double stars. Over seventy of these stars are in the constellation, among them Rigel and δ (delta)-Orionis. There are also multiple stars. θ (theta)-Orionis has already been mentioned. This object appears to the unaided eye as a single star. The telescope reveals the object to be actually composed of four distinct stars which form a compact unit in the shape of a trapezium. See Fig. 4.4a.

Fig. 4.4a. Orion. Note the Great Nebula. Its mass is estimated to be 10,000 times that of the sun.

Rigel is a double star. The bright component has an apparent magnitude of 1.0; its color is yellowish-white. The companion is an 8.0 apparent magnitude of orange hue.

θ (theta)-Orionis is a multiple star. The four companions have apparent magnitudes of 4.0, 10.3, 7.5, and 6.3. The four individual stars form the outline of a baseball diamond or the geometrical form of a trapezium.

B. Auriga. The α (alpha) star, Capella, itself is a binary, but this cannot be determined with the aid of a telescope alone. The binary character of Capella shows up in spectroscopic studies of the star: **such double stars are known as Spectroscopic Binaries.** The two companions of Capella are of about equal mass and are similar in their physical characteristics. The period of one revolution about their common center of gravity for each star is 104 days.

β (beta)-Aurigae, too, is of special interest. It is an **Eclipsing Binary.** The two companions revolve in a plane that is inclined only slightly to the line of sight. They mutually eclipse one another at every revolution. The period of a complete revolution is 3 days, 23 hours, and 2.5 minutes.

A particularly beautiful star cluster is to be found in Auriga. M38 or NGC1912 is usually described as having the shape of an "oblique cross with a pair of large stars in each arm." See Fig. 4.4b.

Fig. 4.4b. Auriga. β (beta)-Aurigae is an eclipsing binary; the two companions are of equal size and brightness. Note the very beautiful M38 star cluster.

4.5 MARCH OBSERVATIONS

A. Gemini. M35 is the object to observe. It is a star cluster of most interesting design.

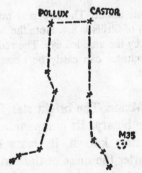

Fig. 4.5a. Gemini. The star cluster M35 can be seen, under excellent weather conditions, by the naked eye. Even a small telescope brings out the extreme beauty of this cluster. The star Castor is known scientifically as α (alpha)-Geminorum, although Pollux is in number one place as far as apparent brightness is concerned. The three known components constituting the star Castor have apparent magnitudes of 2.7, 3.7, and 9.5. Each of the three stars is in itself a spectroscopic binary.

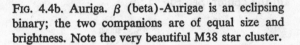

Two streams of small stars run parallel on each side of the cluster.

The star Castor (α (alpha)-Geminorum) is a three component star. Two of these form a binary system with a period of revolution of 300 years. The third component completes one revolution in about 10,000 years. Spectroscopic studies seem to indicate that each of these components is itself a double star. Castor is thus probably a unit consisting of six stars. See Fig. 4.5a.

B. **Canis Major.** Mention has already been made that Sirius is a double star. The companion of this star was described in Sec. 2.43.

Not far from Sirius is the scattered star cluster M41 (or NGC2287), which can be seen by the unaided eye. Fairly good detail can be obtained with a 3-inch telescope. The stars form two distinct groups, joined by a red star in the center. See Fig. 4.5b.

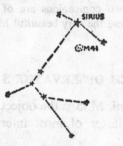

FIG. 4.5b. Canis Major. The apparent magnitude of the companion of Sirius is 8.4. Note the M41 cluster. It can be seen by the unaided eye. The red star in the center of the cluster can easily be observed with a small telescope.

C. **Canis Minor.** The bright star Procyon is a remarkable binary. Its companion is one of the lightest stars known, its mass being less than one quarter the mass of the sun. The star is also extremely faint. It gives only 1/100,000 as much light as Procyon does, and cannot therefore be seen through a small telescope. See Fig. 4.5c.

Fig. 4.5c.

4.6 APRIL OBSERVATIONS

A. **Leo.** The bright star Regulus is a double; the companion is a faint eighth-magnitude star. It is quite possible that Regulus is an "optical" and not a true double star. **An Optical Double consists of two stars that appear close because they are in line of sight of a terrestrial observer but are really at a great distance from one another, along that line.** The stars in an optical double do not, of course, revolve about any common center of gravity as true double stars do. γ (gamma)-Leonis is a true double star. It is acclaimed as one of the finest double stars in the heavens, best observed when not quite dark, or in moonlight. The bright star of this binary system (apparent magnitude 2.6) has a golden tint; the fainter star (apparent magnitude 3.6) is greenish in color. The companions rotate fairly slowly about their center of gravity, a complete revolution lasting more than a thousand years.

A well-known variable star is of interest in this constellation—the long period variable, R-Leonis. At its maximum brightness, visible then to the naked eye, it is a red magnitude 5 star. At its minimum light intensity, when it is

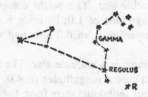

FIG. 4.6. Leo. Regulus is probably an optical double. The two stars appear close because they lie along the same line of sight for a terrestrial observer. A side view of these stars would reveal the true distance between them.

γ (gamma)-Leonis is the double to observe in this constellation. The two companions have apparent magnitudes of 2.6 and 3.6.

The variations in brightness of R-Leonis can easily be observed with a small telescope. A complete period lasts 310 days, while the change from fifth to tenth magnitudes alone takes 144 days. R-Leonis forms an equilateral triangle with two nearby stars of apparent magnitudes 9.0 and 9.6. The changing brightness of the variable can be estimated in relation to the two neighbors.

observable only with a good telescope, it is a tenth-magnitude star. See Fig. 4.6.

4.7 MAY OBSERVATIONS

Telescopic observations for Ursa Major were detailed in Sec. 4.3.

4.8 JUNE OBSERVATIONS

A. Boötes. Many interesting double stars can be observed with the aid of a small telescope. A partial list of these would include the stars π (pi), δ (delta), ι (iota), κ (kappa), ξ (xi), and ε (epsilon). The last double is particularly beautiful: one of its components is a bright yellow; the other is a faint green. See Fig. 4.8a.

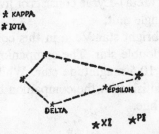

FIG. 4.8a. Boötes, The two components of ε (epsilon)-Boötis have apparent magnitudes of 3.0 and 6.3. The brighter star is distinctly yellow; the dimmer is greenish in color.

ξ (xi)-Boötis is also a double star; the two components are yellow and purple-red, respectively. The yellow companion is the brighter, its apparent magnitude is 4.7; the red star has an apparent magnitude of 6.6.

The information for the other objects follows:

	App. magn.	Color		App. magn.	Color
Kappa	4.6	white	Pi	4.9	white
	6.6	blue		6.0	white
Iota	5.0	yellow	Delta	3.6	yellow
	7.5	white		8.0	blue

B. Virgo. This constellation is rich in nebulae, for which reason this region of the sky has been called the Field of the Nebulae. Several hundred of these clouds have been discovered in Virgo.

A double star is also of interest. It is the third brightest star in the constellation, γ-Virginis. In 1756 the angular distance between the two components was 6 seconds of angle. In 1836 the two stars were so close together that they could not be distinguished by the largest telescopes. In 1936 the separation between the stars was again 6 seconds of angle. A complete revolution of these stars, lasting 180 years, had been under observation. See Fig. 4.8b.

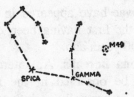

FIG. 4.8b. Virgo. γ (gamma)-Virginis is a famous double star. Its period of revolution is 180 years, and it has been under observation for nearly that length of time. Both components are alike in color (yellow) and in brightness (3.7).

4.9 JULY OBSERVATIONS

A. Scorpius. The bright red star Antares is a double. The companion is 3 seconds of angle distant from the bright star. A 4-inch telescope is needed to distinguish this binary system. Other doubles in Scorpius are the stars β (beta) and ν (nu)-Scorpii.

Several interesting star clusters are also ob-

FIG. 4.9a. Scorpius. Antares is a binary. The bright 1.2 red member of the system has a green companion of apparent magnitude 5.2. The stars β (beta)-Scorpii and ν (nu)-Scorpii are also doubles in field glasses, and small telescopes. The Nu star is actually a quadruple star, as can be seen with a 4-inch telescope.

servable. The one catalogued as Messier 80 is one of the richest in the number of stars it contains. See Fig. 4.9a.

	App. magn.	Color		App. magn.
Beta	{ 2.0	yellow		
	{ 6.0	green	Nu	{ 4.2
				{ 6.7
				{ 7.0
				{ 8.0

M80 is a cluster, rich in stars, globular in shape.

Many novae have appeared in this region of the sky, the first having been observed more than 2,000 years ago.

B. **Corona Borealis.** An interesting variable star can be observed in the middle of the crown. It is normally a sixth-magnitude star, and may keep this brightness for many months. Then, fairly rapidly, it declines in brightness; and in a few weeks, it becomes a fourteenth- or fifteenth-magnitude star. At the end of the minimum period, it begins again to become a sixth-magnitude star. See Fig. 4.9b.

FIG. 4.9b. Corona Borealis. An object of great interest to amateur astronomers is the star marked R in this constellation. It is an irregular variable star. It is normally a sixth-magnitude star, barely visible to the unaided eye. The periods of normality are interrupted from time to time, when the star dims to a magnitude 14 or 15 star. It is one of the enigmatic stars in astronomy.

4.10 AUGUST OBSERVATIONS

A. **Hercules.** The great star cluster in Hercules, M13, NGC6205, has been described in Sec. 2.60. The outer stars of the cluster are resolved into separate units even with a small telescope. But it takes a large instrument to see the full majesty of this globular cluster.

Several fine double stars in this constellation are of interest. α (alpha)-Herculis is one of

these, as are ρ (rho)- and γ (gamma)-Herculis. The δ (delta) star in this constellation looks like a double, but is only an optical double. The two stars are actually moving in different directions, and in several thousand years will be widely separated. See Fig. 4.10.

4.11 SEPTEMBER OBSERVATIONS

A. **Lyra.** The beta star in this constellation was described in Sec.2.62. It is one of the variable stars that can be observed by the unaided eye. Telescopic observations indicate that it is a multiple star, probably consisting of six components. The apparent magnitude of the individual components ranges from 3.0 to 14.3.

There are several other multiple stars in Lyra. ζ (zeta)-Lyrae consists of five stars forming a single unit.

The bright star Vega in this constellation is also a double star. The companion to Vega is a faint 10.5-magnitude star. While Vega is a blue-whitish star, the companion has a distinct orange hue.

FIG. 4.10. Hercules. α (alpha)-Herculis is a beautiful binary. The bright star (apparent magnitude 3.0) is intensely yellow, while the dimmer companion (app. magn. 6.1) is very blue.

The vital data for γ (gamma)-, δ (delta)-, and ρ (rho)-Herculis follow:

	App. magn.	Color		App. magn.	Color
Gamma	{ 3.8	white	Rho	{ 4.0	green
	{ 8.0	lilac		{ 5.1	green
Delta	{ 3.0	green			
	{ 8.1	gray			

The feature of the constellation is M13, the great globular star cluster. It is barely visible to the unaided eye, resembling a fairly hazy fifth-magnitude star. It takes at least a 5-inch telescope to perceive its real beauty, and a much larger telescope to realize the full scope of its majesty.

The cluster probably contains about 500,000 stars.

ε (epsilon)-Lyrae is a double double star. The main double can be seen without optical aid by persons of excellent eyesight.

Each star in the main double is resolved into two components with the aid of a telescope. The four stars in ε-Lyrae have the apparent magnitude of 5.1, 6.0, 5.1 and 5.4.

The Ring Nebula, M57, is so called because of its similarity to a smoke ring when observed with a 5- or 6-inch telescope.

Larger telescopes reveal its greater similarity to a soap bubble than to a flat ring.

The nebula derives its illumination from a fifteenth-magnitude star located at its center.

M57 is one of a large group of planetary nebulae: the adjective "planetary" refers to their slight resemblance in shape to terrestrial planets. See Fig. 4.11a.

FIG. 4.11a. Lyra. The Ring Nebula is an object of great interest to astronomers. It can be seen fairly well nearly halfway between β (beta)- and γ (gamma)-Lyrae with a 3-inch telescope. To set its true annular shape a telescope of at least 5 inches is needed.

β (beta)-Lyrae is a most interesting star. It consists of at least six companions of magnitudes 3.0, 6.7, 13.0, 14.3, 9.2, and 9.0. The variation of brightness of this composite star from 3.4 to 4.3 can be detected by the unaided eye.

ζ (zeta)-Lyrae consists of two bright stars (apparent magnitudes of 4.2 and 5.5) and three faint companions.

Vega is a double, the faint companion being a 10.5-magnitude star with a distinct orange color.

ε (epsilon)-Lyrae is a double double. One of the doubles, ε (epsilon)[1], consists of a 5.1-magnitude star green-white and a 6.0-magnitude star blue-white. The other double, ε (epsilon)[2], consists of a 5.1-magnitude star white and a 5.4-magnitude star very white.

B. Cygnus. This is the most marvelous region of the sky for an amateur observer.

The Milky Way separates into two great parallel branches in Cygnus; a multitude of stars, star clusters, and occasionally dark gaps can be seen there. The region is probably one of the richest in stars in all the sky.

Cygnus has also an unusually large number of variable stars. Several novae have appeared in this constellation in the last three centuries.

Double stars, too, are plentiful in Cygnus— one of which is β (beta)-Cygni. It is one of the most beautiful of all double stars, with contrasting colors of gold and blue. See Fig. 4.11b.

FIG. 4.11b. Cygnus. β (beta)-Cygni is probably the most beautiful of all the double stars. The two companions can be seen even with a magnification of 20 times of a 2-inch telescope. The bright yellow star is of apparent magnitude 3.0, while its bluish partner is a dim 5.3.

C. Sagittarius. The presence of the Milky Way in this constellation results in a beautiful array of globular clusters, open star clusters, and nebulae.

M17, the Horseshoe Nebula—a large cloud of gas and dust, of arched form—is one of the few that can be observed with a small power telescope. Many interesting stars provide the lighting for the nebula.

That part of the sky also contains a very

FIG. 4.11c. Sagittarius. M17, the Horseshoe Nebula, can be observed even with a small power telescope.

M22 (or NGC6656) is one of the finest known globular clusters.

fine globular star cluster, M22, the individual stars of which are faint. Typical magnitudes are 10, 11, etc. The sum total of all their light is great, making the cluster visible to the unaided eye. See Fig. 4.11c.

D. Aquila. Of interest to observers is the variable star η (eta)-Aquilae. It changes from a bright 3.5 to a faint 4.5 magnitude and vice versa every 7 days, 4 hours, and 12 minutes.

There are also many fine doubles in Aquila. Altair, the bright star of the constellation, is one of these. Its companion is a magnitude 10 star at an angular distance of 2.5 minutes of angle from Altair. See Fig. 4.11d.

FIG. 4.11d. Aquila. η (eta)-Aquilae is a Cepheid variable. Its maximum brightness is 3.5 apparent magnitude.

Alpha-Aquilae, or Altair, is a double star.

4.12   OCTOBER OBSERVATIONS

Telescopic observations for Cepheus have been detailed in Sec. 4.3.

4.13   NOVEMBER OBSERVATIONS

A. Pegasus. Many interesting doubles can be observed here. A fine contrast of colors is to be seen in the binary system of Epsilon-Pegasi. The bright star (magnitude 2.7) is yellowish in color; its companion (magnitude 8.7) is a clear violet. The two are more than

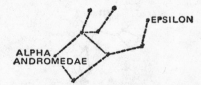

FIG. 4.13. Pegasus. ε (epsilon)-Pegasi is a double star. The bright (2.7) companion is yellowish in color; the dim partner (8.7 apparent magnitude) has a violet hue.

two minutes of angle distant from one another. See Fig. 4.13.

4.14   DECEMBER OBSERVATIONS

A. Andromeda. The Great Galaxy, M31, seen in the background of this constellation was described in Sec. 2.73. Its first observers considered it to be a cloud, or a nebula, and reference to the Queen of the Nebulae dates back more than a thousand years.

With low telescopic power, this galaxy leaves the impression of a bright elliptical object. The true nature of this grand spiral of billions of stars is revealed only by a large telescope. See Fig. 4.14a.

FIG. 4.14a. Andromeda. The Great Galaxy in Andromeda is also known as the Great Nebula in Andromeda. Its Messier number is M31; it is item number 224 in the New General Catalog. It is likely that it greatly resembles our own Milky Way galaxy.

B. Cetus. The chief object of interest is the long period variable ο (omicron)-Ceti, the star also known as Mira, the Wonderful Star. It varies in brightness from a second magnitude

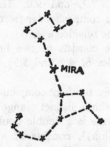

FIG. 4.14b. Cetus. Mira, or ο (omicron)-Ceti, is a long period variable. The star is distinctly red in color, of the giant variety of stars.

to a faint tenth-magnitude star. Its period is irregular, averaging 330 days.

The star has been under study for more than 350 years, and its brightness is still being studied by amateur observers. See Fig. 4.14b.

4.15 JANUARY OBSERVATIONS

A. **Perseus.** The eclipsing variable star β (beta)-Persei, also known as Algol, has been described in Sec. 2.76. Its light intensity varies from a bright 2.2 magnitude to a faint 3.5 magnitude, repeating every 2 days, 20 hours, 48 minutes. The changes in its brightness are very regular. It remains most of the time at its brightest, while the eclipse lasts 9¾ hours. The star then returns very rapidly to the 2.2 magnitude. It is a classic example of an eclipsing binary. Both stars have been studied at length and reasonably accurate data concerning them are available. The brighter has a diameter of 2,500,000 miles, and a mass five times that of the sun. The fainter has a diameter 20 per cent greater and a mass equal to that of the sun. The stars are very close to one another, the distance between their centers being about 7 million miles. They revolve about their common center of gravity, com-

FIG. 4.15a. Perseus. The variations of Algol can be observed by the unaided eye.

η (eta)-Persei is a double star. The bright component has an apparent magnitude of 4.0, the dimmer of 8.5. The colors of the two are very distinct; the bright one is very yellow, the dim—very blue.

The double cluster NGC869 and NGC884 are of great interest. They are located beyond the star Eta-Persei in the direction of Cassiopeia, and are visible to the naked eye. The pair is one of the most beautiful clusters of stars in the sky.

pleting a revolution in 2 days, 20 hours, 48 minutes. The plane of their orbit is not quite in our line of sight; it is inclined nearly 8° to that line. The eclipse is partial. When the star appears at its dimmest, more than half of the brighter component is eclipsed. Observations of β (beta)-Persei can be made by the unaided eye.

Another object of interest in Perseus is a double star cluster. The two close clusters can be seen with the aid of telescope just beyond η (eta)-Persei, in the direction of Cassiopeia. See Fig. 4.15a.

B. **Taurus.** The seven stars in this constellation, known as the Pleiades, or the Seven Sisters, are an object of great interest to the amateur astronomer. To the unaided eye, seven stars are visible, but even a small telescope aids in detecting more than a hundred. On a photographic plate, there are thousands of stars. The stars in the Pleiades group appear to be enveloped in a tenuous nebula, the latter being illuminated by the light of these stars.

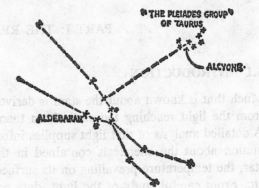

FIG. 4.15b. Taurus. The brightest star in the Pleiades group of this constellation, Alcyone, is a triple star in small instruments, and a quadruple star when observed with large telescopes.

Aldebaran, the brightest star of the whole constellation, has as a companion an 11.2-magnitude star.

Taurus also contains many double and multiple stars. The bright star Alcyone in the Pleiades subgroup is a quadruple star. The brightest star in the constellation, Aldebaran, is accompanied by an 11.2-magnitude, orange-hued star, which can be seen under good atmospheric conditions with a 3-inch refractor. See Fig. 4.15b.

4.16 SOUTH CIRCUMPOLAR OBSERVATIONS

In the constellations that are not visible in middle northern latitudes, there are many objects of interest to telescopic observers.

Alpha-Crucis is a double star. The Alpha star of the Centaurus constellation is a triple star, the three components having magnitudes of .3, 1.7, and 11.0, respectively. A description of *a* (alpha)-Centauri was given in Sec. 2.82.

The skies "down under" are also rich in clusters and nebulae. One of the closest globular clusters of stars is listed as number 104 in the New General Catalog—an almost perfectly round ball, closely packed with a countless number of magnitude 12 and fainter stars.

A "must" object for observations are two galaxies close to the South Celestial Pole. These galaxies have been known for centuries by the names Greater Magellanic Cloud and Lesser Magellanic Cloud: both can be seen by the unaided eye. The larger galaxy has a diameter of about 30,000 light-years; the smaller less than 25,000 light-years. Strong moonlight obliterates the smaller galaxy, but the Greater Magellanic Cloud remains visible even in strong moonlight.

CHAPTER 5

TELESCOPES AND THEIR USES

PART I: THE REFRACTING TELESCOPE

5.1 INTRODUCTION

Much that is known about the stars is derived from the light reaching the earth from them. A detailed analysis of that light supplies information about the chemicals contained in the star, the temperature prevailing on its surface, etc. From careful study of the light, data are obtained about the mass and velocity of the star, as well as a great deal of other information.

Vital to this research is the telescope, which aids the astronomer in three distinct ways: (a) by gathering the light emanating from a star, thus making the star appear brighter—this property of the instrument is called the **Light-gathering Power;** (b) by bringing out details, e.g., separating the components of a double star—this property is called the **Resolving Power;** and (c) by magnifying, or "enlarging" the section of sky under observa-

tion—this is the **Magnifying Power of the telescope.**

There are two major classes of telescopes: **Refracting Telescopes,** and **Reflecting Telescopes.** This section is devoted to the refracting telescope—its composition, properties, and characteristics.

5.2 THE PROCESS OF "SEEING"

Human beings "see" as a result of the light emanating from an object falling upon the light-sensitive inner lining of the eye, the retina. Thus, part of the light emerging, say, from the flame of a candle finds its way through the pupil of the eye, to the retina, which converts the light into a nervous impulse. The optic nerve then transmits these impulses to the brain, producing the sensation of vision.

Non-luminous objects, such as books and chairs are seen by light reflected by them—the reflected sunlight, or artificial light, reaches the observer's retina.

The visual image formed on the retina is on a point to point relationship with the object observed. Thus every point of the flame must illuminate one, and only one, point on the retina.

This idea may be clarified by an example.

Let the object under observation be a luminous arrow, AB. The light emitted by a given point of this arrow, say point C, goes off in all directions in space. A small part of that light enters the observer's eye. The part that enters the eye is in the form of a cone.

To produce clear vision, all the light in the cone must converge on a single point in the retina—a task performed by the crystalline lens in the eye, located just inside the pupil. The point on the retina is the image of the point C on the object—hence, C′.

Images of all the other points of the object are formed on the retina in a similar manner, accumulating to form the image of the luminous arrow, A′B′. See Fig. 5.2a.

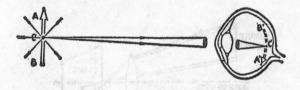

FIG. 5.2a. The process of seeing. AB is a luminous arrow, every point of which is a minute source of light.

The light emanating from one of these points (point C) goes off in all directions (seven rays of light are indicated). Some of that light enters the observer's eye. The rays so entering form a cone. The crystalline lens in the eye converges all the rays to one point C′, on the retina. C′ is the image on the retina of point C on the object. Every other point on the arrow will form a similar image on the retina.

The sum total of all the points on the retina produces the complete image A′B′.

The lens makes use of the curvatures of its surfaces to perform this task. To see how this is done, let us follow two of these rays on their route from point C to point C′. Ray 1, emanating from point C, is refracted at the front surface of the lens, goes through the lens, and is refracted a second time on crossing the rear surface of the lens, falling on the retina at point C′.

This refraction is similar to the refraction (the breakage) that a ray of light undergoes in passing from air into water, or from water into air; or in passing through a glass prism. See Fig. 5.2b.

FIG. 5.2b. Refraction of a light ray on going through a thin prism. The direction of the ray is changed on going from air (A) into glass. The direction is changed again on going from the glass into air (B).

Ray 2, emanating from point C, undergoes similar experience: (a) It is refracted at the front surface of the lens. (b) It passes through the lens. (c) It is refracted a second time on crossing the rear surface. To obtain a clear image of point C, ray 2 must intersect ray 1 at the retina. The lens in the eye adjusts its curvatures to assure the two rays intersecting at the precise point.

Similarly, all other rays emanating from point C on the object, and entering the eye through the pupil, meet at point C′. See Fig. 5.2c.

All that has been said about the crystalline lens in the human eye holds true for the glass lens used in telescopes. There is, however, an

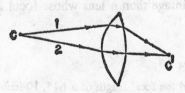

FIG. 5.2c The lens. All the rays reaching the lens from point C are refracted by the lens to converge at point C′. Each ray, such as 1 or 2, is refracted both on entering the lens and on leaving it.

important difference between the two. The eye lens is able to change the curvature of its surfaces. This changes the distance from the focus to the lens. In the case of a glass lens, the focus is fixed.

5.3   LENS SPECIFICATIONS

A lens is specified by indicating the aperture, focal length, and focal ratio (of f number).

These three specifications are related through the formula

$$\text{f number (or focal ratio)} = \frac{\text{focal length}}{\text{aperture}}$$

The aperture is the clear diameter of the lens through which light can get through. It usually denotes the size of the telescope (e.g., 40-inch).

The focal length is the distance between the center of the lens and the focus.

A Focus of a lens is the point on the axis where all the rays parallel to the axis meet. See Fig. 5.3.

FIG. 5.3. The focus of a lens. The focus is a point on the axis of a lens where all the rays parallel to the axis meet. (Only part of the paths of the rays is shown.)

The size of the image varies with the focal length—it increases as the focal length increases. A focal length of 70 cm will form a larger image than a lens whose focal length is 60 cm.

PROBLEM 5.3:

Find the focal length of a f-15, 10-inch aperture lens.

Answer: 150 inches.

The focal length of a lens is often about 15 times the aperture.

5.4   A SIMPLE REFRACTING TELESCOPE

The simplest kind of a refracting telescope consists of only two lenses. The one that is exposed to the object (the star, moon, etc.) is called **the Objective.** Its function is to produce an image of the object under observation. The other lens, through which the observer views the image, is called **the Eyepiece.**

The objects of interest in astronomy are, as a rule, at great distances. The light entering the objective from each point of the object is in the form of parallel rays, the image produced by these rays forming in the focal plane.

The Focal Plane is a plane passing through the focus, perpendicular to the axis of the lens.

The image produced by the first lens is called the **First Image.**

The function of the eyepiece is to magnify the first image. To achieve magnification, the eyepiece is placed so that the first image is just inside its focus—i.e., between the eyepiece and its focus, very close to the focus.

Note that the **Final Image** subtends a larger angle at the observer's eye than did the object.

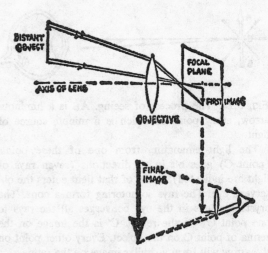

FIG. 5.4. A simple refracting telescope. The objective forms an image in the focal plane of the lens. This is known as the first image.

The eyepiece (shown here in the lower part of the picture as actually *in line* with the objective lens) forms the final image which is a magnification of the first image.

The enlarging of the angle is known as **Angular Magnification.** See Fig. 5.4.

One of the primary functions of a telescope is to produce angular magnification.

PROBLEM 5.4:

An object subtends an angle of 20° at the eye of an observer. The final image subtends an angle of 80°. Find the angular magnification.

Answer: The magnification is 4 times.

The simple type of astonomical telescope described, composed of two lenses, will be used only for small values of magnification. Such a telescope may be used for magnifications up to 10 times **for each inch** of diameter of aperture of the objective. Thus, if the aperture of the objective has a diameter of 2.38 inches, the telescope will be used for angular magnification of 20 to 25 times. The "aperture" of an objective is the transparent part of the objective. It does not include part of the edge of the lens that is cemented to the holder, through which light cannot pass.

To obtain higher magnification (say 40 to 60 times) per inch of diameter, the objective lens will have to be designed so as to remove two common defects. These defects are known as "aberrations" and are usually present in simple lenses. One of these is known as **Chromatic Aberration;** the other as **Spherical Aberration.** The eyepiece, too, will have to be of a more complex design.

5.5 CHROMATIC ABERRATION (COLOR DEFECT OF LENS)

A ray of ordinary light, upon passing through a lens, is not only refracted, but also dispersed into its component colors. This is a highly undesirable feature of the lens. Every ray of "white" light entering the lens from the left is dispersed into a small rainbow of colors.

The term "white light" signifies the ordinary light given off by the sun, stars, etc. This light is actually a combination of all the colors of a rainbow, well mixed. The lens "unmixes" the colors, as each color included in this white ray

of light is refracted at a slightly different angle.

From Figure 5.5a it can be seen that the violet component of the white ray of light is refracted the most; and the red part of the white ray, the least. As a result of this difference in refraction, the violet components of the light will focus closer to the lens than will the red parts.

The "trouble" caused by this defect is obvious. The point to point relationship no longer holds. Rays emanating from one point in the object no longer converge on one point of the image. Each color of the original light converges at a different distance from the lens.

This defect of the simple lens, by which light of different colors fails to arrive at the same focus, is called Chromatic Aberration.

FIG. 5.5a. Chromatic aberration. The violet component is refracted most, while the red component of the white light is bent least. All the other colors are intermediate between these extremes.

To reduce the effects of chromatic aberration, lenses are now made from two component parts, cemented together with Canada balsam or airspaced to form one unit. See Fig. 5.5b.

FIG. 5.5b. A compound lens. Such a lens consists of two (or more) components cemented together with transparent Canada balsam, or airspaced. Chromatic aberration can be greatly reduced by a proper choice of the quality of glass for each component.

One component is in the form of a converging lens; the other, a diverging lens.

NOTE: A converging lens is thicker at the center than at the circumference. Its function is to converge rays of light, that is, to bring the rays closer. A diverging lens is thinner at the center than at the circumference. Its function is to diverge rays. See Fig. 5.5c.

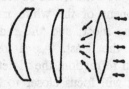

FIG. 5.5c. Three types of converging lenses. Any lens that is thicker in the middle than at the edges is a converging lens. As its name implies such a lens converges rays of light going through it.

The converging lens is produced from crown glass, a very serviceable material for refracting light, dispersing white light into colors only slightly.

The diverging lens is made from flint glass, which is much better for dispersing light than for refracting it. This lens nullifies the dispersion that was produced by the converging lens; it does not, however, remove all the refraction that was produced by the first lens. See Fig. 5.5d.

FIG. 5.5d. Three types of diverging lenses. Any lens that is thinner at the center than at the edges is a Diverging Lens. As its name implies such a lens diverges light rays going through it.

As a result the light is refracted, but not dispersed, thus eliminating chromatic aberration.

This compound lens is known as an **Achromatic** or a **Color-Free Lens,** and is commonly used for objective lenses in telescopes.

A compound lens is actually "color free" for only *two* colors, say green and red or blue and violet. The two colors chosen for perfect focusing are determined by the use to which the telescope will be put. Green and red are best for an objective used primarily for visual purposes, as the human eye is most sensitive to

colors at the red end of the spectrum. An objective in a telescope designed primarily for photographic work will have the compound lens calculated to bring blue and violet to the same focus, as common photographic emulsions are sensitive at the blue end of the color spectrum.

5.6 SPHERICAL ABERRATION (SHAPE DEFECT OF LENS)

This is a defect of lenses with spherical surfaces. See Fig. 5.6a. Most lenses have such surfaces. Both the front and back surfaces of these lenses are portions of spheres. Light cannot properly be focused by such a lens. The light rays passing close to the edges of such lenses are refracted more than light rays passing through the center. Thus, the rays marked A on Fig. 5.6b come to a focus closer to the

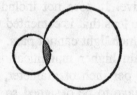

FIG. 5.6a. Spherical lenses. Both the front and the rear of an ordinary lens have the shape of a portion of a sphere. Such lenses cause a defect in the image known as spherical aberration.

FIG. 5.6b. Spherical aberration. Light ray A, close to the edge of the lens, is refracted more than light ray B. Parallel rays thus do not converge to one focus. This defect has nothing to do with the color of light. Spherical aberration is present even when the light is monochromatic.

lens than the ray marked B. Again, the point to point relationship is no longer valid, and the result is a blurred image.

This defect is entirely independent of chromatic aberration; spherical aberration may be present even when there is no dispersion.

The defect is adjusted by making each face of the lens paraboloid in form rather than spherical. A paraboloid lens is curved less at the edges than at the center, and converges parallel rays to a single sharply defined focus.

5.7 CORRECTED OBJECTIVES

Achromatic objectives can now be designed to remedy spherical as well as chromatic aberrations. The components of such a lens need not have paraboloid surfaces, but instead can use spherical surfaces. There are two steps in its design: To begin, the lens maker chooses the spherical curvatures and type of glass needed for each component of the achromatic lens. Then, he employs available scientific data to choose the proper combination of curvatures to eliminate the spherical aberration.

In one such design the converging lens is made of crown glass. The radii of its spherical surfaces are in the ratio of 2 to 3; and the diverging lens is made of flint. One of its sides is a plane; the other side is constructed to fit the surface with shorter radius. This compound lens has no spherical aberration and is also corrected for chromatic aberration.

As a telescope objective the three-lens "Apochromat" lens is by far superior to the ordinary achromatic lens. In an apochromatic lens, three or more colors are focused simultaneously, rather than two colors, as with the ordinary achromatic lens. The former is also entirely free of spherical aberration.

5.8 EYEPIECES

An eyepiece is simply a magnifying glass of short focal length and usually consists of two lenses—one, the **Field Lens;** the other, the **Eye Lens.** The observer's eye is placed next to the eye lens. The two lenses are permanently mounted in a draw tube that can be moved forward and backward inside the main tube of the telescope.

The chief purpose of the field lens is to collect the light rays from the objective and direct them toward the usually smaller eye lens.

The primary purpose of the eye lens is to magnify.

Many eyepieces have been designed and marketed in recent years. Three useful ones are the **Huygenian,** the **Kellner,** and the **Orthoscopic.**

The quality of an eyepiece is determined by:

a. Make
b. Focal length
c. Apparent field of view

A complete description of a typical eyepiece would, for example, be: Huygenian, 27-mm focal length, apparent field of view 50°; or: Kellner, 40-mm focal length and apparent field of view 40°.

NOTE: 1. The focal length refers to the whole eyepiece, that is, the combination of field lens and eye lens.
2. The apparent field of view is just that—the angle subtended by the diameter of the circular view, seen through the eyepiece. See Fig. 5.8.

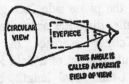

FIG. 5.8. Apparent field of view. Looking through the eyepiece the eye sees a circle of light. The angle subtended at the eye by the diameter of that circle is called the apparent field of view. This angle is a constant for any eyepiece.

The angle that the diameter of the view subtends at the observer's eye is constant for each eyepiece, whether it is used with a telescope or independently.

5.9 THE HUYGENIAN EYEPIECE

This eyepiece consists of two plano-convex lenses, the convex sides away from the eye. See Fig. 5.9. A typical eyepiece of 25-mm focal length may consist of an eye lens 12-mm diameter, 16-mm focal length, and a field lens 26-mm diameter, 48-mm focal length, with a spacing of 32 mm between the lenses.

Good Huygenian eyepieces have an apparent field of view of 50°, and are used primarily when such large angles are needed. The Huygenian eyepieces are often not too well corrected for optical defects; consequently, their use is limited to low magnifications.

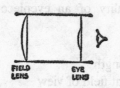

FIG. 5.9. The Huygenian eyepiece. Such an eyepiece consists of two plano-convex lenses spaced about an inch apart. The plane side of each lens is toward the eye.

5.10 THE KELLNER EYEPIECE

This eyepiece, which is an improvement of a prototype known as the **Ramsden** eyepiece, is very popular for medium range magnifications. The eyepiece consists of a plano-convex field lens, the plane side facing the objective, and a smaller diameter achromatic eye lens. A typical Kellner eyepiece of 25-mm focal length would consist of a field lens 28-mm diameter, 41-mm focal length, and an achromatic eye lens 18-mm diameter, 32-mm focal length, with a separation of 20 mm between the lenses. See Fig. 5.10a.

FIG. 5.10a. The Kellner eyepiece. This eyepiece consists of a plano-convex field lens, the plane side facing the objective, and an achromatic eye lens.

The earlier Ramsden eyepiece had no correction for chromatic aberration; and it looked like this (Figure 5.10b):

FIG. 5.10b. The Ramsden eyepiece.

5.11 THE ORTHOSCOPIC EYEPIECE

This eyepiece is one of the best eyepieces available, especially for high magnifications. It consists of a field lens of three components, and a single plano-convex eye lens. The three components of the field lens are a double concave flint lens cemented in sandwich style between two double convex crown lenses. The single plano-convex eye lens is located close to the field lens and has its plane side next to the eye. The lens is corrected for both chromatic and spherical aberrations, and produces a brilliant image in normal proportions. See Fig. 5.11.

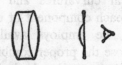

FIG. 5.11. The orthoscopic eyepiece. The field lens consists of three components, crown glass, flint glass, and crown glass, glued together with Canada balsam. The eye lens, very close to the field lens, is plano-convex in shape, the plane side being next to the eye.

When a telescope intended for visual purposes is used for photography, a plate holder replaces the eyepiece.

5.12 COATING OF LENSES

Only part of the light entering the telescope is actually transmitted through the several lenses; a sizable fraction is *reflected* from each optical surface. These reflections from curved surfaces produce troublesome secondary images, and reduce materially the brilliance and clarity of the desired image.

In recent years, this shortcoming has been reduced by coating the glass surface with a thin transparent film, usually of magnesium fluoride, so as to produce interference between the light waves reflected at the top of the coating and the light waves reflected from the bottom, thus eliminating the reflected light. Such destructive interference will happen only if the coating is precisely one quarter of a wavelength thick. Figure 5.12 details what happens.

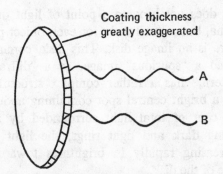

Coating thickness greatly exaggerated

A

B

FIG. 5.12. Coating of lenses. Wave A is reflected from the top of the coating layer, wave B from its bottom (i.e., from the lens itself). The thickness of the coating is adjusted so as to bring about interference between these two waves, and thus eliminate the troublesome reflection from both surfaces.

Ray B is reflected from the bottom of the coating, hence it goes through that layer twice, once going in and once after reflection from the lens surface, and will be out of step by half a wavelength with ray A which is reflected from the top of the coating.

The crests of ray B will destructively interfere with the troughs of ray A and thus eliminate the reflected light.

NOTES: 1. Many light phenomena are explained by the theory that light is an electromagnetic wave. The so-called "rays of light" are merely lines to indicate the direction of the wave's propagation.

2. The phenomenon of interference (i.e., two rays of light when out of step by the proper amount producing darkness), is one of the arguments that light is a wave.

3. The thickness of the film is usually designed to be equal to one quarter of a wavelength of yellow-green light to which the human eye is most sensitive.

A set of lenses properly coated may increase the brightness of the image as much as 30 per cent.

5.13   THE THREE POWERS OF THE TELESCOPE

Telescopes have three functions to perform:

1. To increase the apparent brightness of the object. This increase in brightness depends on the light-gathering power of the telescope.

2. To bring out detail that cannot be seen with the unaided eye. How well a telescope performs this function depends on the resolving power.

3. To magnify the object, or to make it appear that the object is closer. How well a telescope performs this function depends on the magnifying power of the telescope.

5.14   THE LIGHT-GATHERING POWER OF A TELESCOPE

The most important function of a telescope, probably, is to gather a large quantity of light from a star. The telescope "squeezes the light together" into a beam narrow enough to enter the pupil of the eye. See Fig. 5.14.

OBJECTIVE

FIG. 5.14. Light-gathering power of a telescope. All the rays that go in through the large objective come out through the small eyepiece.

This concentration of lights increases greatly the apparent brightness of the object.

The light-gathering power makes it possible to see stars of magnitude higher than 6, the stars that are too faint to be seen by the naked eye. This light-gathering power depends only on the objective lens—it is proportional to its area. **Or: the Light-gathering Power is proportional to the square of the diameter of the objective lens.**

At night, the pupil of the eye has a diameter of approximately ¼ inch. A telescope having an objective of 1 inch diameter admits into the eye $4^2=16$ times more light than does the unaided eye. A 2-inch telescope would admit $8^2=64$ times more light, and so on. Experience verifies this theory. Thus, with a 2-inch telescope, one can observe stars 64 times dimmer than a sixth-magnitude star. These are stars classified as magnitude 10.5.

Similarly, it can be computed that with a 6-inch objective, stars of 12.9 magnitude can be seen; and with a 15-inch objective, stars of 14.9 magnitude can be seen.

5.15 THE RESOLVING POWER OF A TELESCOPE

The resolving power is intimately connected with the clarity with which details can be seen.

The greater the resolving power of a telescope, the clearer will be the detail.

Thus a point of light that appears to the naked eye as one star may be separated (resolved) into two or more close stars when viewed through a telescope with high resolving power.

It is important to have a clear understanding of that power, so we'll dwell on it a bit more.

Consider two pinpoints of light—say, two candles. At a distance of several feet, the two will appear as separate and distinct sources of light. At a greater distance, the two will merge into *one* relatively fuzzy point of light. Experiment shows that the pinpoints of light can no

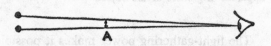

FIG. 5.15a. Resolving power of a telescope. When the angle A subtended at the eye by two points of light is less than 6 minutes, the eye ceases to note them as two distinct points. This can also be stated by saying that at angles smaller than 6 minutes the eye is unable to resolve the object it sees into separate units.

longer be separated when the angle A subtended by them at the eye is less than about 6 minutes of angle. Otherwise stated: **The resolving power of the normal eye is 6 minutes of angle.** See Fig. 5.15a.

The inability to separate points subtending an angle smaller than 6 minutes is due to a basic property of light, known as **Diffraction.** Due to diffraction, a point of light on the ob-

ject does not become a point of light on the retina, but a small disk; for each object point, there is an image disk. This disk, commonly called a "spurious" image, or a "diffraction pattern," has a rather complex structure. It has a bright central spot containing about 85 per cent of total light surrounded by alternating dark and light rings, the light rings decreasing rapidly in brightness toward the edge of the disk.

Thus, the light emanating from point C does not form in reality a point C′ but rather a "spurious" image C′ on the retina. See Fig. 5.15b.

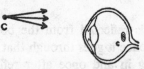

FIG. 5.15b. Spurious image. Light emanating from a point C does *not* converge to a point C′ on the retina, as is usually assumed for the sake of oversimplification. The image of every point of light on the retina is a minute system of concentric light and dark circles.

If a second point of light E (not shown in the figure) is closer than 6 minutes of angle to point C, the spurious image due to it, E′, will materially overlap C′. The brain is no longer able to distinguish two separate points. The eye cannot resolve E from C and will see the two as only one slightly elongated point of light.

The "point to point" relationship between object and image oversimplifies the truth. In reality, it is a point to disk relationship. It is not difficult to see that the smaller the size of these disks, the more detail will be obtained. Optical theory shows that the larger the objective lens, the smaller will be the diameter of the disk.

Optical theory, as well as practice, also shows that the resolving power of a telescope depends **only** upon the diameter of the objective. Thus, stars that appear as one unit in a small telescope may resolve into two or more close neighbors when viewed by a telescope with a larger objective.

There is a simple formula relating the diameter of the objective with the resolving power:

$$\text{Resolving power} = \frac{5}{\text{Diameter of objective}}$$

In this formula, the diameter should be stated in inches; the resolving power in seconds of angle.

A telescope with a 2-inch objective can resolve two stars that subtend an angle of 2.5 seconds of arc at the eye of the observer.

5.16 THE MAGNIFYING POWER OF A TELESCOPE

Telescopes magnify angles. **One of the primary functions of the instrument is to magnify the angles subtended by the objects under observation, a process known as Angular Magnification.** Thus, if without a telescope, an object subtends an angle of 3°, and when viewed through a telescope, the image subtends an angle of 45°, the magnification is 15 times. See Fig. 5.16a.

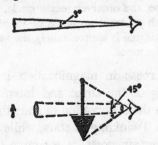

Fig. 5.16a. The magnifying power of a telescope. The object as seen by the unaided eye subtends an angle of 3°.

The image of the same object (lower figure) in the telescope subtends an angle of 45°.

The magnifying power of this telescope is

$$\frac{45}{3} = 15 \text{ times.}$$

Angular magnification is the only magnification that a telescope performs. The increase in the angle gives the impression of nearness, thus making the image appear to be nearer than was the object.

PROBLEM 5.16a:

The moon subtends an angle of approximately ½ a degree of angle at the observer's eye. When viewed through a telescope, the moon's image subtends an angle of 4°. Compute the angular magnification.

$$Answer: \frac{4}{\frac{1}{2}} = 8 \text{ times.}$$

The magnifying power of a telescope depends both on the focal length of the objective lens and on the focal length of the eyepiece.

The angular magnification of a telescope is stated by the simple formula:

$$\text{Angular Magnification} = \frac{f_{\text{eyepiece}}}{f_{\text{objective}}}$$

$f_{\text{objective}}$ represents the focal length of the objective. This distance is usually stated in inches or millimeters. f_{eyepiece} represents the focal length of the eyepiece, the distance usually stated in the same units as the $f_{\text{objective}}$. **Focal length of a lens is the distance from the focus to the center of the lens.**

(The image in most telescopes appears inverted. A star, even with the highest magnification obtainable, appears as a point of light. The fact that it is inverted is of no importance.)

The formula for magnification seems to indicate that there is no limit to magnification, that any desired magnification, say a million times, can be obtained in three ways:

(A) By making the focal length of the objective large. This implies a lens that is only a little thicker at the center than at the edges.

(B) By making the focal length of the eyepiece small. In practice, this would mean that the lens would have to be much thicker at the center than at the edges.

(C) By combination of (A) and (B).

The indications of the formula are correct. Theoretically, there is no limit to possible magnifications.

There are, however, four important limitations to the use of high values of magnification:

a. Magnification decreases the clarity of the picture by increasing the size of the spurious image. The higher the magnification, the greater the decrease in the clarity and distinctness of the picture. **It does no good to force magnification beyond the resolving power of the telescope.**

b. Increase in magnification causes decrease in brightness of the image. The same quantity of light is spread out over a larger area with resulting faintness of image.

c. Increase in magnification decreases the actual field of view of the sky. On doubling the magnification, the angular diameter of the view is cut in half.

The relation between magnification and actual field of view is illustrated in Figure 5.16b (A), (B), and (C). In all three views the telescope pointed in the same direction.

With low magnification, the tops of two houses and a large portion of the sky were in the field of view. (A)

With higher magnification, only the tower of one of the houses can be seen through the telescope. (B)

With still higher magnification, one window occupies the whole view. (C)

The technical term **field of view** is often used in connection with telescopes. **By definition, it is the ratio of two other quantities inherent to every telescope.** These quantities are: (1) the apparent field of view of the eyepiece, and (2) the angular magnification of the telescope.

$$\text{Actual field of view} = \frac{\text{apparent field of view of eyepiece}}{\text{magnification}}$$

The apparent field of view is a fixed quantity for each eyepiece, information that the manufacturer usually supplies with the product, in terms of degrees of angle. Magnification can easily be determined by dividing $f_{objective}$ by $f_{eyepiece}$.

PROBLEM 5.16b:

The eyepiece of a telescope has an apparent field of view of, say, 40°. Its focal length is 10 millimeters. The objective has a focal length of 800 millimeters. Find: (a) the magnifying power; and (b) the actual field of view.

Solution:

a. Magnifying power $= \dfrac{f_{objective}}{f_{eyepiece}} = \dfrac{800}{10}$
    $= 80$ times.

b. Actual field of view $=$

$$\frac{\text{apparent field of view}}{\text{magnification}} = \frac{40}{80} = \frac{1}{2} \text{ degree.}$$

The ½ degree means that, looking through this telescope, the observer sees a circle, the diameter of which subtends an angle of ½ of one degree. Half a degree is approximately the angular diameter of the moon.

d. Increase in magnification increases the twinkling of the stars, and interferes materially with the observation of stars that are close together. Twinkling of stars, while very attractive to certain poets, is a source of great annoyance to an astronomical observer. **The twinkling is actually a rapid variation of the star's apparent brightness and colors accompanied by rapid fluctuations in its apparent posi-**

FIG. 5.16b. (A) Left, (B) Center, (C) Right.

tion. These variations and fluctuations are wholly due to the effect of the earth's atmosphere on the starlight going through it; and they are greatly magnified in a large telescope. It is not unusual that a great telescope is rendered practically useless on a perfectly cloudless night, due to bad "seeing" conditions.

Because of these four reasons, there is a practical limit for maximum magnification. **Maximum magnification is usually kept well within 50 times for each inch of the diameter of the objective.** A 4-inch telescope would be used at the most for magnification up to 200 times.

There is also a **minimum to useful magnification, usually 4 times for every inch of diameter of objective.** If the magnification is less than this, the column of light coming out of the eyepiece will be too large to enter the pupil of the eye and some of the light will be wasted.

5.17 TELESCOPIC MOUNTINGS

One of the most important parts of a telescope, and one to which much engineering skill and ingenuity are devoted, is the mounting.

A long tube has a tendency to vibrate, making the stars "dance." A good rigid mounting greatly minimizes vibrations.

The mounting must be designed so that the telescope can be directed to any point in the sky, from the horizon to the zenith, and to every azimuth from 0° to 360°. The simplest unit to accomplish this is a combination of vertical and horizontal axes—the telescope is attached to a fork through horizontal bearings, and thus can be rotated from horizon to zenith through various altitudes. The fork, in turn, is able to rotate on a vertical axis through the 360° of a horizontal circle. This is the **Alt-Azimuth Mounting.** See Fig. 5.17a.

An alt-azimuth mounting is often used to obtain instantaneous values of the altitude and azimuth of stars or other celestial bodies. It cannot easily be used for long-time observations or long-exposure photography, as the stars constantly change both their altitude and

FIG. 5.17a. Alt-azimuth mounting. The telescope can be rotated about the horizontal axis A, and can thus be directed to any altitude from the horizon to the zenith.

The telescope together with the horizontal axis can be rotated about the vertical axis B to any azimuth from 0° to 360°.

azimuth. The telescope in an alt-azimuth mounting would have to be adjusted continuously for both the vertical and horizontal angle.

NOTE: An alt-azimuth mounting is used in the 236-inch U.S.S.R. telescope. Its use there is justified by the tremendous weight (750 tons) of the moving parts. A digital computer is programmed to make adjustments.

The Equatorial Mounting is specially designed for the purpose of keeping a star in view for long periods of time. See Fig. 5.17b. Only one angle has to be adjusted con-

FIG. 5.17b. The equatorial mounting. The telescope is rotated about the declination axis to the desired declination, and clamped firmly at that position.

The telescope together with the declination axis rotates about the polar axis to keep the object continuously in the field of view.

tinuously; this adjustment is usually performed by a small motor. In this mounting, there are also two axes, and they are also at right angles. One axis is known as the polar axis and is constructed to be parallel to the axis of the celestial sphere. The other axis, known as the declination axis, rotates about the polar axis. The telescope is attached to the end of the declination axis, and can be turned about this axis to any declination desired. Once a star of a given declination is brought into view, the telescope can be firmly clamped to the declination axis, as the declination of a star is an invariable quantity. To keep the star in view, the telescope together with the declination axis must rotate about the polar axis. Once this motion is properly adjusted on the motor, the telescope will follow the star continuously along its path and will have the star in its field of view at all times.

The motor must be adjusted to complete one revolution in one day.

A telescope on an equatorial mounting can also find a given star, for which the data needed are the declination and sidereal hour angle. The telescope is rotated about the declination axis to the given declination and clamped in that position. The declination axis and telescope are then rotated about the polar axis to the proper sidereal hour angle.

PART II: THE REFLECTING TELESCOPE

5.18 INTRODUCTION

Newton's name is associated with the invention of this type of telescope. In the reflector, the function of the objective lens is performed by a mirror. The incoming light is converged by a concave mirror rather than a lens. The image formed by the mirror is viewed with an eyepiece, which is basically the same as that of the refracting type of telescope. Almost everything that was said about the refracting telescope applies here.

5.19 THE SILVERING OF THE MIRROR

Unlike the ordinary household mirror, the silver on the telescopic mirror is put on the front, or concave, side of the mirror, the glass merely acting as a support for the silver. Having the metal in front of the glass eliminates absorption. The light does not pass through the glass and does not lose part of its intensity by absorption in it.

The disadvantage is that the unprotected silver layer becomes tarnished so often and the mirror must be resilvered periodically.

In recent years, an "aluminizing" process has gradually replaced silvering. It has been recently found that vaporized aluminum condensing on glass forms a brilliant surface that is in many respects superior to that of silver. The coating must be made in a vacuum; aluminum thus applied does not tarnish. Upon its first exposure, it becomes coated with a transparent, extremely hard, thin film of oxide of aluminum, which protects the aluminum under it from any further interaction with air.

Another superior feature of the aluminum coating is that it reflects ultraviolet light. Silver is a very poor reflector for that shortwave radiation.

Red light, however, is reflected better by silver; also, in overall reflection, silver is somewhat superior. Silver, at its best, reflects 95 per cent of the total light; aluminum, only 90 per cent.

5.20 LAYOUT OF OPTICAL PARTS

The mirror is placed at the lower end of the tube. The reflected light forms the image in the middle of the incoming rays. To be able to view this image through the eyepiece, it must be moved. Two arrangements that are often used were devised by Newton and his French contemporary Cassegrain, respectively.

In Newton's arrangement, the converging rays of light are intercepted just before the focal plane by a plane mirror. The mirror diverts the rays through the side of the tube to the eyepiece. A reflecting prism is sometimes used instead of a mirror. See Fig. 5.20a.

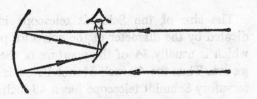

FIG. 5.20a. The arrangement of the objective (mirror) and the eyepiece in the case of a reflecting telescope.

The mirror is at the lower end of the tube (the objective in a refractor, of course, is in the upper end).

The image produced by the mirror is amid the incoming rays. An eyepiece could not be placed there as the observer would materially interfere with the incoming light.

In the Newtonian-type telescope, the one shown here, a little plane mirror diverts the rays through the side of the tube to the eyepiece.

In a Cassegrainian arrangement, a convex mirror is doing the diverting. The converging rays are intercepted by the convex mirror and brought to a focus through an opening cut in the objective. One of the advantages of this arrangement is the flexibility in the focal length of the objective mirror. A complete set of convex mirrors used in conjunction with the objective offers a variety of focal lengths. See Fig. 5.20b.

Some telescopic reflectors are geared to handle both the Newtonian and Cassegrainian arrangements.

Inevitably, the small mirror or prism cuts off some of the incoming light. Relatively, the loss in light is small, a minute fraction of the total amount falling on the objective lens. The obstruction cannot be seen at the eyepiece. It does not, as one might suspect, interfere with the image.

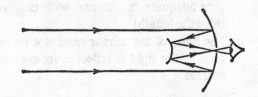

FIG. 5.20b. The Cassegrainian arrangement. Diverting of the image produced by the objectives is done by a small concave mirror. The converging rays reflected by the objective are reflected by this concave mirror once more and brought to a focus just beyond an opening cut in the objective.

A particular reflector may be equipped with several convex mirrors having different curvatures. The focal length of the whole telescope is altered by changing the value of the curvature of the convex mirror.

5.21 REFRACTOR OR REFLECTOR?

Except for the objective and the arrangement for rerouting the reflected light, there are no major differences between a refracting and a reflecting telescope: the light gathering power, the resolving power, the magnifying power, and their respective formulas are identical; as are their mountings.

Each telescope has its advantages and disadvantages; each is used for the kind of research most suitable to it.

Historically, the refracting telescope was the first kind invented. Practically, it is still in wide use and for good reasons:

A. The good definition obtainable with the use of lenses
B. The wider view obtainable
C. The smaller liability to damage from handling
D. Its readiness for instant use

However, the reflecting telescope, using a mirror instead of a lens for the objective, is becoming more and more popular. Its popularity is due to

a. Its freedom from chromatic aberration.
b. Its shorter telescope tube. In the case of refractors, focal ratios of 15 are used to avoid objectionable residue of chromatic aberration. Reflectors of focal ratio of 5

give adequate results and with only one third the length!

c. The glass of the mirror need not be perfect, as the light is reflected from coated surface.

d. Only one surface has to be shaped with precision.

e. No light is lost by absorption in passing through glass.

f. Lower cost.

PART III: MIRROR-LENS (CATADIOPTRIC) TELESCOPES

5.22 THE SCHMIDT TELESCOPE

The mirror of a reflecting telescope has to be in the shape of a paraboloid in order to eliminate spherical aberration.

In 1931 Bernhard Schmidt invented a lens-mirror arrangement which makes it possible to use an easily produced spherical mirror. The deviation of the spherical shape from the paraboloid shape is corrected by a thin lens known as a "corrector plate" placed at the center of curvature of the mirror. See Fig. 5.22.

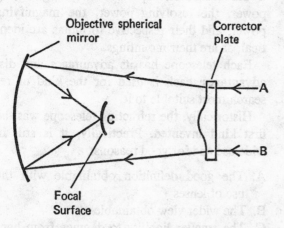

FIG. 5.22. Rays A and B are deflected slightly by the corrector plate, causing them to arrive at the same point C. Point C is also reached by rays close to the axis (not shown).

The corrector plate diverges the rays close to the edge of the corrector plate (rays A and B) so as to bring them, after reflection, to the same point reached by rays close to the axis. The rays close to the axis are not shown in Figure 5.22.

The size of the Schmidt telescope is indicated by the diameter of the corrector plate, which is usually ⅔ of the aperture of the objective. Thus the 48-inch Mount Palomar Observatory Schmidt telescope has a 48-inch correcting lens and a 72-inch (1.83 meters) objective. The radius of curvature of the mirror is 6.10 meters; the focal length is ½ of the radius of curvature of the mirror, i.e. $\frac{6.10}{2}=3.05$ meters, and its focal ratio is a very small $\frac{3.05}{1.83}=1.7$.

NOTE: Telescopes with a focal ratio of less than 8 are called astrographs. They are used primarily to photograph large areas (e.g., 10°×10°) of the sky, containing many thousands of stars.

The photographic plate is curved to fit the curvature of the focal surface and an excellent picture of the entire field of view is thus obtained.

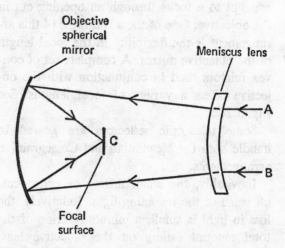

FIG. 5.23. The diverging of the rays is accomplished by the meniscus lens. This lens has spherical surfaces, and hence is easy to manufacture.

5.23 THE MAKSUTOV-BOUWERS TELESCOPE

Like the Schmidt telescope, it uses an easily manufactured spherical mirror.

The necessary divergence of the rays for proper focusing is achieved by using a thick lens, called a **Meniscus Lens,** having spherical surfaces. Spherical surfaces are much easier to produce than the complicated surface of the corrector plate of the Schmidt telescope.

The focal plane is flat. See Fig. 5.23.

PART IV: A TELESCOPE ACCESSORY

5.24 IMAGE TUBE

An image tube is an electronic attachment to the telescope that makes it possible to

A. Photograph much fainter stars, and other celestial objects than would otherwise be possible; and/or

B. Shorten the exposure time for photographing *any* object.

What is going on in the tube is:

a. The light, i.e., photons, from the star comes to a focus not on the photographic film but on a photoelectric-sensitive plate and sets free electrons from the plate (photoelectric effect). The number of electrons set free is proportional to the intensity of light; say five electrons are freed by each photon.

NOTE: At times we speak about "rays" of light. At other times light is thought of as waves or, to be accurate, electromagnetic waves. There are phenomena in science that can be explained only by the assumption that light consists of minute particles called photons.

b. The freed electrons are made to multiply in a photomultiplier tube. The five can be multiplied to many thousands. (This is the important step!)

c. This large number of electrons produces on a fluorescent screen an image that is much brighter than the image due to the original light.

d. This bright image can, of course, be photographed.

PART V: GREAT TELESCOPES AND THEIR USES

5.25 THE 200-INCH TELESCOPE*

In his eternal search for knowledge, the astronomer designs ever larger telescopes, which enable him to see stars too faint to be seen with smaller instruments.

Larger telescopes make visible greater detail, even of remote galaxies, the study of which assists the understanding of our galaxy.

Thus, the astronomer hopes to answer fundamental problems of his science. Such knowledge supplies important evidence concerning the past history as well as the probable future of the universe.

The largest optical telescope in the United States, completed in 1948, is located on Mount Palomar, California: its objective is a mirror 200 inches in diameter.

The physical principles involved in a 200-inch telescope are the same as those of a small telescope. But the engineering problems that arise in making a mirror of nearly 15 tons and in the design of the complete instrument of nearly 500 tons are immense.

* A still larger telescope was completed in the early 1970s in the U.S.S.R. northwest of Tiflis. The mirror is 236 inches in diameter and is housed in an 82-foot tube. It uses an alt-azimuth mounting and a complicated digital computer control when tracking a stellar object.

The basic problems of its construction and design were:

A. The choice of material for the mirror.
B. The casting and annealing process.
C. The grinding, polishing and aluminizing.
D. The design and construction of the mounting.
E. The choice of a suitable location.

A. The material used for the mirror must be hard, stony, homogeneous. It should be easy to polish and should retain the polish for a long time, expanding but little under normal variations in temperatures. All these factors are of great importance as the face of the mirror must be accurate to within about two millionths of an inch.

After testing numerous materials for suitability, the choice narrowed to two: fused quartz and a special variety of pyrex glass. Fused quartz has an ideally low coefficient of thermal expansion, five times lower than pyrex; however, an attempt to cast a quartz disk lasted two years and was discarded. The final choice was a variety of pyrex glass especially developed for the project.

B. The casting of the first 200-inch disk took place on March 25, 1934, using large ladles to pour 20 tons of molten glass into the prepared molds—in itself a full day's work. Blasting jets of incandescent gas kept the glass both in the furnace and in the mold at a temperature of 2,000° F.

Despite all the precaution and care in design, a minor accident spoiled the pouring of the first disk.

The second disk was cast on December 2 without mishap, and after ten hours, was successfully completed. Then it was placed in the annealing oven to cool very gradually. Such a mode of cooling is important to prevent stresses and strains in the glass which might form on rapid cooling. The temperature of the oven was electrically controlled and carefully lowered by a fixed amount every twenty-four hours. After ten months, the disk was cooled to room temperature and was proved to be as perfect a structure as could be hoped for.

C. The grinding and polishing were done by a specially designed machine, employing a cutting abrasive against the surface of the disk.

For the initial grinding, which was to give the disk a spherical concave surface, a coarse carbide abrasive, Natalon, mixed with water, was used. Later, increasingly finer grades of abrasive were used to produce a perfect paraboloid surface.

To minimize the effect of heat resulting from the friction of grinding, the process was rather slow—four years of nearly continuous grinding and polishing were necessary to prepare the mirror for the final aluminum coating.

D. The design and construction of the mounting are evidence of the great progress engineering has made in recent years.

The polished mirror, weighing nearly 15 tons, can be pointed in any direction without the slightest sagging.

The telescope "tube" which carries the mirror so perfectly is also an imposing piece of structural design, exceeding a hundred tons in weight. It is actually a rigid, hollow square center section with strong rigid rings at each end, so well-balanced that it can easily be moved in any direction by hand—although it is usually moved by small electric motors.

E. Careful research led to the choice of the proper location.

The zone between 30° and 35° north latitude is an ideal location. From these latitudes one can observe important areas in the southern celestial hemisphere and still have the north circumpolar stars appreciably above the horizon. This consideration narrowed the search to parts of California, New Mexico, Arizona, and other states lying within that zone.

There are many other determinants of proper location: (a) an elevation of 6,000–8,000 feet above sea level; (b) a large number of cloudless nights a year; (c) a complete absence of earthquakes or even minor tremors of the earth; (d) easy access to a large city.

Careful evaluation of various possible sites led to the choice of Mount Palomar, eighty miles northeast of San Diego in California.

There, the "greatest eye," as it has been called, has been engaged in the tremendous task of unravelling the mysteries of the universe.

5.26 THE GREATNESS OF THE 200-INCH TELESCOPE

The powers of this telescope are enormous. It gathers as much light as do a million human eyes; with its aid, one can see candlelight at a distance of 10,000 miles.

It penetrates twice as far into space—a distance of 2,000 million light-years—than the 100-inch telescope on Mount Wilson.

5.27 THE PROGRAM OF RESEARCH

The instrument is intended to study three major problem areas: the evolution of stars; the structure of the universe; and the constitution of matter.

5.28 ACCOMPLISHMENTS

An important result was achieved in the first years of its operation. The new telescope demonstrated the previous yardstick for astronomical distances to be incorrect—the distance to the Great Galaxy in Andromeda, heretofore estimated as 750,000 light-years, was fixed in 1952 at 1,500,000 light-years and at a later date at 2 million light-years.

The 200-inch telescope was used in the 1960s in the study of the enormous red shift in the optical spectra of stellar-appearing objects identified with radio-emitting sources, the so-called quasars. (Quasars are discussed in some detail in Sec. 10.16.)

5.29 PHOTOGRAPHY

Much of the "observation" is photographic: the astronomer removes the eyepiece from the telescope, attaches a photographic plate in its place, and photographs the object under observation. The objective of the telescope is thus used to form the image on the photographic plate.

Photography has many advantages over direct vision. These include the following:

A. Photographic plates can detect stars that are many times dimmer than the faintest star seen through the same telescope—primarily because the change in the chemicals of the plate is a cumulative effect: the sum total of light reaching the plate during the period of exposure. The eye sees all it can at one instant; the light energy does not accumulate on the retina.

B. A long-period exposure produces details unseen by visual observation, a result of the cumulative effect of the chemicals on the plate. Much of our knowledge of remote galaxies is yielded by the detail made possible by photography.

C. Permanency of record is especially important in studying changes in brightness and the relative displacement of stars. Some unimportant star may suddenly become prominent; the records can be examined for its past history.

D. Study at leisure. Some stars are above the horizon for rather brief periods; photographs taken then can be studied at the convenience of the astronomer.

E. Enlargements. Photographs can be magnified with the aid of a microscope, especially helpful in the mechanical task of counting stars, and of particular interest for globular clusters of stars.

F. In the study of our own solar system, much use is made of photography. Thus, the newest member of the planetary system, Pluto, was first discovered on a photograph. Stars show up as single points while moving objects such as planetoids photograph as short lines, even in an exposure of several hours.

PART VI: THE RADIO TELESCOPE

5.30 INTRODUCTION

Stars emit not only visible radiation (light) but also shorter wavelength radiation (X-rays) and longer (heat, radio). Indeed stars, like all hot bodies, emit radiation in all parts of the electromagnetic spectrum.

The earth's atmosphere, however, is transparent only to light and radio waves. All the other radiations emitted by stars do not reach us, as they are absorbed for the most part by the atmosphere.

The wavelengths of light that can get through the atmosphere (the optical window) run from about 4×10^{-7} meter (violet) to 7×10^{-7} meters (red).

The radio waves that the atmosphere lets through (the radio window) has wavelengths running from 10^{-2} meters to about 30 meters.

Optical telescopes aid in the study of the universe by using the radiation entering through the optical window.

Radio telescopes provide additional information on the universe around us by means of the radiation that enters through the radio window of our atmosphere.

5.31 SIMILARITIES TO A REFLECTOR

The similarities between a radio telescope and an optical reflector telescope are:

A. Both have mirrors, usually in the shape of a paraboloid.

B. Both use equatorial mountings.

C. Both are used to collect energy from the celestial object under study.

D. Both are designed to have as large a resolving power as feasible.

5.32 DISSIMILARITIES

The dissimilarities are:

A. While the optical mirror of a reflector telescope is made of glass covered by a thin coating of aluminum, the radio mirror is made of wire mesh or accurately machined metal sheets.

B. Some radio telescopes (e.g., the 305-meter diameter one in Arecibo, Puerto Rico) have no mounting at all and can be used only during the time when the object under study is in a convenient position for observation. Other radio telescopes (e.g., the 91-meter diameter one at Green Bank, West Virginia) can only be maneuvered in altitude and are of use only during the time that the object is on or near the local meridian.

C. The power intercepted by the whole earth from intense radio sources is about 100 watts; of this only 10^{-14} watt is intercepted by giant radio telescopes. The power collected by the radio telescope has to be amplified a trillion times or so before being used in the recorder.

D. The resolving power is much larger (i.e., we cannot obtain as much detail) than in the case of an optical telescope. The formula for resolving power is:

$$\text{Resolving power (in seconds of arc)} = \frac{10^5 \times \text{wavelength (cm)}}{\text{Diameter of mirror (in)}}.$$

The resolving power of even the 600 foot radio telescope for 20 cm waves is:

$$\text{Resolving power} = \frac{10^5 \times 20}{600 \times 12} = 280 \text{ seconds of arc}$$
$$= 4 \text{ minutes } 40 \text{ seconds}$$

Thus two radio sources emitting 20-cm radio waves can just be resolved as two separate emitters if the angular distance between them is 4 minutes 40 seconds.

Several means to improve resolving power, i.e., to make it smaller, are available to the astronomer. Two of which are

I. Use of a radio interferometer. The interferometer consists of two (or more) telescopes separated by a distance of a few or many kilometers. The distance of separation is used in such a case for the diameter of mirror in the above formula, thus greatly increasing the resolving power. These instruments made it possible to determine exact position of many radio sources.

II. Multielement array of fixed dipole antennas such as that in the Mills Cross radio telescope operated by the University of Sydney, in Australia. Greater resolving power can be obtained from such an array at reasonably low cost.

Other dissimilarities between optical and radio telescopes are:

E. Whereas light from stars can be studied only during the night, radio waves can be studied twenty-four hours a day. These waves pass almost unhindered through the clouds in our atmosphere as well as through the interstellar gas and dust that pervades large portions of the universe.

F. Whereas the final product of the optical telescope is either a photograph or a visual observation, the information obtained from the radio telescope is in the form of fluctuating electrical currents read on a meter. The radio waves reflected from the paraboloid disk reach the receiver, placed at the focus of the paraboloid. After amplification the signal is delivered to the meter.

G. Whereas an optical observatory is usually placed on top of a mountain to be above a large part of the atmosphere, the primary consideration in siting a radio observatory is distance from radio and television signals as well as static from car and airplane ignition systems.

CHAPTER 6

SPECTROSCOPY

6.1 INTRODUCTION

Astronomers can determine

A. What the temperature is on the surface of any star.
B. What chemicals are available on the surface of any star and in what quantities.
C. If the star has a magnetic field, and if so, how intense is it?
D. Whether the star approaching us or receding from us and how fast.

All this information, as well as a great deal of other data about the stars, is derived from careful analysis of the radiation that reaches us from the stars. The branch of science that deals with such analysis is called **Spectroscopy** and its basic instrument is the **Spectroscope**.

6.2 THE SPECTROSCOPE

The function of a spectroscope is to disperse a ray of light into its constituent colors—a

process similar to the one performed by the water droplets in clouds to form a rainbow.

The dispersion of the white light, say, into its several colors is done either by a glass prism or by a grating.

6.3 THE PRISM SPECTROSCOPE

A single ray of ordinary light, say sunlight, will be dispersed upon entering the glass of the prism into a continuous array of colors. It will be further dispersed on emerging from the prism into the air. **Such an arrangement of colors is called a Spectrum.** In the case of sunlight, the spectrum will contain all the seven principal colors: violet, indigo, blue, green, yellow, orange and red. All the intermediate color transitions will also be present. See Fig. 6.3a.

Two basic physical principles govern the dispersion into the several colors:

A. **Light is a form of energy that can be thought of as consisting of waves. The experi-**

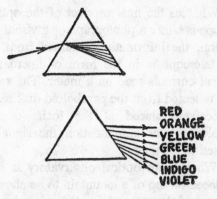

FIG. 6.3a. The prism. Sunlight upon entering the prism is dispersed into a complete spread of colors, called a spectrum. Upon coming out of the prism the colors are spread out still further. A screen held perpendicular to these rays would show a color parade very much similar to a rainbow.

mental evidence is that red light differs from blue light only in wavelength. Red light has the longest wavelength in the visible spectrum; violet, the shortest.

B. **Wavelength, as the name indicates, is the horizontal distance between crests of two adjacent waves.** See Fig. 6.3b. It is usually stated in terms of an extremely small unit of length, known as an angstrom. One angstrom is equal to 1/10,000,000,000 of a meter. In these units, wavelengths of red light are approximately 7,000 angstroms; the wavelength of violet light is about 4,000 angstroms.

FIG. 6.3b. Wavelenth. Light may be thought of as waves. Technically light is known as one branch of a very large group called electromagnetic waves. As far as we know the only basic difference between violet and blue light is in wavelenth.

C. The refraction suffered by light on entering glass depends on the wavelength: the short wave violet is refracted more than the long wave red light. The several colors originally contained in the ray of white light are thus refracted by different amounts and hence, dispersed.

In addition to the prism, the other essential elements of a prism spectroscope are a narrow slit, a collimator, and a telescope.

The narrow slit is the gate through which the light enters the spectroscope. The slit is made fairly narrow to prevent overlapping of colors in the spectrum.

The narrow slit is placed at the focus of an achromatic lens called the collimator, the function of which is to reroute the rays of light into parallel paths. See Fig. 6.3c.

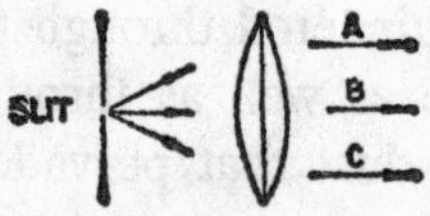

FIG. 6.3c. The slit and the collimator. The slit is placed at the focus of the collimating lens (the word collimate means "to straighten out"). The diverging light rays are brought into parallel tracks by that lens.

Each parallel ray, on passing through the prism, is dispersed into the various colors. Thus, ray A produces a complete red-to-violet spectrum; similarly, ray B produces a complete red-to-violet spectrum; and so on.

The task of collecting the red components of all the rays in one place is performed by the objective of the telescope: it brings together all the dispersed red components as well as the dispersed components of the other colors, and places them side by side. The eye, looking through the eyepiece of the telescope, sees the procession of colors that is the spectrum—consisting, of course, of images of the narrow slit, each image formed by light of a particular wavelength. See Fig. 6.3d. If the light admitted through the narrow slit contains all the wavelengths, the images form a continuous succession. If some wavelengths are missing in the light entering the spectroscope, the spectrum will not be continuous. The place usually occupied by the missing wavelengths will appear black.

Some sources of light, e.g., a neon light, emit only a few definite wavelengths—the spectrum will appear as a series of bright lines separated by wide black bands. Each bright line is an image of the slit in one of the wavelengths that was present in the light.

In the above discussion, light was described variously as a wave motion, and as a ray. The wave is the more correct picture; the ray is used only to indicate the direction in which the wave of light is moving.

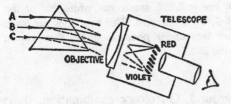

FIG. 6.3d. The telescope part of the spectroscope. Each ray is dispersed into a complete spectrum. The objective of the telescope collects all the red components into one place, all the violet components into another place. Looking through the eyepiece, an observer sees the complete spectrum of colors, from red to violet.

6.4 THE GRATING SPECTROSCOPE

In a grating spectroscope, the prism is replaced by a grating—in its simplest form, a piece of glass on which a large number of parallel lines have been engraved. The more lines per inch, the better the grating: good gratings have as many as forty thousand lines per inch. Light going through a grating will be dispersed into its various colors; the dispersion, however, in this case is not based on refraction as with the prism, but is rather due to interference between light waves that are transmitted in the spaces between the rulings.

6.5 COMPARISON OF SPECTROSCOPES

The grating spectroscope is superior to the prism spectroscope in that it gives a larger spread to the spectrum.

The prism spectroscope concentrates the light within a narrow space, producing a brighter spectrum than does the grating spectroscope. It is used exclusively for examining the light coming from faint stars and other celestial objects.

6.6 KINDS OF SPECTRA (VISUAL)

There are several kinds of spectra: continuous, bright line, and dark line.

A Continuous Spectrum is, as the name implies, a parade of all the colors from the deepest red to the ultraviolet—of which the rainbow in the sky is a good example. In the laboratory a continuous spectrum can be produced by heating a solid, a liquid, or a dense gas to a fairly high temperature—several thousand degrees Fahrenheit. Light from the electric lamp filament, for example, produces such a spectrum. See Fig. 6.6a.

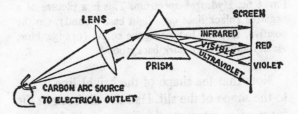

FIG. 6.6a. Continuous spectrum. The visible light from a carbon arc lamp will produce a continuous spectrum with a color spread from red to violet. Note that the visible spectrum is only one part of the complete spectrum.

Beyond the visible violet, there is ultraviolet light that is invisible to the human eye; it can be detected either by a fluorescent screen or by use of photographic plates.

Beyond the visible red there is a wide region of radiation, invisible to the human eye, known as infrared.

One of the ways of detecting infrared radiation involves the use of a thermocouple. The radiation heats one junction of the thermocouple, producing an electric current in it: this current can be measured with a galvanometer.

When light emitted by a gas through which an electrical discharge is passing produces a spectrum consisting of a few isolated parallel lines, it is known as a Bright-Line Spectrum. See Fig. 6.6b.

The spectrum produced by hydrogen consists of several bright lines, on a black background. See Fig. 6.6c.

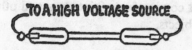

TO A HIGH VOLTAGE SOURCE

FIG. 6.6b. Production of a bright-line spectrum. One of the ways of producing a bright-line spectrum is to: (a) fill this tube with the gas desired (low pressure); (b) attach it to a high (several thousand volts) electric potential.

The light given off by the gas forms a bright-line spectrum, when viewed through a spectroscope.

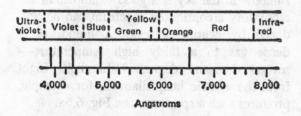

FIG. 6.6c. Hydrogen spectrum. This is a picture of a negative (black lines on a light background). On the positive, the lines indicating the colors (orange, blue, violet) appear on a dark background.

Note that the shape of the bright line is due to the shape of the slit. Had the slit been in the form of a crescent, the lines would be crescent-shaped.

The characteristic color of neon signs is due to bright red and orange lines in its spectrum. See Fig. 6.6d.

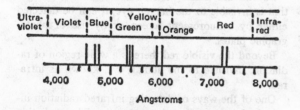

FIG. 6.6d. Neon spectrum. The typical color of neon signs is due to the great intensity of the red and orange lines; these lines overshadow the other colors present in the spectrum. This is a negative of the spectrum seen. On the positive the lines have the indicated colors, while the background is black.

Bright lines of any element can also be produced by placing a volatile salt of that element in a flame.

The spectrum due to sodium vapors shows only one visible yellow line against a dark

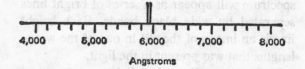

FIG. 6.6e. Sodium spectrum. The yellow light typical of sodium lamps is due primarily to the two very bright lines in the yellow region of the spectrum. Spectral lines are often denoted by letters and numbers. The two lines of the sodium spectrum are known as the D_1 and D_2 lines. The wavelength of the D_1 line is 5,896 angstroms, while that of the D_2 line is 5,890 angstroms. The two lines are so close together that under poor resolution they appear as one wide line.

background. On closer examination, the yellow line turns out to be a doublet, that is, two very close lines, denoted by the symbols D_1 and D_2. See Fig. 6.6e.

It should be carefully noted that each element always gives the same pattern of lines. Each element, so to speak, has its own fingerprints, possessed by no other element. This fact is utilized in chemical analysis and in many other applied fields.

A Dark-Line Spectrum, also known as absorption spectrum, is due to absorption of light of particular wavelength by relatively cool gases. The wavelengths absorbed are identical to the wavelengths that the gas would emit when properly excited.

Cool sodium vapor would remove the two yellow D_1 and D_2 lines from a continuous spectrum. See Fig. 6.6f.

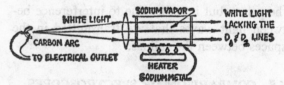

FIG. 6.6f. Dark-line spectrum. Ordinary light, having a continuous spectrum, would lose some of its components on going through a "cool" gas. The components lost are always identical with the ones the gas would emit when giving off light. Thus sodium vapor removes the D_1 and D_2 lines from the continuous spectrum. One way of producing such a dark-line, or absorption, spectrum is indicated here.

FIG. 6.6g. A dark-line spectrum due to sodium vapor. This is a reverse of the bright-line spectrum. The D_1 and D_2 yellow lines appear dark, on a background of a continuous spectrum. (Note that this is a negative and hence dark and light are reversed.)

The spectrum of sodium would then appear as two close dark lines on a background of an otherwise continuous spectrum. See Fig. 6.6g.

Star spectra are of the "dark line" kind. The continuous spectrum originates at the surface of the star; the dark lines are caused by the relatively cooler outer atmosphere of the star.

A typical spectrum of light coming from a star is shown in Figure 6.6h.

FIG. 6.6h. A typical spectrum of a star. Most spectra are dark-line spectra. Some of the dark lines are due to hydrogen, others to helium, still others to other elements. From a careful study of these lines, the chemicals present on a star, as well as other information, are obtained.

6.7 STAR SPECTRUM

An analysis of such a spectrum would resolve the lines into several sets, each due to one of the ninety-two natural elements. Thus, spectroscopy aids in determining the chemicals contained in each star and the relative proportions of these elements—determined from the relative brightness of the various sets of lines.

The analysis refers to the elements in the atmosphere of the star. It is probable that the composition of the interior of a star is similar to that of its atmosphere.

6.8 KINDS OF SPECTRA (ENERGY)

In some studies (e.g., to find the temperature of a star) it is important to know not only what wavelengths (colors) appear in a spectrum, but also how much energy is available in each wavelength.

An energy versus wavelengths curve for a continuous spectrum is indicated in Figure 6.8a (symbol for wavelength is λ).

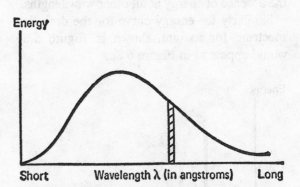

FIG. 6.8a. An energy curve. This is a typical curve showing the amount of energy in ergs (plotted vertically) that is available at any wavelength in angstroms (plotted horizontally).

An energy curve of a spectrum is obtained by:

A. Producing the spectrum on the screen.
B. Changing the light into heat energy for each wavelength by allowing the light to be absorbed by a good absorber (black body, see Sec. 7.3).
C. Determining the amount of heat energy for each wavelength.
D. Plotting the curve of energy against wavelength.

NOTES: 1. It is important to note that the spectrum runs from the shortest wavelength (X-rays, etc.) to the longest (infrared, radio) and that at both extremes the energies are rather small. It is also important to note that research is being done at these several parts of the spectrum, each part requiring specialized equipment and technology. Thus there is a field of X-ray astronomy, radio astronomy, and so on.

2. When the emitter is at a higher temperature, two changes come about in the curve:
A. The area under the curve gets larger, i.e., there is more energy emitted at every wavelength.
B. The maximum (the peak) has moved toward the shorter wavelengths.

An energy curve for the bright-line sodium spectrum (see Fig. 6.6e) is indicated in Fig. 6.8b.

One notes the two lines of energy due to the yellow light emitted by sodium as well as the absence of energy at all other wavelengths.

Similarly the energy curve for the dark-line spectrum for sodium, shown in Figure 6.6g would appear as in Figure 6.8c.

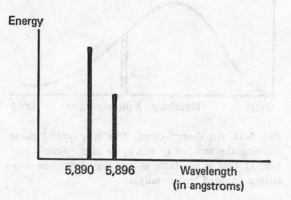

Fig. **6.8b.** An energy curve for sodium would indicate that only at two wavelengths (5,890 and 5,896 angstroms) is energy being emitted. There is zero energy at other wavelengths.

This curve is a composite of a continuous curve less two lines which have been eliminated. The wavelength of the removed lines are also 5,890 and 5,896 angstroms.

Finally, an energy curve for a star would show many lines removed from the continuous curve by absorption. See Fig. 6.8d. Those

lines can be resolved into several sets, each set due to one of the ninety-two naturally occurring elements.

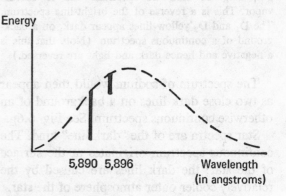

Fig. **6.8c.** The absorption curve for sodium. This consists of a continuous distribution from which two lines have been removed. The wavelengths of the missing lines are identical with the wavelengths of the emitted lines in Fig. 6.8b.

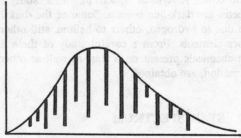

Fig. **6.8d.** Energy curve for a star. A continuous curve from which many lines have been removed by absorption of the starlights in the stars own atmosphere.

CHAPTER 7

PHYSICAL PROPERTIES OF THE STARS

PART I: TEMPERATURE OF STARS

7.1 INTRODUCTION

The spectrum derived from a star's light is also used to determine the star's temperature at its surface, the layer known as "photosphere." The temperatures of stellar photospheres are very much lower than the temperatures in the interior of the stars.

Temperatures are usually stated in the **Absolute (or Kelvin) scale,** denoted by ° A (or ° K. To change from the absolute scale to the centigrade scale, subtract 273° from the former. The temperature of the photosphere of the stars is in the thousands of degrees absolute.

Typical temperatures of stellar surfaces are about 5,000 to 7,000° A. Extremely hot stars, like ζ (zeta)-Puppis, have a temperature of 30,000° A, and there is reason to believe that some stars have surface temperatures as high as 50,000° A. On the other extreme, the coolest known star, χ (chi)-Cygni, a variable star, at the time of its minimum brightness has a temperature of a mere 1,800° A, or about 1500° C.

NOTE: To change from centigrade to the common Fahrenheit scale, multiply the former by $\frac{9}{5}$ and add 32. The temperature of Chi-Cygni on the Fahrenheit scale would be

$$1,500 \times \frac{9}{5} + 32 = \text{approximately } 2,700° \text{ F}$$

7.2 COMPUTING STELLAR TEMPERATURES

One method used to determine the temperature of a star from its spectrum involves three preliminary steps: (A) to determine the energy distribution of the spectrum; (B) to find the wavelength of maximum energy; and (C) to use Wien's law.

A. Determining the energy distribution of spectrum. See Sec. 6.8.

B. Finding the wavelength of maximum energy. See Fig. 7.2. This wavelength is denoted by the symbol λ_{max} and is used to compute the star's temperature.

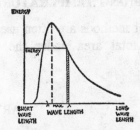

FIG. 7.2. Distribution of energy in a spectrum. The various colors in a spectrum differ greatly in their intensity, i.e., in the amount of energy contained in them. This graph shows the amount of energy (vertical scale) that is available at any wavelength, e.g., at λ the amount of energy is indicated by the vertical crosshatched column. The particular wavelength for which the curve has its maximum is denoted as λ_{max}. This number is used in Wien's law to determine the temperature of the star's surface.

C. Using Wien's law. Wilhelm Wien (1864–1928) derived a simple formula relating λ_{max} to temperature:

$$T = \frac{289 \times 10^5}{\lambda_{max}}$$

This formula states that the wavelength at which the energy is at a maximum is inversely proportional to temperature, or, the higher the temperature, the smaller the value for λ_{max}. This can easily be verified. When iron is heated, it gives off first a dull red heat (long wavelength); then, as the temperature rises, the color of the light changes to orange, yellow, and blue (short wavelength).

Once λ_{max} has been determined, Wien's formula enables us to compute the temperature of stellar bodies.

In the case of our sun, the wavelength of maximum energy is 4,700 angstroms. The temperature of the solar photosphere is

$$T = \frac{289 \times 10^5}{4,700} = 6150° \text{ A.}$$

The temperature determined in this manner is known as the "black body" temperature. (**Black body** is a physical concept of a body that is a perfect absorber of radiation.)

7.3 OTHER METHODS OF DETERMINING TEMPERATURES

Two other methods are often used—one involves the total area under the curve; the other, energy values taken at several wavelengths along the energy curve.

In the first case, the total energy under the curve, rather than merely the maximum, is used to determine the temperature of the sun. The value obtained is 5,750° A. This value is referred to as the **Effective Temperature.**

In the second case, the relative intensity of light at several different wavelengths is used. The temperature derived by this method is known as **Color Temperature.** The sun's color temperature is close to 7,000° A.

NOTES: 1. It is repeated here that these are the temperatures of the surface layers emitting stellar light. The temperatures in the interior of the stars are of an entirely different order of magnitude. Interior temperatures range not in the thousands but in the **millions** of degrees. These temperatures will be discussed later.

2. The three methods of computation give three different values for the temperature of the sun's surface; the true temperature is probably some average of these.

PART II: STELLAR DISTANCES

7.4 INTRODUCTION

Some stars are fairly close to us; light emanating from them reaches us in a few years; the remoteness of other stars staggers the imagination.

This section deals with the direct method of determining distances of stars.

Several indirect methods of finding distances to stars use information obtained from special kinds of stars such as Cepheids, RR-Lyrae, etc. These methods will be outlined in the discussion of those stars.

7.5 DIRECT METHOD

One method used to find the distance to a star is known as **Triangulation,** or the direct method. See Fig. 7.5a. In this method, often used by surveyors, a distance such as AC is determined by measuring three quantities—the length of an arbitrarily chosen line, such

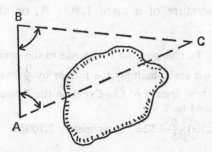

FIG. 7.5a Finding distances by the method of triangulation. To find the distance between points A and C which may happen to be on opposite sides of a lake, say, a line of position, AB, is laid out. Knowing the length of the line AB, and the two angles A and B, it is easy to compute the desired length AC.

as AB, and two angles, A and B. The line AB is known as a line of position. Using the line of position and the two angles, the distance AC is computed.

Standard formulas from elementary trigonometry are involved in these computations.

Accuracy is obtained when the line of position is comparable in size to the distance to be determined. Thus, if AC is 2 miles, the line of position should also be about 2 miles long.

In finding distances to stars, the astronomer is handicapped by the lack of a "long enough" line of position. The largest line available to the astronomer in the diameter of the earth's orbit about the sun (186 million miles), which is only a minute fraction of the distance to even the closest star.

Using this 186-million-mile line of position, as shown in Figure 7.5b, the angle at A is carefully measured. Six months later, when the earth is at point B, the angle B is also carefully measured. Using these data and proper trigonometric formulas, one can compute the angle at C and the distances AC, BC, and OC.

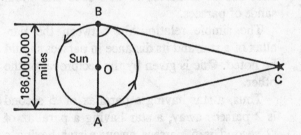

Fig. 7.5b. Method of determining the distance from the sun to a nearby star C.

This method, which can only be used to determine the distance to the nearby stars, is based on the fact that the faraway stars do not change appreciably their relative positions in a six-month period.

NOTES: 1. Distance to a star usually signifies the distance between the center of the star and the center of the sun. At times the distance between the center of the star and the center of the earth is used. The difference between the two, the radius of the earth's orbit, is insignificant in measuring the stellar distance.

2. By agreement among astronomers, the radius of the earth's orbit, and not the diameter, is taken as a line of position.

3. The angle D subtended by the star on the radius (i.e., half the angle C) is known as the "parallax": the more distant the star, the smaller its parallax. See Fig. 7.5c.

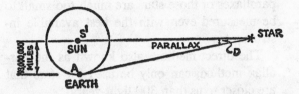

Fig. 7.5c. The angle D is known as the parallax.

The parallaxes of stars are extremely small angles. Even the nearest star, a (alpha)-Centauri, has a parallax of only .756 seconds of angle. This is a much smaller angle than the diameter of a dime would subtend at a distance of a mile. Other stars subtend angles of .1 second and less.

Measurement of such extremely small angles is a very exacting and laborious job.

In the process of finding the parallaxes for the various stars many corrections have to be applied to the readings taken by the observer. (Some of these corrections are now automatically carried out by techniques developed in measuring parallaxes.)

Some of these corrections are due to the motion of the star; others are due to the motion of the observer; still others are due to refraction of light by the earth's atmosphere.

During the six months' interval between observations, the star itself may have moved slightly, relative to other stars. In the same interval, the whole solar system, together with the observer, may have changed position. To obtain a reasonable estimate of the magnitude of these corrections, several sets of measurements extending over a period of several years are taken for each star under study. From measurements taken a full year apart, estimates can be made on the correction necessitated by the motions. Corrections due to the refraction of light by the earth's atmosphere have to be carefully computed, otherwise serious errors in the distance determination may be introduced. In routine parallax work several of these corrections are automatically accounted for.

The distances to the vast majority of stars *cannot* be found by this method, because the parallaxes of those stars are much too small to be measured even with the best available instruments.

The direct method, also known as the parallax method, can only be used for stars that are closer to us than 300 light-years.

7.6 UNITS OF STELLAR DISTANCES

The distances to stars are so great that the ordinary units—miles—are no longer practicable. The nearest star is 25,000,000,000,000 miles away—a number rather awkward to write, to remember, and to use.

Three units are commonly used in Astronomy: (A) the **Astronomical Unit**; (B) the **Parsec**; and (C) the **Light-Year.**

A. The astronomical unit is, by definition, equal in length to the distance from the earth to the sun—93 million miles.

This unit, astronomically speaking, is a fairly small one, and is used primarily in stating distances within the solar system. Thus, the distance of the planet Pluto is 40 astronomical units, or 40×93,000,000 miles (3,720,000,000).

(AU is the proper abbreviation for astronomical unit.)

B. The definition of a parsec is based on the triangle indicated in Figure 7.6.

If the parallax D is equal to 1 second of arc,

then the distance between the star and the sun is, by definition, 1 parsec.

A parsec is an extremely large distance. In terms of miles, one such unit is equal to about 20 million million miles.

The vastness of the parsec does not show up too well in Figure 7.6, because the triangle is not drawn to scale.

When properly drawn, angle A is very close to a 90° angle (it is 90° minus 1 second); the sides BD and AD are almost parallel and the point D will be far from the side AB.

One parsec is 206,265 times as large as an astronomical unit.

PROBLEM 7.6a:

Find the number of miles in 1 parsec.
1 parsec=93,000,000×206,265 miles
=19.2 trillion miles=19,200 billion miles
=19.2×10^{12} miles.   *Answer*

In terms of this unit, the closest star, Alpha-Centauri, is at a distance of 1.3 parsecs. Other stars are at distances of hundreds and thousands of parsecs.

The simple relationship between the parallax of a star and its distance in parsecs should be noted. One is given by the reciprocal of the other.

Thus, a star having a parallax of .5 second is 2 parsecs away, a star having a parallax of .2 second is 5 parsecs away, a star having a parallax of .1 second is 10 parsecs away, and so on.

(C) Another unit of astronomical distance is **the light-year, defined simply as the distance traveled by a ray of light in a period of one year.** It has already been shown in Sec. 1.19 that 1 light-year is equal to 5.88 trillion miles (5.88×10^{12} miles).

Using this unit of distance, α-Centauri is at a distance of 4.2 light-years; or, the light by which we see the star has been en route for 4.2 years.

Distances in parsecs can easily be converted into distances in light-years.

FIG. 7.6. Definition of a parsec. If: (I) The angle B is 90°; (II) the side of AB is 93,000,000 miles long; and (III) the angle D is 1 second, then: the side BD is equal in length to one parsec.

One parsec = 3.26 light-years,
Two parsecs = 6.52 light years,
Ten parsecs = 32.6 light-years; and so on.

PROBLEM 7.6b:

Sirius is 8.6 light-years away. Find its distance (a) in parsecs, (b) in astronomical units, and (c) in miles.

In addition to the sun and α-Centauri, the following are among the stars closest to us: Barnard's star is 6.1 light-years away; Wolf 359 is 7.6 light-years away; and Lalande 21185 is 8.1 light-years away. (Barnard's star, etc., are known by the names of the astronomers who investigated them.)

PART III: SIZE OF STARS

7.7 INTRODUCTION

Stars are of various sizes; the smallest* known one, with a diameter of a mere 4,000 miles, is technically identified by its catalog number AC +70° 8247 (Astrographic Catalog, star number 8247, declination 70° N).

The largest known star, ε (epsilon)-Aurigae B, has a diameter nearly 3,000 times that of the sun. (The sun's diameter is 864,000 miles.)

The diameter of a star cannot be measured directly with the aid of a telescope. Even through a large telescope, stars appear simply as points of light having no measurable diameter. Methods have recently been developed to measure the true linear diameter of a star.

7.8 SIZE OF STARS AS DETERMINED BY THE INTERFEROMETER

An ingenious method—based on light interference—has been used in recent years to measure the diameter of stars. This method actually measures only the angular diameter; but this is not a drawback, since the true diameter can easily be computed once the angular diameter *and* the distance of the star have been determined.

The angular diameter is the angle subtended by its diameter at the observer's eye.

The method, originally suggested by Michelson, was used as early as 1920 at

* Neutron stars, as we shall see in Sec. 7.34, probably have diameters of about 5 miles.

Mount Wilson. The interferometer attached to the upper end of the 100-inch telescope consists basically of a beam of structural steel carrying four mirrors: the two outer ones, A and D, can be moved along the beam to a maximum separation of 20 feet; the two inner ones, B and C, are fixed.

The function of the moving mirror is to get two beams, I and II, from the same star separated by as large a distance as possible (length of steel beam).

The function of the fixed mirrors is to divert both beams into the telescope. See Fig. 7.8a.

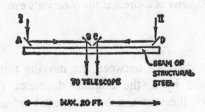

FIG. 7.8a. A Michelson interferometer. The mirrors I and II are moved in unison inward or outward until the dark and light fringes, seen through the eyepiece of the telescope, disappear. The angular diameter of the star is easily computed once this particular distance between the mirrors has been determined.

It has been pretty well established that two such beams, coming, so to speak, from two different regions of the same star would produce interference. The image of the star in the telescope will no longer be a point of light, nor a spurious round diffraction disk, but a set of very fine bright and dark fringes, which appear somewhat like the teeth of a comb.

It has been determined theoretically and proven experimentally that for a certain separation between the moving mirrors, the fringes disappear. At that distance, if the star is large, the bright fringes caused by one half of the star overlap the dark fringes caused by the other half. At this separation of the mirrors, the image appears equally bright throughout. See Fig. 7.8b.

FIG. 7.8b. The image of a star as seen through the combination of telescope and interferometer. The star appears as a little disk covered by alternating light and dark fringes. For one and only one setting of the moving mirrors the fringes disappear, and the disk is equally bright throughout.

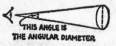

FIG. 7.8c. Angular diameter is the angle subtended by the diameter of a circle at the observer's eye.

If this distance between the moving mirrors is denoted by S, the angular diameter (Fig. 7.8c), of the star can be computed from the formula:

$$\text{Angular diameter} = 12 \, S$$

The distance S must be stated in centimeters; the answer for the angular diameter is in seconds of angle.

This method is applicable only to the largest, nearest, and brightest stars. Fewer than twenty stars have had their angular diameters measured by the interferometer method. Small angular diameters would require mirror separations in hundreds of feet. However, even the few that have been measured are important as

they verify the diameters of stars computed from less direct methods.

Among the stars that were measured with the interferometer are the variable star Betelgeuse, whose angular diameter varies from .034 seconds of arc to .042 seconds of arc and Arcturus and Aldebaran, each of which indicates an angular diameter of .020 seconds of arc.

As the distance to these stars is known, their linear diameter can be computed by multiplying the angular diameter by the distance. The diameter for Betelgeuse is equal to 800 times the diameter of the sun. The linear diameters for Arcturus and Aldebaran are 25 and 40 times the diameter of the sun, respectively.

7.9 SIZE OF STARS AS DETERMINED FROM LUMINOSITY

Another method for determining diameters of stars is based on the relationship between **Luminosity (L), Temperature (T), and Diameter (D)** of a star.

Luminosity is a measure of a star's true brightness and is a quantity that, as we shall see, can easily be found for many stars.

Luminosity is usually stated in multiples or submultiples of the sun's brightness. The most luminous star is one in the Greater Magellanic Cloud, known as S Doradus. Its luminosity of 600,000 means that it is 600,000 times brighter than our sun; that is, if the sun and S Doradus were placed at equal distances from us, say, one parsec, the latter would appear 600,000 times brighter. It also means that it sends 600,000 times as much light per second into space as does the sun.

The intrinsically faintest known star is the companion to BD +4° 4048 (star number 4048 in the Bonn Catalog. Its declination is 4°N). Its luminosity is only about 1/500,000 that of the sun.

The luminosity of a star depends on two factors: (1) the size of the star; and (2) the amount of visible radiation it emits from each square mile of surface, which in turn depends on the surface temperature.

The formula relating the three is:

$$D=\left(\frac{5,750}{T}\right)^2\times\sqrt{L}$$

D is in units of the solar diameter.

T is the temperature of the surface of the star in degrees absolute; and L is, as usual, in terms of sun's brightness.

5,750 is the effective temperature of the sun's surface (photosphere).

PROBLEM 7.9:

Sirius has a luminosity of 27 and a temperature of 9,800° A. Find its diameter.

Substituting the given data in the formula gives the following equation:

$$\left(\frac{5,750}{9,800}\right)^2\times\sqrt{27}=1.8 \text{ times the diameter of the sun.}$$

Still another method to measure size of stars makes use of lunar occultation. In this method the important measurement is the time it takes for the limb of the earth's moon to occult (hide) the distant star.

Over the last ten years a procedure known as Speckle Interferometry has been developed. In this procedure many short ($\frac{1}{100}$ second) exposures of a star are taken. Mathematical techniques are now available to compute the diameter of a star from these (speckled) exposures.

PART IV: STELLAR MASSES AND DENSITIES

7.10 INTRODUCTION

The stars show only small variations in mass. The vast majority have masses between one fifth and five times that of the sun.

The range is also limited. The heaviest known star HD 698 (star number 698 in a catalog of stellar spectra prepared at Harvard Observatory and named after the great American scientist Henry Draper, 1837–82) has a mass 113 times that of the sun. One of the lightest known stars is Luyten 726-8B, with a mass only $\frac{1}{25}$ that of the sun.

At present, there is no direct method of finding the mass of a star. There are, however, several indirect methods; one of these can only be used in the case of pairs of stars known as visual binaries.

7.11 MASS OF VISUAL BINARIES

A binary is a pair of stars which, like the earth and moon, revolve about a common center of gravity. **If the two stars of the pair are separately visible, the pair is called a Visual Binary.** Some 50,000 visual binaries are now known.

The principle involved in finding the mass of a binary is based on Kepler's harmonic law, which can be expressed in terms of a simple formula relating the sum of the two masses,

the distance between them, and the period of revolution.

The formula is: $M+m=\dfrac{p^2}{a^3}$

where M+m is the sum of the two masses expressed in units of the sun's mass; p, the time needed for the line joining the stars to complete one revolution (which should be stated in years); and a, the mean distance between the two stars (in astronomical units). Both the distance, "a," and the period, "p," are determined by direct observation; the mass of the binary system, M+m, is computed with the aid of the formula.

To compute the masses of the individual stars in the pair, additional observations must be made. These concern the absolute motion of each star in the binary system about the common center of gravity. The heavier partner will describe a small ellipse about this center, while the lighter will describe a larger one. From the sizes of these ellipses, the ratio of the two masses is determined, which, with the sum of the masses, is all that is needed to determine the mass of each star.

If the sum is, say, 8 solar masses, and the ratio is 3 to 1, then their individual masses are 6 and 2 times that of the sun.

PROBLEM 7.11:

The sum of the masses, M+m, for a (alpha)-Centauri A and $\propto$-Centauri B is 1.96.

The ratio between the masses is 1.23. Find the mass of a (alpha)-Centauri A and the mass of $\propto$-Centauri B.

Answer: The mass of a (alpha)-Centauri A is 1.08 times the mass of the sun. The mass of $\propto$-Centauri B is .88 times the mass of the sun.

Masses can also be determined for another type of binary system known as "spectroscopic binaries."

A **Spectroscopic Binary** is a pair of stars that appear as a single unit even in a large telescope. The true character of the unit shows up only in a spectroscopic study. The spectrum (see Sec. 7.15) indicates that the unit consists of two stars which are alternately approaching and receding from the terrestrial observer, their motion being similar to the two masses of a rotating dumbbell. There are more than 1,500 known spectroscopic binaries.

Capella, the fifth star in apparent brightness, is a spectroscopic binary. The mass of the brighter member is 4.18, and that of its companion 3.32, times the sun's mass.

7.12 MASS OF STARS OF HIGH SURFACE GRAVITY

This method of determining the mass of a star is applicable to cases of stars that have a very high surface gravity. Large values of gravitational force are present in several kinds of stars; one of them is known as **White Dwarfs.** The high surface gravity in the white-dwarf type is due to the fantastically high values for the density of the matter composing these stars.

White dwarfs have a fairly normal value for mass but a greatly sub-normal (hence the name, "dwarf") value for volume.

The masses of these stars can be computed with the aid of **Einstein's General Theory of Relativity.**

According to this theory, light undergoes a slight change in its wavelength upon departing from a star having a high value of gravitational pull at its surface. Every light wavelength is slightly increased on departure. This shift of all the wavelengths of the spectral lines to the red is known as the "relativistic shift," and is usually extremely small, though measurable. The measured values are used in computing the masses of the stars producing these shifts in the wavelengths.

7.13 DENSITIES

Density, as usual, is determined by dividing the mass by the volume. The quotient indicates how closely the matter of which the star consists is packed.

Stars vary greatly in density, primarily because of the wide range of volumes.

It strains the human imagination even to try to visualize the extreme values in star densities. One of the high density stars is the Pup, the companion of Sirius. In mass it is equal to the sun; however, its volume is only $\frac{1}{30,000}$ as great. Since the average density of the sun is 1.5 times that of water, the average density of the Pup is 50,000 times that of water. A tablespoon of this substance would weigh a ton! And the Pup is not the densest star known.

Neutron stars, as we shall see, have central densities of 10^{14} to 10^{15} times that of water. A cubic centimeter of water would have a mass of 10^{12} kilograms, i.e., a million million kilograms.

On the other extreme, there are stars that have densities less than $\frac{1}{1,000}$ of that of air. The density of these is less than the density of an ordinary vacuum obtainable in the laboratory. They are often called, in fact, "red-hot vacuum." The largest known star, ϵ (epsilon)-Aurigae B, has also the distinction of having the smallest density. The value given for it is $\frac{1}{100,000,000}$ that of water.

PART V: STELLAR MOTIONS

7.14 INTRODUCTION

It is now fairly common knowledge that the "fixed" stars move, and do so at rather high speeds; and that in the course of, say, a century, these movements will change slightly the shape of the constellation. The fact that these high speeds have not materially disarranged the constellations is, of course, due to the great distance of the stars; and also to the rather brief period of time (in astronomic terms) that the stars have been under systematic observation.

The measurement of stellar speeds requires great precision, and is further complicated by the motion of the observer. Not only does the star move, but the observer, too, participates in several motions: (a) daily revolution of the earth about its axis; (b) slight changes in direction of the earth's axis; (c) annual rotation of the earth around the sun; (d) the movement of the sun and the whole solar system in space. These motions cause displacements of the stars, called "common motions," which have, of course, nothing to do with the real movement of the stars.

Common motions must be subtracted from the total displacements of stars to obtain the true motions.

The true speed of a star, known as space velocity, is computed from its two components: one is in line of sight and is known as the radial velocity of the star; the other is perpendicular to the line of sight and is known either as cross motion or tangential velocity.

7.15 RADIAL VELOCITY

The value for this velocity is determined from the spectrum of the star. The computation makes use of a basic principle in physics, known as the **Doppler Principle, according to which the spectrum of an approaching source of light has all its wavelengths shortened.** The change in each wavelength, denoted by Δλ, is given by the formula

$$\Delta\lambda = \lambda \times \frac{V}{c}$$

In this formula:

λ is the original wavelength of the light,
V is the relative velocity of approach, and
c is the velocity of light.

In the formula, c and λ are known. The shift in the wavelengths can easily be measured and the relative velocity of approach computed. The same formula applies to the recession of a star, in which case the shift is toward the longer wavelength. The lines, instead of appearing in their normal place in the spectrum show up in new positions; the new positions of all the lines are closer to the red end of the spectrum.

In practice, photographic methods are used in this kind of work. Two spectra are photographed simultaneously on one plate, one above the other. The spectrum of the star under study is placed together with a comparison spectrum, usually one due to iron. If the star has no radial velocity, the iron lines in the stellar spectrum will coincide with the lines in the comparison spectrum. These lines will be arranged in both spectra in identical patterns.

In the case of a star having radial velocity, the lines will be displaced. The value of this displacement Δλ for any line of wavelength λ is obtained directly from the plate. These values when substituted in the Doppler formula, indicate the radial velocity of the star.

PROBLEM 7.15:

One of the lines due to iron in the comparison spectrum has a wavelength of 5,270 angstroms. On the stellar spectrum, the same line is displaced toward the blue end of the spectrum by .527 angstrom. The velocity of light is 3×10^5 kilometers per second. Find the radial velocity of the star.

Solution: $\Delta\lambda = \lambda \times \dfrac{V}{c}$ or $V = \dfrac{\Delta\lambda}{\lambda} \times c$

$$V = \frac{.527}{5,270} \times 3 \times 10^5 = 30 \text{ km/sec.}$$

Answer: The radial velocity is 30 km/sec, or 18 miles per second. The star is approaching us at that rate, since the displacement is toward the blue end of the spectrum.

The greatest radial velocity known is 547 km/sec, or 340 miles per second, possessed by star CD −29° 2277 (Cordoba Catalog, star number 2277, declination 29° S).

7.16 TANGENTIAL VELOCITY

The tangential velocity of a star is also known as Cross Motion, referring to the velocity of a star in a plane perpendicular to the line of sight. It is usually stated in miles per second or in kilometers per second.

Tangential velocity cannot be found directly; it is obtained by multiplying the angular velocity of the star by its distance. It is common to call that angular velocity **Proper Motion,** and to state its value in seconds of angle per year.

7.17 PROPER MOTION

The greatest proper motion is exhibited by Barnard's star (named after its discoverer, Edward Emerson Barnard, 1857–1923). The star traverses about 10.5 seconds of angle each year, and will move ½ degree (angle subtended by the moon) in about 180 years. Most stars are too remote to manifest measurable proper motions.

Out of 25,000,000 stars that have been in-vestigated to date, fewer than ⅓ of 1 per cent have shown evidence of proper motion.

The task of studying so large a number of stars is greatly simplified by using photographic methods together with a special kind of microscope known as a blink microscope. Photographs are taken of large regions of the sky at intervals of thirty years. The two pictures are then viewed through a blink microscope. There is a device in the microscope to illuminate alternately one and then the other view, in rapid succession. Stars that have moved as much as 6 seconds of arc in those thirty years seem to blink, while all the others remain steady.

As indicated above, the product of proper motion, times the star distance, gives the tangential value of the stellar velocity.

7.18 SPACE VELOCITY OF STARS

Knowing the radial and tangential components, it is easy to find the true space velocity of the star. The velocity is the diagonal of a rectangle of which the radial and tangential velocities are the sides. See Fig. 7.18.

The highest known space velocity of a star is 660 km/sec, or 410 miles per second.

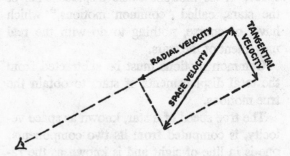

FIG. 7.18. Space velocity. (a) The velocity of the star in line of sight, i.e., radial velocity, is determined with the aid of Doppler's formula. (b) The velocity perpendicular to line of sight is obtained by multiplying the angular velocity of the star by its distance. (c) The true velocity of the star in its motion through space given to scale, by the diagonal of the rectangle having radial and tangential velocity for sides.

PART VI: SPECTRA

7.19 SPECTRAL CLASSES

When spectra of many stars are analyzed, it is found that they can be naturally grouped into several classes. The present classification is based on extensive research pursued at Harvard College Observatory, involving a comparative study of spectra from more than 300,000 stars. Ten distinct classes are recognized and are denoted by letters O, B, A, F, G, K, M, R, N, S.

These letters have been chosen rather arbitrarily and the best way to remember the first nine is by the jingle: "Oh, Be A Fine Girl, Kiss Me Right Now." The last letter has several versions: "Smack," "Sweetheart," etc.

Subdivisions of each of these classes are recognized and designations like B2, K5, G8, etc., are used for them. K5 stands for a spectrum with characteristics halfway between K and M.

The stars Sirius and Vega are class A stars, while the star Altair is designated as A5. Class A spectra are emitted by white stars having surface temperatures of nearly 10,000° A. Characteristics of class A stars are: (a) very strong dark lines due to hydrogen; (b) no helium lines; (c) very few and weak lines due to metals. See Fig. 7.19.

Other classes, too, have well-defined characteristics. The characteristics of the groups may be summarized as follows:

A. Helium lines are present in classes O and B, reaching their maximum in B2 and fading out before reaching class A.

B. Hydrogen is the only element present in all ten series. The lines are strongest in spectra of class A.

C. High temperature metallic lines make their first appearance in class A, rising to maximum strength in class G. (The sun is a class G star.)

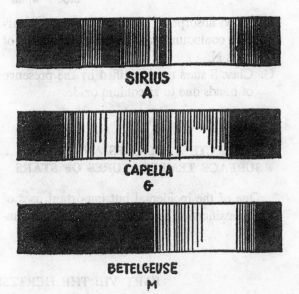

FIG. 7.19. Sirius is a class A star. Spectra emitted by these stars have:

   (a) wide lines due to hydrogen,

   (b) no line due to helium, and

   (c) very few and very thin lines due to metals.

Capella and our own sun are class G stars. Spectra emitted by these stars contain many lines due to iron and other metal. Two lines due to ionized calcium are quite eminent, while the lines due to hydrogen are much less outstanding than in class A stars.

Betelgeuse is a class M star. Low temperature lines are strong—that is to say, spectral lines that can be produced by low temperature sources of light are prominent in this spectrum.

High temperature lines, like those which require a hot electric spark for their production in the physics laboratory, are either very weak or entirely missing.

Whole bands of lines due to titanium oxide are present in spectra of class M stars.

D. Low temperature metallic lines become evident in class G and rise to great prominence in class M.

E. Titanium oxide bands are prominent in class M stars. (Betelgeuse and Antares are class M stars.)

Table 7.19:

Spectral Class	O	B	A	F	G	K	M
Temperature (in degrees absolute)	25,000	23,000	10,000	7,000	6,000	5,000	3,200
Color	very blue	bluish-white	white	yellowish-white	yellow	orange	red

F. Broad absorption bands of carbon and carbon compounds are present in spectra of class N.

G. Class S stars are identified by the presence of bands due to zirconium oxide.

7.20 SPECTRAL CLASSES AND SURFACE TEMPERATURES OF STARS

One of the incidental but important uses of this classification is to determine stellar temperature. The variation from class to class is due, to a very large degree, to the temperature of the surface of the star. Thus, class G spectra come from stars having surface temperatures of 6,000° A; class B, 23,000°; class M, 3,200° A; and so on. As a matter of fact, the surface temperature of any star is easily determined by a glance at its spectrum—the values thus derived are fairly accurate estimates. The relationship between spectral classes, temperature, and color is given in Table 7.19 for classes O through M.

PART VII: THE HERTZSPRUNG-RUSSELL DIAGRAM

7.21 INTRODUCTION

On a clear night some 2,500 stars are visible to the naked eye; through a small telescope, millions; and through the Mount Palomar telescope, billions of stars are visible. It is estimated that the number of stars in our galaxy alone is close to a hundred billion, and there are probably more than ten billion galaxies in the universe.

Questions naturally arise from the above:

Does any organizing principle govern that multitude of stars? Can the stars, like flowers or birds or human beings, be grouped into classes, each class with its own typical characteristics?

Do stars, like human beings, get born, go through infancy, mature, get old . . . and eventually die? Can a credible life history of a star be designed?

A reasonable answer to the last two questions is probably available in a diagram known as the **Hertzsprung-Russell Diagram,** designed independently by the Danish astronomer Ejnar Hertzsprung (1873–1967) and the American astronomer Henry N. Russell (1877–1957) early in the twentieth century.

We shall study the design of the diagram, also known as the HR diagram, in what follows and shall see its connection with the life history of stars in Chapter 9.

7.22 THE DESIGN OF THE HR DIAGRAM

The vertical axis in the Hertzsprung-Russell diagram (see Fig. 7.22) is graduated either in absolute magnitudes or in luminosities; the horizontal axis is graduated either in temperatures or in spectral classes. (It could also be graduated in colors.) The meaning of absolute magnitude and luminosity will be explained next, followed by the discussion of the design of the diagram itself.

Absolute Magnitude. The apparent magnitude of a star depends upon both its intrinsic brightness and its distance.

To be able to compare intrinsic brightness of

different stars it is necessary to eliminate the dependence upon distance.

The concept of absolute magnitude does just that. In this concept it is assumed that all the stars were removed from their real location to a new place, exactly 10 parsecs away from the terrestrial observer.

Naturally, stars that are brought closer to the terrestrial observer will appear brighter, while stars that had to be "pushed" to the 10-parsec line will now appear dimmer. The new magnitude assigned to the stars when they are 10 parsecs away is known as absolute magnitude. Most stars are at distances greater than 10 parsecs; the sun, however, with an apparent magnitude of −26.7, when moved to a distance of 10 parsecs, would have an absolute magnitude of +4.8. It would then appear as one of the fainter stars and would be invisible to observers with below-average vision.

The symbol for absolute magnitude is M, while m is usually used to denote the apparent magnitude of a star.

Luminosity. As indicated in Sec. 7.9, one of the definitions of luminosity is based on the total energy output of a star per unit of time, i.e., total power output.

In the case of the sun, the total power output is 3.9×10^{33} ergs/sec, implying that 3.9×10^{33} ergs are emitted into space by the surface of the sun every single second.

Luminosities of stars are usually stated in multiples or submultiples of the sun's power output. The total power output from the star Sirius is 27 times larger than that of the sun, hence the luminosity of Sirius is 27 (if the luminosity of the sun=1).

The symbol for luminosity is L.

NOTES: 1. It should be noted that luminosity and absolute magnitude are closely related, thus if we know one we can find from either a chart or from a formula the other. The formula is

$$M = 4.8 + 2.5 \log \frac{1}{L},$$

when M stands for the absolute magnitude of the star and L its luminosity relative to the sun.

PROBLEM 7.22:

Find absolute magnitude of Vega, given that its luminosity is 60.

$$M = 4.8 + 2.5 \log \frac{1}{60}$$

Using pertinent rules for logarithms this can be written as

$$M = 4.8 - 2.5 \log 60$$
$$= 4.8 - 2.5 \times 1.8 = +.4$$

Answer: The absolute magnitude of Vega is +.4.

2. It should also be noted that brightness of stars can be stated in various ways. Three distinct measures are often used: (a) apparent magnitude, (b) absolute magnitude, and (c) luminosity.

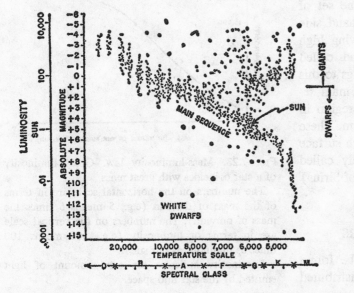

FIG. 7.22. The HR diagram for neighboring stars. On a complete diagram there are several thousand dots. Each dot represents the luminosity and the stellar spectrum of one star. The values of absolute magnitude may be used instead of the values of luminosity for the vertical scale. Similarly the surface temperature (in °A) of the star may be used instead of the spectral class for the horizontal scale.

The dot representing our sun is indicated in the proper place; the sun has an absolute magnitude of 4.8 and is in the G spectral class.

Stars brighter than +1 absolute magnitude are classified as giants; all the other stars are classified as dwarfs.

The values of these for the five stars that appear brightest to us are given in the following list.

Star	Apparent magnitude	Absolute magnitude	Luminosity (sun=1)
Sirius	—1.58	+1.3	30
Canopus	— .86	—3.2	1,900
α(alpha)-Centauri	+ .06	+4.7	1.3
Vega	+ .14	+ .5	60
Capella	+ .21	— .4	150

This list shows that if these stars were all placed at a distance of 10 parsecs (to obtain absolute magnitude), Canopus would be by far the brightest star.

The list also shows that Vega is twice as luminous and Capella five times as luminous as Sirius.

In the HR diagram each star is indicated by a dot. The position of the dot is determined by the star's luminosity and spectral class. A careful plot of the dots for stars that are in the neighborhood of the solar system brings out two very important features of the diagram in Figure 7.22:

A. The vast majority of the stars fit within a narrow band that runs from the upper left-hand corner to the lower right-hand corner of the diagram. It is known as the **Main Sequence,** and the stars belonging to it, including our sun are known as main-sequence stars.

B. The marked regularity in the main sequence has two very important exceptions. The dots for two well-defined types of stars fall far from the main sequence. One set of dots is scattered in the upper right-hand side of the diagram. These are stars having high luminosity but low temperature and called **Red Giants.** (The star Capella belongs to this class.) The other set of dots off the main sequence are concentrated in a small region in the lower left-hand side of the diagram. These are stars with low luminosity, but high surface temperatures. They are appropriately called **White Dwarfs.** The Pup (companion of Sirius) is a classic example of a white dwarf.

7.23 THE MAIN-SEQUENCE STARS

The fact that these stars are to be found only along a narrow band and not distributed in a disorderly manner all over the diagram suggests a close relationship between them. The stars in this sequence are presumably similar in some of their characteristics. Their spread along the sequence is most likely due to differences in masses, the more massive stars being the more luminous.

NOTE: The mass of a star is closely related to its luminosity. The relationship between the two can be derived from purely theoretical considerations. Figure 7.23 indicates graphically this relationship. It is known as **Mass-Luminosity Law. Thus the more massive the star, the more luminous it will be.**

The stars of high luminosity occupying the upper portion of the HR diagram are known as giants. The low luminosity stars are called dwarfs. The dividing point between giants and dwarfs is sometimes based on absolute magnitude of brightness. Stars that are brighter than absolute magnitude +1 are giants; those that are dimmer than absolute +1 (i.e., magnitudes +2, +3, etc.) are dwarfs. The main sequence runs the whole gamut from blue giants to red dwarfs.

We shall see, in Chapter 9, that the main-sequence stars are mature stars, producing energy through a thermonuclear reaction. We

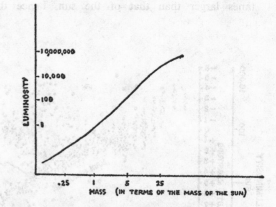

Fig. 7.23. Mass-luminosity law. Great luminosity of a star coincides with great mass.

The numbers on the horizontal scale are in terms of the mass of the sun (e.g., 5 means 5 times the mass of our sun). The numbers on the vertical scale are in terms of luminosity (e.g., 100 means 100 times as luminous as our sun).

Luminosity indicates the total amount of light emitted by the star into space.

shall also see there that all stars spend most of their lifetime on the main sequence.

7.24 THE OFF-MAIN-SEQUENCE STARS

Off the main sequence in the Hertzsprung-Russell diagram one finds the red giants, and the even larger red supergiants, as well as the white dwarfs.

The red giants, and particularly the red supergiants, are of extremely large volume. Some of the latter are big enough to accommodate much of the solar system. The masses of some are only five or ten times the mass of the sun, their bulkiness being due to the unusually small densities. The star Arcturus is classified as a red giant, while Antares is typical of the Supergiant variety. The temperature of these stars is approximately 2,000° A. Most of the radiation emitted by them is in the red and in the infrared. We shall see, in Chapter 9, that these stars are in their "later years," have used up much of the fuel needed for thermonuclear reactions, and have departed from the main sequence.

The white dwarfs are similar in color to the white stars of spectral class A; their luminosity, however, is extremely small. Many white dwarfs have a luminosity less than $\frac{1}{100,000}$ that of a normal class A star. This is not due to lack of mass, as they compare well in this respect with the mass of the sun. Their faint luminosity is due to their small size. Naturally, stars with fair-sized masses and small volumes have high values of density. These high values were already noted in the consideration of the red shift in the light leaving these stars; it was noted there that a tablespoon of matter of a white dwarf would weigh tons.

Theoretically, there is a limit to the mass of the white dwarf: one cannot be greater than 1.2 times that of the solar mass.

Theory also suggests a relationship between the mass of the dwarf and its diameter—namely, the larger the mass, the smaller the diameter.

Several hundred white dwarfs are now known. They are no doubt much more numerous than we have thus far observed; but their small luminosity makes them invisible at any great distance.

It will be noted in Chapter 9 that the white dwarf stage is one of the last episodes in the normal evolution of a star.

7.25 THE VARIABLE STARS

The main-sequence stars are permanent objects. Their masses and hence their luminosities don't change materially even in millions of years. This is also true of the white dwarfs and of some red giants and red supergiants.

There is, however, a reasonably large number of stars (more than 10,000) whose intrinsic brightness and spectral characteristics vary with time.

The changes in intrinsic brightness are due in some cases to pulsations (the star swells and shrinks periodically), in other cases to explosions (the star ejects part of its mass into space).

The pulsating stars include several groups: Cepheids I; Cepheids II, RR-Lyrae variables, and long-period variables.

Of the exploding stars we shall mention just two groups: novae and supernovae.

7.26 CEPHEIDS

A Cepheid is a type of star whose brightness varies periodically. At the beginning of a period, for a typical Cepheid, its brightness increases very rapidly, for as long as several hours. That is followed by a gradual dimming which may continue for several days. This cycle is then repeated. See Fig. 7.26a. The Cepheids are very punctual and regular in their variation. The change in brightness from minimum to maximum is usually not very great; a change in one magnitude, say, from 5.3 to 4.3, is a fairly representative value.

The first Cepheid known was the δ star in Cepheus—hence the derivation of its name. Since the discovery of the first Cepheid in 1784, hundreds of similar stars have been dis-

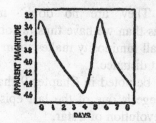

FIG. 7.26a. Cepheids. The variation in the apparent magnitude of δ (delta)-Cephei is shown. The maximum brightness of this particular Cepheid is 3.3; at its dimmest it has an apparent magnitude of 4.5. The complete cycle repeats every 5 days 8 hours.

covered. They are luminous supergiants, spectral classes F and G.

Cepheids and other variable stars are named according to a fixed set of rules: the first variable star discovered in any constellation is given a prefix, R (e.g., R-Leonis); the second bears the prefix S; Z is followed by RR, then by RS, RT, etc.; RZ by SS, ST, and so on. AA follows ZZ in that scheme, until QZ. As no combinations with the letter J are made, this scheme allows for 334 variables in any one constellation. Additional variable stars are denoted by a much simpler scheme: V335, V336, etc.; e.g., V357-Cygni.

Periods of Cepheids (or the spans of time between maximum brightness and maximum brightness) range from a small value of 1 hour 28 minutes for CY-Aquarii to 45 days 4 hours for SV-Vulpeculae.

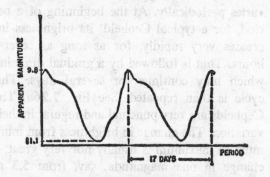

FIG. 7.26b. Light curve typical of a Cepheid II star. Neither the brightening part of the curve nor the dimming part is smooth. There are characteristic leveling off intervals in both parts of the curve.

The numbers given are for the star W-Virginis.

Later research indicated that there really are three kinds of Cepheids. These are identified as **Cepheids I**, **Cepheids II**, and **RR-Lyrae Variables**.

Cepheid I stars are on the average 1.5 magnitudes brighter than Cepheids II. They brighten rapidly, dim rather gradually. See Fig. 7.26a. Their periods range from 1.5 to 40 days, the most frequent being 5 days.

Cepheid II have characteristic leveling off intervals both in the brightening and in the dimming parts of the curve. See Fig. 7.26b. Their periods are from 10 to 25 days.

7.27 PERIOD OF CEPHEIDS AND ABSOLUTE MAGNITUDE

A remarkable relationship has been discovered between the period of a Cepheid and its absolute magnitude.

The discovery dates back to the research in 1908 of Miss Henrietta Leavitt at the Harvard College Observatory concerning Cepheid stars in the Lesser Magellanic Cloud. The Lesser Magellanic Cloud as well as the Greater Magellanic Cloud are, in reality, galaxies—close neighbors to our galaxy.

The clouds, named after the Portuguese navigator, appear to the naked eye as two faint patches of light. They cannot be seen from the United States as they are within 20° of the South Celestial Pole.

The important result of the discovery made by Miss Leavitt is that all the Cepheid stars having the same period have the same absolute magnitude. Stars having long periods have high values for absolute magnitude; short-period stars, low values.

It also means that all one has to do to find the absolute magnitude of such a star (usually a difficult task) is to measure the period (a rather easy job).

This relationship can best be expressed in the form of graphs, one for each Cepheid type in which absolute magnitudes are plotted on the vertical axis and the period on the horizontal. See Fig. 7.27.

NOTE: Magnitudes, in the case of variable-brightness stars, are taken to be the mean of the maximum and minimum values.

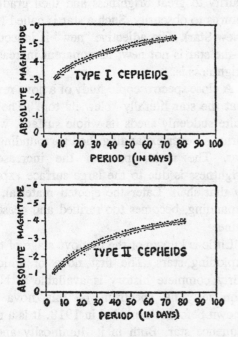

FIG. 7.27. Two curves of absolute magnitude vs. period. The curve relating the absolute magnitude of a Cepheid I with its period is similar to the curve for a Cepheid II; the difference between the two curves is in brightness. For the same period a Cepheid I star is 4 times as bright as a Cepheid II. This can also be stated by saying that Cepheid I stars have values of absolute magnitudes smaller by 1.5 than Cepheid II stars having the same period of variation.

7.28 INDIRECT METHOD FOR MEASURING STELLAR DISTANCES

A basic formula in astronomy links apparent magnitude (m), absolute magnitude (M), and distance (Dps; distance measured in parsecs).

If any two of these are known, the third can be determined.

The formula is

$$M = m + 5 - 5 \log Dps$$

The formula can also be written as

$$\log Dps = \frac{1}{5}(m - M) + 1$$

PROBLEM 7.28:

Given M = .6, and
m = .14
Find distance
Substituting, one obtains
$$\log Dps = \frac{1}{5}(.14 - .60) + 1 = .91$$
and using a table of logarithms to the base 10, one finds that Dps = 8.1 parsecs.

In the case of Cepheids, we do know both m, and M.

The first is obtained by averaging the apparent magnitude of the star, the latter by using the observed period together with the proper period-absolute magnitude curve. Hence we can determine the distance to the Cepheid or to any group of stars that that particular Cepheid happens to be associated with.

7.29 RR-LYRAE VARIABLES

These are Cepheids of very short period, the longest known being 29 hours, the shortest, a little less than an hour and a half. The first star of this type to be discovered was a seventh-magnitude star in the constellation of Lyra; hence, the name. These Cepheids were formerly known as "cluster type Cepheids" because they were first discovered in globular star clusters. This name is obsolete now as they are known to be present in all parts of the sky. Some 3,000 of these are known. They are fifty times more luminous than the sun and are of spectral class A or F.

7.30 ANOTHER INDIRECT METHOD FOR MEASURING STELLAR DISTANCES

Studies of RR-Lyrae variables indicate that they all have an absolute magnitude (M) close to +.6.

Using this value and the observed average apparent magnitude (m), one can find the distance in parsecs (Dps) from

$$\log Dps = \frac{1}{5}(m - M) + 1$$

This is the distance to this star or to any group of stars that the RR-Lyrae star happens to be in.

7.31 LONG-PERIOD VARIABLES

These variables are usually giant red stars with periods longer than 100 days. Their light variation is not quite as regular as in the case of other variable stars. The most famous of the long-period variables is certainly o (omicron)-Ceti. Discovered in 1596, the star was soon thereafter called Mira, the Wonderful. At maximum brightness, Mira has been known to reach an apparent magnitude of 1.5; at that stage, it is the most brilliant star in that part of the heavens. At minimum brightness, its magnitude is about +9, totally invisible to the naked eye. Its average period is 330 days. Individual periods may be less than 300 days or more than 350.

7.32 CEPHEIDS ON THE HR DIAGRAM

Figure 7.32 indicates the approximate locations of the three kinds of Cepheids. These areas are known as the instability strips.

When stars following their treks on this diagram reach these areas, they somehow become unstable and pulsate.

7.33 NOVAE

Occasionally a star rises from relative obscurity to great brightness and then gradually returns to obscurity. Such a star is called **Nova (New Star)**. The adjective "new" is inaccurate —the star is not new; its apparent increase in brightness is.

A close spectroscopic study of a nova reveals that the star literally "blew its top." The star quite suddenly sheds its whole surface, which forms an ever expanding shell surrounding the star. The major part of the increase in brightness is due to the large surface exposed by that shell. Later the ejected material, still expanding, becomes too rarified and ceases to shine.

Little is known of the prenova stage of these exploding stars. The first nova of which a fairly complete history is available is Nova-Aquilae. The spectrum of this nova was known before it exploded in 1918. It is a main sequence star. Both in its luminosity and its spectral characteristics, it is fairly similar to our sun. No irregularities could be detected in these spectra, thus indicating that an ap-

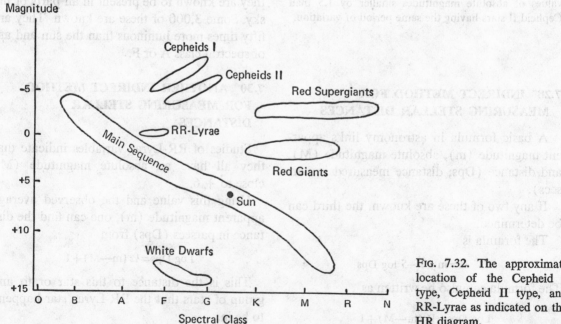

Fig. 7.32. The approximate location of the Cepheid I type, Cepheid II type, and RR-Lyrae as indicated on the HR diagram.

parently normal star, such as our sun, can burst into a terrific explosion unpredictably.

The probability that this will happen is extremely small. Computations show that the chance of such a solar cataclysm (that of course would in a matter of days bring life on earth to an end) is extremely small—one in many billion.

The probability is further decreased by the fact that such explosions are much more likely to occur in massive hot white stars having spectra of type O and B than in a fairly "low mass" cool yellow star of type G, like our sun.

Also, this explosion most likely occurs toward the "end of life" of the star—in the case of our sun, in about 5 billion more years.

In recorded history over 200 novae have been observed in our galaxy. Currently, with improved observational techniques, one or two novae are discovered every year, while ten times as many probably escape detection.

A schematic light curve for a nova would indicate (a) an almost abrupt increase in luminosity by as much as 10,000 times its value in the prenova stage; (b) a brief pause followed by a further increase in brightness by a factor of ten; (c) a decline in brightness to prenova stage. The decline varies in shape with the individual nova. See Fig. 7.33.

The initial rise may be concluded in several days. The final decline may continue for several years. In terms of apparent magnitude, some of these novae are bright enough to be seen in broad daylight; others are visible only through a telescope.

When the nova reaches the postnova stage, it resumes its former luminosity. Apparently no permanent damage has been done. The loss in mass has been estimated to be a small and rather unimportant fraction of the star.

One of the explanations for novae is that this particular kind of a star generates at a certain stage in its development more energy than its surface can radiate. The star gets rid of this excess by ejecting a thin shell into space.

A more fundamental explanation deals with

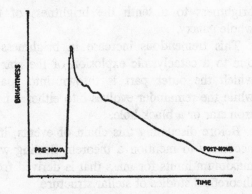

Fig. 7.33. Schematic light curve for a nova. An increase in brightness by a factor of as much as 10,000 may take place in several days. This increase is usually followed by a day or so of no change in brightness, and another increase in brightness by a factor of ten. The decline is less regular and usually lasts several years.

the fact that slightly more massive stars (from 1.2 times the mass of the sun) have to lose this excess mass before they can enter the stage of evolution known as white dwarf.

This loss of mass may be accomplished by a star's ejecting one or more thin shells and hence becoming a nova or a recurrent nova.

7.34 SUPERNOVAE, NEUTRON STARS, PULSARS, BLACK HOLES

Records show several cases of exceptionally bright stellar explosions. The increase in luminosity in these cases is more than 10,000 times greater than that of ordinary novae. These are known as **Supernovae.** The brilliant star that suddenly manifested itself in the constellation of Cassiopeia in 1572 and led Tycho Brahe to devote his life to astronomy is of that classification. The last recorded supernova in our galaxy was observed in 1604, and closely studied by another great scientist, Johannes Kepler.

The data on supernovae seem to indicate that there is about one supernova per century in our galaxy. More than 200 supernovae have also been recorded in other galaxies. One of these, in the Andromeda galaxy, was recorded in 1885. That star increased in brightness to a tenth the brightness of the whole galaxy.

This tremendous increase in brightness is due to a cataclysmic explosion of the star in which the outer part is thrown into space, while the remainder evolves into either a neutron star or a black hole.

Before discussing this chain of events, it is necessary to mention a theorem dealing with maximum limits for mass that is derived from theoretical studies of stellar structure.

THEOREM: A star approaching the end of its thermonuclear life cannot evolve into the white dwarf stage (the "normal" way for a star to end its life) if its mass is larger than 1.2 times the mass of the sun. Stated slightly differently, a star with a mass larger than 1.2 times the mass of the sun cannot reach the equilibrium conditions prevalent in a white dwarf. This limit of 1.2 suns' masses is known as the Chandrasekhar limit (named after the Indian astronomer Subrahmanyan Chandrasekhar [1910–]).

Similarly, the limit for a neutron star (see below) is 3.2 times the mass of the sun.

The chain of events for a supernovae is as follows:

A. A star of mass very much larger than the sun (say, 5 times larger), having used up all its thermonuclear energy, starts to contract.

B. The internal pressure is unable to support the various layers of this massive star, the star collapses, and a tremendous amount of heat is produced.

C. The outer part of the star explodes, throwing into space a large part of the star, probably more than half its mass, which becomes a supernova nebula. A classic example of a supernova nebula is the Crab Nebula in Taurus, which had its origin in a supernova of A.D. 1054.

D. The inner part, the core of the star, evolves at the high temperatures (billions of degrees) and pressures prevalent, into (1) a neutron star (pulsar) if its mass is between 1.2 and 3.2 times the mass of the sun, or (2) a black hole if the mass is larger than 3.2 times the mass of the sun.

NOTES: 1. At the extreme pressures and temperatures in the core, protons and electrons combine to form neutrons, hence the name neutron stars.

Neutron stars are extremely small (diameters of a few miles) and almost unimaginably dense (100 thousand million kilograms per cubic centimeter).

In such a star, the neutrons, acting like a "gas," create enough pressure to prevent the core from totally collapsing.

A neutron star when rotating produces a strong magnetic field. Outside electrons injected into this field decelerate and emit radiation. Beams of this radiation, upon reaching the earth, produce the pulses associated with pulsars. Hence, pulsars are fast rotating neutron stars, the emissions of which reach the terrestrial observer.

Theory also shows that when material particles interact with a fast-rotating neutron star, radiation of X-ray wavelength should be emitted. This has been verified by observation.

The first pulsar was discovered in 1967 by astronomers at Cambridge University and has a period between pulses of 1.3 seconds. More than a hundred pulsars have been discovered by 1974; one of these is the pulsar connected with the Crab Nebula. The Crab Nebula pulsar is identified as NP 0532, the P indicating that it is a pulsar, the N 0532 that it was discovered by members of the National Radio Astronomy Observatory near right ascension 05 hours 32 minutes. This pulsar is also an X-ray star. The period of the X-rays is identical with the period of rotation of the star.

2. When the pressure created by the neutrons is insufficient to offset the contractional forces, the core may gravitationally collapse to zero volume and become a **Black Hole**. The surface gravity of a black hole is so great that it prevents light or anything else from escaping into space.

CHAPTER 8

INTERSTELLAR MATTER AND NEBULAE

8.1 INTERSTELLAR MATTER

Stars are usually enormous in size; but spaces between stars (interstellar space) are even larger.

Very tenuous matter consisting of gases and minute (radius 10^{-5} cm) dust particles pervade this interstellar space.

While spectroscopic and radio emission studies indicate that the gas consists mainly of hydrogen, with minute additions of other elements, such as carbon, nitrogen, oxygen, sodium, iron, and titanium, the composition of the dust particles is less well known. One theory suggests that the particles consist of clusters of a large number of carbon atom joined together to form graphite. Another suggestion is that the dust particles actually consist of icy crystals, of H_2O, NH_3, and CH_4 or a combination thereof.

The density of that interstellar matter is extremely small. Reasonable figures are one atom of gas per cubic centimeter and about ten dust particles per cubic kilometer.

The total mass of interstellar matter, though, compares well with total mass of stars. Computations show that in the neighborhood of the sun, for example, the interstellar mass is equal to about one quarter the mass of the neighboring stars.

The interstellar matter is responsible for both the dimming and reddening of distant stars. The reddening effect is due to the fact that the interstellar matter scatters the shorter wavelengths (blue, violet) much more efficiently than it does the red. Hence the blue colors get scattered and the red goes through.

8.2 NEBULAE

In many parts of interstellar space there can be found rather heavy concentrations of interstellar matter. These are called **Nebulae** (*nebula* is the Latin word for cloud).

The density of nebulae is 1,000 times or more the density of interstellar matter.

Nebulae are classified as (1) **Emission**; (2) **Reflection**; (3) **Dark**.

An **Emission Nebula** is a cloud of matter that happens to have one or more extremely hot, luminous, spectral types O or B stars imbedded in it. The ultraviolet light from the stars excites the hydrogen and oxygen to emit its characteristic light. An excellent example of an emission nebula is the Great Nebula of Orion.

If the star (or stars) imbedded in the nebula is cooler than a type B1 star, the matter in the cloud will not emit light of its own; it will, though, reflect light from the star. These are known as **Reflection Nebulae**. The spectrum of such a nebula is of course identical with that of the star. Excellent examples of reflection nebulae are the clouds surrounding the several important stars of the Pleiades.

If the nebula has no nearby star to supply it with light, it is known as a **Dark Nebula**. A striking example of this type is the Horsehead Nebula, also in Orion.

CHAPTER 9

THE STARS: ENERGY AND EVOLUTION

PART I: ENERGY

9.1 ENERGY MAGNITUDES

It is estimated that the stars have been emitting light energy and heat energy for several billion years. Where did all that energy come from? Where does it come from now?

Many theories have attempted an answer; but, before theories are considered, it is well to get an idea of the magnitude of the energies involved. A fairly exact value for the total amount of energy produced in one minute by one of the stars (our sun) can easily be computed.

A. Every minute, each cm² of the earth's surface perpendicular to the sun's rays receives a total amount of heat and light energy equal to 1.94 calories. (This number is known as the Solar Constant of Radiation.) Solar energy reaches the surface of the earth at the rate of nearly 5 million horsepower per square mile. The total amount of energy received yearly by the entire surface of the earth is fantastic. It exceeds by nearly 5 million times the annual production of energy obtained from coal, gas, waterfalls, fuel oil, and all other artificial sources of energy.

B. Knowing the distance of the earth's surface from the sun, it is possible to compute the total energy radiated by the sun per minute: 472,300 billion billions of horsepower! (The earth intercepts only one two-billionths of the energy radiated by the sun.) 472,300 billion billions of horsepower of energy for several billion years!

Ordinary combustion such as coal could not account for it. It the sun were made of the best coal, it would have turned to ashes a long time ago.

9.2 THE GRAVITATIONAL THEORY

Until the beginning of this century, there was only one rational explanation, the one formulated by the German physicist Hermann Helmholtz (1821–94). According to Helmholtz's theory, stars were gradually shrinking in diameter. A small decrease in volume could supply the amounts of energy needed. It can be computed that, in the case of the sun, a shrinkage of the diameter by 200 feet per year would account for the emission of energy. This theory is often referred to as the gravitational theory, because the primary cause of shrinkage is the gravitational pull on the outer layers towards the center of the sun.

9.3 ENERGY FROM NUCLEAR SOURCES

Modern explanations are based on nuclear reactions. That energy can be derived on earth from annihilation of part of the mass of atomic nuclei is a pretty well established fact. It is very likely that stellar energy is produced in a similar way. Such processes could easily explain the data we possess.

The conversion of mass to energy is, of course, governed by the famous Einstein equation:

$$E = mc^2$$

m, measured in grams, is the amount of mass annihilated; c, measured in cm/sec., is the velocity of light; and E, measured in ergs, is the energy obtained in return.

PART II: LIFE HISTORY OF A STAR

9.4 INTRODUCTION

It is now possible to make a preliminary sketch of the life history of a star. Research yet to be done may, of course, alter facets of that sketch, though at present the sketch seems reasonable and complete.

The life of a star can conveniently be divided into seven periods:

A. Birth (local concentration of nebular matter).
B. Infancy (contracting stage).
C. Maturity (main sequence).
D. Later years (red giant).
E. Still later years (variables).
F. Last stages (white dwarf, neutron stars, and blackholes).

The life history of a star depends greatly on its mass. So does life expectancy.

Life expectancy of stars varies from several millions (for very massive stars) to many billions of years (for the least massive).

We see in the sky stars of different masses, those of each mass in all stages of development. Some, astronomically speaking, have just been born, others are in the prime of life, still others are in their declining years. If we synthesize these stages, it is possible for us to obtain a set of reasonably complete pictures for all the stars.

As with all theories of development, an assumption must be made about the starting point.

Our starting point is a nebula in interstellar space. The average density of matter in the nebula in several thousands atoms per cubic centimeter (or 5×10^{-21} grams per cubic centimeter). The temperature is just a few degrees above zero absolute, say $3°$ A.

Originally, i.e., when the first generation of stars was formed, a nebula was composed of only hydrogen and helium (mostly hydrogen plus a minute percentage of helium).

The other ninety or so natural elements were produced in the cores of massive ultra-hot stars. These elements found their way from the core of a star into the nebula during outbursts of novae and during catastrophic explosions of supernovae.

Later generation stars contained, in addition to hydrogen and helium, small percentages of all (or almost all) other natural elements.

9.5 BIRTH

Slight motions within the nebula create local concentrations of matter. Gravitational forces greatly aid the building up of matter in these concentrated regions and thus give birth to an autonomous chunk of matter, maybe 10^{27} (a billion billion billion) tons in mass—a protostar.

NOTE: It is considered likely that the small dark globules often seen at edges of some nebulae are in actuality protostars. Much smaller masses than the one cited above would not possess enough gravitational effectiveness to become a unit; masses much larger would become unstable and split into a number of small stars.

Thus then a star is born. The first stars, maybe some 10 billion years ago; the latest, right now. There is no doubt that this process continues and that stars are continually being born.

At birth the star is much too cold to emit visible light. Emission of waves of radio wavelength is much more likely.

9.6 INFANCY

The large mass of nebular matter, under the influence of self-gravitational pull, shrinks and thus changes mechanical potential energy into heat. The principal emission changes from radio to infrared waves; the object is now referred to as an infrared star.

This shrinking and heating up process takes place quickly (astronomically speaking), within a mere 30 million years, and involves three basic stages:

A. The large mass which originally extended for trillions of miles will decrease to only several hundred million miles.
B. The pressure at the center will increase from almost zero to several thousand million atmospheres.
C. The temperature at the core will rise from several degrees absolute to about 20 million degrees absolute, high enough to initiate the thermonuclear transformation of hydrogen into helium.

The star's infancy is over. It's now a mature star. In scientific terms, it has reached the main-sequence line on the HR diagram (see Fig. 7.23).

NOTES: 1. The time required for the transition from birth to maturity depends materially on the mass of the star. Massive stars develop rapidly and may reach maturity after several hundred thousand years, while less massive ones may take much longer than the 30 million years mentioned above to become main-sequence stars.

2. Massive stars naturally enter higher on the main-sequence line than less massive ones, as massive stars are more luminous than less massive stars.

9.7 MATURITY (MAIN-SEQUENCE STARS)

Whereas gravity had been the sole source of energy to this stage, the end of infancy is marked by the emergence of a new one: energy from thermonuclear reactions.

Nuclear energy in stars is produced from mass, according to the Einstein formula $E = mc^2$. When m is measured in grams and c (the velocity of light) in centimeters per second, E will be in ergs.

The mass in this formula is actually a difference of masses, i.e., the difference between the sum of the masses of the lighter atoms that go into the reaction and the mass of the heavier atoms that result from it.

When 4 atoms of hydrogen fuse together at high temperatures (thermonuclear, or fusion process) near the center of a star to form one helium atom, the loss of mass is

$$4 \times \text{mass of hydrogen atom} = 4 \times 1.673 \times 10^{-24} \text{ gm}$$
$$= 6.692 \times 10^{-24} \text{ gm}$$
$$\text{Less mass of helium atom} = 6.644 \times 10^{-24} \text{ gm}$$
$$= .05 \times 10^{-24} \text{ gm}$$

The mass that "got lost" was transformed into energy.

$$E = mc^2 = .05 \times 10^{-24} \times (3 \times 10^{10})^2$$
$$= 4 \times 10^{-5} \text{ erg}$$

Thus, on the sun or any other star 4×10^{-5} ergs of energy are produced each time 4 atoms of hydrogen fuse to form 1 atom of helium.

Our sun emits into space every second about 4×10^{33} ergs. To produce this tremendous amount of energy every second, the sun uses up in its core 700,000 million kilograms of hydrogen . . . and produces 695,000 million kilograms of helium in turn.

While these numbers are enormous, they are but a minute fraction of the mass of hydrogen available, hence our sun will most likely shine for quite a few more billions of years.

Science recognizes two distinct processes of hydrogen-into-helium fusion. One is known as the proton-proton and the other as the carbon cycle.

In the proton-proton process the several steps are

A. Two hydrogen atoms combine to form an isotope of hydrogen called deuterium.
B. Deuterium picks up a hydrogen atom forming a light isotope of helium.
C. Two atoms of light helium form the final helium atom.

The carbon cycle is a bit more complicated. Carbon, nitrogen, and oxygen alternately appear and disappear in the reaction. The net effect of six distinct nuclear reactions is that 4 hydrogen atoms fuse to form 1 helium atom, just like in the proton-proton case. And the same amount of energy is released.

It is likely that the proton-proton reaction is predominant in stars like our sun where the core is relatively cool. Minimum temperature needed is 10^6 ° A.

In more massive stars than our sun, with minimum temperatures of 10×10^6 ° A, the carbon cycle is predominant.

Most of a star's life is spent in this stage. During the millions (for a massive star) or billions (for a less massive star) of years spent, the star will move up about one magnitude on the HR diagram.

9.8 LATER YEARS (RED GIANTS)

When the core of the star runs out of hydrogen, it falls back on its alternative source of energy, i.e., gravity. The core begins to contract and get hotter. As a result of this, three things happen:

A. The temperature outside of the core gets high enough for the hydrogen there to fuse into helium.

B. The outer layers of the star expand and the star becomes a giant.

C. The surface temperature of the star decreases . . . and the star becomes a red giant or a red supergiant, depending on the mass of the star.

For a star like our sun, this process may last a billion years. During that time the radius may increase fifty fold and the surface temperature may go down to about 3,000° A.

On the HR diagram this process is indicated by a line going up and to the right from the point of departure on the main sequence. See Fig. 7.22.

9.9 STILL LATER YEARS (VARIABLES)

Simultaneous with the expansion of the star, the helium core was contracting and rising in temperature.

At temperatures of 100 million ° A, a new reaction sets in and the course of evolution is changed again.

At that temperature 3 helium atoms fuse into 1 carbon atom. Later the star again begins to draw on the gravity sources and becomes smaller and smaller. The route followed on the HR diagram is reversed again, i.e., toward the left. See Fig. 9.9.

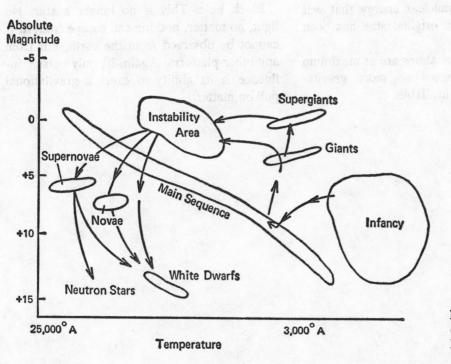

FIG. 9.9. Life history of a star as noted on an HR diagram.

Still later, when moving across the instability strip, the star will start to pulsate and become a Cepheid variable. And finally, depending on the mass, one of three things may happen:

A. If the mass of the star is less than 1.2 times the mass of the sun, the star will become a white dwarf.

B. If the star is slightly more than the 1.2 figure, the star will shed a part of its mass and become a nova or it will shed small parts of its mass several times and become a recurrent nova. Eventually the star will become a white dwarf.

C. If the star's mass is a great deal more than 1.2 times the mass of the sun, it will shed a major part of its mass into space, thus producing a supernova nebula as well as either a white dwarf, neutron star, or black hole, depending on the size of the mass being imploded. This topic has been discussed at some length in Sec. 7.34.

9.10 LAST STAGES

White dwarf. To become a white dwarf, the following events have taken place:

A. All the thermonuclear energy that was available to the original star has been fully used up.

B. The nuclei of the atoms are at maximum compression, hence no more gravitational energy is available.

C. The free electrons are not able to supply any energy. The only remaining source of energy is from the random motion of the nuclei.

The positively charged nuclei are little by little slowing down, and the kinetic energy is the source of heat and light for the white dwarf. Eventually, this source will disappear, too.

After several billion years, the light will cease. Visual contact with the earth will be severed. Only by its gravitational pull does the dying star make known its existence—only by its disturbance of the path of another star would we be made aware that there is then an object there that once shone for billions of years.

Neutron star. The star loses energy into space and its rotational rate decreases. The decreases in spins or the increases in periods have been observed in the case of many of these stars. Eventually this type of star, too, will lose all its energy and, like the white dwarf, will move through space as a dark chunk of material with only a gravitational field around it.

Black hole. This is no longer a star. No light, no matter, nothing can escape from it. It cannot be observed from the earth, nor from any other platform. Again, its only outside influence is its ability to exert a gravitational pull on matter.

CHAPTER 10

THE GALAXIES

PART I: OUR GALAXY

10.1 INTRODUCTION

The sun and some 100 billion other stars, plus a great deal of interstellar matter, plus many nebulae, form the object known as **Our Galaxy.**

The study of distribution of stars in our galaxy has demonstrated that this vast collection resembles a somewhat flattened disk; in fact, it is often represented as a gigantic grindstone or a double convex lens.

Viewed from above, it would appear circular in outline, the stars forming a spiral, or pinwheel, design; a side view would reveal its thinness. See Figs. 10.1a and 10.1b.

The most reliable figure for the diameter of the galaxy is 100,000 light-years. The maximum thickness is estimated at 10,000 to 15,000 light-years.

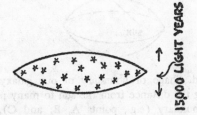

FIG. 10.1b. Side view of our galaxy points up its relative thinness.

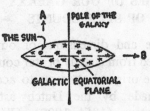

FIG. 10.1c. Two views of the galaxy. Looking from the solar system along the smaller dimension (direction A) stars are seen against a black background.

The nearby stars along direction B are seen against the background of the Milky Way. The luminosity of the latter is due to the merging points of light produced by tens of billions of stars. The galactic equatorial plane slices the galaxy horizontally in two equal parts. The pole of the galaxy is perpendicular to the galactic equatorial plane at its center.

Our sun with its system of planets occupies an unspectacular position. The solar system is located about 30,000 light-years from the center, and fairly close to the galactic equatorial plane.

Looking from our own small planet at this multitude of stars, one gets two distinct views. See Fig. 10.1c. In the direction parallel to the pole of the galaxy, due to thinness of the latter, individual stars are seen against a dark

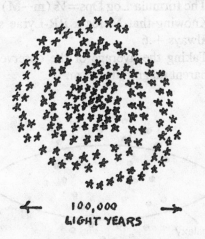

FIG. 10.1a. Top view of our galaxy reveals its circular outline. The stars are not evenly distributed over that area. There is a concentration of stars in the center of the galaxy as well as along two arms that start at opposite sides of the center and spiral about it.

background. The view along the equatorial plane is different—the closer stars are seen against a faint luminous band (Milky Way), which owes its existence to the merging light of the billions of stars present in the thick part of our galaxy.

This band of light thus indicates the direction of the equatorial plane of our galaxy.

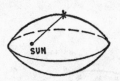

FIG. 10.1d. Shape of boundary of our galaxy. By computing the distance from the sun to many points on the boundary (e.g., points A, B, and C), the shape of the galaxy can be visualized.

10.2 STUDIES OF OUR GALAXY WITH THE AID OF STAR COUNTS

The shape and dimensions of our galaxy can be derived from a study of star counts.

One of the original attempts to accomplish this was made by the Dutch astronomer Jacobus Kapteyn (1851–1922). His method consisted of four steps:

A. Finding the relative number of stars of different absolute magnitudes in spaces near the sun.

B. Assuming that the same relative numbers, i.e., the same mix, prevails in spaces far from the sun.

C. Computing how many such groups have to be in each direction in order to account for the actual number and magnitude of stars for that particular angle and thus finding the distance to the edge of the galaxy for that direction.

D. Repeating the same computation for all other directions and thus getting the outline of the galaxy. See Fig. 10.1d.

Modern analysis introduces a correction because of the effect of interstellar matter in Kapteyn's calculations and arrives at the pic-ture of a double convex lens, 100,000 light-years in diameter, as previously outlined.

10.3 STUDIES OF OUR GALAXY WITH THE AID OF GLOBULAR CLUSTERS

Another method of estimating the size of our galaxy is based on globular star clusters, which, as the name implies, are **swarms of stars crowded together in the shape of a globe.** See Fig. 10.3.

One of the most beautiful globular clusters —barely visible to the naked eye—is M13, in the constellation on Hercules. Telescopic studies reveal that it probably consists of more than 500,000 stars, 50,000 of which can be counted individually. The remaining number can only be estimated since the stars are too close together to be able to be counted separately.

Many of the globular clusters contain RR-Lyrae variables. (Others have Cepheid II variables among them.) We have already seen (Sec. 7.30) how easy it is to compute a distance to a cluster containing a RR-Lyrae variable, using

A. The formula Log D_{ps}=⅕ (m—M)+1

B. Knowing that M for a RR-Lyrae star is always +.6

C. Taking the average of the observed apparent magnitudes as m.

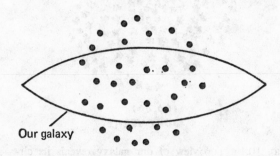

FIG. 10.3. Distribution of globular star clusters. A symbolic representation of these star clusters would show them to be distributed in the form of a sphere about our galaxy. The diameter of the sphere is equal to the diameter of the Milky Way.

A study of the distance of the hundred or so known globular clusters brings out the fact that they are distributed to form a sphere about our galaxy, the Milky Way cutting this sphere in two equal halves. The diameter of the sphere agrees quite well with the value of the diameter of the Milky Way (100,000 light-years), which serves as an additional check on our knowledge of the size of our galaxy.

10.4 ROTATION OF OUR GALAXY

The shape of the galaxy implies that it is rotating; in fact, it could not exist as a flat disk without rotation. The axis of rotation is perpendicular to the equatorial plane of the galaxy. This motion of the galaxy as a whole is superimposed on the movement of its individual stars. In this respect it is similar to the rotation of the earth about its axis, while all kinds of movements proceed on the surface of the earth. However, there is a great difference between these two rotations. The galaxy does not rotate as a solid body. The stars rotate around the center of the galaxy in much the same way as the planets move around the sun; the stars close to the center of the galaxy move at great orbital velocities; stars far from the center, at small velocities. Our sun has an orbital velocity of 160 miles per second. Stars close to the center seem to outrun the sun. Stars closer to the edge of the galaxy seem to move at slower speeds. Relative to the sun, these latter seem to be going to the opposite direction.

The period of revolutions, of course, will depend on the distance of the star from the center. It takes the sun 224,000,000 years to complete one revolution.

10.5 STUDIES OF OUR GALAXY WITH THE AID OF RADIO TELESCOPES

Our knowledge of the structure of our galaxy has been greatly extended through the study of 21-cm radio waves emitted by interstellar hydrogen.

NOTE: Neutral hydrogen emits radiation of 21-cm wavelength when the electron spin changes its orientation.

An atom of hydrogen in which the electron spins in the same direction as the proton has slightly more energy than an atom in which the spin of the electron is opposite to the spin of the proton. See Fig. 10.5. When the electron "flips" from the former to the latter arrangement, a quantum of electromagnetic energy is given off. Its wavelength is 21 cm.

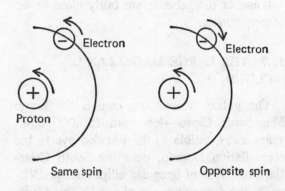

FIG. 10.5. Electron flip. On the left side of the illustration, the electron and the proton are both spinning in the same direction (counterclockwise). After the electron "flips," electron and proton spin in opposite directions.

A study of the distribution of hydrogen in our galaxy again confirms its size and shape as obtained by previous methods.

Research using 21-cm waves also indicates that much of the hydrogen is confined to a rather thin layer of a 1,000-light-year thickness and that it seems to concentrate in certain areas, especially in the spiral arms.

PART II: OTHER GALAXIES

10.6 INTRODUCTION

Our galaxy is not alone in this celestial world. The universe is probably populated by more than 10 billion galaxies. Several terms are used interchangeably for these galaxies. Sometimes they are referred to as **Island Universes** (implying that the universe is interspersed with islands that are similar to our own Milky Way galaxy). Sometimes they are referred to as **Extragalactic Nebulae** (in spite of the fact that they are galaxies of stars and not nebulae).

Some of the galaxies are fairly close to us; others, remote.

10.7 THE LARGE MAGELLANIC CLOUD

The galaxy nearest our own is the **Large Magellanic Cloud**—less than 150,000 light-years away, visible to the unaided eye in the constellation Dorado, near the South Celestial Pole. It is of irregular elliptic shape. Visually, the dimensions are about 12° by 4°; its actual large axis is 30,000 light-years in length.

The Large Magellanic Cloud contains many objects of great interest. Of particular interest are the almost 1,500 Cepheid variables, more than 100 intense, discrete radio sources, as well as the Great Looped Nebula, designated as 30 Doradus. 30 Doradus is the largest known gaseous nebula, much larger than the Great Nebula of Orion. That it is also extremely bright would be much more apparent if it had been in our galaxy. In fact, if 30 Doradus were placed at the distance of Orion, it would appear 200 times brighter than Sirius.

NOTE: It should be emphasized that the Greater Magellanic Cloud, the nearest extragalactic nebula, is neither a cloud nor a nebula. It is a galaxy. That is, it is a large island universe consisting of light-emitting stars, globular star clusters, nebulae, and all other entities that can be found in any galaxy, including our own.

The star, S-Doradus, in the Large Magellanic Cloud, is by far the most luminous star known, one of a group known as "irregular variables." At its maximum brightness, it is 600,000 times (some computations indicate 2,000,000 times) as bright as our sun.

The Large Magellanic Cloud recedes from us at a velocity estimated to be more than 160 miles per second.

10.8 THE SMALL MAGELLANIC CLOUD

The **Small Magellanic Cloud's** estimated distance of 180,000 light-years places it only slightly farther than the Large Magellanic Cloud; it is visible to the unaided eye in the constellation Tucana, also near the South Celestial Pole. However it has only about half the diameter of the Large Magellanic Cloud. A study of its Cepheids, it should be remembered, led to the discovery of the period-absolute magnitude curve. This "cloud" contains a great number of faint stars, ranging from magnitude 11 to the faintest known stars.

It also includes one or more X-ray binary stars.

NOTE: An X-ray binary consists of a pair of close stars one of which is in a collapsed form (neutron star?) at the end of its life cycle, attracting matter from its companion. This matter, as it approaches the enormously hot collapsing star, emits X-rays.

The recessional velocity of the Small Magellanic Cloud is appreciably less than that of the Large Magellanic Cloud, approximately 100 miles per second. Both the Large and Small Magellanic Clouds are often regarded as satellites of our galaxy.

10.9 THE LOCAL GROUP OF GALAXIES

The Milky Way galaxy seems to be a member of a cluster of galaxies known as the

Local Group. Our galaxy is at one end of this cluster and M31, the galaxy in Andromeda, is at the other extreme. There are twenty-three galaxies in this group. Most of these have rather low luminosity and are seen by us because of their nearness.

Several members of the local group are indicated in Table 10.9.

Table 10.9

Name	Type	Distance (in light years)
Our galaxy	Spiral	0
Large Magellanic Cloud	Irregular	150,000
Small Magellanic Cloud	Irregular	180,000
M31, Andromeda	Spiral	2,000,000
M32, satellite of Andromeda	Elliptical	2,000,000
NGC205, satellite of Andromeda	Elliptical	2,000,000
M33, Triangulum	Spiral	2,000,000

10.10 THE ANDROMEDA GALAXY

Of particular interest in the local group of galaxies is the Great Galaxy of Andromeda (also known either as M31 or NGC224)—an interest due to its great resemblance to our galaxy, about which it provides information.

Although slightly larger than our galaxy, from a 2,000,000-light-year distance it appears to the naked eye as a fairly hazy patch of light of apparent magnitude 4.3.

Long-exposure photographs reveal its real beauty. On such photographs the galaxy appears as a flat, elliptical disk, making an angle of 15° with the line of sight. The center of the ellipse is extremely bright and surrounded by two spiraling arms that encircle the nucleus more than four times. The arms contain many nebulae.

The spiral arms had been resolved into individual stars as early as 1923, but efforts to distinguish individual stars in the center were unsuccessful for nearly twenty years. The center of the galaxy appeared on all photographs as uniform bright mass without any detail.

The bright mass in the center was successfully resolved in 1943 when pictures were made on a new type of red-sensitive plates, instead of the regular blue-sensitive plates used up to that date. The individual stars were clearly resolved into distinct units on the new type of plates.

This discovery led to new conclusions, chief among which is that the stars can be divided into two general classes, known as Population I and Population II stars.

Population I stars are usually to be found in the arms of spiral galaxies, as well as in irregular galaxies, such as the Magellanic Clouds. This class of stars is characterized by the fact that the brightest stars in it are blue in color and have high surface temperatures.

Population II stars are usually found in globular clusters, elliptical galaxies, as well as at the centers of spiral galaxies. The brightest stars of this class are not blue and hot, but red and cool.

In the past twenty years, more than a hundred novae have been discovered in the galaxy of Andromeda, most of them close to the center of the galaxy. Of particular interest, however, was the supernova sighted in 1885.

The galaxy is moving with a speed of close to 180 miles per second toward the sun; most of its velocity, however, is due to the rotation of our own galaxy, which brings the solar system closer to the galaxy in Andromeda by nearly 200 miles each second.

10.11 REMOTE GALAXIES

The twenty-three galaxies that form the local group are only a minute fraction of all existing island universes, the total number of which is estimated to be more than 10 thousand million.

The 200-inch telescope at Mount Palomar can detect galaxies as far as 2 billion light-years away. There are more than 2 thousand million galaxies within that distance from earth.

New techniques, using image tube scanners (see Sec. 5.24) and computers that subtract the effects of the night sky, have been developed in the early 1970s.

The combination of image tube scanners and computers enabled scientists to find a galaxy nearly 8 thousand million light-years away.

10.12 CLASSIFICATION OF GALAXIES

A. **Irregular.** Typical of these galaxies are the Magellanic Clouds. These have no simple geometric form or clear design.

B. **Elliptical.** These galaxies take on the shapes of more or less flattened disks. No spiral arms are discernible. About 25 per cent of all galaxies are in this group.

C. **Spirals.** Typical of these galaxies are the Andromeda galaxy and our own galaxy. Spiral galaxies are usually divided into two subgroups: (a) **Normal Spirals** and (b) **Barred Spirals.** In the case of normal spirals, the two arms begin their spiraling immediately upon coming out of the core of the galaxy. In the case of barred spirals, the two arms extend straight out at first, and begin to spiral at the end of the extension.

10.13 RADIO GALAXIES

All galaxies emit radio waves. Some galaxies, though, are extremely strong radio emitters sending out into space radio waves hundreds of thousands times more intense than the average galaxy.

An extremely intense source is 19N4A (19 means right ascension 19 hours; N stands for International Astronomical Union Catalog; 4A means declination 40° north, serial letter A), commonly known as Cygnus A. The intensity of radiation is in the order of 10 million times that of our galaxy or of the Great Galaxy of Andromeda.

At one time it was suggested that the enormous intensities of the radiation were derived from a collision between two galaxies. Statistical studies, however, indicate that chances for such a collision are close to zero.

The best interpretation available at present is that the radio emission comes from clouds of gas that had their origin in explosions of the central regions of giant elliptical galaxies, explosions that are probably a million times more intense even than an explosion of a supernova. These clouds of gas, often in pairs, interact with magnetic fields located tens of thousands of light-years away from the illuminated part of the galaxy, thus causing the emission of the intense radio waves.

10.14 THE RED SHIFT

A remarkable feature known as the **Red Shift** is exhibited by all galaxies. Red shift, it will be recalled, means that all the lines of the spectrum are shifted from their normal positions toward new positions that are closer to the red end of the spectrum. This shift is interpreted as a Doppler displacement, indicating a recession of the galaxies from the earth.

Further studies of the red shift brought out the fact that there is a close relationship between the velocity of recession and the distance of the galaxy. The farther the galaxy is from the earth, the faster it recedes.

The relationship is known as Hubble's constant, and its value is 100 kilometers per second for every megaparsec. (A megaparsec is a million parsecs or about 3.25 million light-years.) Thus a galaxy that is at a distance of 20 megaparsecs from our galaxy will recede at a speed of 2,000 kilometers per second from us. These velocities have to be corrected for ordinary random motion of galaxies. This correction is particularly important in the case of nearby galaxies. In the case of a few of the nearby galaxies, the random motion toward us outweighs the velocity of recession, thus resulting in a net motion toward our galaxy.

It has been difficult to explain reasonably why our insignificant earth or our galaxy should be the point from which all galaxies recede. The explanation now widely accepted is included in the concept of the expanding universe.

10.15 THE EXPANDING UNIVERSE

This concept implies that not only do all the galaxies move away from our galaxy, but every galaxy is moving away from every other galaxy. This increase in distance is due to the fact that the whole universe is expanding and the distance between any two galaxies is increasing at a constant rate.

A one-dimensional analogy may help to clarify this concept. Suppose one marks a 10-inch rubber string at three points: A, B, and C. A and C are at the ends; B is in the middle, 5 inches away from A and C. That is, AB=BC=5 inches. Now suppose that the string is stretched to 16 inches. Then AB= BC=8 inches. Now suppose the stretching was done at a constant rate, and it took 2 seconds to complete. B would, in such a case, seem to move away from A at a rate of 1.5 inches per second and C would be increasing its distance from A at a rate of 3 inches per second. Thus if A is our galaxy and B and C are neighboring galaxies, then C would seem to recede from us at twice the speed that B would.

The theory of the expanding universe makes it possible to compute its age. Assuming that the expansion has always proceeded at the present rate, it is possible to determine the date the expansion began—about 10 or 15 billion years ago.

10.16 QUASARS (QUASI-STELLAR RADIO SOURCES)

Several major surveys of the intensities of radio waves from outer space have been made.

These surveys indicate that in addition to radio galaxies there are several hundred points in the sky from which very intense radiation is emitted. These points are now referred to either as quasi-stellar radio sources or, more commonly, as **Quasars.**

The following information about quasars has been ascertained so far:

A. They have very small angular diameters. Most of them have angular diameters of .1 to .2 second of arc. Some have angular diameters of less than .001 second.

B. They exhibit enormous red shifts (see Sec. 10.14), indicating recession velocities as high as 90 per cent of the velocity of light, and hence, according to Hubble's constant, they are at tremendous distances from us. Indeed, quasars are probably the most distant objects in the universe.

C. Using values for angular diameter and values for distances, astronomers have made computations of the linear diameters of quasars. Some have diameters of less than 5 light-years.

D. A large percentage of quasars have been identified, through the largest optical telescopes available, with photographed objects in the sky.

E. Inserting the observed values of visual apparent magnitudes (m) and the computed values for distances in parsecs to quasars (Dps) in the formula $M=m+5-5 \log Dps$, values for the absolute magnitude (M), as well as for the luminosities of the optically visible objects, have been determined. Thus, quasar 3C273 (item number 273 in the third Cambridge University list of radio sources) which has an apparent visual magnitude of +12.7 at a distance of 1.5 thousand million light-years has an absolute magnitude (M) of −26!

The M=−26, of course, means that if 3C273 were placed at a distance of 10 parsecs it would appear to us almost as bright as our sun. The apparent magnitude of our sun is −26.7.

F. The intensity of the radio waves is more than a million times that received from a galaxy such as the galaxy in Andromeda.

This and similar data raises the question:

How does such a small object, only a few light-years in diameter, produce so much energy both in radio and in visible wavelength?

Or, to put it in a different way, what are the mechanics of energy production whereby a "little" quasar can produce more energy than the brightest galaxy hundreds of thousands of light-years in diameter?

Possible answers to the preceding questions are:

a. The red shift due to surface gravity. The major part of the red shift is gravitational in origin and is not due to recessional velocity at all.

NOTE: We have seen (Sec. 7.12) that light emitted from stars of high surface gravity has its wavelength shifted to the red end of the spectrum.

If the red shift due to recessional velocity is only part of the shift, then the quasars are nearer to us than previously computed and the values for visual and radio luminosity are much smaller . . . and no problem exists.

Theoretical studies indicate that this explanation of red shift in the case of quasars is not realistic.

b. Antimatter. The energy is derived from a collision between a cloud of ordinary matter and a cloud of antimatter. Antimatter consists of particles with electrical charges opposite to the usual ones. E.g., a positron is similar to an electron, except that it has a positive charge. An antiproton is similar to a proton, but is negatively charged. And so on. When matter meets antimatter, they annihilate one another, with a resultant release of tremendous amounts of energy.

Few scientists believe that the energy emitted by quasars is derived by this method.

c. Gravitational collapse. According to this theory, the energy of quasars is obtained from gravitational contraction due to a collapse of superstars. Each superstar is millions of times more massive than an average star and releases tremendous amounts of energy in the process of gravitational contraction.

The search for a definitive, well-proven theory that will fully explain quasars is still on. Such a theory may very well open a new chapter of research in this science.

PART III: THE BIRTH AND DEVELOPMENT OF THE UNIVERSE

10.17 CURRENT THEORIES

There are three theories offered at this time to describe the birth and the development of the universe. They are known as (A) the **Big Bang Theory**, (B) the **Oscillating Universe Theory**, and (C) the **Steady State Theory**.

A. THE BIG BANG THEORY

According to this theory, "once upon a time" there was a vast fireball of extremely hot, dense gases consisting mostly of hydrogen and some helium.

And then some 10 or 15 billion years ago that fireball exploded (big bang!), and this expansion is still going on as evidenced by the red shift.

As time went on, "concentrations of matter" developed in many places in the expanding mass of gases. These concentrations grew in size by attracting more and more material from their surroundings, thus breaking up the universe into large masses of gas—each mass destined to become a galaxy. These masses continue to take part in the ever-expanding universe.

Eventually each large mass of gas fragmented again to form stars. The first-generation stars consisted of the two gases then present in the universe, hydrogen and helium. With the passage of time other elements were generated at the cores of massive stars (massive stars have extremely high core temperatures and evolve very rapidly). These new elements were then ejected by the first stars into the interstellar gas, to be used as raw material in the formation of later stars.

B. THE OSCILLATING UNIVERSE THEORY

This theory suggests that the expansion that began with the big bang will gradually come to a halt because of gravitational force. Then collapse will begin bringing back all the material to the original fireball. A second big bang will then occur, and the evolutionary process will commence all over again.

C. THE STEADY STATE THEORY

The picture suggested by the proponents of this hypothesis can be summarized as follows:

a. There is no beginning and no end to the universe.
b. The universe always appeared and always will appear the way it appears to an observer now.
c. As some galaxies recede and get old, new galaxies are formed in the empty spaces left behind.
d. The gases, dust, and energy (also a form of mass, according to Einstein) given off by stars as they age are the raw materials from which new stars are produced.

At present the big bang theory is the most accepted, followed by the steady state theory. A great deal more research will have to be pursued before a definitive decision can be made.

CHAPTER 11

THE SOLAR SYSTEM

PART I: THE SUN

11.1 BASIC DATA

Symbol: ⊙
Diameter: 864,400 miles; 109 times that of the earth.
Distance from earth:
    Min. 91,500,000 miles
    Mean 93,000,000 miles
    Max. 94,500,000 miles
Apparent angular diameter:
    Min. 31 minutes, 28 seconds
    Mean 31 minutes, 59 seconds
    Max. 32 minutes, 30 seconds
Mass: 2.2×10^{27} tons; 333,400 times that of the earth.
Density mean: .25 times that of the earth
Surface gravity: 900 ft per sec^2; 27.9 times that of the earth
Temperature, photosphere (effect): 5,750° A
Temperature at center of sun: 14×10^{6}° A
Apparent magnitude (m): −26.7
Absolute magnitude (M): +4.8
Spectral class: G-0
Inclination of solar axis to ecliptic: 7°10′
Period of spinning, at equator: 24 days, 16 hours

Solar constant (energy received at earth's surface): 1.94 calories per cm^2 per minute
Energy output (of whole sun): 5×10^{23} horsepower

11.2 INTRODUCTION

Compared to many of the billions of stars in our galaxy, the sun is an average star. Its apparent brightness and apparent size are due entirely to its closeness to the earth. The next nearest star, α (alpha)-Centauri is 270,-000 times farther from earth than the sun. α (alpha)-Centauri is the third brightest star in the sky; and by sheer coincidence, it and our sun are almost identical in their characteristics.

Of the vast amount of data concerning the sun, two facts seem particularly startling:

A. The sun, unlike the earth, is completely gaseous. A boundary called the photosphere (sphere of light) exists between the sun and its atmosphere, and from this sunlight originates. The photosphere is quite opaque, making it impossible to see anything beneath it. **The solar atmosphere consists of three layers: the Reversing Layer, the Chromosphere, and the Corona, all fairly transparent to the light emitted by the photosphere. See Fig. 11.2.**

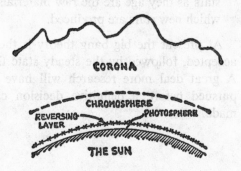

FIG. 11.2. The solar atmosphere. Three layers are recognized in the solar atmosphere; no sharp and definite boundaries exist between them.

The layer immediately above the photosphere (the surface of the sun) is known as the reversing layer. It is only 1,000 miles thick, but materially affects the quality of light given off by the photosphere, by removing some components from it.

The intermediate layer about 6,000 miles thick is known as the chromosphere. It is here that prominences and chromospheric flares, which cause radio fadeouts, have their origin.

The outer layer is known as the corona. It forms a pearly gray layer, a million or so miles thick about the sun.

B. The other "startling" fact is that the sun does not spin about its axis at constant angular speed. A point on its equator completes a full revolution in 25 days, while a point at 60° North or South of the equator takes 31 days to complete a revolution.

11.3 DISTANCE

The average distance of the sun from the earth (derived by triangulation) is 93 million miles, less in January than in July by as much as 3 million miles.

11.4 DIAMETER

Given its distance from the earth and its angular diameter, it is easy to compute its real diameter.

The average distance is 93,000,000—more precisely 92,955,700 miles.

The apparent diameter of the sun at that distance is slightly over a half degree of angle—precisely 31 minutes, 59½ seconds, or 1919.5 seconds of angle.

The linear diameter is obtained from the formula:

$$\text{Linear diameter} = \text{distance} \times \text{angular diameter}.$$

Angular diameter must be stated in a special unit, known as a radian, equivalent in size to 206,265 seconds of angle.

Substituting the known values in the formula, linear diameter $= 93{,}000{,}000 \times {}^{1919.5}\!/_{206265}$, the result is that the diameter of the sun is 864,400 miles.

The solar diameter is more than a hundred times larger than that of the earth—the earth, together with the moon revolving about it in its orbit, could easily be contained by the sun.

Compared to other stars, the sun is of average size: very small stars have diameters of only 4,000 miles; very large, diameters estimated to be nearly 3,000 times greater than that of the sun.

11.5 VOLUME

Given the diameter of the sun, its volume can be determined: it is 1,250,000 times greater than that of the earth.

11.6 MASS

The mass of the sun may be computed with the aid of a simple formula known as Newton's form of Kepler's third law.

The formula relates the mass of the sun

with the period of earth's orbit around it which is usually stated as

$$P^2 = \frac{4\pi^2 a^3}{G(M_1 + M_2)}$$

In this formula:

P is the period, in seconds, of one revolution of the earth around the sun, namely 3.16×10^7 seconds.

π has to do with the ratio of a circumference to a diameter in a circle. Its value is 3.14.

a is the mean distance between the sun and the earth, in cm. Its value is 1.5×10^{13} cm.

G is a physical constant known as the universal constant of gravitation. Its value is 6.67×10^{-8} in the proper units of centimeter-gram-second system.

M_1 is the mass of the sun to be determined by using this formula.

M_2 is the mass of the earth, which may be neglected (i.e., zero substituted for it), since the mass of the earth is only $\frac{1}{333,400}$ (almost zero) that of the sun.

The mass of the sun thus computed as 2×10^{33} grams, or 2×10^{30} kilograms, or approximately 4.5×10^{30} pounds, or 2.2×10^{27} tons, or more than 2 billion billion billions of tons.

That is one third of a million times more massive than the earth. Placed on one side of a balance, the sun would equal in weight 333,400 earths placed on the other.

Compared to other stars, however, the sun's mass is rather average. There are stars close to a hundred times as massive; others have a mass $\frac{1}{25}$ or less that of the sun. The vast majority of stars, though, have masses within the range of 5 times to $\frac{1}{10}$ the mass of the sun.

11.7 DENSITY

Knowing the mass of the sun and its volume, it is easy to compute its density.

$$\text{Density} = \frac{\text{mass}}{\text{volume}}$$

The result of such a computation can be stated in two ways:

A. The density of the sun is 1.4 times that of water. A cubic foot of its matter would weigh $62.4 \times 1.4 = 87.4$ pounds.

B. The density of the sun is about .25 that of the earth.

The density of the sun is not constant. The density close to the center is much greater than it is near the surface because of the sheer weight of overlying matter. The weight of the material of which the sun is made would cause a pressure of about 10 billion atmospheres at the center of the sun, and the density of the gas at the center is 100 times that of water, or nearly 10 times that of lead.

NOTE: Despite this pressure and density, the sun is gaseous throughout because of the temperature at its center, which is about 14 million degrees absolute.

11.8 SURFACE GRAVITY

Knowing the mass of the sun and its radius, it is easy to compute the surface gravity.

The simple formula is:

Surface gravity $= G \times \dfrac{M}{R^2}$ where G is the universal constant of gravitation which has a value of 6.67×10^{-8} in centimeter-gram-second units; M is the mass of the sun (2×10^{33} grams); and R the radius of the sun (6.96×10^{10} cm). Substituting these figures and comparing the result to the surface gravity of the earth, it is found that surface gravity on the face of the sun is 28 times that on the face of the earth: a ten-pound baby would register 280 pounds on a spring balance there.

This surface gravity is due primarily to the mass of the sun, which exerts a strong gravitational pull. This strong gravitational attraction is somewhat diminished by the sun's large radius.

11.9 PHOTOSPHERE

Looking at the sun through dark glasses, one sees a bright disk known as the **Photosphere,** the surface of the sun.

Actually, the photosphere is not a geometrical surface, but rather a shell about 150 miles thick from which light is emitted into space.

Light originating beneath this layer is totally absorbed within the 150-mile thickness; little light is produced in the rarified gases above the photosphere.

The top of this photospheric layer has an average temperature of less than 6,000° A and a density of .001 of the density on earth of air at sea level.

The uniform brightness of the disk is only approximately correct. Careful study of the photosphere reveals that the photosphere is not uniformly bright, but rather speckled or marked by granulations, with diameters hundreds of miles long. These granules, probably covering the whole area of the photosphere, are not fixed on the surface; they change constantly in size and in structure.

NOTE: The heat energy produced in the core of the sun is transmitted to the surface in part by radiation, in part by convection (i.e., by moving gases or by upward-moving hot bubbles and downward-moving cool ones).

It is this up and down motion breaking through the surface of the sun that is responsible for the granulations.

Also appearing from time to time are (A) sunspots, and (B) faculae.

A. **Sunspots** are gigantic areas on the solar disk that appear dark by comparison to surrounding regions, and have diameters of tens of thousands of miles.

B. **Faculae** are areas on the surface of the sun that appear brighter by comparison to surrounding regions.

11.10 SUNSPOTS

Since Galileo first discovered them in 1610, sunspots have been under study. The result of this research may be summarized as follows:

A. **Structure.** Most spots consist of two portions that differ greatly in "darkness."

The inside portion—the technical name of which is **Umbra** (Latin for shadow)—is the darker of the two. Surrounding the umbra is the semidark portion, the **Penumbra.**

NOTE: The terms "dark" and "semidark" as applied to sunspots need clarification. Actually, the dark

umbra emits brighter light than the most efficient electric arc. The area *appears* dark against the background of the still brighter solar disk. The umbra is 2,000° A cooler than the rest of the photosphere. But its temperature is still tremendous: 4,000° A.

B. **Size.** Sunspots vary greatly in size—from 2,000 miles across to more than ten times that figure. The largest known spot, seen in April 1947, covered an area larger than 30 times the surface of the earth.

C. **Latitude.** Spots occur in two belts of the solar surface: one, between 5° N and 40° N solar latitudes; the others occur between 5° S and 40° S solar latitudes. There are, of course, a few exceptions to this rule.

D. **Duration.** More than 50 per cent of sunspots have a life span of less than 4 days; occasionally, however, spots last for more than 100 days.

E. **Magnetic Field.** Each spot is a center of a magnetic field, the strength of the field varying with the size of the spot. Some spots have a "north-seeking" polarity; others, the opposite polarity.

Studies of magnetic fields are based on the Zeeman effect. (Pieter Zeeman, of Holland, discovered in 1896 the effect of a magnetic field on spectral lines.) **Spectral lines either split into several components or widen materially under the influence of a powerful magnet.** See Fig. 11.10a.

The mode of splitting or the amount of widening is dependent upon the magnetic field. Information about the magnetism of sunspots is based on the widening of the spectral lines in the light coming from the spots.

Indeed, the first indication that a sunspot is about to form is a many-thousandfold increase in the intensity of the magnetic field in that particular area. Also, as the sunspots grow, so does the intensity of the magnetic field, which, furthermore, outlives the sunspot by many days, weeks, or months.

F. **Shape and Movements.** To the best of our knowledge, the sunspot has the shape of a vortex, its motion being counterclockwise in the northern hemisphere of the sun and clockwise in the southern.

FIG. 11.10a. Effect of magnetic field on spectral lines (Zeeman effect). The upper half of the picture shows two lines in a spectrum of the element vanadium as they appear without a magnetic field. The lower part of the picture shows the effect of inserting a large magnetic field (about 15,000 gauss) parallel to the light producing the spectrum. One of the lines "splits" into four components; the other into two.

Gases are flowing outward at the base of the vortex and inward at upper levels. The height of the vortex may be 100 miles and magnetic effects are most likely the gases' main driving forces.

G. Variation in Spottedness. The area of the sun covered by spots varies greatly. Weeks may pass without a single spot, followed by the appearance of scores of sunspots on the solar disk.

The Royal Observatory at Herstmonceux, Sussex, keeps a close watch on these areas. Every day, precise determinations are made. The results are stated in terms of 1/1,000,000 of the visible disk of the sun, and are averaged over the year. The mean daily spot area in 1933 was 88; and 2,019 for 1937. The latter means that on the average 2,019/1,000,000 of the visible disk of the sun was covered by spots.

H. Cycles. A definite cycle in sunspottedness was suggested as early as 1843, and has since been verified. The period of a complete cycle is 22 years; each complete cycle is divided into two halves, 11 years each. The half-cycles are alike in their variations in spot area, as shown in Figure 11.10b. They differ in the

magnetic polarity. The details of one such hypothetical cycle are as follows:

1. The beginning of the cycle is at a minimum of spottedness, marked by the appearance of two spots in latitude 35° N, and two spots in latitude 35° S. Each pair of spots lies along an east-west axis—one is called a "leader," the other, a "follower." The two are about 3 or 4 degrees apart.

The magnetic properties of the two pairs are different. If the leader of the 35° N pair

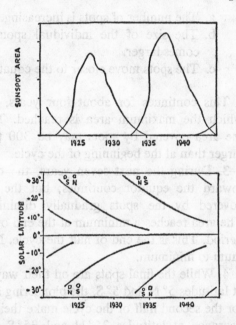

FIG. 11.10b. Sunspot cycles. The upper diagram shows the variation in area of the sun covered by spots during one complete cycle (1922–1946). The complete cycle consists of two half-cycles, with maxima in the years 1928 and 1937. The lower diagram points out the variations in latitude, and in magnetic polarity.

At the beginning of the cycle one pair of spots appears in latitude 35° N; the western spot has a south-seeking magnetic polarity, the other a north-seeking; another pair appears at 35° S with reverse polarities. About 1928 the area covered was at a maximum (1,390 parts in a million of the visible area of the sun were covered on the average). The spots moved closer to the equator: their mean latitude was only about 18°. In the early 1930s the sunspottedness was at a minimum, and the location was within a few degrees of the solar equator: a new half-cycle is in the making, though at higher latitudes. The only difference between the second half-cycle and the first is in the reversed magnetic polarity.

has the property of a north-seeking pole, the follower will act as a south-seeking pole. The polarities of the pair at 35° S will be reversed. The leader of the group below the equator will be a south-seeking pole, and the follower, north-seeking. The arrangement of spots at the beginning of the cycle is shown in the lower half of Figure 11.10b.

2. The original spots last several days; others then make their appearance. Three changes should be noticed:

a. The number of spots is increasing.
b. The size of the individual spots becomes larger.
c. The spots move closer to the equator.

This continues for about four years, after which the maximum area is reached. Then, the area covered by spots may be 300 times larger than at the beginning of the cycle.

3. During the next seven years, the travel toward the equator continues; but the area covered by the spots gradually diminishes. The area reaches a minimum at the end of this period. This is the end of half the cycle. Minimum to minimum.

4. While the final spots are on their way out at latitudes 5° N and 5° S, the pioneering spots for the second half of the cycle make their appearance at latitudes 35° N and 35° S. One pair appears in the northern latitudes, the other in the southern. The second half of the cycle is similar to the first, with one major difference: the magnetic polarity of each spot is now reversed. Thus, if the leader at 35° N eleven years ago was a north-seeking pole, it will now show the properties typical of a south-seeking pole.

At the end of twenty-two years, a new cycle begins. Recent minima took place in the years 1933, 1944, 1954, 1964, and 1972. The most recent maximum was in 1968.

NOTES: 1. The characteristics of sunspot cycles become evident only in an averaging process. During a period of maximum sunspot activity, the sun may be perfectly clear; during a period of minimum activity, a large proportion of the sun may be covered with spots. The two half-cycles, therefore, become apparent only in averaging a large amount of data.

2. The figure of eleven years for a half-cycle is also an average; observed periods may differ materially. Half-cycles of only eight years are known; as are half-cycles of fourteen years.

11.11   ROTATION OF THE SUN

Sunspots also yield information about the spinning of the sun on its axis. That the sun spins on its axis is suggested by two facts:

A. All sunspots move across the sun in the same direction.
B. Sunspots are behind the solar disk for as much time as they are in front of it.

Chief among other proofs is the one based on the Doppler effect. The spectra of light from opposite sides of the sun show marked differences: that from the edge of the sun "going away" from the observer indicates a red shift; that from the limb of the sun approaching the observer indicates a shift of its lines toward the blue end of the spectrum.

The direction of the sun's spinning is the same as that of the earth. For an observer on the sun, the stars would rise on the eastern horizon and set in the west. Or, an observer outside the sun, looking down at its north pole, would see it spinning in a counterclockwise direction.

The period of one complete revolution about its axis is *not* a constant, but varies with the latitude. At the equator, it is 24.6 days. The period for other latitudes is given in the table.

Solar latitudes	Period of one revolution
Equator 0°	24.6 days
30°	26.0 "
45°	28.4 "
60°	31.0 "
80°	33.5 "

The study of astronomy would be far more complicated if this were true of the earth—if, say, a day at the equator were twenty-four hours, and a revolution about the axis of the earth at latitude 60° took thirty hours.

11.12 INCLINATION OF THE SUN'S AXIS

Furthermore, sunspots yield information about the inclination of the sun's axis, based on the slight curvature in the route followed by the spots: the solar axis is inclined by 7° 10′ of angle to a line making 90° with the earth's orbit. In March the sun's north pole is tilted away from the earth; in September, toward the earth.

11.13 FACULAE

Faculae (Latin for small torches) seem to be plateaus above the photospheric surface.

They are slightly brighter than the photosphere but can be seen well only when they are near the dimmer background of the limb of the sun.

These small torches precede by a day or so the appearance of the sunspot but usually stay on and on, sometimes for months, after the sunspot. Their average life time is about two weeks.

11.14 THE REVERSING LAYER

Reversing Layer is the name given to the lowest of the three layers in the sun's atmosphere. The base of the layer is the surface of the sun; the top extends to about 1,000 miles above the surface. This thickness has been determined from studies of solar eclipses; the time it takes the moon to cross that layer and the known value of the moon's speed are used in that computation.

The density of the reversing layer greatly decreases, while the temperature increases, toward the top of the reversing layer. The best values for density and temperatures for the top of the layer available are 5×10^{-18} grams per cm^3 and 7,500° A.

The reversing layer is responsible for the many (thousands) dark lines in the otherwise continuous spectrum of sunlight, since the gases in the reversing layer absorb these particular wavelengths. A curve showing the distribution of the sun's energy indicates that absorption. At certain wavelengths the energy normally present was "ripped out." See Fig. 11.14.

The wavelengths that have been ripped out (i.e., the dark lines on the spectrum) identify

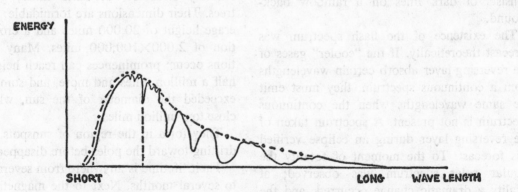

FIG. 11.14. Distribution of solar energy. The smooth dot-dash curve indicates the distribution of energy with wavelength of the light leaving the photosphere of the sun. The vertical distance to the curve indicates the amount of energy present at any particular wavelength.

The solid line curve indicates the distribution of solar energy reaching the terrestrial observer. The dips in the curve imply that energy has been "ripped out" at these particular wavelengths.

Some of the dips in the solid curve are due to the gases in the reversing layer; others are due to absorption by water vapor and carbon dioxide in the earth's atmosphere.

clearly the chemical composition of the reversing layer. The identification is obtained by comparing these wavelengths with those in spectra produced in the laboratory by chemical elements, thus identifying the presence of sixty-five out of the ninety-two elements present on the earth. Among the sixty-five elements present in that layer are hydrogen, carbon, nitrogen, oxygen, aluminum, iron, cobalt, cadmium, lead, and platinum. It is very likely that more than sixty-five elements will eventually be identified.

From a study of the intensity of the spectral lines, reasonable values can be obtained for the percentages of the various elements at the solar surface.

Recent figures indicate that the mix of elements consists of 90 per cent hydrogen, 10 per cent helium, with minute fractions of percentages of oxygen, carbon, neon, nitrogen, and so on.

During a solar eclipse a flash spectrum of the reversing layer—which has the same number of lines and the same wavelengths as the dark lines in the solar spectrum—can be obtained. The difference between the flash spectrum and the solar spectrum is that the flash spectrum consists of bright lines on a dark background, while the normal solar spectrum consists of dark lines on a rainbow background.

The existence of the flash spectrum was forecast theoretically. If the "cooler" gases of the reversing layer absorb certain wavelengths from a continuous spectrum, they must emit the same wavelengths when the continuous spectrum is not present. A spectrum taken of the reversing layer during an eclipse verified this forecast. To the moment of totality the regular solar spectrum was observed; at totality a dramatic change occurred, and the flash spectrum appeared. The flash spectrum lasts only two or three seconds.

11.15   THE CHROMOSPHERE

The name for the middle layer in the sun's atmosphere is the **Chromosphere,** the average thickness of which is about 6,000 miles. In some zones of the sun the thickness may be as much as 8,000 miles, in others, as little as 5,000.

The chromosphere (i.e., color sphere) owes its name to its very bright color (rose-pink), which is due largely to a line in the spectrum of hydrogen, denoted by "H-alpha" of wavelength 6,563 angstroms.

Going upward through the chromosphere, both the density and the temperature continue to decrease, the density slowly, reaching a value of about 10^{-15} grams per cm³ at the top of the chromosphere, the temperature rapidly, reaching an extreme of 1,000,000° A. The hydrogen in this layer is close to 100 per cent ionized.

Studies of the chromosphere indicate that the top layer is in a continuous state of great turbulence in which large masses of gas are thrown upward, often to great heights.

11.16   PROMINENCES

Prominences can best be described as curtains of rose-colored flame perpendicular to the surface of the sun—at times resembling a feathery structure, at other times, gigantic trees. Their dimensions are formidable: an average height of 20,000 miles and a cross section of 2,000×100,000 miles. Many exceptions occur: prominences can reach heights of half a million miles and more, and some have exceeded the diameter of the sun, which is close to a million miles.

They form in the region of sunspots, many drifting toward the poles before disappearing.

Their lifetime is anywhere from several days to several months. Next to the magnetic field they are the longest lived associate of a sunspot.

Another outstanding characteristic of a prominence has to do with its speed (i.e., the value of the speed and the way it changes).

Speeds of 200 or 300 miles per second are common. In September 1937 a great eruptive prominence was timed at a maximum speed of 450 miles per second, and ascended to a height of three quarters of a million miles in less than half an hour.

The change in speed is abrupt, and new velocity is a single multiple of the former. Thus a prominence may be rising at a speed of 80 miles per second, then rather suddenly change speeds to 160 miles per second, continue for a while at that speed, and then again suddenly start moving at 240 miles per second. Prominences when viewed with the solar disk as a background appear as dark, snakelike filaments.

11.17 CHROMOSPHERIC FLARES

Extremely bright clouds known as **Flares** appear from time to time above the chromosphere differing from prominences in brilliance, size, and duration.

A. **Brilliance.** At maximum intensity, they are the brightest white spots on the sun.

B. **Size.** They are smaller than prominences and usually reach a height of only 10,000 miles.

C. **Duration.** Unlike prominences, they develop (near active sunspot groups) and disappear extremely rapidly. Flares reach their maximum brightness in several minutes and disappear in an hour or more. Five to ten flares per day is not uncommon.

The scientific interest in chromospheric flares is due to the fact that these flares, in their short lifetime, emit intense radiations in X-ray, ultraviolet, and radio wavelengths that reach the earth with the speed of light and affect radio transmission as well as the magnetic field of the earth. Similarly, the chromospheric flares discharge into space clouds of ionized particles (plasma) moving at a speed of 650 miles per second, which also affect the magnetic field of the earth as well as causing the northern and southern lights (aurorae).

11.18 RADIO FADEOUTS

Radio fadeouts are caused by strong ultraviolet light emitted by chromospheric flares.

Radio reception on earth over long distances is made possible by the presence in the earth's atmosphere of electrified layers, which, like mirrors, reflect electromagnetic waves back to the earth. Several such concentric shells are present at various heights up to about 200 miles above sea level. **The group of shells collectively is known as the Ionosphere.** See Fig. 11.18.

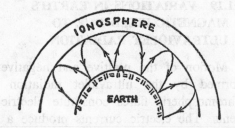

Fig. 11.18. The ionosphere. The ionosphere acts as a mirror for radio waves. Waves emitted from a transmitting antenna at point A on the earth's surface are reflected back and forth between the earth's surface and the ionosphere, and thus manage to reach all the way around the globe.

In the absence of such reflection radio transmission is only possible in line of sight. No signal could thus be received around the curved surface of the earth.

The maintenance of electrified shells is attributed to the action of ultraviolet rays from the sun, the function of which is to maintain the right number of **electrified particles known as Ions** in these layers. When some of these particles lose their electric charge, the ultraviolet rays provide replacements, which are produced by interaction between the radiation and normal oxygen and nitrogen atoms at those levels. In these interactions the atoms lose electrons (negative charged particles), and the remaining atoms become positively charged ions.

The ultraviolet radiation from the flares ionize nitrogen and oxygen atoms below the ionosphere, thus creating a barrier at a height of about 40 miles that disrupts the normal radio transmissions.

These interruptions have a duration identical with the lifetime of the flare, i.e., an hour or more.

Interruptions in radio performance are, of course, of great interest to the military. Attempts have been made at various times to forecast these disturbances, but the forecasts, based materially on sunspot activity, are not yet 100 per cent reliable.

11.19   VARIATIONS IN EARTH'S MAGNETIC FIELD DUE TO ULTRAVIOLET RADIATION

Motion of the positive and negative ions formed by the ultraviolet radiation from chromospheric flares constitute electric currents. The electric currents produce a magnetic field which combines with the earth's normal magnetic field. The combined field at times is at great variance with the normal field.

Ordinary navigational compasses may be of little use during the periods of activity of these chromospheric flares.

11.20   VARIATIONS IN EARTH'S MAGNETIC FIELD DUE TO CHROMOSPHERIC FLARES

Chromospheric flares discharge into space clouds of ionized particles consisting primarily of protons and electrons. Measurements indicate that about 500 protons and 500 electrons per cubic centimeter arrive at the earth with speeds of 650 miles per second or more at the time of the eruption.

NOTES: 1. These ions caused by the flare are over and above the five or so protons and electrons per cubic centimeter that arrive on the earth with a speed of 300 miles per second when the sun is quiet (i.e., no flares). This motion of protons and electrons is called the solar wind.

2. The normal solar wind causes the sun to lose mass at the rate of millions of tons per second. At times of solar flares the loss of mass is many times the normal rate.

The protons and electrons coming from the sun constitute electric currents. The magnetic field (known as a magnetic storm) resulting from these currents plays havoc with instruments on earth that depend on magnetic fields for proper readings. The magnetic storm shows up on the earth 24 hours (or more) after the solar eruption, as it takes the solar wind (traveling at 650 miles per second) over a day to cover the 93 million miles between earth and sun.

11.21   THE AURORAE

The aurora seen in the northern hemisphere of the earth is known by one of two names: the Latin **Aurora Borealis** or, translated into English, Northern Lights. The corresponding names for the aurora in the southern hemisphere are **Aurora Australis,** or Southern Lights. Aurorae are most frequently seen at 70° N or 70° S latitudes, respectively. They are among the most dramatic of terrestrial phenomena, resembling gigantic curtains hundreds of miles high of multicolored light, most often green, but also rose, lavender and violet.

On rare occasion an aurora covers the whole visible sky, from horizon to zenith.

To the best of our knowledge, aurorae result from the solar wind (electrons, protons) interacting with the outlying gases of the earth's atmosphere. The shape of an aurora is greatly influenced by the earth's own magnetic field. The incoming solar particles are directed the last several thousand miles by the magnetic field of the earth.

11.22   RADIO EMISSIONS

There are several radio sources on the sun:

A. Emission from the undisturbed sun.
B. Facular emission.
C. Noise storms.
D. Flare storms.

A. **Emission from the undisturbed sun.** The sun's photosphere, like any other heated object, emits radio waves (see Fig. 6.8a). The temperature of the photosphere being 6,000° A, the intensity of these waves is very low. Very low-intensity radio waves are also emitted by the solar atmosphere.

B. **Facular emission.** These radio waves are several times more intense than emission from the undisturbed sun. They are emitted from localized sources and seem to originate above faculae. Facular emissions may last two or more months.

C. **Noise storms.** These, too, are highly localized emissions and are as much as a hundred times more intense than emissions from the undisturbed sun. There seems to be a close correlation between the intensity of noise storms and size of sunspots on the photosphere. The larger the one, the stronger the other.

D. **Flare storms.** These are by far the most intense emissions from the sun—from hundreds of thousands to over millions of times more intense than the emissions from the undisturbed sun.

There is excellent reason to believe that these radio emissions from the sun are the result of interaction between the plasma (moving protons and electrons), which is ejected at speeds of 650 miles per second by the chromospheric flares, and the upper solar atmosphere.

11.23 THE CORONA

The **Corona** is the uppermost layer of the solar atmosphere, visible to the naked eye during a total eclipse of the sun. It can also be seen and photographed at other times with special equipment such as a coronagraph, which produces an artificial solar eclipse. The corona is a pearly gray halo of intricate design surrounding the body of the sun, vastly larger than the two layers beneath it, being close to a million miles in thickness.

The shape of the corona is closely connected with the eleven-year period of sunspots. At sunspot maximum, it is circular and few pronounced rays protrude; at sunspot minimum, it is elongated, with enormous streamers radiating. See Fig. 11.23.

FIG. 11.23. The corona. A drawing of the corona during the eclipse of the sun in the year 1900. Sunspots at the time were at a minimum and the corona is fairly elongated. The thickness is greatest in the equatorial regions of the sun.

One of the remarkable characteristics of the corona is that it has an enormously high temperature. The temperature obtained by several independent methods turns out to be 1,000,000° A.

How this temperature was obtained, in one of the methods, and what a temperature of $10^{6°}$ A means is explained as follows:

A. Several bright lines in the spectrum of the corona had no counterparts in the photosphere. For years it was thought that these lines were due to a chemical element that is present in the solar corona and nowhere else. This element was even given a name—Coronium.

B. Further studies, however, indicated that these "mysterious" lines were due to well-known chemical elements, such as iron and calcium, when the elements were in a highly ionized state. Ionized iron, for instance, has thirteen of its normal twenty-six electrons removed, and ionized calcium has six of its normal twenty electrons removed.

C. The ionization of the corona was assumed to be accomplished by collisions between atoms having high kinetic energy or having high kinetic temperature. Computations show that to obtain that high an order of ionization the kinetic temperature has to be 1,000,000° A.

NOTE: **Kinetic temperature** is a temperature in absolute degrees which is used to indicate the **kinetic energy** of a particle (expressed in **ergs**, a unit of work in the cm/gram/second system of measurement). Either kinetic temperature or kinetic energy can be used to describe the probable energy of a particle (for example, a particle at room temperature—20° C or 293° A—has a kinetic energy of $.4 \times 10^{-13}$ ergs and a kinetic temperature of 293° A). Using this relationship, we can calculate that a particle having an energy a thousand times larger—i.e., $.4 \times 10^{-10}$ ergs—has a kinetic temperature of 293,000° A.

D. The energy that the fast-moving atoms acquire seems to have its origin in the 100,000-km convective shell underlying the photosphere. Waves originating in that shell "shake" up the atoms in the corona, causing the collisions—which will eventually result in ionization.

11.24 THE SPECTROHELIOGRAPH

Much of the knowledge about the sun and its atmosphere was obtained with the aid of an instrument known as a **Spectroheliograph.** Introduced by Professor George E. Hale (1868–1938) in 1890, it has been invaluable, enabling the astronomer easily to obtain the distribution of any element on the disk of the sun. In a few moments an astronomer can determine the distribution of hydrogen, oxygen, calcium, or any other element on the part of the solar surface facing the earth.

The spectroheliograph determines not only the location of the element on the sun's surface, but also the nature of its motion. Spectroheliograms taken of sunspot areas indicate, for example, the whirling motion of the hydrogen gas there present.

The instrument consists of an ordinary spectograph, to which an additional slit has been added, called the **Spectrum Slit;** the slit on the spectrograph proper is called the

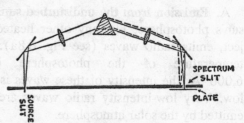

FIG. 11.24. The spectroheliograph. The source slit and the spectrum slit are rigidly connected. As the first one is moved across the solar disk, the second moves in step across a photographic plate.

The source slit admits light from a very narrow strip of the solar disk. The light admitted is resolved into a multitude of wavelengths by the prism. The spectrum slit is adjusted for one particular wave length characteristic of one of the elements, say hydrogen.

As the two slits are moved in unison, each time hydrogen is present on the surface of the disk, its characteristic wavelengths will go through the spectrum slit and react with the chemicals on the photographic plate. Wherever the element is absent on the surface of the solar disk, no light will go through the spectrum slit and this particular part of the negative will remain unexposed.

Thus the locations of hydrogen, for instance on the surface of the sun, can be found by moving the source slit clear across the solar image.

Source Slit. The function of the spectrum slit is to exclude all but the desired single wave length of light, characteristic of the element (say hydrogen) under study. If hydrogen is not present in the source, no light will enter the spectrum slit.

A photographic plate is placed next to the spectrum slit, connected to the source slit. Both move synchronously. As the source slit is made to move across the image of the solar disk, the plate will follow that motion across the spectrum slit. The developed photographic plate will show the areas on the sun where hydrogen, say, is present. See Fig. 11.24.

The working of the spectroheliograph can also be explained as follows:

A. The source slit admits light from a small area of the solar disk.

B. The prism disperses that light into a spectrum.

C. The spectrum slit allows only one narrow line of the spectrum, due to one element, to enter into the plate and affect its chemicals. If this area of the solar disk does not contain that element, no light enters. The chemicals on the plate are not exposed.

D. The source slit, in unison with the plate, is then moved to another area on the solar disk, and then still another, until the whole disk of the sun is covered.

NOTE: This instrument is used primarily with an image of the solar disk. It cannot be used with stars, as they appear only as points of light, even at great magnification. It is of little use with planets, as theirs is merely reflected sunlight.

PART II: THE MECHANICS OF THE SOLAR SYSTEM

11.25   INTRODUCTION

The solar system consists of the sun; the planets and their satellites; the planetoids, comets, meteorites, and dust. Both the adjective "solar" and the noun "system" are appropriate.

"Solar" indicates that the sun governs: it contains nearly 99.9 per cent of all the matter in the system. (The mass of all the planets, satellites, etc. comprises the other .1 or 1 per cent.) As a result of this division of mass, the "massive" sun is nearly stationary while all the "lighter" bodies revolve around it.

The word "system" implies that all the bodies observe great regularity in their motions. The laws governing these motions have been known for several centuries. Of great importance among the several laws are the three that are known by the name of their discoverer (Johannes Kepler) and the Universal Law of Gravitation (first stated by Isaac Newton).

11.26   KEPLER'S FIRST LAW OF PLANETARY MOTION

This law states that the orbit of every planet is an ellipse which has the sun as one of its foci.

DEMONSTRATION:

Object: To draw an ellipse.
Equipment: Pencil, piece of string, two thumbtacks, paper.
Procedure:
1. Place string to form an angle, ABC.

2. Fix the ends A and C with the thumbtacks, and place the pencil at B.
3. Keeping the string taut, move the pencil around to form the oval curve. See Fig. 11.26a.

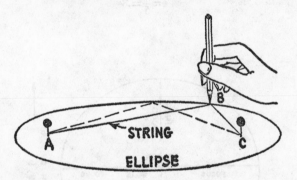

FIG. 11.26a. Drawing of an ellipse. Fix the end of the string at points A and C. Stretch the string to form the angle at B. Keeping the string taut at all times move the pencil about to form the oval curve. A is one focus of this ellipse, C is the other.

Result: The curve described by the pencil is an ellipse. The two points that were kept fixed by the thumbtacks are called the foci of the ellipse (sing. focus).

PROBLEM 11.26a:

Given an ellipse. Its major axis is 5 inches long, its minor axis is 3 inches long.
Find: 1. The distance between the foci; 2. the eccentricity of the ellipse.
Solution: 1. The major axis, the minor axis, and the distance between the foci are related by a simple formula. If the length of the major axis is denoted by a; if the length of the minor axis is denoted by b; and the distance between foci is denoted by c; the formula is:

$$b^2 + c^2 = a^2 \text{ or } c = \sqrt{a^2 - b^2}.$$

In this case, $c=\sqrt{5^2-3^2}=4$ inches. The distance between the foci is 4 inches. See Fig. 11.26b.

2. **"Eccentricity" of an ellipse is defined as the ratio of distance between foci to length of major axis. It is denoted by e.**

$$e=\frac{c}{a}$$

This ratio, in the case of an ellipse, is always larger than 0 and less than 1. It indicates how "eccentric," compared with a circle, the ellipse is. When the ratio is small, say .1, the ellipse is very little eccentric. It is almost circular. When the eccentricity is large, say .8, the ellipse is highly elongated. In this problem the eccentricity is given by:

$$e=\frac{4}{5}=.8$$

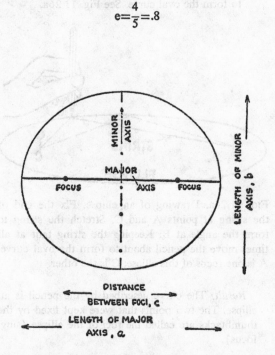

FIG. 11.26b. In an ellipse the length of the major axis, a, the length of the minor axis, b, and the distance between the foci, c, are related by the formula—

$$b^2+c^2=a^2$$

Planets move in nearly circular orbits. The eccentricities of Venus and of the earth are .01 and .02, respectively.

Comets move in elongated orbits. The orbit of Halley's Comet is an ellipse, with an eccentricity of .97.

11.27 KEPLER'S SECOND LAW OF PLANETARY MOTION

This law deals with the speed of the planets in their respective orbits. The speed is not constant, the planets moving faster the closer they are to the sun. The maximum speed of any planet is attained when it is closest to the sun, the minimum when it is farthest. The point on the orbit closest to the sun is known as perihelion, the farthest, aphelion.

Though the speeds of the planets in their orbits are not constant, another feature closely connected with speed *is* constant—namely, the speed with which the line connecting the sun and any particular planet passes over areas.

This is expressed in the formal version of Kepler's second law: **The radius vector of each planet passes over equal areas in equal intervals of time.**

The radius vector is an imaginary line that connects the sun with a planet—short at the perihelion and long at the aphelion.

The second law indicates that at aphelion,

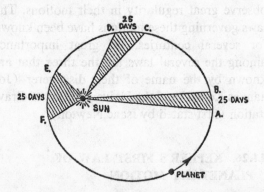

FIG. 11.27. Kepler's second law of planetary motion. The radius vector would cover equal areas (three such areas are shown here shaded) in equal times (25 days).

At aphelion the planet moved relatively slowly to get from A to B. At perihelion the planet had to move at a relatively high speed to cover the distance from E to F.

The term radius vector used in the formal version of the law is an imaginary line joining the sun with the planet. The line connecting the sun to A, or the sun to B, or the sun to D, etc., is a radius vector.

the planet moves slower than at perihelion in order to pass over equal areas of the ellipse. See Fig. 11.27.

The earth's average velocity along its orbit about the sun is 18.5 miles per second. Since the orbit is almost a circle, its speed does not vary materially along the path. At aphelion, the earth moves only by ½ a mile per second slower than at perihelion.

In the case of highly eccentric orbits, such as those pursued by comets, the orbital speed varies greatly. Halley's Comet, when at perihelion, has a speed of 100 miles per second; and at aphelion, of less than 1 mile per second.

11.28 KEPLER'S THIRD LAW OF PLANETARY MOTION

The third law deals with the relationship between the period of a planet and its mean distance from the sun.

The "period" is the time that it takes a planet to complete one revolution about the sun. For the earth, this is 365.26 days; for the planet Mercury, only 88 days; for Pluto, the farthest planet, 248 *years*.

Kepler's third law states that **the squares of the periods of any two planets are proportional to the cubes of their mean distances to the sun.**

This can be stated as an algebraic equation: Let the two planets be designated as A and B.

$$\frac{(\text{period of A})^2}{(\text{period of B})^2} =$$

$$\frac{(\text{mean distance of the sun to A})^3}{(\text{mean distance of the sun to B})^3}$$

If the known data for the earth are used for one of these planets, say B, the equation becomes:

$$\frac{(\text{period of A})^2}{(365.26)^2} =$$

$$\frac{(\text{mean distance of the sun to A})^3}{(93,000,000)^3}$$

This equation has two variables: the period of a planet and its mean distance. If one of

these is obtained by observation, the other can be computed algebraically.

PROBLEM 11.28:

The period of the planet Mars is 687 days. Compute the mean distance of Mars from the sun.

Solution: Inserting the given data in the equation:

$$\frac{(\text{mean distance of mars from sun})^3}{(93,000,000)^3} = \frac{(365)^2}{(687)^2}$$

Answer: The distance of Mars from the sun is 142,000,000 miles.

NOTE: Kepler's third law is not quite complete. The complete form was evolved by Newton. In the complete form, "the squares of the periods" have to be multiplied by the combined mass of the sun and the planet. The corrected equation reads:

$$\frac{(\text{period of A})^2(\text{mass of sun \& planet A})}{(\text{period of B})^2(\text{mass of sun \& planet B})}$$

$$= \frac{(\text{mean dist. of A})^3}{(\text{mean dist. of B})^3}$$

11.29 EVALUATION OF KEPLER'S THREE LAWS

The discovery of these laws was a milestone, not only in the history of astronomy, but also in the history of science in general. It is an eternal monument, not only to the brilliance of Kepler, but also to his devotion to science, to which he committed infinite patience and labor.

There was one shortcoming to these laws, however—a very important shortcoming. Kepler's laws did not explain the behavior of the planets, why they move in elliptical orbits, or why their speeds change as they do.

The answers were soon forthcoming in Sir Isaac Newton's epoch-making book, *Mathematical Principles of Physics*. There, Newton showed that the planets behave as they do because of a most fundamental universal law—the law of gravitation; and that Kepler's three laws are merely consequences of that universal law.

11.30 NEWTON'S UNIVERSAL LAW OF GRAVITATION

The law, dealing with forces between material objects, states that every particle of matter attracts every other particle of matter with a force, depending on three factors:

A. Mass of one object.
B. Mass of the other object.
C. The distance between the objects.

These factors are often denoted as M, m, and r, respectively.

The formal statement of the law is: **Every particle of matter in the universe attracts every other particle with a force that is proportional to the product of their masses, and inversely proportional to the square of the distance between them.**

The law can also be expressed as an algebraic equation:

$$FG = (\text{force of gravity}) \times \frac{Mm}{r^2}$$

G is known as the universal gravitational constant. Its value is 6.7×10^{-8} if M and m are expressed in grams, r in centimeters, and F in dynes. The formula for the Universal Law of Gravitation will then be:

$$F = 6.7 \times 10^{-8} \frac{Mm}{r^2}$$

PROBLEM 11.30:

A mass of 2,000 grams, about 4.4 pounds, is at a distance of 2.54 centimeters (about 1 inch) from another mass of 5,000 grams. Find the force of attraction between these two bodies.

$$F = 6.7 \times 10^{-8} \frac{2000 \times 5000}{(2.54)^2} = .1 \text{ dyne.}$$

Answer: The force with which each mass attracts the other is .1 dyne.

A dyne is an extremely small force, much smaller than a pound of force. Approximately 500,000 dynes are equal in value to one pound of force.

11.31 APPLICATION OF THE LAW OF GRAVITATION

The law was of enormous aid in solving a host of problems. Chief among these are:

A. Freely falling bodies. Any body not properly supported, will fall toward the center of the earth.
B. Ocean tides and tides in the atmosphere.
C. Motion of comets.
D. Precession of equinoxes.
E. Motion of planets. If the gravitational force between the earth and the sun ceased to operate, the earth would go off on a tangent. It is the direct result of this law that planets revolve about the sun as they do. This result is shown in Figure 11.31.

The nine planets move in elliptical orbits at various distances from the sun, counterclockwise.

Although gravitation applies, of course, to the stars and galaxies as well, its effect is easier to see in the case of planets because of the presence of *one* large mass (the sun) acting on several close, smaller masses (the planets). The perturbation on these motions by distant stars is extremely small.

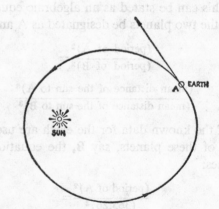

FIG. 11.31. Effect of gravitational attraction. It is due to the gravitational attraction of the sun that the earth continues to move in its orbit.

In the absence of this attraction the earth would leave its elliptical orbit and go off on a tangent, such as at point A, farther and farther away from the sun.

11.32 APPARENT MOTION OF PLANETS AS SEEN FROM THE EARTH

The true motion of the planets cannot be observed from the earth, because the earth itself is constantly in motion. Observations indicate only the motion of the planets relative to that of the earth. At times a planet's relative velocity, with respect to the earth, is greater than its true velocity, as when the earth and the planet move in opposite directions; at other times the planet's relative velocity is less than its true velocity, as when a planet and the earth move in the same direction.

Of particular interest in the apparent motion of planets is the retrograde phase in which planets seem to move in a direction opposite to their normal one. See Fig. 11.32a

FIG. 11.32a. Retrograde motion. As seen against the background of the celestial sphere the planet was moving at A in the normal direction (this is called "direct motion"), and continued to do so until point B. From B to C the motion is in a direction opposite to normal (retrograde motion). At point C, the planet makes a U-turn and continues in direct motion.

The backward or retrograde motion of several of the planets puzzled astronomers for many centuries, until finally it was explained by Copernicus. An example is of great aid in visualizing the apparent retrograde motion.

Let the inner circle in Figure 11.32b represent the orbit of the earth around the sun. Let the large circle represent the orbit of Mars. The earth, being closer to the sun, moves faster than Mars. Let the top of the figure represent part of the celestial sphere. The sphere serves as a background upon which the movements of Mars are observed.

When the earth is in position 1, Mars will be seen in place 1 on the celestial sphere. Several weeks later, both the earth and Mars will

have moved in their orbits. Mars is now at point 2. As the earth moves through positions 3 and 4, the line described by Mars on the celestial sphere will be of a body in retrograde motion.

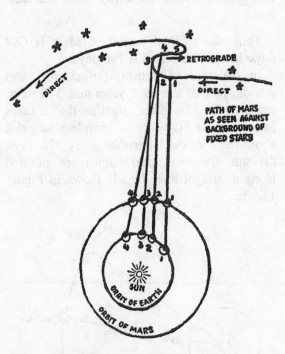

FIG. 11.32b. Explanation of retrograde motion. The earth, being closer to the sun than Mars, moves faster than Mars (the earth completes its circle in 365 days, Mars in 687). At point 1, Mars is "ahead" of the earth; its motion is direct. At point 4 the earth is "ahead" of Mars, and the latter seems to retrograde.

11.33 SIDEREAL AND SYNODIC PERIOD OF A PLANET

In connection with planets, there are two definitions of period: (A) sidereal period; and (B) synodic period. These differ in length due to the motion of the earth.

A Sidereal Period is the time it takes the planet to complete one revolution in its orbit. Another way of saying the same thing is: It is the time required by a planet to complete a circle on the celestial sphere, as seen from the sun.

B. The Synodic Period, which involves the

motion of the earth, is the interval between one time that the sun, the earth, and planet are aligned and the next time. Since both the earth and the planet are in motion, the synodic period differs materially from the sidereal.

Thus, the sidereal period of Mars is 687 days; its synodic period is 780 days.

In the case of Saturn, the sidereal and synodic periods are 29.5 years and 378 days, respectively. The former signifies that it takes Saturn nearly 30 years to complete its orbit about the sun; the latter that every 378 days, the sun, the earth, and Saturn are situated along a straight line. This is shown in Figure 11.33a.

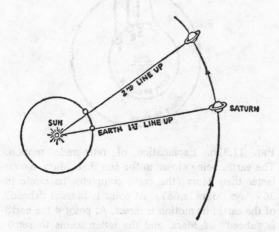

FIG. 11.33a. The synodic period of Saturn. This period is the interval of time between one lineup of sun-earth-Saturn to the next time these planets form a straight line. The synodic period of Saturn is 378 days. It consists of 365 days for a complete revolution of the earth plus 13 days needed for the earth to catch up with Saturn, which in the meanwhile has moved on to a new position.

The 378 days are composed of (a) 1 revolution of the earth about the sun (365 days); and (b) 13 days to catch up with Saturn which, in the meanwhile, has moved to a new position in its orbit.

There are two simple formulas to compute the synodic periods of planets. One formula is to be used for inferior planets, the other for superior.

Mercury and Venus are Inferior Planets. They are closer to the sun than the earth.

The orbits of the superior planets are outside the earth's orbit. See Fig. 11.33b.

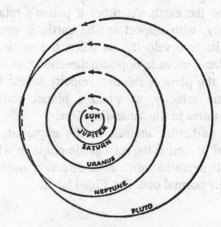

FIG. 11.33b. Orbits of five superior planets. The orbits are ellipses of small eccentricity, hence closely resemble circles. All the planets move in a counterclockwise direction, as shown by the arrows. The length of the arrow indicates the distance the planet travels in one year. The four other planets (not shown) move along orbits inside the orbit of Jupiter.

The formula for an inferior planet is:

$$\text{Synodic period of planet} = \frac{360}{P-E}$$

P is the number of degrees of arc that a planet moves in its orbit in one day; E is the number of degrees that the earth moves in its orbit in one day.

For Mercury,

$$P = \frac{360}{88}$$

$$E = \frac{360}{365\frac{1}{4}}$$

Substituting these numbers in the formula, we then get:

$$\text{Synodic period of Mercury} = \frac{360}{\frac{360}{88} - \frac{360}{365\frac{1}{4}}}$$
$$= 116 \text{ days}$$

For a superior planet, the formula is:

$$\text{Synodic period of superior planet} = \frac{360}{E-P}$$

where E and P have the same meaning as in the previous formula.

The proof of this second formula is fairly simple. The denominator E−P stands for the number of degrees that the earth gains on a planet in *one* day. But in a synodic period, the earth gains a complete revolution (360°) on the planet; hence, that period is equal to the number of times (E−P) is contained in 360.

PROBLEM 11.33:

Compute the synodic period of Mars.

Given: The sidereal period of the earth is 365¼ days, or $E = \frac{360}{365\frac{1}{4}}$;

and the sidereal period of Mars is 687 days, or

$$P = \frac{360}{687}$$

Answer: 780 days.

PART III: BASIC PLANETARY DATA: HOW DO WE KNOW?

11.34 INTRODUCTION

For each planet there is now available a large number of data. These include dimensions as well as other physical and orbital data.

The methods used to obtain several of these values are indicated in this part.

11.35 DISTANCE TO SUN

One fairly accurate way to determine the mean distance of a planet to the sun makes use of Kepler's third law (see Sec. 11.28).

If distances are measured in astronomical units and sidereal periods in years, the third law can be written as

$$(\text{period of a planet})^2 = (\text{mean distance of planet to sun})^3$$

PROBLEM 11.35:

The sidereal period of the planet Mars is 687 days. Find the mean distance of Mars from the sun.

Solution: Changing days into years and inserting in above formula,

$$\left(\frac{687}{365.25}\right)^2 = (\text{mean distance of Mars to Sun})^3$$

The answer for mean distance is 1.52 astronomical units, or (multiplying 1.52 by 93,000,000) 142,000,000 miles.

11.36 ECCENTRICITY

The eccentricity of a planet's orbit can be found

A. By determining the distance of the planet from the sun at different times of the year.

B. By plotting a graph of date versus distance from the sun. The graph will be an ellipse.

C. By computing the eccentricity e, using the formula $e = \frac{c}{a}$ where c is the distance from either focus (the sun is at one of the foci) to the center of the ellipse and a is the length of half of the major axis.

NOTE: Computing actual (as opposed to mean) distances from the sun for a planet other than the earth is a more arduous task.

11.37 INCLINATION OF ORBIT TO ECLIPTIC

can be obtained from observations on the celestial sphere. The inclination is equal to the maximum angle the planet reaches above or below the ecliptic.

11.38 PERIOD OF ONE REVOLUTION, SIDEREAL

The sidereal period can be obtained by using the formulas from Sec. 11.33 and the observed synodic period (see Sec. 11.39).

11.39 PERIOD OF ONE REVOLUTION, SYNODIC

This period can be obtained by noting the interval of time between two successive conjunctions of the planet with the sun, i.e., two successive times that the planet is on the line that joins the sun and the earth.

11.40 ORBITAL VELOCITY

An average value can be found by dividing the length of the circumference by the time it takes to cover that distance, i.e., by the sidereal period.

11.41 DISTANCE OF A PLANET FROM EARTH

One method that can be used to determine the distance of a planet from the earth is triangulation. In this method a line of position, say, 1,000 km long, is established on earth (see Fig. 7.5a). The angles from both ends of the line to the planet are measured. Standard formulae from elementary trigonometry are used to find the distance to the planet.

Another method is to measure the time elapsed for a radar signal to make a round trip to the planet. The distance to the planet is obtained by multiplying half the time for the round trip by the velocity of light.

PROBLEM 11.41:

A radar signal was sent to the planet Venus early in 1958. The round trip took about 5 minutes (300 seconds). Find the distance to the planet at that time.

Solution: Since the velocity of light, or the velocity of radar, is 186,000 miles per second, then

$186,000 \times 150 =$ approximately 28,000,000 miles.

11.42 ANGULAR DIAMETER

The angular diameter of a planet is determined by measuring the size of the photo-graphic image obtained with a telescope of known focal length.

11.43 LINEAR DIAMETER

The linear diameter of a planet is obtained by multiplying the angular diameter (in radians) by the distance to the planet. The formula is:

Linear diameter = angular diameter × distance to planet

The angular diameter in this formula has to be in radian units. (A radian is an angle that subtends an arc of a circle equal to the radius of that circle; 1 radian is slightly more than 57°.) The rate of conversion from degrees to radians is 1 radian $= \dfrac{360°}{2\pi}$. The diameter will be in the same unit as that used for distance to the planet.

11.44 VOLUME

Assuming that the planet is a sphere, the geometrical formula for volume of a sphere can be used:

$$\text{Volume} = \frac{4}{3}\pi \times \text{the radius}^3$$

where π has a value of 3.14.

11.45 MASS

The mass of a planet that has a satellite orbiting around it is obtained from Kepler's third law (see Sec. 11.28) as amended by Newton (see note following Problem 11.28).

One form of this amended law is $P^2 = \dfrac{4\pi^2 a^3}{G(M_1 + M_2)}$

where
P is the sidereal period of the satellite
a is the distance from center of satellite to center of planet
G is the universal gravitational constant (in the meter-kilogram-second system $G = 6.7 \times 10^{-11}$ newtons × meters^2 × kilograms^{-2}).
M_1 and M_2 are the masses of the planet and the satellite, respectively. The mass of the satellite

(M$_2$) is usually so much smaller than the mass of the planet (M$_1$) that it may be omitted from the formula.

PROBLEM 11.45:

Find the mass of Mars, given that its satellite Phobos is at a distance of 5,820 miles=9,400 km=9.4×10^6 meters and it orbits the mother planet in 7 hours 39 minutes=27,500 seconds.

Solution: Using meters for the unit of distance and seconds for the unit of time, then

$$M_1 = \frac{4\pi^2 \times (9.4 \times 10^6)^3}{6.7 \times 10^{-11} \times 27,500^2} = 7 \times 10^{23} \text{ kg, approxi-}$$

mately, for the mass of Mars, or about 11 per cent the mass of the earth.

The mass of planets that do not have natural satellites (e.g., Venus) is obtained by the use of either (A) an artificial satellite that orbits the planet or (B) determining the perturbation exerted by the planet on a close passing planetoid or spacecraft.

11.46 DENSITY

Mean density of a planet is obtained by dividing the mass by the volume. The value of a density is often stated in terms relative to the density of the earth.

11.47 SURFACE GRAVITY

The acceleration due to gravity at the surface of a planet is derived from Newton's Universal law of gravitation (Sec. 11.30) by dividing both sides of the equation by m. The equation then reads $\frac{F}{m} = a = 6.7 \times 10^{-8} \frac{M}{r^2}$. In the meter-kg-sec. system, the mass of the planet M should be expressed in kgs. and the radius of the planet r should be in meters.

11.48 VELOCITY OF ESCAPE

The speed that an object must acquire in order to escape from the gravitational field of a planet is obtained from

$$V = \sqrt{\frac{2 \text{ GM}}{r}}$$

In the centimeter-gram-second system, G=6.7×10^{-8} the mass has to be stated in grams, and the distance of the object from the center of the planet in centimeters. The escape velocity will be in units of centimeters per second.

11.49 PERIOD OF ROTATION ABOUT AXIS

The period of rotation of planets that have identifiable features (e.g, Mars) is determined by timing a complete rotation of such a feature.

The Doppler shift in radar waves between the approaching limb and the receding limb of a planet is used to determine the period for planets that do not have identifiable features (see Sec. 12.7 for the period of rotation of Mercury).

11.50 INCLINATION OF PLANETS EQUATOR TO ORBIT

This is usually derived from the study of an arc described by a surface marking on the planet.

11.51 TEMPERATURE

Spectral analysis of the light emitted by a planet is used to determine its surface temperature. The method is similar to the one described in Sec. 7.2.

11.52 ALBEDO

Albedo pertains to the ability of an object to reflect light. Some objects—e.g., tops of clouds—reflect most of the light falling upon them; others absorb most of the light, reflecting little. Stones, rocks, and soil are poor reflectors of light.

Albedo is defined as the ratio of the quantity of light reflected to the light received by the object.

In reference to the planets, albedo is equal to the ratio:

$$\frac{\text{light reflected by the planet}}{\text{sunlight falling on the planet}}$$

The denominator can be computed from the known value of the sun's luminosity and the planet's distance from the sun. The numerator is derived from the observed brightness of the planet.

CHAPTER 12

THE INFERIOR PLANETS

12.1 INTRODUCTION

The nine planets can be divided into two distinct groups: **Terrestrial Planets** and **Jovian Planets.** Mercury, Venus, earth, Mars, and Pluto are terrestrial planets similar to the earth in size.

Jupiter, Saturn, Uranus, and Neptune are Jovian (Jupiterlike) planets and are much more massive than the terrestrial ones.

The planets can also be grouped according to distance from the sun. Mercury and Venus are known as the **Inferior Planets,** as they are closer to the sun than the earth. The planets from Mars through Pluto are known as the **Superior Planets,** as they are farther from the sun than the earth.

PART I: THE PLANET MERCURY

12.2 BASIC DATA

Symbol: ☿
Distance to sun:
  Min.   28,500,000 miles
  Mean 36,000,000 miles
  Max. 43,500,000 miles
Eccentricity of orbit: .2056
Inclination of orbit to ecliptic: 7°0'14.6"
Period of one revolution about the sun:
  Sidereal 88 days
  Synodic 116 days
Orbital velocity (mean): 29.8 miles per second
Distance from earth:
  Min.   57,000,000 miles
  Max. 129,000,000 miles
Angular diameter (at mean inferior conjunction):
  10.88 seconds
Diameter: 3,010 miles
Volume: .06 times that of the earth
Mass: .054 times that of the earth
Density: .99 times that of the earth
Surface gravity: .37 times that of the earth
Velocity of escape: 2.6 miles per second

Period of rotation about axis: 58.7 days
Inclination of planet's equator to orbit: 28°
Temperature:
  Min. −280° F
  Max. 700° F
Albedo: .06
NOTE: Methods used to derive the above data are detailed in Secs. 11.34 to 11.52. See also Glossary.

12.3 TIMES FOR OBSERVATION

Mercury is the planet nearest the sun. It can be observed in the sky with the naked eye only when the sun is well below the horizon.

The synodic period of Mercury is 116 days. Half of this time Mercury leads the sun, i.e., it is west of the sun; the other half, the planet trails.

NOTE: The true orbit of Mercury is an ellipse. The terrestrial observer sees this ellipse almost edgewise; hence it appears to him as almost a straight line.

Mercury thus seems to us to oscillate east and west of the sun along that line.

The planet when west of the sun can be seen just before sunrise; when east of the sun it can be seen just after sunset.

NOTE: The ancient Greeks thought that they were observing two different planets. They used the name Mercury for the object they saw after sunset, and gave the name Apollo to the object visible before sunrise.

The farthest that Mercury can be from the sun is 28° of angle. The technical formulation is: The maximum elongation of Mercury is 28°.

(Elongation is the angle subtended at the earth by the sun and one of the planets.)

The length of time that Mercury can be observed is further reduced by the slant of this elongation.

The elongation is never perpendicular to the horizon, but somewhat inclined toward it. March, April, August, and September, when the elongation is closest to being vertical, are the best months in which to observe Mercury.

Astronomers do not limit their observations to the twilight hours. By eliminating diffuse sunlight from the telescope, observation of Mercury can be pursued during the daytime, particularly when Mercury is far to one side of the sun. Greater accuracy in observations is attainable at the time the planet is high in the sky (instead of near the horizon), as its light is less affected by the atmosphere.

12.4 WHAT DO WE SEE?

In naked-eye observations, Mercury, under favorable conditions, appears as a bright star —brighter than any star, except the sun, in the sky.

Twinkling, due primarily to the smallness of the disk and to its closeness to the horizon, can also be observed.

Through a telescope Mercury appears as a diffuse whitish object, going through phases (see Sec. 12.6). A large number of gray surface markings are also visible.

Excellent pictures of the surface of Mercury were obtained in a flyby of the United States space probe Mariner 10 in March 1974. The pictures taken as the craft was at a distance of less than 500 miles reveal that half the surface is heavily covered with craters while the other half consists primarily of smooth plains.

Cliffs hundreds of miles in length and several miles high were also visible.

12.5 TRANSITS

Occasionally, the planet crosses between the earth and the sun; **such a crossing is called a Transit and not a solar eclipse, as the planet covers only a small portion of the solar surface.** Transits can only be observed by telescope. The observer sees a small black circle, less than 1 per cent the diameter of the sun, slowly crossing the solar disk.

Transits only occur either in May or November. (The next transits of Mercury will occur November 12, 1986 and November 14, 1999.) Transits occur so rarely because the large (7°) inclination of Mercury's orbit to the orbit of the earth results in the planet usually passing either north or south of the sun.

Accurate measurements of transits are used not only in exact determination of the orbit of Mercury, but also in computing the earth's period of rotation—which latter indicates that the earth is slowing down. (The period of one rotation about its axis will increase by one second in the next 100,000 years.)

12.6 PHASES

Mercury goes through a series of phases, from full to new, similar to those of the moon. When it is beyond the sun, most or all of its illuminated face can be seen by telescope; but when it is on the same side of the sun as is the earth, only a small crescent is visible.

The brightness of the planet varies with changes in phase, although when "full" it is far from the earth and the "fullness" is offset by the distance.

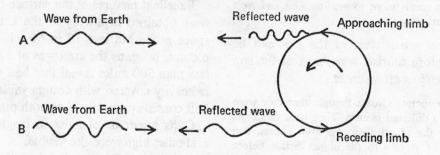

FIG. 12.7a. Wave A is reflected by approaching limb. Its wavelength is changed to shorter waves. Similarly wave B is changed to longer wavelength. From the amounts of change, one can compute the period of rotation of the planet.

12.7 PERIOD OF ROTATION ABOUT ITS AXIS

Both because of Mercury's small size and the poor quality of surface markings, astronomers had difficulty in determining the period of rotation. The best estimate available, until 1965, was that the period is 88 days, an estimate obtained in inconclusive experiments in the late nineteenth century. This period is equal to the sidereal period of revolution about the sun (also 88 days).

A recent method of measuring Mercury's rotation is by means of radar astronomy and using the Doppler shift. Radar waves reflected from the limb of the planet approaching the terrestrial observer are shifted toward shorter wavelengths. Similarly, radar waves reflected from the receding limb are shifted toward longer wavelengths. The amount of shift depends on the velocity of approach (or recession) and hence on the speed of rotation of the planet. For a schematic outline, see Fig. 12.7a.

With the Arecibo, Puerto Rico, dish operating as a radar telescope in 1965 the value of 58.7 days direct sense for the rotation of Mercury was obtained. "Direct sense" means that the rotation is counterclockwise as seen from above the north pole of Mercury.

The sidereal period of revolution (88 days) is exactly at a ratio of 3 to 2 to the period of rotation about the axis (58.7 days). This sim-

ple ratio is probably not a coincidence and a reasonable explanation follows:

A. Mercury is not a perfect sphere; one of its diameters is longer than the others.
B. The gravitational pull of the sun constrains this elongated diameter at perihelion to be in line with the sun every 1.5, 3, 4.5, 6, etc. rotations of the planet. See Fig. 12.7b.

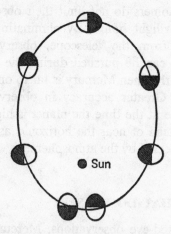

FIG. 12.7b. The revolution (about the sun) and the rotation of Mercury. Note that the bulge of the elongated diameter of Mercury is again in line with the sun after 1.5 rotations.

12.8 TEMPERATURE

From the intensity of the 3.4-mm and 19-mm radio waves from Mercury, astronomers have determined that its average temperature at full phase is 700° F, or 650° A. A high temperature is to be expected on Mercury since, due to its proximity to the sun, it receives seven times as much energy per unit area as the earth does.

At night on Mercury its skin temperature drops down to a low of 100° A.

Of interest are the radio measurements below the surface of the planet. Even at one meter below the surface the temperature remains almost always the same, about 350° A.

12.9 ALBEDO

Mercury's albedo is found to be .06—i.e., 6 per cent of the light received by Mercury from the sun is reflected back into space, and 94 per cent of the light is absorbed by the planet.

12.10 SURFACE GRAVITY AND VELOCITY OF ESCAPE

The surface gravity of Mercury is about .37 times that of the earth—i.e., the gravitational force is only about ⅓. A 9-pound object would indicate 3 pounds on a spring balance there.

Its surface gravity explains the absence of a gaseous envelope (atmosphere) around Mercury.

Because of the low value of surface gravity, the velocity of escape from the surface of the planet is only 2.6 miles per second: any object leaving Mercury with a velocity of 2.6 miles per second would leave forever. (On earth, the velocity of escape is 7 miles per second.)

Gases have the property of expansiveness—every gas spreads in all directions and occupies ever larger volume. The surface gravity of earth is strong enough to counteract the expansive tendency of the atmosphere. On Mercury, however, the gravitational force is too weak to prevent the escape of gases. Gas molecules that usually have a speed in excess of 2.6 miles per second can thus escape from the planet. If there had been any atmosphere on Mercury, it must have escaped a long time

ago, materially aided by the intense temperature on part of the planet. And yet theoretical and experimental considerations seem to indicate that there is a most tenuous atmosphere on Mercury. The theoretical research deals with the higher-than-expected temperature of the planet at quarter phase; the experimental, with the rather weak absorption lines of carbon dioxide obtained in spectral studies of that planet, as well as with the findings of Mariner 10 in 1974 that Mercury has a magnetic field. The interaction of this field with the solar wind brings about a most tenuous atmosphere. Estimates of the surface pressure due to the atmosphere are in the neighborhood of 10^{-12} atmospheres, i.e., one million millionth of the terrestrial sea-level pressure.

12.11 ADVANCE OF MERCURY'S PERIHELION

The major axis of Mercury's orbital ellipse rotates (precesses) slowly in space. In one hundred years the direction of the axis and hence the perihelion will change direction by 574 seconds of arc.

The rotation is counterclockwise as seen from above the solar system and is due to the gravitational effect of the sun and the other planets on Mercury.

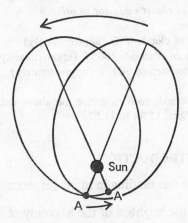

FIG. 12.11. The major axis of the orbit of Mercury advances in space and so does the perihelion (A). The rate of advance (precession) is 574 seconds of arc per century.

Computations using classical (Newtonian) physics can account for 532 seconds of arc per century. Computations using Einstein's general theory of relativity show that the mass of sun should cause an additional 42 seconds per century. The correct rotation (precession) of the orbital axis, as indicated above, is 574 seconds of arc per century. See Fig 12.11.

PART II: THE PLANET VENUS

12.12 BASIC DATA

Symbol: ♀
Distance to sun:
    Min. 66,500,000 miles
    Mean 67,270,000 miles
    Max. 67,500,000 miles
Eccentricity of orbit: .007
Inclination of orbit to ecliptic: 3.4°
Period of one revolution about the sun:
    Sidereal 225 days
    Synodic 584 days
Orbital velocity: 22 miles per second
Distance from earth:
    Min. 26,000,000 miles
    Max. 160,000,000 miles
Angular diameter:
    Min. 11 seconds
    Max. 61 seconds
Diameter: 7,650 miles
Volume: .902 times that of the earth
Mass: .82 times that of the earth
Density: .9 times that of the earth
Surface gravity: .87 times that of the earth
Velocity of escape: 6.5 miles per second
Period of rotation about axis: 243 days (retrograde)
Inclination of planet's equator to orbit: 3°
Temperature:
    At top of clouds 0° F (approximately)
    At bottom of clouds 400° F (approximately)
    At planet surface 900° F (approximately)
Albedo: .8
NOTE: Methods used to derive the above data are detailed in Secs. 11.34 to 11.52.

12.13 INTRODUCTION

Venus is outstanding in many respects:

A. It is the brightest of the heavenly objects, with the exception of the sun, the moon and extremely rare comets. At its brightest, it is visible during daytime and is strong enough to cast shadows of objects after dark.

B. It comes closest to earth, approaching to a distance of 26,000,000 miles.

C. It has the most nearly circular orbit: the eccentricity of its ellipse is a mere .007.

And yet, as we shall see, very little is known about Venus. It is still the "mysterious" planet.

12.14 TIMES FOR OBSERVATION

The synodic period of Venus is 584 days. Half of this time (a bit less than ten months) it rises ahead of the sun, and the other half, it sets after it.

NOTES: 1. In this case, too, the ancients thought that they were observing two different objects. They referred to the morning object as Lucifer, and to the evening "star" as Hesperus. Venus is named after the goddess of love and beauty.

2. The orbit of Venus is a circle (eccentricity .007). The projection of the orbit on the celestial sphere is a very flat ellipse, almost a straight line. Venus appears to oscillate east and west of the sun on that line.

The greatest angular distance between Venus and the sun is about 46°, and therefore Venus sets (or rises) at most 3 hours after (or before) the sun.

Consideration of the angle made by the planet's apparent path indicates that morning observations in the fall are the most favorable in the northern hemisphere.

The planet can also be seen during daylight, when it is not too close to the sun.

12.15 WHAT DO WE SEE?

To the unaided eye Venus appears as a bright stellar object. It shines with a steady white light. At its brightest it reaches an apparent magnitude of —4.4 and is then more than twelve times as bright as Sirius.

The telescopes reveal the fact that Venus, like Mercury and the moon, goes through a complete cycle of phases, as well as major changes in apparent diameter. See Sec. 12.16.

The telescope also reveals a bright diffuse object with no permanent markings on it.

The Mariner 2 spacecraft, launched in August 1962, passed within 22,000 miles of Venus in December 1962. Its observations confirmed that the planet is completely covered with yellowish-white clouds and that no glimpse of any solid surface is available through any break in the clouds.

The Mariner 10 craft investigated Venus in February 1974 at a height of less than 4,000 miles and found that the clouds swirl around the planet in a zonal motion with speeds exceeding 150 miles per hour and that in the region of Venus facing the sun large scale convection interacts with that zonal motion.

On October 22, 1975, a probe from the unmanned U.S.S.R. spacecraft Venera 9 landed on Venus and, notwithstanding the lethal extremes of temperature and pressure, succeeded in transmitting, for 53 minutes, photographs of the landscape, as well as a flood of other data from the surface of the planet. Three days later a similar probe from a twin spacecraft, Venera 10, landed 1,375 miles away from the Venera 9 probe and returned its findings for 65 minutes. These were the first photographs ever taken from the surface of another planet.

Preliminary studies of these data revealed the following information:

A. The extreme value for atmospheric pressure is 90 to 92 times the earth's surface atmospheric pressure.

B. A surface temperature of 905° F was reported by Venera 9 and 870° F by Venera 10.

C. Surface wind speeds were found to be low. These ranged at both sites from 2 to 6 miles per hour.

D. The amount of sunlight transmitted through the clouds turned out to be much greater than originally expected. Shadows of objects on the surface were clear and distinct in the photographs.

E. Jumbles of large rocks (12 to 16 inches across) are strewn over the landscape, which had previously been thought to consist of sandy deserts. The rocks at the Venera 9 site included both smooth rounded specimens as well as angular rock fragments, while the ones near Venera 10 were flat "pancake-type" stones.

12.16 PHASES AND APPARENT DIAMETER

As the planet approaches the line joining the earth and the sun, it reveals a crescent, which grows narrower as it approaches—the length increasing as the width decreases. Just before the light is entirely cut off from Venus (as with a new moon), its crescent is six times larger than when it is full. **When the planet is directly between the sun and the earth, it is**

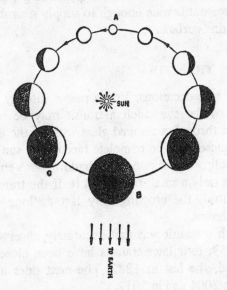

Fig. 12.16. Phases of Venus. Venus appears as a circular disk of light (full) when it is at superior conjunction (A on diagram).

As it moves toward position B (inferior conjunction), less and less of the illuminated surface of Venus can be seen by a terrestrial observer.

However, because its diameter increases, Venus will appear at its brightest 36 days before (position C) or 36 days after inferior conjunction.

said to be at **Inferior Conjunction.** Venus is full (as with a full moon) when it is on the opposite side of the sun from the earth. **That point on the orbit of an inferior planet is called Superior Conjunction.** See Fig. 12.16.

12.17 BRIGHTNESS

Venus' remarkable brightness results from several favorable factors:

A. Its closeness to the sun.
B. Its closeness to the terrestrial observer.
C. The high value of its albedo. Nearly 80 per cent of the light received by Venus from the sun is reflected back into space.

Venus does not appear at maximum brightness in its full phase, because of its remoteness from earth at that time. It appears brightest just before and just after it passes inferior conjunction. (Specifically, it is brightest 36 days before and 36 days after it crosses the line joining the earth with the sun.) Then, it is close enough to the earth to appear large, and the crescent is wide enough to supply a sizable reflecting surface.

12.18 TRANSITS

On rare occasions, Venus passes directly in front of the sun; such a transit may be observed through a smoked glass without the aid of a telescope. The complete face of the sun is not eclipsed because the shadow of Venus covers only a small portion of it. If the transit is central, the crossing may last as long as eight hours.

Such a transit was first accurately observed in 1639; four later transits have been closely studied, the last in 1882. The next ones are due in 2004 and in 2012.

Transits of the sun do not occur at every inferior conjunction because of the inclination (3°) of the orbit in which Venus travels to the orbit of the earth. As a result, Venus is sometimes on one side and, sometimes, on the other side of the earth's orbit, i.e., half the time it is slightly above the ecliptic and the other half

slightly below the ecliptic. During the time of inferior conjunction when Venus is either above or below the ecliptic, no transit will occur. It is only when Venus is (a) just crossing the ecliptic, and (b) at inferior conjunction, that transit is possible—the two occurring simultaneously on the average of once every 50 years.

The two points of intersection between the orbit of a planet and the plane in which earth revolves (the ecliptic) are called Nodes—one point is called an "ascending node"; the other, a "descending node." The line joining the two points is called the nodal line.

The conditions for the occurrence of a transit of Venus can also be stated as follows: A transit will occur if the line joining the earth and the sun coincides with the nodal line.

12.19 PERIOD OF ROTATION ABOUT ITS AXIS

As there are no fixed markings on the clouds surrounding Venus, it was impossible for a long time to determine either the period of rotation of the clouds or the period of rotation of the planet itself.

The definitive answer was arrived at by using Doppler shifts in radar wavelengths, a technique similar to the one used in the case of Mercury (see Sec. 12.7). Venus rotates in a retrograde (clockwise) direction, once every 243 days. The spin axis is several degrees away from the perpendicular to the orbital plane.

Of interest is the fact that the values 584 (synodic period) and 243 retrograde (rotational period) result in the same face of Venus being exposed to the earth at each inferior conjunction.

12.20 THE SURFACE OF THE PLANET

The permanent cloud cover made it impossible until late 1975 to see any part of Venus's surface.

Techniques were available, though, to map the surface, to measure its temperature, and to find the atmospheric pressure without seeing it.

A. Mapping. Radio waves from the earth easily penetrate the clouds on Venus and are reflected by the solid surface of the planet back to earth. Waves reflected by high ground return before waves from low ground and thus a map of the topography can be constructed.

The completed map showed that Venus, like Mercury, has a rather rough surface, that there are several high mountains, as well as a multitude of craters at various points on the planet.

B. Surface temperature and pressure. Observations taken by the U.S.S.R. spacecraft Venera 7 and Venera 8 in 1972 upon landing on the surface of the planet indicate a temperature of close to 900° F, with only a small difference between the illuminated and dark sides of the planet, and a surface pressure of 90 atmospheres. The high value of surface temperature is most likely due to the greenhouse effect.

NOTE: The greenhouse effect, best demonstrated in greenhouses, can be observed on the earth, as well. The glass roof acts as an energy trap very readily admitting sunlight, mainly of wavelengths between 4,000 and 7,000 angstroms, at which wavelengths it is perfectly transparent. It does not permit the radiation coming from the warmed earth inside the house to leave, being opaque to that "dark heat" which has wavelengths of, say, 100,000 angstroms. The result is that energy in the form of heat is accumulated in the greenhouse. This effect is also clearly felt upon entering a car that was standing in the summer heat with the windows rolled up.

In the case of Venus, the incoming solar radiation is able to diffuse through the clouds and atmosphere to the surface; the outgoing infrared radiation is absorbed by the carbon dioxide in the atmosphere. Carbon dioxide (CO_2) is quite opaque to infrared radiation.

The surface temperature and pressure thus obtained coincided very well with the data obtained from the Venera 9 and 10 probes (see Sec. 12.15).

12.21 THE CLOUDS AND THE ATMOSPHERE

That the visible outline of Venus consists of a dense layer of clouds is evidenced by the following:

A. The brightness of Venus. Clouds are good reflectors, while rocks are poor reflectors.
B. No fixed surface marks on Venus have ever been photographed from the earth. The usual photograph reveals a smooth, uniform yellowish disk.
C. Information from spacecraft that came close to the planet.
D. A study of the variation in brightness of the star Regulus when Venus passed in front of it in 1959.

To the best of our knowledge, the base of the clouds is 20 miles and the top of the clouds about 45 miles above the surface.

There being no, or extremely little, water vapor on Venus, the cloud droplets are not of the water variety. Suggestions for their makeup run all the gamut from dust to sulphuric acid. (The sulphuric acid hypothesis successfully explains most of the properties of Venutian clouds.)

Other indications from research on the envelope of Venus:

A. The lower atmosphere (surface to base of clouds at 20 miles) is very hot and dry. There are strong up and down (convective) currents prevalent there.
B. There are only slight horizontal winds in the lower atmosphere. Two to six miles per hour is a reasonable figure.
C. The upper atmosphere has very strong horizontal winds. Values of 150 miles per hour have been registered.
D. Temperature at the top of the cloud layer is close to 0° F and the pressure is a small fraction of terrestrial sea-level pressure.
E. Upward from the top of the clouds, the pressure keeps on decreasing; the temperature continues at the same 0° F.

F. The main chemical component of the atmosphere is carbon dioxide, which accounts for nearly 97 per cent of its weight. The other 3 per cent comprises small amounts of oxygen, carbon monoxide, water vapor, nitrogen, hydrochloric and hydrofluoric acid, a trace of ammonia, and a lot of dust particles.

G. Venus has no magnetic field, or if it does have one, its intensity is less than 1 per cent of that of the earth's magnetic field.

Nor is there a belt of trapped high-energy particles.

H. There is an ionosphere and it interacts intensely with the particles imported by the solar wind.

Truly, Venus is no tourist paradise, at least not for terrestrial beings. With a surface temperature of 900° F, pressure of 90 atmospheres, little oxygen, no water, lots of dust in the air, and bleak-looking clouds . . . no attraction.

CHAPTER 13

THE EARTH AND ITS MOON

PART I: THE EARTH

13.1 BASIC DATA

Symbol: $\oplus$
Distance to sun (mean): 92,955,700 miles
Eccentricity of orbit: .17
Period of one revolution about the sun: Sidereal 365.256 mean solar days (1 year)
Orbital velocity (mean): 18.5 miles per second
Diameter: Min. (polar) 7,900 miles
    Max. (equatorial) 7,927 miles
Surface area: 195 million square miles
Volume: 260 billion cubic miles
Mass: 6.6×10^{21} tons
Density: 5.5 times that of water
Velocity of escape: 7 miles per second
Period of rotation about axis: 23 hours, 56 minutes, 4 seconds
Inclination of equator to orbit: 23.5°
Incoming solar radiation: 1.94 calories per cm² per minute
Albedo: .36
Acceleration at sea level: 32.2 feet per second per second

13.2 INTRODUCTION

The earth is one of the smallest of the nine planets revolving about the sun, ranking fifth in diameter, fifth in mass, and third in distance

from the sun. Otherwise, it is very like several other planets.

So far as is observed, it is the only place in the universe on which "life" exists.

As a base for astronomic observation, it is far from excellent, its major drawback being that it is not stationary, so that all observations must be corrected for its motion. Nor is its motion simple; it is, rather a highly complex combination of at least *six* elementary motions:

A. It rotates about its axis (once a day).

B. The axis revolves about the sun (once a year).

C. The axis precesses.

D. The axis nutates.

E. The sun, with the earth and the other planets, speeds through the local cluster of stars at a speed of 12 miles per second.

F. The local cluster of stars takes part in the rotation about the center of our galaxy at a speed of hundreds of miles per second.

The senses do not make one aware of these motions, much as passengers in a smoothly running train are hardly aware of its speed.

Only when measurements are made of the movements of other heavenly bodies does the effect of the motion of the earth have to be carefully considered.

13.3 ROTATION ABOUT ITS AXIS

The earth spins counterclockwise about its axis, completing one revolution in a sidereal day, the duration of which is 23 hours, 56 minutes, and 4 seconds. (The sidereal day is shorter than the "clock" day, which is known as the "mean solar day.")

Many experiments prove that the earth spins about its axis; one of the most decisive is that devised by the French physicist, J. B. L. Foucault, in 1851, in which the rotation of the earth becomes directly visible.

The only necessary equipment is a pendulum, which may consist of a sphere of lead, and a suspension wire. To obtain accurate results:

A. The suspension wire should be long;

B. the lead sphere should be heavy; and

C. the pendulum suspended on good bearings.

According to the theory on which the experiment is based, a freely swinging pendulum maintains its plane of oscillation—that is, if a pendulum is started in a North-South direction, it will continue to swing in that direction until air resistance or friction bring it to rest. See Fig. 13.3.

The procedure as performed above the North Pole is as follows:

A. Start the pendulum swinging.

B. Mark a line on the ground indicating the trace of the pendulum's bob.

C. Observe that an hour later, this line has turned 15° in a counterclockwise direction, relative to the plane in which the pendulum swings.

D. Observe that in one sidereal day, the line completes one revolution, counterclockwise.

The original experiment was performed in the Pantheon in Paris, with a 200-foot length

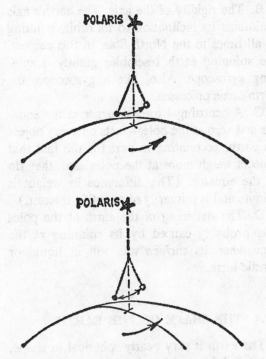

FIG. 13.3. The Foucault pendulum. Above, experiment as performed above the North Pole. Note the line traced at the start of the experiment.

Below, the pendulum continues to swing in the same plane. The line has moved on in a counterclockwise direction. At the end of six hours the trace makes an angle of 90° with the plane in which the pendulum swings. (To obtain a complete circle in 24 hours the experiment has to be performed at the earth's North Pole.)

of suspension wire. At the Paris latitude, the experiment is slightly more complicated; the consequence, though, that the earth spins about its axis is inescapable.

NOTE: We are not aware of the true motion of the earth. What is observed is an apparent one, consisting of an apparent rotation of the celestial sphere—that is, the stars and the sun rise on the eastern horizon and set on the western horizon. This relationship between true and apparent motion has its counterpart in a moving train. Looking from a window of a northbound train, one sees the apparent due south motion of the neighboring terrain.

Several effects are directly due to the spinning of the earth:

A. The procession of day and night. Every place on earth alternately faces the sun (day) or is on the opposite side of the sun (night).

B. The rigidity of the axis. The earth's axis maintains its inclination to its orbit, pointing at all times to the North Star; in this respect, the spinning earth resembles greatly a spinning gyroscope. Also, like a gyroscope, the earth's axis precesses.

C. A centrifugal force—larger at the equator and zero at the poles—acts on every object on earth, accounting in part for the fact that objects weigh more at the poles than they do at the equator. (The difference in weight is minute and is primarily of scientific interest.)

D. The flattening of the earth at the poles was probably caused by its spinning at the time when its surface was still in liquid or plastic form.

13.4 THE SHAPE OF THE EARTH

The earth is very nearly spherical in shape, only slightly modified by its mountains and valleys; in fact, if it were scaled to the size of a billiard ball, it would be a more perfect ball.

The sphere is slightly flattened at the poles: the polar diameter is 27 miles less than that of the earth at the equator. This flattening is the "oblate spheroid" which describes the shape of the earth.

The oblateness of the earth is also responsible in part for the variation of weight with latitude; since an object at the pole is closer to the center of the earth, it is greater in weight. The change in weight from equator to pole is about ½ of 1 per cent.

NOTE: Data obtained by artificial satellites indicates that the earth is slightly pear-shaped. Its South Pole is indented, the North Pole slightly extended.

13.5 REVOLUTION ABOUT THE SUN

The earth also revolves about the sun, counterclockwise. (The orbit of the earth is shaped like an ellipse, with the sun as one of its foci.) See Fig. 13.5.

Again, we see not the **true** motion, but rather the **apparent** motion of the sun, which appears, in the course of a year, to make one

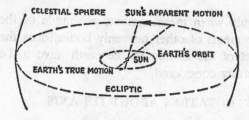

FIG. 13.5. The true motion of the earth is its revolution about the sun. This results in an apparent motion of the sun about the earth. The path of the sun as projected against the celestial sphere is known as the ecliptic. The latter term (the ecliptic) can also be defined in two other ways: (1) The ecliptic is the path of the earth as seen from the sun against the background of the celestial sphere; or (2) the ecliptic is the intersection of an infinite plane containing the earth's orbit with the celestial sphere.

revolution about the earth. **This apparent orbit of the sun is called the Ecliptic; a belt 8° wide on each side of the ecliptic is called the Zodiac.** There are twelve prominent constellations within the belt (zodiacal constellations), through which the sun, in its apparent motion, passes once every year. These are: Aries, Taurus, Gemini, Cancer, Leo, Virgo, Libra, Scorpio, Sagittarius, Capricorn, Aquarius, and Pisces. The sun is in the constellation Pisces toward the end of March.

If the bright sunlight could be eliminated, the sun could actually be seen within that constellation in March. Aries and Taurus serve next as temporary hosts. During the summer months, the sun passes through Gemini, Cancer, and Leo, and so on, to complete the twelve zodiacal constellations.

This apparent motion of the sun about the earth is used to define "year." **Year is the time it takes the sun to complete the circuit of the stars.** This is a **Sidereal Year**, not the year we normally think of, which is known as **Tropical Year** and is twenty minutes shorter than the sidereal year.

13.6 INCLINATION OF EQUATOR TO ECLIPTIC

The path in which the sun follows its apparent motion on the celestial sphere is inclined to the celestial equator, the angle between the two circles being 23 degrees and 27 minutes.

One of the points at which the circles intersect is designated by the symbol ♈ and is known as the First Point of Aries; here, the sun crosses the celestial equator on its way from the southern to the northern portion of the Ecliptic.

The other point is designated by the symbol ♎ and is known as the First Point of Libra. When the sun is at either point, day is equal in length to night, everywhere on earth.

The sun is at ♈ on or about March 21; this point is also known as the **Vernal Equinox** (translation: Spring equal night). It is at ♎ on or about September 23; the First Point of Libra is also known as the **Autumnal Equinox.** See. Fig. 13.6a.

The inclination between the two paths is the primary cause of terrestrial seasons. When the sun is north of the equatorial plane, it is warm

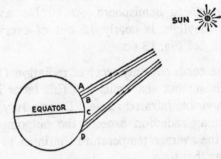

FIG. 13.6b. The rays in the northern hemisphere are concentrated in the small arc AB. The same group of rays falling on the southern hemisphere are spread out over the large arc CD. This is the primary reason for the warm season in the northern hemisphere.

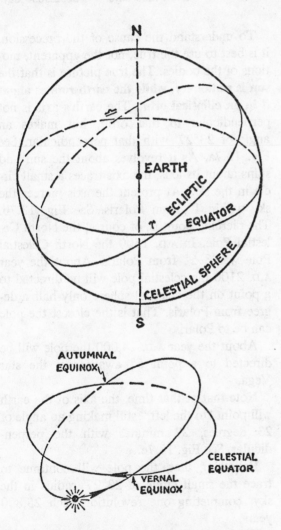

FIG. 13.6a. The apparent path traced out by the sun on the celestial sphere is known as the ecliptic. It is inclined 23°27′ with the earth's (or celestial) equator. The points of intersection of the two orbits are called equinoxes.

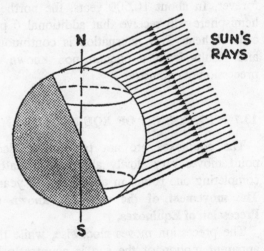

FIG. 13.6c. Daytime is more than 12 hours in the northern hemisphere, and less than 12 hours in the southern. This is a contributing factor to the warm season, while the sun is above the celestial equator. On June 21 the sun is farthest from the equator. The hottest weather in middle latitudes occurs later: average temperatures in the United States, say, do not reach their height until late July or early August. This lag results from the balance of radiation.

in the northern hemisphere, and cold in the southern for two major reasons:

A. The sun's rays are more concentrated. This is illustrated in Figure 13.6b. In the northern hemisphere, the rays supply the heat for the small arc AB; in the southern, they are distributed over a much larger arc CD. The southern hemisphere receives less heat per unit area.

B. The sun is above the horizon longer in the northern hemisphere. At 40° N, say, in June, daylight is nearly 15 out of every 24 hours. See Fig. 13.6c.

The earth not only receives radiation (light and heat) but also emits it. (This latter is in the invisible infrared range.) During July, the incoming radiation exceeds the outgoing, so that the average temperature continues to rise during that time.

The earth, moving in its true elliptical orbit, is closest to the sun during the southern summer. Due to the difference in distance, the southern hemisphere receives about 6 per cent more solar energy than does the northern.

This increment of heat will not continue forever. In about 10,500 years, the northern hemisphere will receive that additional 6 per cent of heat. This alternation is continuous, and results from a phenomenon known as precession of equinoxes.

13.7 PRECESSION OF EQUINOXES

The equinoxes are not permanent. Each point moves very slowly along the equator, completing one round in about 25,800 years. **The movement of the points is known as Precession of Equinoxes.**

The precession moves clockwise, while the apparent motion of the sun is counterclockwise. Thus, when the sun is approaching the vernal equinox the latter moves forward to meet the sun.

The vernal equinox is used to define the **Tropical Year** (from the Greek word "trope," which means "turning") or the **Season Year**— what we normally mean by "year." Techni-

cally, Tropical Year is: **The period of time elapsed between two successive passages of the sun through the vernal equinox.**

Because of the motion of the equinox to "meet the sun," this year is shorter than the sidereal year, based on the fixed stars. The comparison is:

	Tropical year	*Sidereal year*
Days	365	365
Hours	5	6
Minutes	48	9
Seconds	46.0	9.5
	365.24220 days	365.25636 days

To understand the cause of the precession, it is best to use the true, not the apparent, motions of the bodies. The true picture is that the **sun is stationary, while the earth rotates about it in an elliptical orbit.** The earth's axis is not perpendicular to that orbit, but makes an angle of 23°27′ with that perpendicular. See Fig. 13.7a. As it revolves about the sun and spins about its axis, the axis traces a small circle in the sky. At present the axis pierces the sky within 1° from Polaris. See Fig. 13.7b. The piercing point is, of course, the North Celestial Pole. In A.D. 1500 the North Celestial Pole was 3½° from Polaris. About the year A.D. 2100 the celestial pole will be directed to a point on the celestial sphere only half a degree from Polaris. That is the closest the pole can be to Polaris.

About the year A.D. 14,000 the pole will be directed to a point 5° away from the star Vega.

Note that at that time, the axis of the earth will point "to the left," still making an angle of 23 degrees, 27 minutes with the perpendicular. See Fig. 13.7c.

Following that, the pole will continue to trace the small circle of 23°27′ radius in the sky, completing one revolution each 25,800 years.

The path of the celestial pole among the stars is indicated in Figure 13.7d.

The cause of the motion of the earth's axis is the same as that of a spinning top.

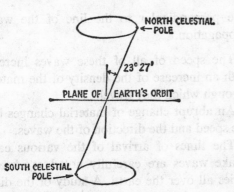

FIG. 13.7a. The celestial poles trace out two circles each of 23°27′ radius.

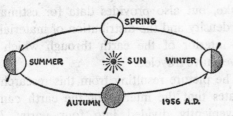

FIG. 13.7b. The axis of the earth at present points toward the North Star. On this picture the axis is "up to the right."

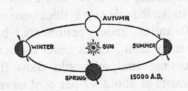

FIG. 13.7c. In the years about A.D. 14,000 the earth's axis will point "up to the left." Compare this to the present "up to the right" inclination. Note that the magnitude of the angle 23°27′ did not change.

The pull of gravity causes the leaning axis of the top to precess, describing the surface of a cone. See Fig. 13.7e. The force that causes the earth's axis to precess is exerted by the sun and the moon on the slight equatorial bulge.

The effect of this force is to change the *direction* of the axis, not its inclination; the axis remains at 23°27′ while it describes a complete surface of a cone once every 25,800 years.

The equinoxes move with the rotation of the axis, also making one revolution in 25,800 years.

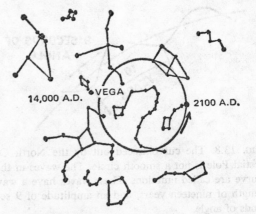

FIG. 13.7d. In the year A.D. 2100 the North Celestial Pole will be within half a degree of Polaris. In the year A.D. 14,000 the pole will be within 5° of Vega. Vega will be the North Star at that time.

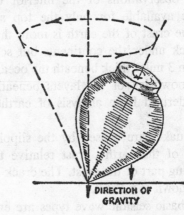

FIG. 13.7e. In the case of a spinning top it is the force of gravity that causes the axis to "precess," that is, to describe a cone.

13.8 NUTATION

The curve traced by the earth's axis is not a smooth circle. It has small waves, due to the "nodding" of the earth's axis about the mean position of 23°27′. The true motion of the axis is a combination of precession and the nodding motion—the latter motion is known as **Nutation** (from the Latin word for "nodding"). The period of one such complete wave is nineteen years; the nod at its maximum is 9 seconds of angle. See Fig. 13.8. The gravitational pull of the moon is the primary cause of nutation.

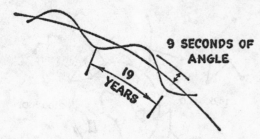

FIG. 13.8. The curve traced out by the North Celestial Pole is not a smooth circle. The waves in that curve are called nutations. These waves have a wave length of nineteen years, and an amplitude of 9 seconds of angle.

13.9 THE INTERIOR OF THE EARTH

Direct observations of the interior of the earth are available for only the top several miles. The crust of the earth is more than 30 miles thick under the continents but scarcely more than 3 miles thick beneath the oceans.

Our knowledge of the layers beneath this crust is derived from analysis of earthquake waves.

Earthquakes are caused by the slipping of one part of the earth's crust relative to the neighboring part of the crust. The crack in the crust is known as a **Fault.**

Three basic seismic wave types are emitted at the time of the slipping:

A. The surface wave.
B. The primary wave.
C. The secondary wave.

A. The surface wave, as its name implies, travels like an ocean wave on the earth's surface. It is the slowest of the three waves and is by far the most destructive.

B. The primary wave, next in speed, travels through both solid and liquid materials. It is a longitudinal (compressional) wave, similar to a sound wave. The solid or liquid particles oscillate to and fro along the line of the wave's propagation.

C. The secondary wave is the slowest of the three and can travel only through solid material. This is a transverse wave, similar to an ocean wave. The particles oscillate along a line perpendicular to the line of the wave's propagation.

The speed of all of these waves increases with an increase of the density of the material through which they travel.

An abrupt change of material changes both the speed and the direction of the waves.

The times of arrival of the various earthquake waves are carefully noted at observatories all over the earth. A study of the differences in time of arrival at several of these observatories by the primary and the secondary waves not only pinpoints the focus of the quake, but also provides data for estimating the density and the distribution of materials in the interior of the earth through which the waves have traveled.

The picture resulting from this research indicates that the interior of the earth can be conveniently divided into four parts: (A) crust; (B) mantle; (C) outer core; and (D) inner core.

A. **The Crust,** the layer best known to us, has, as indicated above, a thickness of more than 30 miles under continents, but are scarcely more than 3 miles under the oceans.

A chemical analysis would show that the crust consists of about 47 per cent oxygen, 28 per cent silicon, 8 per cent aluminum, 5 per cent iron, and smaller percentages of a large number of the other elements.

B. **The Mantle** extends to a depth of between 1,800 and 1,900 miles. Chemically, it is primarily made up of silicates that are rich in magnesium and iron.

NOTE: The Moho discontinuity, named for its discoverer, the Yugoslavian geophysicist Andrija Mohorovičić, is the boundary between the crust and the mantle.

C. **The Upper Core** is more than 1,200 miles deep. It consists most likely of nickel-iron, and since secondary waves cannot go through it, the nickel-iron is probably in liquid form.

D. **The Inner Core** has a radius of about 800 miles. It, like the outer core, probably consists of nickel-iron.

Changes in transmission of the primary waves indicate that this metal alloy is in solid form.

NOTE: The average density of the earth is 5.5 grams per cubic centimeter. The density of the material near the surface is 2.7, or less than half the earth's average density.

The assumption of nickel-iron in the core will account for the high value of the earth's average density. The rotation of this metal will also account for the earth's magnetic field. See Fig. 13.9.

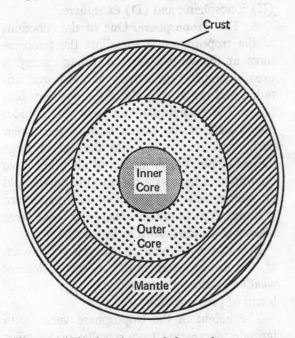

FIG. 13.9. The four layers of the earth: crust, mantle, outer core, and inner core.

13.10 MAGNETISM OF THE EARTH

The earth's magnetic field is, to a first approximation, similar in form to a field in the neighborhood of a bar magnet. The axis of the earth's magnetic field is inclined 12° to the earth's geographic axis. One of the magnetic poles is near Hudson Bay, the other in Victoria Land in Antarctica. Their locations seem to change from time to time.

The explanation given for the earth's magnetism is that it is due to moving currents of liquid iron in the core of the rotating earth.

One of the uses we make of the earth's field is to orient the needle in a magnetic compass. The compass needle orients itself parallel to the local magnetic line.

Artificial satellites and space probes have shown that the magnetic field around the earth is much more complicated than the first approximation indicated above.

The complication is due to the interaction between the magnetic field associated with the solar wind and the earth's "normal" magnetic field.

The result of this interaction is a field known as the **Magnetosphere,** which extends about 50,000 miles in the direction toward the sun and more than a 150,000 miles in the direction away from the sun. The presence of the 150,000-mile "tail" was revealed from the data obtained by the Explorer 10 satellite in 1961.

13.11 HIGH-ENERGY-CHARGED PARTICLE BELT

In addition to the magnetic field, the earth is surrounded by two belts of high-energy-charged particles, mostly high-energy protons and electrons that get trapped by the earth's magnetic field.

These belts, named for the American physicist James A. Van Allen, were discovered in one of the research projects of the Explorer 1

FIG. 13.11. The two doughnut-shaped regions of the Van Allen belt. In these regions there is a concentration of trapped high-energy-charged particles.

in 1958 and further verified by the data obtained by Pioneer 3 in 1959.

The belts are doughnut-shaped. The innermost one is at a distance of about 2,000 miles, the outer one at 10,000 miles from the earth's surface.

The trapped high-energy protons and electrons spiral along the magnetic lines of force of the earth, then bounce from one hemisphere to the other during the several days or weeks of the entrapment. See Fig. 13.11.

13.12   THE ATMOSPHERE

Surrounding the earth's surface is an envelope of air. It protects man from ultraviolet radiation from the sun and aids in equalizing temperature extremes.

The air is a mixture, not a chemical combination, of several gases. The composition, by volume, is 78 per cent nitrogen, 21 per cent oxygen, less than 1 per cent argon, and minute parts of carbon dioxide and water vapor. It is probable that these percentages are different in the upper air and that hydrogen and helium play an important part in the composition of the air at heights of about 30 or 40 miles.

The average pressure exerted at sea level by this atmosphere is 14.7 pounds per square inch, or 1,013.2 millibars, the units used in meteorology. This is an average value—the actual value varies with time. Usually, high pressures—say, 1,030 millibars—are associated with good weather, low pressures—say, 980 millibars—with precipitation.

The pressure at sea level is caused by the weight of the overlying air. At elevations above sea level, the pressure is less; at 3.5 miles the pressure is half of 14.7 pounds per square inch; at 7 miles the pressure is one quarter of 14.7; and so on. Every 3.5 miles, the pressure decreases to 50 per cent of its previous value.

The density of the air follows the same rule as does pressure. At 3.5 miles above sea level it is 50 per cent that of sea-level value. At 100 miles the density of the air is less than that obtainable in the best laboratory vacuum. Data

from the satellites Vanguard 1 (1958) and Explorer 9 (1961) clearly indicate that densities at any given altitude vary greatly from day to day, primarily because of variations in solar activity.

The earth's atmosphere has no sharply defined upper level. A study of meteors indicates the presence of air at levels up to 100 miles; a study of aurorae indicates the presence of air at least 400 miles above sea level. The atmosphere can be divided into four layers, or shells: (A) troposphere; (B) stratosphere; (C) ionosphere; and (D) exosphere.

A. **The Troposphere.** One of the functions of the troposphere is to adjust the temperatures at the earth's surface. Solar energy is usually supplied excessively at the lower latitudes, and rather sparsely in the northern latitudes. The exchange of air between latitudes moves part of the excess heat to the cooler parts, and vice versa, with the aid of large masses of air. Warm masses of air bring large quantities of heat with them to the north; cold air masses move south, to cool off the southern latitudes. **The boundaries between these large masses of air are known as Fronts.**

It is at the boundaries between air masses, at the fronts, that most of the inclement weather takes place—clouds, fog, and all forms of precipitation.

The height of the troposphere varies with latitude, decreasing from a value of 10 miles above sea level at the equator to 5 miles or less at the poles.

The temperature of the troposphere decreases from an average of 56° F at sea level to a value of −60° F at the top.

The tropopause is the dividing boundary between the troposphere and the next layer.

B. **The Stratosphere** extends about 40 miles above the troposphere. The temperature here stays constant an average −60° F for the first 10 miles upward, then increases to 32° F in the next 10 miles, and finally decreases to −160° F in the top 20 miles of the layer.

The air currents in the stratosphere are primarily horizontal, i.e., parallel to the earth's surface.

Chemically, the stratosphere is similar to the lower reaches of the atmosphere (see Sec. 13.12), with the following two exceptions:

  a. There is less water vapor.

  b. There is much more ozone. The ozone (O_3) forms in the lowest 10 miles of the stratosphere through the action of the sun's ultraviolet rays on oxygen (O_2) molecules.

NOTE: Ozone, composed of molecules containing three atoms of oxygen, is opaque to the extreme ultraviolet radiation from the sun.

The absorption of ultraviolet radiation by the ozone is important as this radiation is extremely harmful to all kinds of life on the earth.

The stratosphere contains about one fifth of the mass of the entire atmosphere.

C. **The Ionosphere.** This layer varies in thickness between 50 and 100 miles. It contains substantial numbers of ionized atoms, the ionization being caused by ultraviolet and X-ray radiation from the sun. There are three reasonably distinct layers in the ionosphere, universally referred to as the D, E, and F layers, each layer with its own characteristics.

All three layers, though, are of great importance in long-range radio broadcasting. Multiple reflections between these layers and the earth makes it possible to send radio signals around the earth.

The D layer, at a height of about 60 miles above sea level, is instrumental in reflecting back to the earth long-wave radio broadcasting. The E layer, at 80 miles above sea level, is most efficient in reflecting medium-wave radio broadcasts. Similarly, the F layer, at about 150 miles, is involved in reflecting short-wave radio broadcasting.

As indicated in Sec. 11.8 above, radiation from solar flares seriously interferes with the broadcasting during the lifetime of such a chromospheric flare.

D. **The Exosphere** is the layer above the ionosphere, and it continues into outer space. This is the region in which atomic and molecular escape from the earth's atmosphere becomes significant. Lighter atoms and molecules can escape from the base of the exosphere, heavier particles from higher alti-

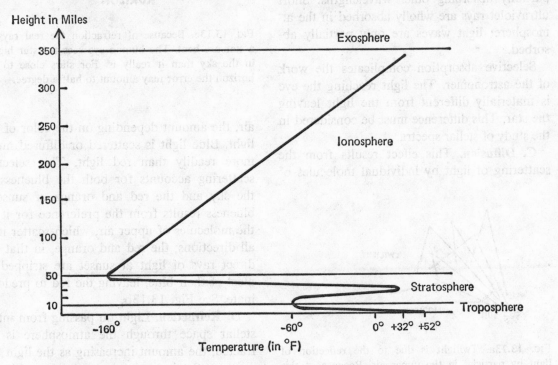

FIG. 13.12. The four layers of the atmosphere. Note in particular the variation of temperatures with height in the stratosphere.

tudes. Ionized particles are prevented from escape by the earth's magnetic field.

These four layers of the earth's atmosphere are diagrammed in Figure 13.12.

13.13 THE ATMOSPHERE IN ASTRONOMY

The earth's atmosphere affects in several ways incoming radiation: (A) reflection, (B) absorption, (C) diffusion, and (D) refraction.

A. Reflection. The phenomenon of twilight is a direct result of reflection by very small particles of dust and smoke which reflect the rays from the sun after it sets, or before it rises, back to the earth, thus providing additional daytime. See Fig. 13.13a. Astronomical twilight lasts until the sun's center is 18° below the horizon: then, even the faintest stars may be seen.

B. Absorption. The earth's atmosphere is a selective absorber, absorbing nearly 100 per cent of some wavelengths of light; but only partially absorbing other wavelengths. Short ultraviolet rays are wholly absorbed in the atmosphere; light waves are only partially absorbed.

Selective absorption complicates the work of the astronomer. The light reaching the eye is materially different from the light leaving the star. This difference must be considered in the study of stellar spectra.

C. Diffusion. This effect results from the scattering of light by individual molecules of

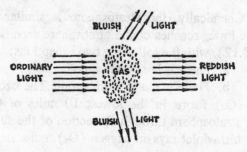

FIG. 13.13b. Ordinary light on going through a gas is partly diffused and partly transmitted. The diffused light is richer in the bluish wavelength; the transmitted part appears reddish because of its deficiency in the blue wavelengths.

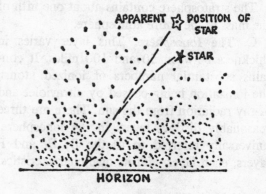

FIG. 13.13c. Because of refraction the real rays of a star are bent. The human eye sees the star higher in the sky than it really is. For stars close to the horizon the error may amount to half a degree.

air, the amount depending on the color of the light. Blue light is scattered or diffused much more readily than red light. This selective scattering accounts for both the blueness of the sky and the red and orange of sunsets: blueness results from the preference for it by the molecules of upper air, which scatter it in all directions; the red and orange, in that the direct rays of light at sunset are stripped of most of their blue, leaving the red to predominate. See Fig. 13.13b.

D. Refraction. Light on passing from interstellar space through the atmosphere is refracted, the amount increasing as the light approaches the denser layer close to the earth.

As a result, all celestial bodies appear higher

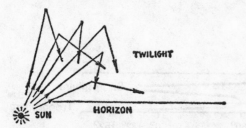

FIG. 13.13a. Twilight is due to the reflection of light by particles in the upper air. Because of this reflection, daytime continues for long after the sun has set, or considerably before the sun rises.

than they really are. The amount of elevation is greatest near the horizon and diminishes rapidly as it approaches the zenith overhead. Close to the horizon, it is slightly over half a degree. See Fig. 13.13c. At altitudes of 10° above the horizon, the amount diminishes to 1/10th of a degree; at zenith, of course, the amount is zero.

Refraction permits the stars and the sun to be seen shortly before they rise and for a short while after they have set.

Refraction also produces the twinkling of the stars. The density of the air at various levels changes fairly rapidly due to the winds prevailing at those levels. Starlight on its way through is refracted in amounts that vary from second to second. This accounts for the "high speed jumping," the "twinkling," of stars.

PART II: THE MOON

13.14 BASIC DATA

Symbol: ☾
Eccentricity of orbit: .055
Inclination of orbit to ecliptic: 5°9′
Period of one revolution about the earth:
  Sidereal 27.32 days
  Synodic 29.53 days
Orbital velocity: .64 miles per second
Distance from the earth:
  Min. 226,000 miles
  Max. 252,000 miles
Angular diameter: Mean 31 minutes, 5.2 seconds
Diameter: 2,160 miles
Volume: 1/50 times that of the earth
Mass: 1/81.3 times that of the earth
Density: .61 times that of the earth
Surface gravity: 1/6 times that of the earth
Velocity of escape: 1.48 miles per second
Period of rotation about axis: 27.32 days
Inclination of equator to orbit: 1.5°
Temperature:
  Min. −225° F
  Max. 225° F
Albedo: .07

13.15 INTRODUCTION

The earth has one satellite revolving continuously about it, while it is pursuing its own journey about the sun. Although its volume is only 1/50 and its mass 1/81 that of the earth, it affects the latter in a rather striking way. The periodic rise and fall of the ocean—the tides—is one instance of the moon's effect on the earth.

The extreme closeness of the moon has made possible its study since the early days of astronomy. The average distance is a mere 60 times the earth's radius.

Some data had been obtained by telescope; but much of what is known is from naked eye observations—much of this is, in fact, common knowledge—for example, the fact that the moon goes through a complete set of phases every month, from new to crescent, to quarter, and so on; and also that the moon moves in almost the same path as the sun.

That the moon rises each day an average of 51 minutes later than on the previous day is well known, as is the fact that part of the moon always faces the earth, while another part is always hidden.

13.16 THE MOON IN ITS ORBIT

The moon moves about the earth in an elliptical orbit, with the earth as one of its foci. **The point on the ellipse nearest the earth is called Perigee**—the distance between the moon at perigee and the earth is 221,463 miles. **The point on the ellipse farthest from the earth is known as Apogee,** and that distance is 252,710 miles. The moon traverses this path counterclockwise. See Fig. 13.16a.

The plane of the moon's orbit lies very close to the plane of the ecliptic, the apparent path of the sun on the celestial sphere and is inclined about 5° with the ecliptic. See Fig. 13.16b. **The two points at which the moon's path intersects the plane of the ecliptic are known as Nodes.** These are not constant in

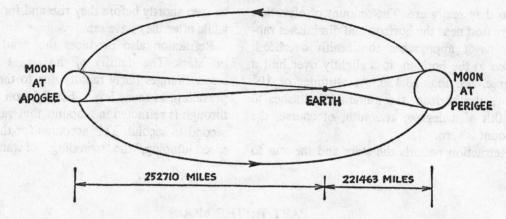

FIG. 13.16a. The moon in its orbit. An observer above the North Pole of the earth would see the moon describe an ellipse in a counterclockwise direction.

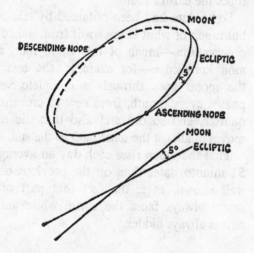

FIG. 13.16b. The orbit of the moon is inclined by 5° to the apparent orbit of the sun (the ecliptic). This can be seen both in perspective (above) and in the side view (below).

space, but move clockwise along the ecliptic, completing one revolution in nineteen years.

The moon seems to move along its orbit much faster than the sun: it takes the latter a full year to complete the circuit; the moon, only one month. Half of this time the moon is above the ecliptic; the other half, below it.

This seemingly faster motion causes the moon to rise and set a little later each day, the average delay being about 51 minutes.

13.17 OCEAN TIDES ON EARTH

The surface of the ocean rises and falls at any given place at more or less regular intervals. On an average, the period between two successive high tides is 12 hours and 25.5 minutes—exactly one half the time it takes the moon to complete the circuit about the earth, i.e., one half of 24 hours and 51 minutes. This is not a coincidence: the ocean tides are caused primarily by the moon's gravitational pull, an effect to which the sun contributes.

The formation of the tides is illustrated in a slightly exaggerated form in Figure 13.17a.

A represents the center of the solid earth; B is a body of water facing the moon; and C is a body of water on the opposite side of the earth.

The gravitational force of the moon is, of course, exerted on B and C as well as on A. The intensity of the force is largest at B, because of B's closeness to the moon and is least at C, because of its remoteness. The arrows on C, A, and B indicate the different sizes of lunar "pull." This difference in "pull" causes:

A. High tide at B, because it is pulled with greater force to the moon than at A.

B. High tide at C, because the earth is pulled away from it, thus leaving the water level high, relative to the earth.

C Low tide at the other two sides of the

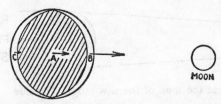

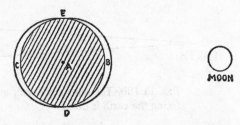

FIG. 13.17a. The formation of tides. The force at A pulling on the solid earth is larger than at C and hence the earth pulls away (toward the right) from C, causing the high tide there. The force at B is larger than at A and hence the body of water at B pulls away from the solid earth causing the high tide on the side of the earth facing the moon.

FIG. 13.17b. The water at B is "escaping" from the earth causing high tide there. The water at C is being left behind by the "escaping" earth causing high tide there. The bodies of water at E and D will be at low tide at that time.

earth, D and E, as the water flows from there to supply the high tide sides. See Fig. 13.17b.

The tides travel with the apparent motion of the moon, from the eastern horizon toward the western horizon of the observer. High tide at any place on the earth occurs when the moon is at the local meridian or at the antemeridian, except for lags (maybe as much as six hours) due to friction and other secondary effects.

The effect of the sun on tides is secondary to that of the moon—the ratio of the tide-raising force of the sun is only about 7 per cent that of the moon—because of its much greater distance.

When the tide-raising forces of the moon and the sun co-ordinate, the resulting tides are at a maximum—i.e., at new moon, when the two are at the same side of the earth. **Maximum tides are known as Spring Tides.** The other extreme is reached when the sun is at 90° to the moon—**the tides are then at a minimum and are known as Neap Tides.**

The moon's closeness also has an influence on the magnitude of the tide. When the moon is at perigee, the tide-raising force is greater than normal by some 20 per cent.

13.18 PHASES

The moon's apparent change in shape from a narrow crescent to a full circle and then again to a narrow crescent, is due to the fact

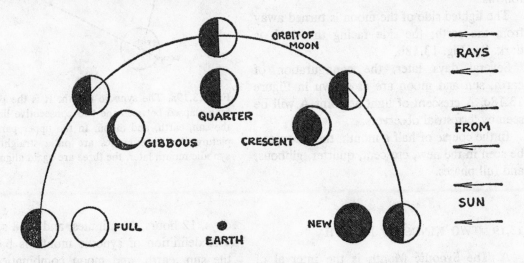

FIG. 13.18a. The moon in its various phases. The five circles along the orbit of the moon indicate the lighted hemisphere on the moon. The inner five circles indicate the corresponding illumination of the moon as seen from the earth.

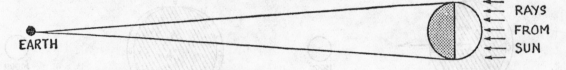

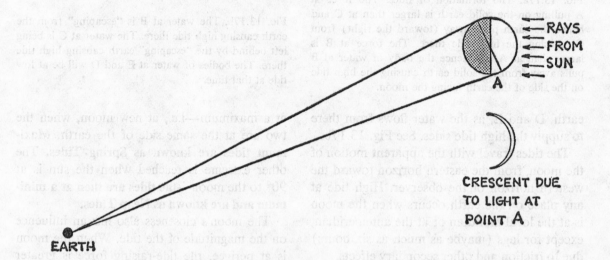

FIG. 13.18b. The sun, the earth, and the moon at the time of the new moon. The side facing the earth is dark.

FIG. 13.18c. The young moon. Part A of the moon's sunlit surface is now seen by terrestrial observers, in the form of a thin crescent.

that it revolves **around the earth** (see Fig. 13.18a), but it receives its illumination **from the sun.** At new moon the configuration is as follows:

The lighted side of the moon is turned away from the earth; the side facing the earth is dark. See Fig. 13.18b.

Several days later, the configuration of earth, sun and moon are as shown in Figure 13.18c. A crescent of light at point A will be seen by terrestrial observers.

In the course of half a month, the moon can be seen in the new, crescent, quarter, gibbous, and full phases.

13.19   TWO KINDS OF MONTH

A. **The Synodic Month** is the interval of time elapsed between two consecutive new moons, or two consecutive full moons: its duration is 29.53 days—or more exactly, 29

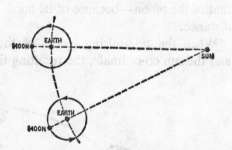

FIG. 13.19a. The synodic month. It is the period of time elapsed between the two consecutive lineups of the sun, earth, and moon. In the upper part of this picture the three bodies are on a straight line; a synodic month later, the three are again aligned.

days, 12 hours, 44 minutes, and 2.78 seconds. The definition of synodic month is based on the sun, earth, and moon combination. Another definition of the synodic month: **It is the average period of time elapsed between one alignment of the sun, earth, and moon and**

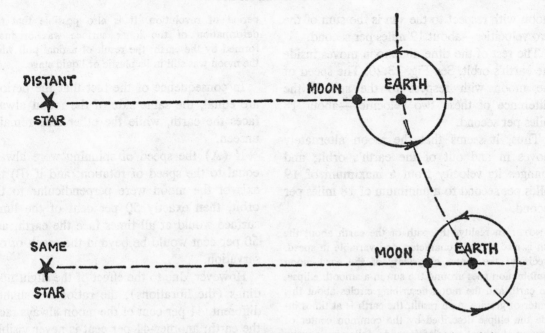

FIG. 13.19b. The sidereal month. This is the period of one complete revolution of the moon about the earth, as seen from a distant star.

the next. The synodic month is also known as the **Lunar Month.** See Fig. 13.19a.

B. **The Sidereal Month, or the Star Month,** is shorter than the synodic, its duration being only 27.32 days, or 27 days, 7 hours, 43 minutes, 11.47 seconds. The definition of the Sidereal Month is based on the fixed stars: **It is the period of time elapsed between two consecutive times that the earth and the moon are in line with the same fixed star.** See Fig. 13.19b.

The synodic month is longer because while the moon goes round the earth, the latter continues to revolve about the sun. The moon must travel a little farther before the three bodies are again in line.

13.20 PATH ABOUT THE SUN

With respect to the earth, the moon moves in a smooth ellipse with a speed that varies only slightly from an average value of .64 miles per second. With respect to the sun, both the path and the velocity of the moon are

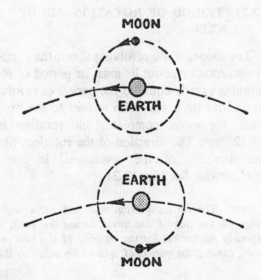

FIG. 13.20. The path of the moon about the sun. Half the time the moon is outside the earth's orbit, and moves in the same direction as the earth; the rest of the time the moon is inside the earth's orbit and moves in a direction opposite to that of the earth.

materially different—the path of the moon is wavy; the velocity, variable.

Half the time, approximately, the moon is outside the earth's orbit. The speed of the moon with respect to the sun is the sum of the two velocities—about 19 miles per second.

The rest of the time, the moon moves inside the earth's orbit. See Fig. 13.20. The speed of the moon with respect to the sun is the difference of these two velocities—about 18 miles per second.

Thus, it seems that the moon alternately moves in and out of the earth's orbit; and changes its velocity from a maximum of 19 miles per second to a minimum of 18 miles per second.

NOTE: In reality, the path of the earth about the sun is also wavy in character, and variable in speed. Precisely: the **center of gravity of the earth-moon combination** goes around the sun in a smooth ellipse, the earth and the moon describing circles about this center of gravity. As a result, the earth is at times inside the ellipse described by the common center of gravity; at other times, it is outside, following a wavy path with variable speed.

13.21 PERIOD OF ROTATION ABOUT ITS AXIS

The moon, while revolving about the earth, is also rotating about its axis. Its period of rotation is exactly equal to the period of revolution about the earth. With respect to the fixed stars, the moon completes one rotation in 27.32 days. The direction of the rotation, like the direction of the revolution, is counterclockwise. See Fig. 13.21.

NOTE: The earth's gravitational pull on a slight bulge on the side of the moon facing the earth is probably responsible for the equality of the two periods, causing the period of spin to be equal to the

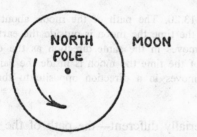

FIG. 13.21. An observer looking *down* at the north pole of the moon would see the moon spinning in a counterclockwise direction about its axis.

period of revolution. It is also possible that this deformation of the lunar surface was originally formed by the earth; the result of a tidal pull when the moon was still in its plastic or liquid stage.

In consequence of the fact that the periods are equal, the same side of the moon always faces the earth, while the other side remains unseen.

If (A) the speed of spinning were always equal to the speed of rotation; and if (B) the axis of the moon were perpendicular to the orbit, then exactly 50 per cent of the lunar surface would at all times face the earth, and 50 per cent would be beyond the reach of observation.

However, due to the effect of the slight noddings (the librations), the ratios are slightly different. 41 per cent of the moon always faces the earth; another 41 per cent is never visible; 18 per cent is sometimes visible and sometimes not.

13.22 LIBRATIONS

These apparent to-and-fro motions of the part of the moon facing the earth are called Librations. There are three kinds of librations: (A) longitudinal, (B) latitudinal, and (C) diurnal. Because of the longitudinal librations, an observer is able to see not only the "face" of the moon but also the "cheeks." Because of the latitudinal librations, the top of the "forehead" and the "chin" are alternately exposed. Diurnal librations depend upon the position of the observer on earth.

A. **Longitudinal Librations** of the moon are due to the fact that the spinning of the moon on its axis is at a constant speed, while its motion around the earth is at a variable speed. Spinning is sometimes ahead of and sometimes behind the revolving, thus alternately exposing the left side and the right side. See Fig. 13.22a.

B. **Librations in Latitude** are due to the inclination of the lunar axis to the lunar orbit. The moon's axis is tilted by 6½° to a perpendicular line to that orbit. Terrestrial observers can see 6½° past the northern pole of the

FIG. 13.22a. Librations in longitude. Because of these oscillatory motions, we are able to see not only the "face" of the moon, but also the right and left cheeks alternately.

FIG. 13.22b. Librations in latitude. Because of the tilt of the moon's axis to its orbit, observations can be made a little beyond the north pole as well as a little beyond the south pole of the moon. This is indicated in these figures by showing that during a period of two weeks the "forehead" of the "man in the moon" is in view, while during the other two weeks the "chin" is to be seen.

moon when that pole is tilted toward the earth; two weeks later, 6½° past the south pole of the moon is exposed. See Fig. 13.22b.

C. **The Diurnal Libration** is a small effect, maximum 1°. It is due to the fact that two widely separated observers on the earth would see slightly different hemispheres of the moon.

13.23 SURFACE

Even the unaided eye notices "marks" on the "face" of the moon, the meaning of which is revealed by the telescope. The surface of the moon is covered with (A) craters, (B) maria (seas), (C) mountains, (D) domes, (E) rills (clefts), and (F) rays (streaks).

A. **Craters.** The outstanding features of the moon's surface are mountain rings, which resemble somewhat craters of terrestrial volcanoes. The mountain rings vary greatly in

size, from about 150 miles in diameter down to mere fractions of a foot in diameter. The rims of these craters also vary considerably in height. Some of the craters are bounded by high walls rising 3 or 4 miles above the surrounding terrain; others have heights of only 1 foot or so.

It is estimated that there are perhaps 100,000 craters with radii greater than 1 mile.

The craters are found everywhere, in the three quarters of the moon's surface covered by rough mountainous regions, as well as in the quarter of the surface occupied by the marias. There are even craters within craters within craters.

Computation shows that the volume of soil piled up on the rim of each crater is equal to the void in the pit.

The prominent craters have been named for noted scientists and philosophers. See Figs. 13.23a and b for the names of some of the craters on both the near and far sides of the moon. (The far side of the moon is that side of the moon not visible from the earth. The first pictures of it were taken by the U.S.S.R. spacecraft Lunik 3 in 1959.)

The origin of the lunar craters is still a mat-

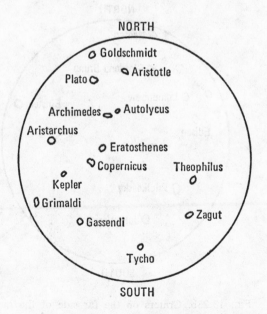

FIG. 13.23a. Craters on the near side of the moon. These can be seen from the earth at all times.

ter of speculation. There are two schools of thought. One assumes the craters to be of volcanic origin, the other suggests that they were caused by the impact of giant meteorites. These ideas will be discussed in detail in Sec. 13.27.

B. Maria. This name (Latin for "seas") was mistakenly given to the darker and smoother areas on the surface of the moon by Galileo in the early seventeenth century. Very likely at one time they were seas of molten lava; if so, they have long since hardened to form a rigid crust. They differ, at present, from the rest of the lunar surface by being poor reflectors of sunlight—i.e., their albedo value is low.

Many of these maria have been definitely outlined and named. Typical names are Mare Crisium (Sea of Crises, or Conflicts), Mare Fecunditatis (Sea of Fruitfulness), and Mare Serenitatis (Sea of Serenity). See Fig. 13.23c. The seas are approximately circular in shape and all but a few are interconnected. The diameter of the seas is in the hundreds of miles.

C. Mountains. There are many mountain ranges on the lunar surface, as well as many isolated mountain peaks. Several of the ranges have been named for terrestrial mountain

FIG. 13.23c. Several Maria on the near side of the moon, i.e., on the side that always faces the earth.

ranges (e.g., Alps, Apennines); others, for eminent mathematicians and astronomers (e.g., Leibnitz). Some of the lunar mountains rise to greater heights than the earthly ones. Several peaks of the Leibnitz range, which lies near the south pole of the moon, rise to heights exceeding that of Mount Everest, the highest peak on earth.

D. Domes. Many domes dot the surface of the moon. They appear not unlike mountains of volcanic origin on the earth.

E. Rills. Rills are long crevices in the surface of the moon. Some narrow, others more than a mile wide, they cut across other surface features, up to distances in the hundreds of miles.

F. Rays. Rays are light-colored streaks on the surface of the moon, radiating in all directions from several of the more prominent craters.

These are best observed, because most conspicuous, near the period of full moon. They are 10 to 15 miles wide and at times stretch over other surface features for 500 to 2,000 miles.

FIG. 13.23b. Craters on the far side of the moon. The first pictures of these craters were taken by the Soviet spacecraft Lunik 3 in 1959.

13.24 SURFACE GRAVITY

The **Surface Gravity** of the moon is only one sixth that of the earth. This can easily be computed from the known figures of the radius of the moon and from its mass. Thus the weight of every object on the surface of the moon is only one sixth its weight on earth, and a body thrown upward would rise six times higher on the moon than on earth.

A direct result of the low value of the surface gravity is a low value of escape velocity, which in turn accounts for an absence of atmosphere. The escape velocity is 1.5 miles per second, so that a particle of gas having an initial velocity of 1.5 miles per second has enough speed to escape from the gravitational pull of the moon. Since 1.5 miles per second is a sufficiently common value for atmospheric gases at temperatures prevalent on the moon, if the moon ever had an atmosphere, it has long since escaped.

Research verifies the absence of atmosphere: experiments performed during a total solar eclipse show conclusively that rays of solar light grazing the surface of the moon are not refracted. Also the spectrum of light from the moon is the same as that from the sun, hence there are no gases on the lunar surface.

13.25 TEMPERATURE

The **temperature range** on the moon's surface is very large. The surface is exposed to the rays of the sun continuously for a period of two weeks and then deprived of sunlight for an equal period of time. The difference in temperature between the light and the dark side is increased by the absence of an atmosphere and by the low value of .07 for the albedo.

Measurements of radiation that reach the earth from the sunlit side of the moon register temperatures well above the boiling point of water (212° F); measurements taken of the dark side of the moon indicate extreme cold there. The temperature of the dark side is probably close to −225° F.

The sun's heat does not penetrate very deeply below the moon's surface. This is evident from studies of lunar eclipses. The temperature at the moon's surface drops rapidly as soon as the supply of sunlight ceases. A change of 100° F in one hour is the rule. The temperature rises with even greater speed soon after the surface emerges from the darkness.

13.26 SPACE AGE STUDIES OF THE MOON

The space age has added several important tools for the study of the moon.

Before that age began, indeed, as late as the 1950s, all our knowledge of the moon was based on analyses of the visible, infrared, and radio waves; that is, the sunlight reflected by the moon, the radiation emitted by the moon, and the radio waves that were reflections of waves originally produced on the earth.

Some of the accomplishments in lunar exploration of the last several decades, presented chronologically, are as follows:

A. October 1959. The Soviet spacecraft Lunik 3 took the first photographs of the far side of the moon, the surface not visible from the earth. The far side turned out to have the same features as the near side, with one exception, namely, it has fewer and smaller maria.

B. 1964 and 1965. The American Ranger spacecraft series transmitted photographs as well as television pictures of the moon, up to the moment of crashlanding on the moon's surface. The photographs brought out clearly a great deal of detail on the lunar surface.

C. 1966 to 1968. The Surveyor space-craft series, also American, soft-landed on the moon and took pictures as well as tested, with the aid of a soil sampler, the chemical and physical properties of the lunar surface.

NOTES: These tests led to the following discoveries:
  a. The lunar surface could support the weight of a vehicle.
  b. The soil was granular, the grains coming in a variety of sizes.
  c. The particles cohered one to another, somewhat as wet sand does on earth.
  d. The soil was compactible and has a den-

sity of about 1.5 grams per cubic centimeter.

e. Numerous objects were scattered all over the surface; some of these were hard rocks, other crumbled easily when struck.

f. The lunar material resembled chemically crushed basalt on earth (this result was achieved using a lab method known as alpha-particle back-scattering procedure).

D. 1966 and on. The American Lunar Orbiter spacecraft series, originally designed to make a complete photographic layout of the surface of the moon, was instrumental in discovering (in 1968) an increase in the downward gravitational pull over one of the large seas.

NOTE: It is now assumed that there are large high-density mass concentrations (mass concentration is abbreviated "mascon") under each of the large maria.

Among the facts about the moon that were determined by expeditions are the following:

A. There is indeed dust in the moon, and it clings to everything and to everyone. It is usually several inches deep. Under the dust is a layer, several feet deep, of large chunks of broken rock, called the regolith, and under that is the bedrock.

B. Some of the rocks strewn on the surface are of igneous origin, probably formed by cooling of lava some 4 billion years ago. Other rocks are of the breccia type, namely, rocks formed by cementing or pressing together small fragments of older rocks, the older rock being 4.5 billion years old.

In addition to the igneous rocks and the breccia, fragments of iron meteorites and glass particles were found.

C. The lunar rocks are by and large similar to rocks formed from magma within our earth. One difference worth noting is that the titanium content is materially higher in lunar rocks as compared to its terrestrial counterpart.

D. Very sensitive seismometers placed on the moon indicated (1) a scarcity of quakes (moonquakes), indicating that the moon is now a solid, and has a relatively cool interior;

(2) that the few quakes which did trigger the seismometer were due either to the tidal effect of the earth (and took place when the moon was either nearest or farthest from the earth) or to the impact of abandoned spacecraft or incoming meteorites.

The lunar module of Apollo 12, which was sent crashing to the lunar surface after the astronauts rejoined the parent craft, caused the moon to vibrate at a rate of one cycle per second for more than half an hour. Similar vibrations were caused by the impact of the lunar module of Apollo 14. The most plausible explanation given at this time is that the vibrations are due to the fact that the lunar material is not homogenous and therefore the waves from the impact arrive at the seismometer via different routes at different times.

E. The magnetometer placed on the moon by Apollo 12 astronauts detected a field of less than 1 per cent the intensity of the earth's magnetic field near the equator. It is not impossible that magnetic fields on the moon are due primarily to the presence of scattered magnetized iron meteorites.

13.27 BIOGRAPHY OF THE MOON

To the best of our knowledge the moon, like the earth and like the sun, was "born" about 4.5 billion years ago. At that time a large chunk of a cloud of gas and dust separated itself from the rest of the cloud and in response to the force of gravity began to contract and therefore to heat up.

It eventually shrank to its present size and shape.

The low surface gravity and the high surface temperature of the moon caused the escape of the light gases.

Heat radiating from the surface of the moon caused the sphere to change into liquid. Then the surface of the moon solidified and a billion years later the interior of the moon solidified as well.

As noted in Sec. 13.23, there are two theories concerning the formation of the lunar surface. The most probable is the following:

The meteorites encountered by the moon along its orbit were responsible for the surface features existing at present. Most of them produced craters, while a few of the very big ones were able to breach the surface when the interior of the moon was still fluid and produced a flow of lava that covered and obliterated all the existing craters in that neighborhood. Radioactive studies of the igneous rock in Mare Tranquilitatis indicate that this flow of lava took place some 3.7 billion years ago.

Evidently at that time a large meteorite breached the lunar surface, and the outflowing lava produced that mare. Craters now seen in this sea are "younger" than 3.7 billion years.

Large meteorites may very well be resting now under all the seas and be responsible for the extra pull of gravity experienced in overflights.

This, then, is the likely series of events of the formation of the surface features several billions of years ago, and with the following two exceptions these are the same features that the moon has now. No wind or rain has brought about erosion in the craters or in the mare, with two exceptions:

A. Possibly there is still a very small residual volcanic activity in the interior of the moon. The presence of domes on the surface is attributed to that activity.

B. The dust, the broken rock, and the stray rocks and rubble on the surface are due to the continuous sweeping by the moon of meteoroids and micrometeoroids encountered along its path.

13.28 A TRIP TO THE MOON

Six manned American Apollo vehicles have landed on the surface of the moon, the first (Apollo 11) launched on July 16, 1969, the sixth of the series (Apollo 17) on December 7, 1972. The approximate landing locations are indicated in Figure 13.28a. All the landing sites were on the near side of the moon.

FIG. 13.28a. Landing sites of the Apollo voyages during the years 1969–1972.

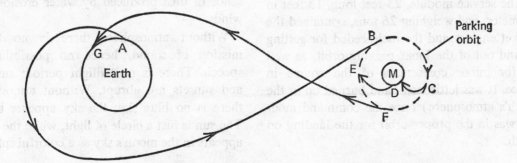

FIG. 13.28b. The trip to the moon (not to scale). A: Lift-off from earth. B: Entering parking orbit. C: Lunar module separates from command module. D: Landing on moon (M). E: Lunar module rejoins command module. F: Spacecraft leaves parking orbit. G: Splash-down on earth.

(There would have been no means of radio communication with a spacecraft landing on the far side of the moon.)

Each Apollo mission carried a crew of three, two members actually landing on the lunar surface, while the third was responsible for circling the mother ship in the parking orbit.

The crew of Apollo 11 consisted of Neil A. Armstrong, Edwin E. Aldrin, Jr., and Michael Collins. The first two were the first humans to have landed on the surface of our satellite (July 20, 1969, at 4:17:20 o'clock P.M., EDT).

The spacecraft in all of the Apollo missions consisted of three main parts: the command, service, and lunar modules. A Saturn V rocket was used to get the spacecraft off the earth and into space on its journey to the moon.

The trip to the moon was in two parts. At the end of the first part the whole spacecraft was placed in a circular orbit about 70 miles above the surface of the moon. In the second part two members of the crew, using the lunar module, descended to the surface of the moon. See Fig. 13.28b.

The command module, 11 feet tall, with a base diameter of 13 feet, and weighing more than 5 tons was the "home away from home" and the communication center during the round trip for the three astronauts. Since it was the only module that returned to the earth, it had a heat shield to screen it from the heat developed during the re-entry into the earth's atmosphere.

The service module, 23 feet long, 13 feet in diameter, and weighing 26 tons, contained the rocket engines and the fuel needed for getting in and out of the lunar parking orbit, as well as for minor corrections of the course in space. It was jettisoned (and burned up in the earth's atmosphere) once the command module was in the proper orbit for the landing on earth.

The lunar module, 20 feet high, 13 feet in diameter, and weighing more than 15 tons, was designed to carry two members of the crew from the lunar parking orbit to the moon and back to the command module. It contained guidance and electronic equipment, two sets of engines, and fuel supplies. One of the engines was designed to slow down the descent to the moon and set the vehicle gently down on its surface. The second set was used to lift the module from the moon and return it to the mother ship. The lunar module, its task completed, was jettisoned and either left behind to circle the moon forever or sent crashing to the surface of the moon so that the effect of its impact on the seismometers on the moon could be studied.

The Saturn V rocket designed especially for the Apollo project was more than 300 feet high, weighed (fuel included) about 3,000 tons, and used up, in the first 2.5 minutes of the flight, more than 2,000 tons of kerosene and liquid oxygen.

13.29　LIFE ON THE MOON

The moon is an arid, barren waste. It has neither atmosphere, water, vegetation, nor animal life.

The absence of water also implies an absence of clouds in the sky, as well as an absence of dust produced by water erosion and winds.

Without atmosphere there is no transmission of sound, hence no possibility of speech. There is no twilight period; sunrises and sunsets are abrupt. Without atmosphere there is no blue sky; the sky appears black. The sun is just a circle of light, while the earth appears in the moon's sky as a colorful sphere.

CHAPTER 14

ECLIPSES OF THE SUN AND THE MOON

14.1 INTRODUCTION

A. Eclipse of the Moon. The earth, in its orbital motion around the sun, is accompanied by its shadow, which extends into space in a direction opposite to that of the sun.

The shadow has the shape of a cone, the base of which is the cross-section of the earth, the average length of which is 858,000 miles. Because of the variation in distance between the earth and the sun, the length of the shadow may differ from the average by about 25,000 miles.

A lunar eclipse occurs when the moon enters the shadow-cone. See Fig. 14.1a.

B. Eclipse of the Sun. The moon, following its path about the earth, carries its shadow along with it.

This shadow, too, has the shape of a cone,

though much slimmer than the earth's shadow-cone, the diameter of its base being a mere 2,160 miles. The length of the moon's shadow is on the average equal to 232,000 miles, varying by about 4,000 miles either way. See Fig. 14.1b.

Often it is not quite long enough to reach the earth. The moon-earth distance varies from 226,000 miles at perigee, to 252,000 miles at apogee; the mean distance being 239,000 miles. See Fig. 14.1c.

A solar eclipse occurs when the earth's surface cuts off part of the shadow-cone, i.e., truncates the cone.

When the shadow-cone does not quite reach the surface, a phenomenon known as **Annular Eclipse or Ring Eclipse occurs.** Under those circumstances, the apparent cross section of the moon is too small to cover the apparent di-

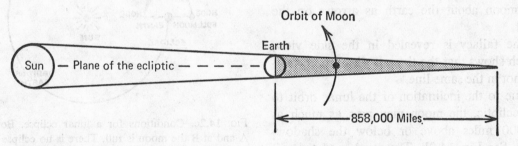

FIG. 14.1a. Lunar eclipse. This kind of eclipse occurs when the moon is inside the shadow-cone of the earth. A lunar eclipse can be observed from any point on the night side of the earth.

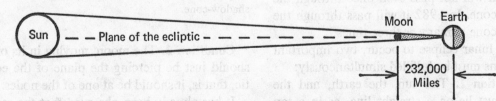

FIG. 14.1b. Solar eclipse. A total eclipse of the sun can be seen by terrestrial observers at all places on the earth touched by the moon's shadow-cone. When the shadow-cone does not quite reach the earth an annular (or ring) eclipse of the sun takes place.

ameter of the sun, and the "outskirts" of the sun, in the form of a bright ring, are visible to the observer.

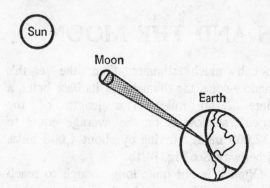

FIG. 14.1c. A total solar eclipse can be seen by terrestrial observers anywhere along the arc described by the truncated shadow-cone of the moon.

14.2 CONDITIONS FOR A LUNAR ECLIPSE

A top view of the ecliptic would mislead one to think that there should be one lunar eclipse a month. This top view is shown in Figure 14.2a. The apparent orbit of the sun about the earth, the ecliptic, is shown in this figure as the heavy line on the left, the orbit of the moon about the earth as arrows on the right.

The fallacy is revealed in the side view, which shows that the three bodies are, in reality, not in the same line.

Due to the inclination of the lunar orbit to the ecliptic, the moon may pass as much as 20,000 miles above or below the shadow-cone. See Fig. 14.2b. The number of times it passed through the shadow is a small fraction of those it crosses above and below it. In 1976 the moon will not pass even once through the shadow-cone. In 1982 it will pass through the shadow-cone as many as three times.

For a lunar eclipse to occur, two important conditions must be fulfilled simultaneously:

Condition 1. The sun, the earth, and the moon must lie on a straight line, as in a top view—that is, the moon must be in its full phase as seen from the earth. This occurs once every month.

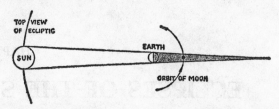

FIG. 14.2a. Top view of ecliptic. Looking down at the apparent orbit of the sun and the orbit of the moon, one gets the mistaken impression that lunar eclipses should occur once every month.

FIG. 14.2b. Side view of the ecliptic. This view points up the fact that the moon is actually not in a straight line with the sun and the earth. The moon in its inclined orbit may pass by as much as 20,000 miles above or below the shadow-cone.

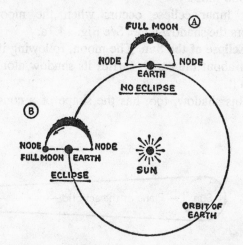

FIG. 14.2c. Conditions for a lunar eclipse. Both at A and at B the moon is full. There is no eclipse at A because the moon is well above the ecliptic; it will pass above the shadow-cone of the earth. There is an eclipse at B because the moon is in the plane of the ecliptic and will have to go through the earth's shadow-cone.

Condition 2. The moon, moving in its orbit, should just be piercing the plane of the ecliptic, that is, it should be at one of the nodes.

It has already been observed that the moon, half a month, is below the plane of the ecliptic and above the other half. **The points at which the moon pierces the ecliptic plane are known** as Nodes: one, the Ascending Node; the other, the Descending Node. **The line joining the two is called the Nodal Line.**

Figure 14.2c shows two positions of the moon in which Condition 1 is fulfilled. Both at A and B the moon is full.

There is no lunar eclipse at A; the moon in its orbit is far above the ecliptic. There will be a lunar eclipse at B because the full moon occurs at the time when the moon is at a node.

14.3 DURATION OF A LUNAR ECLIPSE

A lunar eclipse is of relatively long duration, as the thickness of the earth's shadow-cone where the moon passes through it is nearly 5,700 miles. If the moon passes centrally, it would be totally eclipsed for a period of close to two hours, since the moon's diameter is 2,160 miles and its average speed is 2,000 miles an hour. See Fig. 14.3.

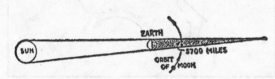

FIG. 14.3. Duration of a lunar eclipse. It takes the moon nearly an hour to enter the shadow. If the moon passes centrally through the cone the total eclipse time will be nearly two hours. The emerging lasts an hour.

The earth's shadow does not hide the moon altogether. Even when totally eclipsed, it is quite visible, its normal brilliance being replaced by a rather dull reddish color. This slight illumination is due to sunlight that is refracted by the earth's atmosphere into the shadow-cone. The blue and violet components of the sunlight are presumably removed by diffusion in the earth's atmosphere, the red components being responsible for the illumination of the lunar disk.

14.4 PARTIAL LUNAR ECLIPSES

In the case of a partial eclipse, only part of the moon passes through the shadow-cone, the normally full moon then appearing with a darkened notch either at its north or south side.

Partial eclipses, of course, precede as well as follow every total lunar eclipse. It takes about an hour for the full face of the moon to enter the shadow, and a similar period to emerge completely from the shadow.

14.5 SERIES OF LUNAR ECLIPSES

Eclipses come in series, a complete series consisting of either forty-eight or forty-nine individual eclipses, extending over a period of 865 years. The interval between two successive eclipses in a series is 6,585⅓ days. Successive eclipses show close resemblance to one another, demonstrating series-membership.

The process of deriving the figure 6,585⅓ follows:

In order to have a repetition of an eclipse:

A. The moon must again be full. This condition occurs every 29.53059 days.

B. The sun must again be in the same position with respect to the nodes. This occurs at intervals of 346.6201 days.

The least common multiple of these numbers is 6,585, that is, that every 6,585 days (or, exactly, 6585⅓ days) the moon, earth and sun will align to repeat a previous eclipse. The time interval of 6,585⅓ days is known as a **Saros,** a word meaning "repetition" in the language of the ancient Babylonians.

Many series of eclipses are going on simultaneously—at present, there are twenty-eight series of lunar eclipses in progress. For this reason, as many as three lunar eclipses may occur in any one calendar year. Three eclipses is the possible maximum; the minimum is, of course, zero.

Total eclipses of the moon in the next few years will take place on Sept. 6, '79; Jan. 9, '82; July 6, '82; Dec. 30, '82; May 4, '85; Oct. 28, '85; Apr. 24, '86; Oct. 17, '86.

14.6 ECLIPSES OF THE SUN

Eclipses of the sun differ in several important ways from those of the moon:

A. Solar eclipses can occur only at new moon; lunar eclipse, only during full moon.

B. All lunar eclipses, both total or partial, can be observed simultaneously from every point on the terrestrial hemisphere that is turned toward the moon. Only the thinnest part of the shadow-cone produced by the moon ever touches the earth. The maximum diameter of the circle intercepted by the earth's surface is less than 170 miles. A much larger diameter is intercepted in the case of penumbra—that diameter is close to 4,000 miles.

The shadow-cone itself is often called the **Umbra** (Latin for "shadow"); the half-tone region in Figure 14.6a is called the **Penumbra.** Observers in that region will see only a partial eclipse of the sun, the percentage of the sun's surface eclipsed depending on the distance to the umbra—the closer it is, the greater the percentage.

As the moon and its shadow-cone move in their assigned orbits, the small circle and the circle due to the penumbra follow. A typical route pursued by an eclipse is shown in Figure 14.6b, taken from the publication by the nautical almanac office of the U. S. Naval Observatory in Washington, D.C., known as *The American Ephemeris and Nautical Almanac.* The moon's shadow-cone first touches the earth near the west coast of South America and, moving eastward, leaves the earth 3¼

hours later near the east coast of Africa. The total eclipse band in this case is less than 100 miles wide.

The speed of the shadow on the earth depends greatly on latitude and the angle the shadow-cone makes with the earth's surface. At the equator, the speed may be only 1,000 miles per hour. In higher latitudes, especially near sunrise or sunset when the shadow-cone is greatly slanted to the earth's surface, it may be 5,000 miles per hour.

C. The duration of the total part of a lunar eclipse is nearly two hours, the greatest possible duration of a solar eclipse at any one point on the earth's surface is 7 minutes and 30 seconds.

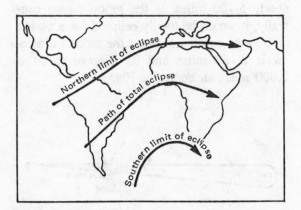

FIG. 14.6b. Path of a typical total solar eclipse. The width of the totality path is less than 100 miles. The northern and southern limits indicate the regions on the earth from which a partial solar eclipse can be observed. The arrows indicate the direction of the eclipse's path.

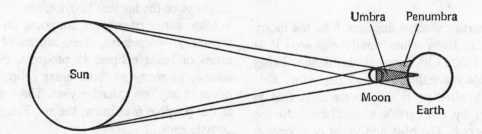

FIG. 14.6a. The umbra and penumbra. The dark cone is the umbra. Observers located at that place on the earth will see a total eclipse of the sun. The half-dark region next to the shadow-cone is the penumbra. Terrestrial observers located there will see a partial eclipse of the sun.

14.7 SERIES OF SOLAR ECLIPSES

Solar eclipses, too, occur in series, a complete series containing seventy or seventy-one eclipses and lasting about 1,260 years. The period of 6,585⅓ days between two successive eclipses in one series is identical in length to that of lunar eclipses.

The seventy or seventy-one eclipses of any solar series follow a pattern. The first one of a series is always a very small partial eclipse near one of the earth's poles. Subsequent ones are less and less partial and occur farther from the pole. The eclipses that occur near the middle of a series are of the "total eclipse" kind; their route on the earth's surface is farther and farther away from the pole at which the series first made its appearance. Toward the end of the series, the eclipses again become progressively partial, the last one of the series appearing at the opposite pole of the earth from which they entered.

Due to the time denoted by the fraction in the figure 6,585⅓, each member of a series appears farther west as compared with its predecessor. The change in longitude is nearly 120 degrees, as the earth has turned ⅓ of a revolution about its own axis during that time. After each three eclipses the trace returns to the original longitude. The latitude will be farther south or farther north, depending on whether the series had its start at the north or the south pole of the earth. See Fig. 14.7.

There is no need to wait almost eighteen years (6,585⅓ days) to see a solar eclipse; at present, eleven solar series are producing eclipses. Two of these, known as numbers 6 and 7, are producing eclipses of particularly long duration. Series 5 is of special interest as its path is along easily accessible places and it is of moderate (2.5 minutes) duration.

The minimum number of solar eclipses in any calendar year is two. The maximum is five.

14.8 CATALOG OF ECLIPSES

The Austrian astronomer Theodor Oppolzer (1841–86) published a catalog in which are

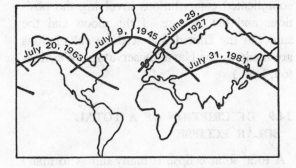

FIG. 14.7. Four members of a series of solar eclipses.
NOTE: (a) The period between successive eclipses in one series is nearly eighteen years (6,585⅓ days).
b) Each member is located one third of a revolution west of its predecessor.
c) If the series started at the North Pole, each successive member would be seen further south on the earth.

detailed descriptions of nearly 8,000 solar eclipses and 5,200 lunar eclipses between 1207 B.C. and A.D. 2162; the tracks of all the solar eclipses are shown on the catalog's nearly 160 charts. Some of those of long duration that will occur in the last quarter of our century are listed below.

Table 14.8. Solar Eclipses of Long Duration, 1976–2000.

Date	Where visible	Duration in minutes
Oct. 23, 1976	Zaire, Indian Ocean, New Zealand	5
Feb. 26, 1979	U. S. Pacific Northwest, Greenland	3
Feb. 16, 1980	Central Africa, India	4
June 11, 1983	Indian Ocean, Eastern Indonesia, Coral Sea	5
July 11, 1991	Marshall Islands, Central Mexico, Brazil	6
Nov. 3, 1994	East Indies, Australia, Argentina	4
Feb. 26, 1998	Central Pacific, Venezuela, Atlantic Ocean.	4

The time of each eclipse can be predicted to within less than two seconds, and its path to within less than a quarter of a mile, based on complicated computations involving the positions and the motions of the moon and the sun. (In the United States, these calculations are made by the Naval Observatory, Washington, D.C.)

14.9 DESCRIPTION OF A TOTAL SOLAR ECLIPSE

A total solar eclipse is many things to many people. To the primitive and the superstitious, it may cause great consternation and fright. Battles have been suspended and peace treaties signed in consequence of solar eclipses. For most of us, however, the total solar eclipse is simply a magnificent spectacle. The scientist is additionally interested since several important observations can be made only during the several minutes of totality, and so he or she may travel halfway across the world to observe the phenomenon at totality.

The shadow-cone of the eclipse moves across the face of the sun from west to east, covering more and more of its western limb. Several important stages may be observed:

The first contact can be observed only by looking at the sun through smoked glass or overexposed photographic film. See A in Fig. 14.9.

As the darkened western limb becomes larger, both the intensity and the quality of the sunlight change—it has less blue than the light from the center of the disk. See B in Fig. 14.9.

In the last stages of the partial phase, the weird color of sunlight proceeding from the crescent is heavily accentuated, the dim, strange light seeming to affect both animals and plants: birds fly about, twittering; roosters crow; and dogs bark excitedly. See C in Fig. 14.9.

Shortly before the phase of totality, fowl go to roost and many flowers close their blossoms, as they normally do at sundown. Images of the crescent sun appear in the shadows of tree leaves. See D in Fig. 14.9.

Several minutes before the beginning of totality, ghostly shadow bands appear to be crossing over any exposed white surface. The

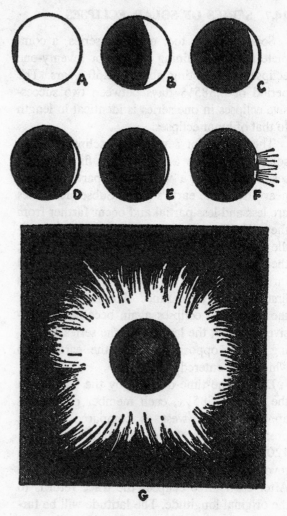

FIG. 14.9.

bands are atmospheric waves made visible by the narrow crescent of sunlight. See E in Fig. 14.9.

A few seconds before totality, only several beams of sunlight reach the earth through the valleys on the moon's limb. (These are the so-called "Baily's Beads.") Those brilliant beads vanish almost at once and their disappearance marks the beginning of totality. See F in Fig. 14.9.

At totality, the full beauty of the corona is on display. The pearly halo surrounds the sun and, often, clearly defined streamers are seen emanating from the corona proper. Stars and planets make their appearance, adding greatly to the majesty of the scene. See G in Fig. 14.9.

Totality may last as much as 7½ minutes. The uncovering of the sun then begins with the appearance of Baily's Beads on its western limb. All the phenomena that were seen at the eclipsing stage are repeated now in reverse order.

14.10 SCIENTIFIC INTEREST IN SOLAR ECLIPSES

Total solar eclipses offer unique opportunities to pursue several kinds of research:

A. The solar atmosphere can best be studied at the time of an eclipse; in particular, many photographs are taken of the flash spectrum, which is used to determine the exact thickness of the reversing layer, and in studies concerning the chemical elements constituting the layer.

B. A careful search is made in the immediate neighborhood of the sun for an intra-Mercurial planet—that is, for a planet closer to the sun than Mercury.

C. Contact times of the moon and the sun during eclipses serve as a check on the formulas used in determining the relative motions of these bodies.

D. Recent total eclipses were used to check the Einstein "bending." According to Einstein's general theory of relativity, light from stars should be slightly "bent" on passing close to the sun, due primarily to the effect of the gravitational pull of the solar mass on the rays of light. The values of the "bending," as forecast by Einstein's theory, correspond very closely to the ones found at the times of solar eclipses.

CHAPTER 15

THE SUPERIOR PLANETS

PART I: THE PLANET MARS

15.1 BASIC DATA

Symbol: ♂
Distance to sun:
    Min.   129,000,000 miles
    Mean 142,000,000 miles
    Max.   154,000,000 miles
Eccentricity of orbit: .09
Inclination of orbit to ecliptic: 1.9°
Period of one revolution about the sun:
    Sidereal 687 days
    Synodic 780 days
Orbital velocity: 15 miles per second
Distance from earth:
    Min.   35,000,000 miles
    Max. 247,000,000 miles
Angular diameter:
    Min. 3.6"
    Max. 24.5"
Diameter:
    Min. (polar)   4,200 miles
    Max. (equatorial) 4,220 miles

Volume: .15 times that of the earth
Mass: .108 times that of the earth
Density: .7 times that of the earth
Surface gravity: .38 times that of the earth
Velocity of escape: 3.2 miles per second
Period of rotation about axis: 24 hours 37 minutes 22.6 seconds
Inclination of planet's equator to orbit: 25.2°
Temperature:
    Min. −150° F
    Max.   80° F
Albedo: .15
NOTE: Methods used to derive the above data are detailed in Secs. 11.34 to 11.52.

15.2 INTRODUCTION

Because Mars is unique in many ways, it is doubtless the most studied planet. Lowell Observatory (near Flagstaff, Arizona) was designed for the express purpose of studying the planets in general and Mars in particular.

It was also the most controversial planet: facts submitted by some astronomers were strongly doubted by others—thus, for example, some claimed to have seen artificial lines of irrigation which could only have been built by intelligent beings; others denied that such lines exist.

(The remote possibility that there is some form of life has been exploited by writers of pseudo-scientific fiction and producers of highly imaginary films and television shows.)

Mars is notable for its red color and its variable brilliance—when close to earth, it is nearly fifty times brighter than when it is at maximum distance from earth.

15.3 THE ORBITS OF MARS AND THE EARTH

The orbit of Mars is just outside that of the earth. Once every synodic period (about 780 days) the two planets are in line with the sun and to one side; and once every period they are in line on opposite sides of the sun. **The first is called Opposition, when Mars and the sun are on opposite sides of the earth; the second is called Conjunction, when the sun and Mars are in the same direction as viewed from earth.**

Because of the eccentricity of Mars' orbit, the two planets do not follow equidistant tracks, the distance at opposition between them varying from a minimum of 35 million miles to a maximum of 63 million miles. See Fig. 15.3. They are closest near the point occupied by earth on August 25 and most distant during February. Oppositions on or near the August date are called "favorable oppositions" and occur at intervals of fifteen or seventeen years—the next ones will be due in July 1986 and September 1988.

Most of our information about the planet is obtained during such favorable approaches.

The farthest Mars can be from earth is at conjunction, when the distance is 247,000-000 miles, more than seven times farther than when at favorable opposition.

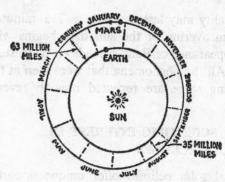

FIG. 15.3. The orbits of Mars and earth.

15.4 THE SURFACE OF THE PLANET

A. THROUGH THE TELESCOPE

The best telescopes show that the surface of Mars is a patchwork of several colors: reddish, gray, and white.

The reddish areas are presumably deserts, their color is uniform and constant and they extend over 60 per cent of the planet's surface. The gray areas, covering about 40 per cent of the planet's surface, change from gray in the Martian winter to blue-gray in the summer. The reddish areas are predominant in the northern hemisphere, the gray in the southern.

The white surfaces are found near both the north and the south poles of the planet and show marked variations with the local season. The white cap appears at the beginning of winter when the particular pole is pointing away from the sun and very often disappears from view during the summer when the same pole points toward the sun. The north and south poles of the planet thus alternate in the possession of white cover.

The white cap builds up at a very rapid rate. In several days it may extend some 20° to 30° from the pole. This period is followed by a long period (the winter season) of stagnation, when it will remain essentially unchanged. With the advent of spring, it contracts greatly and breaks up into several small irregular white spots; these disappear altogether with the approach of summer.

The south polar cap generally becomes larger than the northern one; and it is also the one most likely to disappear entirely during the summer in Mars' southern hemisphere.

B. DATA FROM THE SPACE PROBES

Our present knowledge of the surface of Mars is based primarily on the findings of the Mariner 4, 6, 7, and 9 space probes.

Mariner 4 flew by Mars on July 15, 1965, came within 6,200 miles of its surface, and radioed back twenty-one fine photographs of its surface. Many more excellent pictures were obtained from Mariner 6, which came within 2,000 miles of the surface on July 31, 1969, on an equatorial orbit, and from Mariner 7 which came within 2,000 miles on August 5, 1969, part of its orbit being over Mars' south pole.

Mariner 9, launched in November 1971, was designed to become a satellite of Mars (the first man-made satellite to orbit a planet) and to send back a steady flow of photographs and scientific data from various points along its orbit. The orbit ranged from 1,025 to 10,610 miles above the surface of the planet. By the time the instruments were turned off, nearly a year after its launch, this spacecraft transmitted a vast amount of information, that has enormously enhanced our knowledge of Mars.

The findings of these probes seem to indicate that the surface of Mars is both lunarlike and earthlike, both dead and alive.

Several specific observations based on the four probes are the following: Similar to the moon, the surface of Mars is covered by:

A. **Craters.** Craters come in various sizes. Some are hundreds of miles in diameter, others only a few hundred feet across. The Martian craters differ from their lunar counterparts in that their rims are much less sharp and their floors are shallower. Some of the smaller craters form lines that appeared as artificial channels to early observers. Here, too, as in the case of the moon, the assumption is made that these craters were originally produced by meteoritic impacts. Since then, weather elements on Mars have greatly eroded the original features.

B. **Rills.** Hills wind across the surface here and there on the planet.

Unlike the moon, the surface of Mars has:

C. **Volcanic mountains.** A number of large volcanic mountains on Mars suggest that the planet either now has or once had a very hot interior. The fact that these mountains are all on one side of Mars gives credence to the idea that the heating-up process is new rather than old, the heat being provided through slow radioactive breakdown of uranium and thorium.

D. **Canyons.** At least one of the canyons on Mars is more than 2,000 miles long, 75 miles wide, and 4 miles deep. Some astronomers believe that the canyons provide evidence that Mars, just like the earth, exhibits the phenomenon of continental drift.

E. **Areas of jumbled ridges and depressions.** The ridges on Mars typically are 1 or 2 miles wide and 2 to 7 miles long. This terrain reflects light much more efficiently than the cratered areas.

F. **Featureless deserts.** One of the largest of these deserts is known as the Plain of Hellas. There is not a single crater of diameter larger than 1,000 feet in this 1,200-mile-diameter region.

G. **Dune-like areas.** There are areas on the planet covered by regularly spaced ridges that greatly resemble sanddunes on earth.

15.5 ATMOSPHERE

Both theory and experiment show that a gaseous atmosphere exists on Mars. The theoretical consideration involves the velocity of escape, 3.2 miles per second, high enough to allow the planet to retain an atmosphere. There is experimental evidence from the following:

A. The existence of a twilight zone.
B. The albedo.
C. Comparison of infrared and ultraviolet photographs.
D. The variation in size of the polar white caps.
E. The occasional presence of clouds and mists.

A. **The Existence of a Twilight Zone.** Being an outer planet, Mars does not go through a complete series of phases as do the inner planets. One never sees a crescent of the planet, nor the quarter phase, but only the full and gibbous (slightly less than full) phases. At the gibbous phase, the presence of an atmosphere is observed. That part of the dark side of Mars which is turned toward the earth is slightly illuminated, and extends for about 8° beyond the part of Mars illuminated directly by sunlight. (It is called the Twilight Zone.) Light is derived from reflected sunlight, the reflection caused by the atmosphere of the planet, in a manner similar to the way that twilight reaches the earth.

B. **The Albedo.** Mars reflects sunlight better than an airless planet like Mercury. The albedo of Mars is nearly 15 per cent (i.e., 15 per cent of the incident sunlight is immediately reflected back into space), while that for Mercury is only 7 per cent.

C. **Comparison of Infrared and Ultraviolet Photographs.** Photographs taken of the planet through ultraviolet filters show it to be larger than do photographs taken with the aid of an infrared filter. The radius as computed from the two photographs differed by nearly 60 miles. The infrared picture seemingly corresponds to the solid disk of the planet; the disk appearing on the ultraviolet, to the outer surface of the atmosphere—in perfect agreement with physical theory. Red and infrared rays are transmitted by gases with little or no scattering; blue light is scattered greatly by any kind of a gaseous atmosphere. The infrared

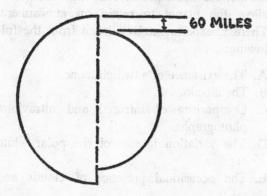

FIG. 15.5 Comparison of infrared and ultraviolet photographs of Mars. The left side was taken with a filter that lets through blue, violet, and ultraviolet light. The right side was taken with the aid of a filter through which red and infrared light passes. The difference in size is to be carefully noted. This difference indicates the thickness of the atmosphere that diffuses the blue and violet light.

filter admits to the photographic plate the red and infrared light coming directly from the surface of the planet; while the ultraviolet filter admits the blue and ultraviolet rays scattered by the atmosphere. The difference in the two radii, i.e., 60 miles, is assumed to be the thickness of the atmosphere on Mars. See Fig. 15.5.

D. **The Variation in Size of the Polar White Caps.** This variation is further direct proof of the existence of an atmosphere: the white caps are probably due to frozen CO_2. In the absence of an atmosphere, the cycles of forming and melting would not be possible.

E. **The Occasional Presence of Clouds and Mists.** This is still further proof of the Martian atmosphere.

Spacecraft readings indicate that the Martian atmosphere is nearly 200 times thinner than the one on the earth. A barometer would read a surface pressure of 5 millibars as compared to 1,000 millibars on the earth's surface.

The fall off of pressure with height is much less on Mars than on the earth. At about 20 miles above the surface of each planet the atmospheric pressures are about equal. Above 20 miles, the pressure on Mars is higher than at the corresponding level above the earth.

A major component of the Martian atmosphere is carbon dioxide (CO_2). Trace quantities of water vapor and oxygen have also been identified. The bulk of the rest is probably nitrogen. (A Russian surface probe of Mars suggests that as many as 30 per cent of the atmosphere might be the inert gas argon.)

Mars has a very weak magnetic field, less than one thousandth of the earth's intensity, suggesting that the core of the planet is solid.

There is no radiation belt around Mars.

Several types of clouds have been observed in the Martian sky. Of these, two are outstanding: (A) cirruslike clouds, and (B) dust clouds.

A. The cirruslike clouds formed from crystals of either ice or frozen CO_2 are just as white as cirrus clouds on earth. They are to be found, however, at a much higher altitude (20 miles) than their earthly counterparts. When observed over the winter polar caps, the clouds were nearly motionless; in mid-latitudes, cloud speeds of 30 or more miles per hour were noted.

B. The dust clouds above Mars more often than not are stationary for long periods of time. They have been known, though, to move at high speeds. Dust storms have been estimated to sweep across Martian deserts at 200 mph. (Mariner 9 was enveloped for nearly 8 weeks in a severe dust storm soon after it reached its assigned orbit.) A careful examination of data on hand seems to suggest that dust storms occur often when Mars is in its perihelion position, i.e., is closest to the sun.

15.6 SEASONS AND CLIMATES

The seasons on Mars are in some respects similar, and in others dissimilar, to those on the earth.

The similarities are:

A. The width of the climatic zones—due primarily to the inclination of the plane of the equator to the plane of the orbit—is similar on both planets. In the case of earth, this inclination is 23.5°; for Mars, it is 25.2°. The inclination of the axes is, of course, primarily responsible for seasons. Both planets have four seasons.

B. The variations in the period of daylight are similar on both planets. The period of one complete rotation of Mars about its axis is slightly more than 24½ hours, as compared with our 24 hours.

The dissimilarities are:

C. Each season on Mars is nearly twice as long as each season on earth. The length of the season depends upon the period of one revolution about the sun. Earth's sidereal period is 365¼ days; for Mars it is 687 days.

D. The average temperatures in each of the climatic zones on Mars are less than those of the corresponding zones on earth, because

Mars is about 50 per cent farther away from the sun than is the earth, so that the intensity of the sun's heat and light is diminished. The temperatures in the equatorial zone of Mars at noontime seldom rise above 80° F, while the lowest midnight temperature is −90° F.

E. Summer on Mars' southern hemisphere is much warmer than summer on its northern hemisphere because of the large eccentricity of the orbit, which is .09 as compared to the earth's .02. That is, the distance from Mars to the sun is closer by 20 per cent at perihelion than at aphelion. The difference in distance for earth is 3 per cent.

F. The changes in temperature from day to night are much greater on Mars than on earth, because of the thinness of Mars' atmosphere.

15.7 LIFE ON MARS

For many decades the idea persisted that certain forms of life exist on Mars. It was this idea that was responsible in part for the special interest that science gave to that planet.

The best that can be said at the present time is that of all the planets in the solar system, Mars is the likeliest place where living things, such as lichens or mosses, could be found.

With conditions such as the following, it is hard to imagine that man or any animal or vegetable could exist:

A. Little or no water.

B. Little or no oxygen.

C. 1/200 of the atmospheric pressure on earth.

D. Intense showers of ultraviolet rays capable of breaking up the simplest of molecules.

E. Meteorite falls, which our own atmosphere shields us from.

Two U.S. scientific vehicles called Vikings have been designed for the main purpose of searching for life on Mars. One of the Vikings is expected to soft-land a spacecraft to search the soil for evidence of living organisms on Mars at latitude 21° N in July 1976; the other Viking is due to perform a similar task at latitude 44° N in September 1976.

In the mid-1970s scientists were divided as to whether the conditions on Mars favored (no matter how primitive) on Mars.

In the late 1970s scientific opinion tends to interpret the Viking lander experiments performed on Mars itself, as not having demonstrated life.

15.8 SATELLITES

Mars has two tiny satellites—Phobos (Fear) and Deimos (Panic), named for the two mythological companions of Mars, the god of war.

Phobos, the larger, has a diameter of about 10 miles, while the diameter of Deimos is only 7 miles. Both revolve about Mars in its equatorial plane in the usual counterclockwise fashion.

Phobos is 5,800 miles from the center of its mother planet and a mere 3,700 miles from the surface. Its period of revolution about the planet is only 7 hours, 39 minutes, this being less than the period of rotation of Mars about its own axis. Phobos rises in the west and sets in the east 4½ hours later.

Deimos is 14,600 miles from the center of Mars. Its period of revolution about the planet —30 hours, 18 minutes—differs only slightly from the period of rotation of Mars about its own axis—24 hours, 37 minutes. Deimos rises in the east, and lagging behind the rotating planet, it goes through two complete cycles of phases before it sets in the west.

15.9 A TRIP TO MARS

At the time of the most favorable opposition, Mars is only 35,000,000 miles from the earth. For reasons of fuel economy, a space ship would follow a curved orbit and not a straight line. Along the greater part of the curved orbit to Mars, the ship would be able to coast and avoid the use of fuel.

An optimum orbit for a space ship to follow is indicated by AB in Figure 15.9. The ship's orbit is an ellipse, with the perihelion at the time of the separation from the earth (point A), and an aphelion at the time it reaches Mars (point B).

To start the ship on its orbit, it would be necessary to supply it with a speed of about 27 miles per second, 20 miles per second to follow the required orbit, and 7 miles per second to escape from the earth's gravitational field.

Because of the velocity of the earth in its orbit around the sun, the ship has a built-in velocity of 18.5 miles per second. This means that the fuel would only have to supply a speed of 8.5 miles per second.

After coasting for much of the route, under the gravitational pull of the sun, the ship will arrive at point B (some 200 or more days after launching) with a speed of about 15 miles per second and come under the gravitational pull of the planet Mars, which would increase this speed by about 3 miles per second. Since the speed of Mars at its perihelion (point B) is about 16.5 miles per second, the relative velocities of the two bodies may amount to as much as 4.5 miles per second (16.5−15+3=4.5). It will be necessary to minimize the velocity before landing on the planet or to leave the main vehicle in a parking orbit and release a landing module to descend to the planet proper.

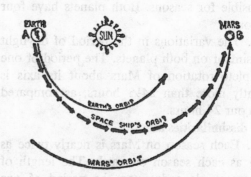

Fig. 15.9. The orbit of the Mars spacecraft is an ellipse with the sun at one of the foci. Point A is the perihelion (closest to the sun) of this orbit, and point B is the aphelion (point of the ellipse farthest from the sun).

PART II: PLANETOIDS

15.10 BASIC DATA

Total number: At least 100,000 with diameters larger than 1 mile

Diameters: Smallest, a fraction of a mile; largest, 500 miles

Total mass of all planetoids: $\dfrac{1}{2000}$ that of earth

Mean distances to sun: 130 to 500 million miles

Period (*sidereal*): 2 to 12 years

Inclinations of orbit to ecliptic: 0° to 48°

Eccentricities: 0 to .66

15.11 INTRODUCTION

One planet is missing. Theoretically, there should be a planet revolving in an orbit between Mars and Jupiter. No planet has ever been found there. Instead, there are a large number of small bodies, known either as minor planets, planetoids, or asteroids, the latter name indicating their resemblance to stars. Some fragments have diameters as large as 500 miles; others smaller than a mile. The first planetoid discovered was Ceres, in the year 1801. The next three (Pallas, Juno, and Vesta) were discovered in 1802, 1804, and 1807. The number of known planetoids is in the tens of thousands—many with unusual shapes suggesting that they might be fragments of a planet that disintegrated under the influence of tidal forces produced by its neighbor, Jupiter.

15.12 THEORETICAL "DISCOVERY"

As so often happens in astronomy, the planetoids were first discovered in theory, later in the sky. The discovery was based on Bode's rule, named for the German astronomer Johann Elert Bode (1747–1826).

Bode's Rule

A. List the planets in order from the sun.
B. Write the number 4 under each planet.
C. Write products of 0×3, 1×3, 2×3, 4×3, 8×3, and so on, under each planet in proper order.
D. Add the vertical columns and divide by 10.

	Mercury	Venus	Earth	Mars	?	Jupiter	Saturn
A.	Mercury	Venus	Earth	Mars	?	Jupiter	Saturn
B.	4	4	4	4	4	4	4
C.	0	3	6	12	24	48	96
D.	.4	.7	1.0	1.6	2.8	5.2	10.0

The bottom row of numbers corresponds very closely to the true distance of the planets from the sun when expressed in astronomical units (1 astronomical unit is equal to the distance of the sun from the earth). The true distances are:

$$.39 \quad .72 \quad 1.00 \quad 1.52 \quad 2.8 \quad 5.2 \quad 9.54$$

According to this rule, there should be a planet at a distance of 2.8 astronomical units from the sun. A systematic search for the "missing planet" along the belt of the zodiac, in which all the planets move, led to the discovery of a multitude of planetoids. The first planetoid, Ceres (for the guardian deity of Sicily), was discovered on January 1, 1801, by the Italian astronomer Giuseppe Piazzi (1746–1826). Its distance from the sun coincided very closely to the one assigned it by Bode's rule.

NOTES: 1. Uranus, Neptune, and Pluto had not been discovered when the rule was published (1772). Uranus was discovered shortly after and was found to conform well to Bode's rule—19.6 by the rule, 19.2 by actual measurement. Neptune and Pluto, however, do not at all fit the rule.

2. An explanation of Bode's law is given in a theory that is known as the theory of dynamical relaxation. According to this theory the planets, when first formed, followed an entirely different set of orbits. Reacting to gravitational forces from its neighbors, each planet altered its orbit until the perturbing forces became minimal. The final arrangement is one that obeys mathematical expressions similar to Bode's rule.

15.13 ORBITS OF THE PLANETOIDS

The vast majority of the planetoids move within orbits that lie between the orbits of Mars and Jupiter. The perihelia of some planetoids, e.g. 433 Eros, lie within the orbit of Mars. Others, known as the Apollo asteroids have perihelia inside the earth's orbit.

NOTE: As soon as a planetoid's orbit is established, it is designated by a number—in order of its discovery—followed by a name (e.g., 1 Ceres, 2 Pallas, 3 Juno, and so on). The name is usually selected by the discoverer. In the beginning, feminine names were taken from mythology. Later, names were taken from Shakespeare's plays and Wagner's operas. Many planetoids were named after wives, friends, and even pet dogs and cats. Feminine names have been used except for several planetoids that have unusual orbits; these were given masculine names.

There are a number of planetoids with aphelia outside the orbit of Jupiter. 944 Hidalgo has an aphelion distance of 9.64 astronomical units.

The inclination of the planetoidal orbits to the ecliptic varies within wide limits, many of them moving in orbits that nearly coincide with the ecliptic; others, in highly inclined orbits. The orbit of Icarus is shown in Figure 15.13. Its orbit is inclined 21° to that of the earth about the sun.

All planetoids move around the sun in direct orbit, i.e., counterclockwise, like the nine planets.

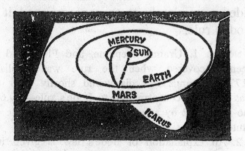

FIG. 15.13. The orbit of Icarus is inclined 21 degrees to the orbit of the earth about the sun.

15.14   THE SIDEREAL PERIODS OF THE PLANETOIDS

The periods of the planetoids vary greatly between a lower limit of two years and an upper limit of twelve years. There are, however, "forbidden" periods—i.e., no planetoids with periods one half, one third, or one quarter the period of Jupiter (11.86 years). This is a direct consequence of a physical phenomenon known as **Gravitational Resonance.** The gravitational attraction of Jupiter on planetoids moving in these orbits is cumulative, causing the small fragmentary masses to move on to other orbits.

15.15   THE TROJANS (The Jupiter Planetoids)

Trojans is the name given to two groups of planetoids that follow the same orbit as Jupiter: one group travels 60° ahead of Jupiter, the other 60° behind.

The location of these planetoids relative to the planet is in accordance with a theoretical solution of the three-body problem derived by the French mathematician Joseph Louis Lagrange (1736–1813).

15.16   OUR INTEREST IN THE PLANETOIDS

The primary interest in planetoids focuses on their close approaches to the sun and the earth. Icarus, discovered in 1949, passes closer to the sun than Mercury by as much as 17 million miles.

Several planetoids have recently been discovered that pass within less than 10 million miles from the earth's orbit. The closest recorded approach took place on October 10, 1937, when the small planetoid Hermes came within half a million miles of the earth.

The planetoids are useful in checking the motion of other heavenly bodies.

PART III: THE PLANET JUPITER

15.17 BASIC DATA

Symbol: ♃

Distance to sun:
Min. 460,100,000 miles
Mean 483,600,000 miles
Max. 507,100,000 miles

Eccentricity of orbit: .048

Inclination of orbit to ecliptic: 1°18′18″

Period of one revolution about the sun:
Sidereal 11.86 years
Synodic 398.9 days

Orbital velocity (mean): 8.1 miles per second

Distance from earth:
Min. 367,000,000 miles
Max. 600,000,000 miles

Angular diameter (mean, at opposition): 48.86″

Diameter:
Min. (polar) 82,970 miles
Max. (equatorial) 88,760 miles

Volume: 1,319 times that of the earth

Mass: 317.9 times that of the earth

Density: .24 times that of the earth

Surface gravity: 2.64 times that of the earth

Velocity of escape: 37.4 miles per second

Period of rotation about axis (mean): 9 hours 54 minutes

Inclination of planet's equator to orbit: 3°7′

Temperature (at top of clouds): −230° F

Albedo: .73

NOTE: Methods used to derive the above data are detailed in Secs. 11.34 to 11.52.

15.18 INTRODUCTION

Jupiter, with Saturn, Uranus, and Neptune, forms the group of major planets—distinguished by their large volumes, large masses and low densities.

Jupiter is the most voluminous: it could accommodate within the space occupied by itself, all the other planets. Its mass, too, is enormous. More than 300 spheres as heavy as the earth would be needed to balance Jupiter.

15.19 WHAT DO WE SEE?

A. **Naked eye.** To the unaided eye Jupiter appears as a bright yellowish object moving slowly through the twelve divisions of the zodiac, completing the circuit in just under twelve years.

One star only, Sirius, exceeds Jupiter in brightness, and only the planets Venus and at times Mars are brighter. For nearly six months of every year Jupiter is in full view every night, a brilliant planet in a field of stars.

B. **Telescopic view.** Telescopic observations of Jupiter show an oblate sphere with prominent markings—either orange or red—running parallel to the equator. These belts—most likely currents within the extensive atmosphere of the planet—resemble the trade wind zones on earth. The equatorial belt is light in color and varies from 12,000 to 15,000 miles in width; on each side of the equatorial belt, alternate dark and light belts assume parallel courses. While maintaining their general outline, the belts vary greatly over time in location, in color, and in form.

The period of rotation of Jupiter has been determined from observations of the semipermanent markings on the belts of the planet, no two of which have the same period.

The period of the planet varies with latitude —it is shortest at the equator (9 hours, 50 minutes) and longest in latitudes far from the equator (9 hours, 56 minutes). The planet's mean period is about 9 hours, 54 minutes. Variation of period with latitude does not increase uniformly, but rather is quite erratic. To complete the confusion, the periods of like latitudes in the northern and southern hemispheres of Jupiter are not equal to one another, nor do the periods remain constant for any long interval of time.

Jupiter's mean period of rotation—9 hours, 54 minutes—and its radius—44,380 miles—imply immense speed for matter located near the planet's surface—in fact, 30,000 miles per hour; the corresponding figure for the earth is about 1,000 miles per hour.

The high speed of rotation of Jupiter is no doubt responsible for its considerable equatorial bulge; the polar diameter is shorter by nearly 6,000 miles than the equatorial diameter.

At times, bright spots appear on Jupiter's dark belts, and at times dark spots appear on the bright belts. One spot—known as the Great Red Spot—made astronomical history. It appeared fairly suddenly in 1878, occupying a region on the outer surface of Jupiter 30,000 miles long and nearly 7,000 miles wide. Soon after its appearance it began to fade, at first rapidly, then gradually; and then it brightened again. The spot has undergone many such cycles since it was first observed. The spot also seems to drift relative to the belt it is in; the rate of drift also varies—at times the spot moves faster, at other times slower, than the belt.

C. **Space-probe observations.** The space probe Pioneer 10 flew by Jupiter on December 3, 1973, and Pioneer 11 made a close approach a year later.

The following observations are based on this research:

A. **Magnetic field.** The planet's magnetic field is most intense. The total energy in that field is 400,000,000 times the energy stored in the earth's field. Jupiter's field is inclined about 10° to the rotational axis and is offset by 5,000 miles from center of the planet.

B. **High-energy particle belt.** There was excellent evidence on the planet of the presence of a very flat, almost disklike belt of high-energy electrons, protons, and alpha particles.

C. **Internal heat source.** The planet emits 2.5 times as much energy as it receives from the sun, which suggests an internal source of heat.

D. **Temperature of cloud tops.** The temperature at the top of the belts facing the sun is about the same as those away from the sun.

E. **Core.** The planet is probably composed entirely of liquid; the temperature at the core is some 50,000° F.

F. **The Great Red Spot** on Jupiter is probably an area of hurricanelike turbulence

trapped between two atmospheric bands flowing in opposite directions.

G. There are most likely many **Convective (up and down) Vortices** in the atmosphere of Jupiter.

15.20 RADIO EMISSIONS FROM JUPITER

There are at least three distinct types of radio emissions from Jupiter: (A) thermal, (B) high-energy particles, and (C) triggered.

A. **Thermal.** This is the normal radiation emitted by any body that has a temperature above zero degrees absolute (−273° C, or −460° F). The intensity of radiation relates well with a temperature of −230° F at the top of the planet's bands.

B. **High-energy particles.** The radio emission in this case is due to the effect of the intense magnetic field on the high-energy particle belt surrounding the planet. This emission shows up particularly well in radio waves of .5 to 3 feet wavelengths.

C. **Triggered.** These radio signals are of very high intensity with a wavelength of about 30 feet. They are emitted in short blasts, each blast lasting a second or so, a complete series of blasts going on for about an hour. The rotation period for this radio "noise," which is shorter than that of non-equatorial, visible features, is 9 hours, 55 minutes, 29 seconds.

The occurrences of these intense radio outbursts from the planet correlates well with the position of the planet's satellite Io. The most intense outbursts occur when Io is at maximum elongation on either side of the planet. One explanation of these radio emissions is that Io triggers a concentration of high-energy particles to emit these pulses of radiation.

15.21 THE STRUCTURE OF THE PLANET

The complete structure of the planet is as yet unknown, but the following can be said:

A. Spectrographic studies indicate the presence of ammonia, methane, and molecular hydrogen (H_2) in the atmosphere of the planet.

NOTE: Ammonia (NH_3) is the strong-smelling substance often used as a household cleaning agent. Methane (CH_4) is known as "fire damp" and is the main constituent of the gases that cause explosions in coal mines.

B. The average density of the planet is about one quarter that of the earth.

Other information available in the mid-1970s leads us to believe that the following is likely:

a. The chemical makeup of the planet is similar to that of the sun, i.e., primarily hydrogen, plus a small percentage of helium (He) and minute quantities of other materials.

b. The interior is probably liquid or solid, but not gaseous, since the temperatures are not high enough to overcome the enormous pressures due to the overlying atmosphere. The pressure at the center of the planet is about 32 million atmospheres. No diameter for this interior can be given at this time. The most often stated figure suggests that it is the same as the diameter of the planet excluding the outermost 2,000 miles of atmosphere.

c. The atmosphere, like the interior, is composed primarily of H_2 (80 per cent), He (20 per cent), and small fractions of percentages of CH_4, and NH_3.

d. Most of the NH_3 is probably in solid, crystalline form; these tiny crystals form the banded clouds, or belts.

e. The temperatures at the top of these banded clouds is $-230°$ F, and the pressure is similar to the pressure at the earth's sea level.

15.22 THE SATELLITES

Fourteen moons revolve about Jupiter. The first four, known as the **Galilean satellites,** were discovered by Galileo in 1610 and are designated either by the names Io, Europa, Ganymede, and Callisto, or simply as JI, JII, JIII, and JIV. The fifth satellite, Amalthea, or JV, was discovered in 1892 by the eminent American astronomer Edward Emerson Barnard (1857–1923); the fourteenth satellite

(JXIV) was discovered in October 1975 by the American astronomer Charles T. Kowal. Satellites JI through JXIII divide naturally into three groups: (A) the inner, (B) the intermediate, and (C) the distant; the classification of JXIV in any one of these groups has not been firmly established by the end of 1975.

A. **The Inner Group.** This group comprises satellites JI through JV, that is, the four Galilean satellites and the one discovered by Professor Barnard.

The Galilean satellites move in nearly circular orbits at distances from Jupiter varying from 262,000 to 1,170,000 miles with periods varying from 1¾ days to 16⅔ days. Their periods of rotation and revolution are identical. Therefore an observer on Jupiter would always see the same faces of the four satellites. All four are large enough to show perceptible disks in a telescope, and were it not for the overpowering brilliance of the mother planet, they could be observed by the naked eye. At times, all four are on the west side of the planet; at other times, only three, two, one, or none are there, the others being on the east side. Frequently, one of the satellites is in eclipse (passing behind the planet) or in transit (passing in front of the planet). The change in position of the four can be detected during a few hours of telescopic observation. The transits themselves are often difficult to follow. However, the shadows they produce on the surface of Jupiter are very clear and can be followed even with fairly small telescopes, when good "seeing" conditions prevail.

The fifth satellite is closer to Jupiter than are the Galilean ones, its distance from the center of the planet being only 112,000 miles and from its outer surface only about 68,000 miles. The period of revolution about the mother planet is less than twelve hours; the orbital velocity, therefore, is 17 miles per second, or nearly 60,000 miles per hour.

B. **The Intermediate Group.** JVI, JVII, JX, and JXIII belong to this group. They are all small in size, having diameters of less than 100 miles and are at an average distance of 7 million miles from Jupiter. Their period of revolution is estimated to be about 270 days.

C. **The Distant Group.** This group comprises JXII, JXI, JVIII, and JIX (listed here in order of increasing distance from the planet). These satellites are characterized by:

a. great distance from the mother planet, estimated to be close to 15 million miles;

b. long periods of rotation, all four exceeding two years; and

c. retrograde motion for all four, that is, they revolve in a direction opposite to the one which all planets and most other satellites move. A view from above the north pole of Jupiter would reveal these four satellites moving in their orbits in a clockwise direction.

PART IV: THE PLANET SATURN

15.23 BASIC DATA

Symbol: ♄
Distance to sun:
  Min.   836,000,000 miles
  Mean 886,700,000 miles
  Max.   936,000,000 miles
Eccentricity of orbit: .0557
Inclination of orbit to ecliptic: 2°29′22.6″
Period of one revolution about the sun:
  Sidereal   29.46 years
  Synodic 378 days
Orbital velocity: 5.99 miles per second
Distance from earth: 744,000,000 miles
Angular diameter (mean, at opposition): 19.27 seconds
Diameter:
  Min. (polar) 66,890 miles
  Max. (equatorial) 74,160 miles
Volume: 735 times that of the earth
Mass: 95 times that of the earth
Density: .128 times that of the earth
Surface gravity: 1.16 times that of the earth
Velocity of escape: 22.5 miles per second
Period of rotation about axis (at equator): 10 hours 14 minutes 24 seconds
Inclination of planet's equator to orbit: 26°45′
Temperature (at top of clouds): −290° F
Albedo: .76
NOTE: Methods used to derive the above data are detailed in Secs. 11.34 to 11.52.

15.24 INTRODUCTION

Saturn is the planet with rings—one of the major planets, large in dimension and massive. Second in size to Jupiter, its mass is 95 times that of the earth. Like the other major planets, its density is low—less than that of

water, that is, it could float on water. (Its mean value of density is .71 that of H_2O.)

Like the other major planets, it rotates at high speed about its own axis completing one rotation in approximately 10.5 hours. This period is not the same for the whole planet. The motion of spots at the equator indicate a period of 10 hours, 14 minutes, while spots at 60° N complete a rotation in 10 hours, 40 minutes. It is not impossible that these are the only two basic periods of rotation. The latitude of the dividing line between the two is unknown as yet.

The values of rotation cited above refer to the planet's outer atmosphere, the top of which because of its opacity is the only "surface" visible to us.

Saturn used to be unique because of the system of surrounding rings, first seen by Galileo in 1610 and first clearly described by the Italian-French astronomer Jean Dominique Cassini (1625–1712). There is now (1977) reason to believe that Uranus, too, has a system of rings around it.

15.25 WHAT DO WE SEE?

A. **Naked eye.** To the naked eye Saturn is a dull yellow in color, steady in light, and always among the brightest objects in the sky. At its brightest it compares well with a less-than-zero magnitude star; at its dimmest it appears like a first-magnitude star. It moves among the constellations at a much slower rate than Jupiter, completing a circuit of the zodiac in thirty years.

B. **Telescopic view.** Saturn is second to Jupiter in interest to the amateur observer, who will find little difficulty in noting the following:

a. Oblateness of the planet.
b. The belts on the surface. These are less pronounced than on Jupiter.
c. Spots, which appear at irregular intervals. An outstanding one appeared in 1933, and was named the Great White Spot. In several months it elongated into a white band around the planet.
d. The rings which are clearly visible. The gap between the two brighter rings, called Cassini's division, can be seen under favorable conditions with a small telescope.
e. The largest satellite, Titan, and the next largest, Iapetus, which are easy to observe. Three other satellites (Rhea, Tethys, and Dione) can be seen under particularly favorable conditions.

15.26 THE STRUCTURE OF THE PLANET

The structure of Saturn in all probability greatly resembles that of the planet Jupiter:

A. Here too hydrogen is the prime constituent.
B. The core is probably liquid or solid.
C. The spectroscope shows
a. lines of CH_4 in the atmosphere, and
b. no lines due to NH_3. All the ammonia, because of Saturn's low temperature, is probably in solid crystalline form in the cloud bands. This does not show up in the spectroscope.
D. The spectroscope shows no lines due to molecular hydrogen (H_2). There are good reasons to believe, though, that H_2 is present in Saturn's atmosphere. One of these reasons is the similarity of Saturn to Jupiter, whose atmosphere contains 80 per cent of that gas.

E. The temperature on top of the banded clouds (or belts) is $-290°$ F.

15.27 THE RINGS

There are four rings encircling Saturn, which are denoted by letters A, B, C, and D. Their dimensions and those of the gaps between them are given on Figure 15.27a.

The rings differ materially in brightness: the middle ring (the B ring) is the brightest of the four; the outer ring (the A ring) is next; and the innermost (the D ring) is the least bright. The C ring is often called the "crepe ring" and the B ring, the "bright ring."

The gap between the B and A rings is known as Cassini's division, in honor of its discoverer.

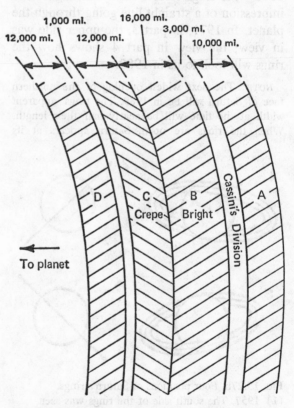

FIG. 15.27a. The rings of Saturn. A top view of Saturn shows clearly the four rings, as well as the gaps between them. The widths of the rings are 10,000, 16,000, 12,000, and 12,000 miles, respectively. The B ring is the brightest, followed by A, C, and D, in order of decreasing brightness. The 3,000-mile gap between A ring and B ring is known as Cassini's division.

The rings are remarkable for their thinness: a cross section would be an extremely thin rectangle—that of the outer ring, for example, would be a rectangle 10,000 miles long and only 5 or 7 miles wide.

The rings are exactly in the plane of the planet's equator, the latter being inclined about 27° to the plane of the ecliptic. Since the axis of Saturn maintains a fixed orientation in space (that is, the axis always points to the same spot on the celestial sphere), terrestrial observers can see the rings at different inclinations. This is shown in the four parts of Figure 15.27b.

Part 1 is the view of the rings as they looked in 1957—the lower side of the rings was in our line of sight. Part 2 is the view in 1965—the rings were sideways and gave the impression of a straight line going through the planet. In 1971, in part 3, the upper side was in view; the view in part 4 shows how the rings will look to us in 1980.

NOTE: The next widest opening of the northern face of Saturn will be in 1989. The rings' apparent width at the time will be nearly half their length. When the rings are open, Saturn appears at its brightest; the rings reflect almost twice as much light as the planet does.

A cycle of the ring phases is completed once every 29.5 years, this being the period of one revolution of Saturn about the sun.

The rings of Saturn are thought to be composed of countless small particles, the size of grains of sand or thin gravel. This supposition is based on two facts: (A) The rings are semitransparent; occasionally a star can be seen shining through. (B) The inner part of each revolves about the planet in less time than the outer part: if the ring were solid or liquid, the period of rotation for each would be constant.

The gaps between the rings are due to gravitational resonance. Here the resonance is between the satellites of Saturn and the revolving sand or gravel. The small particles remain outside orbits in which the period of revolution would be a simple fraction of the period of the satellite. No particles move in the gap between rings A and B because the period of such motion would be exactly half the period of Mimas, Saturn's closest satellite. This phenomenon is similar to Jupiter's effect on planetoids (see Sec. 15.14).

It is now believed that the rings are due either to a satellite that was torn asunder by the tidal forces of the mother planet, or to a satellite that was never quite created: for the former, it is assumed that a satellite extremely close to Saturn was torn to fragments by tidal forces; for the latter, it is assumed that material about to form a satellite was prevented from doing so by the same tidal forces.

Mathematical analysis supports these assumptions, demonstrating that no satellite can exist closer to a planet than 2.44 times the planet's radius, or within a distance of 1.44 from the planet's surface. The figures are known as "Roche's limits," for the French scientist E. A. Roche (1820–83) who discovered them in 1850.

15.28 THE SATELLITES

Saturn is attended by ten satellites—the nearest, Janus, is at a distance of 106,000 miles from the center of the planet. The most

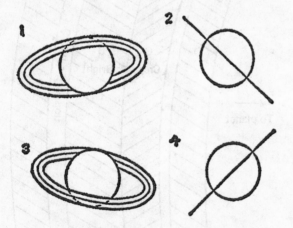

FIG. 15.27b. Four positions of Saturn's rings.
(1) 1957. The south side of the rings was seen.
(2) 1965. The rings were seen sideways. Because of their extreme thinness, the edge gave the impression of a thin straight line.
(3) 1971. The top side of the rings was turned toward the earth.
(4) 1980. The edge of the rings will again be in line of sight for terrestrial observers. Its inclination, though, will be different from the one in 1965.

distant, Phoebe, is more than 8,000,000 miles away from the mother planet.

The periods of the satellites vary from 18 hours for Janus to 550 days for Phoebe, all, with one exception, revolving about Saturn in the normal direction. Phoebe alone shows retrograde motion, thus adding greatly to its orbital stability. Mathematically it can be shown that a distant satellite, whose direction of motion is normal, can more easily be withdrawn from the planet than one whose motion is retrograde.

The diameters of the satellites are fairly small—the largest is that of Titan (about 3,500 miles) and the smallest that of Janus (about 100 miles).

The velocity of escape of gases from Titan is large both because of its large mass and low temperature (due to its distance from the sun). Titan is thus able to retain an atmosphere. Spectroscopic studies indicate the presence of CH_4 (methane) on the satellite.

Recent studies by a team of scientists from the State University of New York at Stony Brook revealed the presence of ethane—one of several molecules necessary for the formation of amino acids, the basic element of life, on Titan.

The satellites appear to rotate with a period equal to that with which they revolve, thus keeping the same face toward the primary (i.e., the mother-planet) and accounting for their observed variation in brightness. The periods of these variations in brightness are identical with the periods of revolution—the brightness of one satellite, Iapetus, changes by a factor of five from minimum to maximum for each revolution.

PART V: THE PLANET URANUS

15.29 BASIC DATA

Symbol: ♅
Distance to sun:
    Min.   1,700,000,000 miles
    Mean 1,782,000,000 miles
    Max.   1,870,000,000 miles
Eccentricity of orbit: .0472
Inclination of orbit to ecliptic: 0°46′23.1″
Period of one revolution about the sun:
    Sidereal 84.01 years
    Synodic 369.66 days
Orbital velocity: 4.2 miles per second
Angular diameter (mean, at opposition): 3.58″
Diameter:
    Min. (polar) 30,000 miles
    Max. (equatorial) 32,000 miles
Volume: 67 times that of the earth
Mass: 14.6 times that of the earth
Density: .23 times that of the earth
Surface gravity: 1.12 times that of the earth
Velocity of escape: 14 miles per second
Period of rotation about axis: 10 hours 49 minutes
Inclination of planet's equator to orbit: 97°53′
Temperature: −350° F
Albedo: .93

NOTE: Methods used to derive the above data are detailed in Secs. 11.34 to 11.52.

15.30 INTRODUCTION

Uranus, named after the Greek deity that sprang from Chaos and became the personification of Heaven, has an apparent magnitude of 5.7—it is thus barely visible to the unaided eye when seeing conditions are particularly favorable. Its faintness is due to its great distance both from the sun, which illuminates it, and from the earth from where we observe it.

It moves in its assigned orbit, however its apparent motion is relatively slow, completing one revolution about the sun in nearly 84 years. Its progress from the western terrestrial horizon toward the eastern is about 4 degrees per year.

The planet greatly resembles the other major planets, Jupiter, Saturn, and Neptune. Its atmosphere, too, very likely consists of a combination of ammonia, methane and hydrogen, the percentage of the ammonia being fairly low as compared with the methane and especially the hydrogen.

Telescopically, because of the abundance of methane in atmosphere of Uranus, it appears as a greenish disk.

From time to time white spots appear on the surface of the planet; these are useful in determining the period of rotation.

Excellent photographs taken by equipment on the unmanned balloon Stratoscope II show the oblateness of Uranus as well as the darkening on its limb. No equatorial belt markings could be detected on these photographs.

Uranus is unique among the planets on several counts:

A. It was the first planet to be discovered with the aid of a telescope.
B. It was discovered by accident.
C. It rotates about its own axis "backward" (i.e., clockwise).
D. Its equatorial plane is almost at right angles with its orbital plane—the exact value of the angle between the two planes is 82°.

15.31   THE DISCOVERY

The planet Uranus was discovered by the Englishman Sir William Herschel (1738–1822), a professional musician and amateur astronomer, on March 13, 1781, with a small 7-inch reflecting telescope of his own construction. It appears in such a telescope as a very small disk, little differing from a point of light typical of a star. This slight difference in size, however, was sufficient reason for Herschel to suspect that the object was **not** a star; and his data confirmed that a new planet revolving about the sun, at a distance of 19 astronomical units, had been discovered.

15.32   PERIOD OF ROTATION ABOUT ITS AXIS

The spin of Uranus is "backward," or retrograde, in contrast to the other planets, which move about the sun counterclockwise and spin similarly about their own axes. Uranus describes the orbit about the sun in the normal counterclockwise manner, but the ro-

tation about its own axis is clockwise, the equator of the planet being inclined 82° to its orbit about the sun. An alternate way of describing the rotation is often used. This states that the equator of the planet is inclined 98° with its orbit. The original north and south poles are thus reversed, and the direction of spin about the axis is normal, not retrograde.

For a clearer picture of the effects of these large angles, either 82° or 98° for Uranus, the

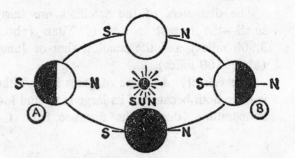

FIG. 15.32a. Effect of large (hypothetical) inclination of earth's axis. If the earth's axis were inclined by 90° (and not 23.5°, as in reality) to the axis of its orbit, then at one time during the year the North Pole would be the warmest place on the earth (position A). Six months later sunlight would shine most directly at the South Pole, and that would be the warmest place on earth (position B).

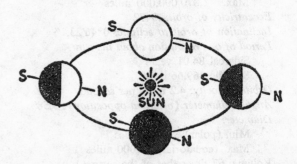

FIG. 15.32b. If the earth's axis were rotated still further from its present inclination of 23.5° to, say, 98°, the poles would interchange their identities. The North Pole would now be below the plane of the ecliptic and would therefore be known as the South Pole. The U.S. would now be in the southern hemisphere. An observer looking down at the new North Pole (the erstwhile South Pole) would see the earth rotating clockwise. Clockwise rotation is the normal direction for the earth's South Pole.

results of large inclinations on the earth may be studied.

Suppose that the earth's equator is inclined, not 23.5° but 90° to its orbit, that is, the axis of the earth would lie in the plane of its orbit.

At one time, the present North Pole would be closest to the sun; six months later, the South Pole would most directly receive the sun's rays. The concept of climatic zones, as we know it, would no longer apply. See Fig. 15.32a.

Suppose then that the angle is still further increased, say, to 98°. The original North Pole would be below the ecliptic; the United States would be in the southern hemisphere; California would be on the East Coast; and a vertical view taken from above the ecliptic would show the earth to spin in a clockwise fashion, i.e., in retrograde motion. See Fig. 15.32b.

15.33 THE SATELLITES AND THE RINGS

Uranus has five satellites: Miranda, Ariel, Umbriel, Titania, and Oberon, all revolving in the plane of the mother-planet's equator, hence, at nearly right angles with the orbit in which the planet moves. All five have retrograde motion, consistent with the planet's spin about its own axis.

The satellites range in size from about 150 to about 600 miles in diameter. The radii of their orbits range from 76,000 miles for the satellite closest to the planet to 364,000 miles for the farthest.

Studies of an occultation of a star by Uranus pursued in 1977 seem to indicate that this planet is surrounded by a system of rings, as is Saturn.

PART VI: THE PLANET NEPTUNE

15.34 BASIC DATA

Symbol: ♆
Distance to sun:
   Min.   2,770,000,000 miles
   Mean 2,794,000,000 miles
   Max. 2,818,000,000 miles
Eccentricity of orbit: .0086
Inclination of orbit to ecliptic: 1°46′23.5″
Period of one revolution about the sun:
   Sidereal 164.8 years
   Synodic 367.49 days
Orbital velocity: 3.4 miles per second
Angular diameter (mean, at opposition): 0°0′2.13″
Diameter:
   Min. (polar) 30,000 miles
   Max. (equatorial) 30,600 miles
Volume: 57 times that of the earth
Mass: 17.2 times that of the earth
Density: .33 times that of the earth
Surface gravity: 1.18 times that of the earth
Velocity of escape: 15.5 miles per second
Period of rotation about axis: 15 hours 48 minutes
Inclination of planet's equator to orbit: 28°48′
Temperature: −350° F
Albedo: .84
  NOTE: Methods used to derive the above data are detailed in Secs 11.34 to 11.52.

15.35 INTRODUCTION

Because of its great distance from the earth, Neptune is invisible to the naked eye. Telescopic observations reveal a small greenish disk equal in brightness to an eighth-magnitude star. Neptune requires nearly 165 years to complete one revolution about the sun. Its eastward drift among the stars is slightly more than 2° per year.

There is little variety of season: the mean temperature is −350° F, summer being not much warmer than winters.

Neptune was discovered first by mathematical computations, then by actual observation.

15.36 THE DISCOVERY

Astronomers were first alerted to the presence of Neptune because Uranus moved strangely in its orbit. By 1845 the discrepancy between the computed and observed positions of Uranus was 2 minutes of angle, an "intolerably large quantity" in astronomy. One explanation was that the motion of Uranus was disturbed by an unknown planet beyond its orbit, which, when ahead, pulled on Uranus, thus increasing its speed; and when behind, acted, by its gravitational pull, as a brake on its motion.

John Couch Adams (1819–92), in the mid-1840s an undergraduate at Cambridge University (England), and a young French mathematician, Urbain Leverrier (1811–77), each independently computed the orbit of the hypothetical planet, both arriving at the same results. Within an hour after the telescopic search began, the planet was found in the exact position indicated by the mathematical calculation.

15.37   THE STRUCTURE OF THE PLANET

Neptune is similar in size and many other physical characteristics to Uranus; indeed, the two are considered to be twins. The structure of the planet is probably similar to the structure of Uranus, Saturn, or Jupiter.

The high value for the planet's albedo indicates that Neptune is surrounded by a dense atmosphere.

Spectrographic studies show strong methane bands, as well as molecular hydrogen absorption lines.

15.38   THE SATELLITES

Two satellites of Neptune have been discovered: the first, Triton, within a few months after the planet's discovery; the second, more than a century later, in 1949.

Triton is unique in being the only satellite close to its mother planet having retrograde motion. Its distance from the mother planet is 220,000 miles, almost the same as the distance between our moon and earth. Triton's retrograde motion may be a direct result of the following two events: (A) Triton and the ninth planet, Pluto, were at one time satellites of Neptune, both moving in a direct way. (B) A close encounter between Triton and Pluto caused the ejection of Pluto (which became an independent planet) and a reversal in the direction of Triton.

Triton has a diameter of about 2,200 miles; a mass about one fifteenth that of the earth; and revolves about Neptune once every 5 days, 20 hours, in an orbit inclined 37° to the plane of the ecliptic.

The second satellite, Nereid (named for a mythological sea nymph-attendant of Neptune, God of the Sea), moves about its mother planet in a direct way. Its sidereal period is 360 days and its orbit is inclined about 5° to the ecliptic.

Nereid is unique for two reasons: (A) It is too faint to be seen even with great telescopes. Observations of this satellite are made primarily by photography. (B) The large eccentricity of its orbit (.75). Its distance from Neptune varies from 730,000 miles at its closest point to 7,000,000 at the farthest point on its orbit.

PART VII: THE PLANET PLUTO

15.39   BASIC DATA

Symbol: ♇
Distance to sun:
　　Min. 2,750,000,000 miles
　　Mean 3,667,000,000 miles
　　Max. 4,600,000,000 miles
Eccentricity of orbit: .25
Inclination of orbit to ecliptic: 17°1′

Period of one revolution about the sun:
　　Sidereal 248.4 years
　　Synodic 367　days
Orbital velocity: 2.9 miles per second
Angular diameter: 0°0′.25″
Diameter: 3,700 (?) miles
Volume: .1 (?) times that of the earth
Mass: .2 (?) times that of the earth
Density: 9 (??) times that of the earth

Surface gravity: .5 times that of the earth
Velocity of escape: 3.2 (?) miles per second
Period of rotation about axis: 6.39 days
Temperature: —400° F (?)
Albedo: ?

NOTE: Methods used to derive the above data are detailed in Secs. 11.34 to 11.52.

15.40   INTRODUCTION

The ninth and most distant known planet is Pluto, named for the mythological god of the underworld. Its distance from the sun is nearly four thousand million miles—thus the benefits from the sun are minute. Pluto receives only $\frac{1}{1600}$ the amount of heat and light the earth does. The pale light from the distant sun probably helps make the frozen wastes of the planet's surface appear more frightful and unreal than it otherwise would.

Pluto, of apparent magnitude 14.8, appears even to very powerful telescopes as a minute yellowish point of light—except to the 200-inch telescope on Mount Palomar, which shows Pluto's apparent disk.

15.41   THE DISCOVERY

As with Neptune, Pluto's fame is connected with its discovery—for which Percival Lowell of Flagstaff, Arizona; W. H. Pickering of Harvard; and Clyde Tombaugh, then a student-assistant in the Flagstaff Observatory, are responsible. The search for the planet occupied more than twenty years. An announcement of its discovery on March 13, 1930, coincided with Professor Lowell's birthday and the anniversary of Herschel's discovery of Uranus. Its symbol, ♇ (P and L) represents the initials of Percival Lowell.

Again, the search for Pluto was provoked by a deviation from computed motions of Uranus and Neptune.

15.42   THE ORBIT

Pluto is outstanding in several respects (see Fig. 15.40):

A. Its orbit has the highest inclination of any of the planets (17°).
B. Its orbit has the highest eccentricity of any of the planets (.25).
C. Near perihelion Pluto is closer to the sun than Neptune so that the latter becomes the outermost planet.

At perihelion Pluto's distance to the sun is 2,750 million miles, while Neptune's distance is 2,794 million miles. Pluto will be at perihelion in 1989, but all during the years 1970 to 2010 Neptune will be farther away from the sun than Pluto.

There is no chance of a collision between the two planets because Pluto's orbit has an inclination of more than 17°. See Fig. 15.40. The closest that one planet gets to the other is about 250 million miles.

This close approach, together with such

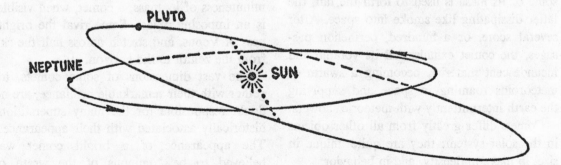

Fig. 15.40. The orbits of Neptune and Pluto. Neptune and all the other planets except Pluto move in orbits that are only slightly inclined to the ecliptic. The large inclination of Pluto's orbit as compared with Neptune's is shown here.

data about Pluto as size (small) and period of rotation (large), are often used as an argument that Pluto was once a satellite of Neptune.

NOTE: A careful search over the entire sky north of 50° south declination to a line at least 35° north

of the ecliptic has proven clearly that there are no planets beyond Pluto.

This gigantic survey, however, was not in vain. While no more planets were found, the survey succeeded in discovering a cluster of 1,800 galaxies, a globular cluster, several galactic clusters, and 700 planetoids.

CHAPTER 16

COMETS AND METEOROIDS

PART I: THE COMETS

16.1 INTRODUCTION

The name "comets" derives from *stellae cometae,* Latin for "long-haired stars." They are perhaps the most remarkable objects in the solar system, their appearances differing greatly from what they really are.

In appearance, a bright comet is a large illuminated moonlike disk, at times visible in broad daylight, followed by a tail millions of miles long, moving like a planet about the sun, in a rather elongated ellipse.

But in reality, **a comet is merely a globular aggregate of stones, which, upon approaching the sun, becomes warm enough to emit light and is converted partially into dust and gas that leave the comet to form the tail.**

Each time a comet passes close to the sun, some of its mass is used to form the tail, the latter dissipating like smoke into space. After several score, or a hundred, perihelion passages, the comet exhausts all its votatile and incandescent material, becoming a swarm of meteoroids roaming in space and supplying the earth intermittently with meteoric showers.

Comets differ greatly from all other objects in the solar system: they are quite unique in size, in mass, in density, and in behavior.

The tail of some comets extend 50 million miles; and some reach a length of 100 million

miles. The width and thickness of a comet are also of colossal proportions; 50,000 miles is a typical figure for either one of these dimensions.

Disproportionately, the mass is insignificantly small, too small to disturb the motion of even the smallest satellites on close encounter: the mass of a large comet is estimated at one millionth that of our earth.

Large volume and small mass make for very low mean density—probably not more than a millionth that of air at sea level. (Comets have been described as "the nearest thing to nothing that anything can be and still be something.") This low density is one reason that it is essentially transparent, so that stars can be observed through it.

Notwithstanding the low density and the minuteness of its mass, a comet, when visible, is an imposing object. Some rival the brightness of Venus, and stretch across half the sky from the zenith to the horizon.

The vast dimensions of some comets, together with their remarkable brilliance, are no doubt responsible for the many superstitions historically associated with their appearances. The appearance of a bright comet was believed to be "ominous of the wrath of Heaven, and harbingers of war and famine, of the dethronement of monarchs, and the dissolution of empires." Myth is further provoked by their characteristic sudden appearances.

Actually, very few bright comets have been recorded: one or two in a lifetime is the average. The last great comet appeared in 1882, was observable for nearly nine months, and was conspicuous for several weeks. No truly spectacular comet has appeared in the present century. Two that appeared in 1910 (one, a return of Halley's comet; the other, the 1910 I comet), and the far southern comet of December 1947 were only "fairly" great comets.

The frequency of faint comets is, of course, much greater than that of great or "fairly" great ones.

About five new comets are discovered every year, most of them too faint to be seen by the unaided eye. There were, by 1975, 625 comets with reliably determined orbits.

Comets are labeled by the name of their discoverer (e.g., Donati's comet) or by the name of the astronomer who made the comet an object of scientific attention (e.g., Halley's comet). Formally, they are provisionally designated by year of discovery and lower-case latter to indicate the order in that year, e.g., Ikeya-Seki 1967n was the fourteenth comet discovered in 1967. After the orbit has been computed they are finally designated by the year of their first observed passage near the sun, together with a Roman numeral to indicate the order in that year. Thus Ikeya-Seki 1967n was given the final designation Ikeya-Seki 1968 I as it was the first comet to pass perihelion in 1968.

16.2 THE STRUCTURE OF A COMET

A comet usually consists of: (A) a nucleus, quite small and bright; (B) a nebulous mass called the coma, surrounding the nucleus; and (C) a tail that gives the appearance of streaming from the coma. The tail is always much dimmer than the head, although there is no sharply defined boundary separating them. See Fig. 16.2.

A. **The Nucleus.** The nucleus is the central

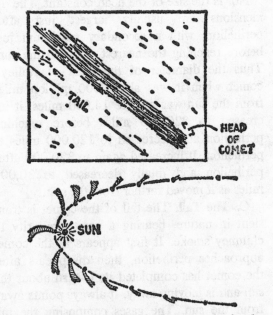

FIG. 16.2. The structure of a comet. The head, or coma, forms the front of the comet, the nucleus being the central part of it. The main bulk of the comet is taken up by the tail. This is a negative of the view, the bright objects appearing black in it.

The tail makes its first appearance when the comet is within several astronomical units distance from the sun. It is longest at perihelion and disappears when the comet is again at a great distance from the sun. Because of the pressure of sunlight the tail at all times points away from the sun.

bright spot, fairly small, rarely exceeding a diameter of a few miles. It differs from the rest of the comet primarily in density, it being the most concentrated part of the comet. Recent studies show that the nucleus is a conglomerate of frozen particles of methane (CH_4), ammonia (NH_3), ice (H_2O), together with a mixture of dust particles and meteoroids.

B. **The Coma.** As a nucleus nears the sun, some of the frozen particles evaporate and become gaseous. The gases emitted form the coma of the comet. Action of solar light transforms some of the molecules into other chemicals, such as carbon, cyanogen, ammonia radicals, and hydroxyl (OH).

Most comets have globular heads, varying greatly in size. The diameter may be less than 10,000 miles or may exceed 1 million miles.

Nor is the size of the head constant. The dimensions are usually largest just after perihelion, with a secondary maximum just before reaching the nearest point to the sun. Thus the diameter of the head of Halley's comet when it was about 300 million miles from the sun was a mere 14,000 miles; it increased to 220,000 miles before reaching perihelion and decreased to 120,000 miles at perihelion. It increased again to 320,000 after perihelion and finally decreased to 30,000 miles as it moved farther from the sun.

C. The Tail. The tail of the comet is transient in nature, bearing a great similarity to chimney smoke. It first appears as the comet approaches perihelion, then disappears after the comet has completed its U-turn about the sun and is moving away. It always points away from the sun. The gases composing the tail were swept out of the coma by radiation from the sun. This radiation also converts some of the original molecules into new ones such as carbon monoxide (CO), carbon dioxide (CO_2) and nitrogen (N_2).

While a length of 100 million miles is fairly common, the tail of the great comet 1843 I was estimated to have been more than 500 million miles long. This large spread is due to the fact that radiation pressure caused by sunlight greatly overcomes the gravitational pull of the coma on these gases.

Radiation pressure, as the term implies, is pressure due to radiation. Its value on terrestrial objects is insignificantly small—the pressure due to solar radiation on a square mile of the earth's surface is slightly less than two pounds. Its effect on the gases volatilized inside the coma, as well as on the fine dust particles, is great. Radiation pressure easily overcomes the gravitational pull acting on these particles, and is thus able to eject them from the coma to great distances. The propelling force due to this pressure follows the particles along their route. Their speed upon leaving the head is approximately .5 miles per second; farther along the tail, velocities of 50 miles per second are quite common.

Another result of the pressure due to the sun's radiation is that the tails always point away from the sun, trailing the comet as it approaches the sun and preceding it when the latter recedes.

16.3 THE ORBIT OF COMETS

A. ELLIPTICAL ORBITS

Of the 625 known comets as of the mid-1970s, nearly 250 are known to move in elongated ellipses; the most famous among these is Halley's comet. Edmund Halley (1665–1742), a contemporary of Sir Isaac Newton, was the first to suggest that the comet observed in 1682 was the same that was seen 76 years and 151 years earlier; and predicted its next visit early in the year 1759. He did not live to see his predictions come true; but the comet appeared in April 1759 and made two subsequent appearances on schedule. See Fig. 16.3a. It is due again in 1986.

B. OTHER ORBITS

The orbits of the other 370 comets have not been definitely ascertained. It is possible that these too move along elongated ellipses; or, more likely that they may move along parabolic or hyperbolic curves.

Figure 16.3b indicates the three types of curves that a comet's path can take. It is of the utmost importance to be able to ascertain the

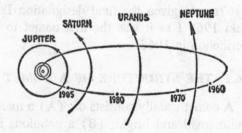

FIG. 16.3a. The orbit of Halley's comet as seen against the background of the orbits of the planets. In 1960 the comet was past its aphelion and on its way to the sun; 1970 found it at a distance about one third of the way between the planets Uranus and Neptune. It will again be visible from the earth in 1986. The actual orbit is inclined about 17° to the plane of the ecliptic.

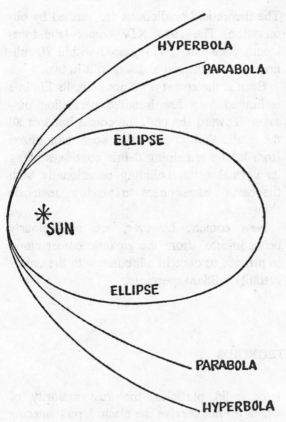

FIG. 16.3b. Possible orbits for a comet. An ellipse is a closed orbit; comets moving on it return time and time again to perihelion and can thus be seen time and time again by terrestrial observers. Both the parabola and the hyperbola are open orbits; the two ends of each never meet. Any object moving in such an orbit comes from infinite space, makes one appearance at perihelion, and then disappears, never to be seen again.

route followed by a comet. Comets that move in elliptical orbits return repeatedly to perihelion. Comets that move on either of the other two orbits appear only once to terrestrial observers; after making a U-turn about the sun they leave the solar system forever.

Regrettably, it is impossible to ascertain the orbits of many comets.

When the comet is close to the sun, the curvature of the three orbits is nearly identical (see arcs in Fig. 16.3b), making it almost impossible to distinguish among them. At great distances from the sun, when the orbits diverge from one another, the comets are too faint for observations.

Orbits of comets are often altered by close approaches to one of the major planets.

As a result, some comets have their periods shortened, others lengthened; still other comets have their orbits changed from an ellipse to either a parabola or hyperbola. Thus in 1886 Brooks's comet passed within about 55,000 miles of Jupiter's surface and underwent a change in period from over twenty-nine years to slightly more than seven years.

The orbits of 250 or more comets that are known to have elliptical orbits lie wholly within the solar system—more than fifty have their aphelia (points farthest from the sun) near the orbit of Jupiter. These are known as "Jupiter's family of comets." Others seem to have their aphelia near Saturn, Uranus, and Neptune and are known as the "families" of the respective planets. Actually, when orbital inclinations are taken into account, these comets "belonging" to Saturn, Uranus, and Neptune actually pass closer to Jupiter than to any of these other three planets.

16.4 LIFE AND DEATH OF A COMET

A study of long-period comets indicates that at a distance of between 50,000 and 150,000 astronomical units from the sun, there is a **Comet Cloud** containing as many as a hundred billion individual comets. Because of perturbation of neighboring stars, some of these are occasionally injected into the domain of the solar system, beginning their stay in the solar system as long-period comets, moving along greatly elongated ellipses.

During their stay in the solar system, both their orbit and their content may be greatly changed.

As noted above, the orbit of a comet is affected during close aproaches to one of the major planets. Such an encounter may change the comet's aphelion from thousands of astronomical units to a distance as small as ten astronomical units from the sun, similarly, the period may be decreased from hundreds of years to a small fraction of that time. (A major planet may also lengthen the aphelion distance or even evict the comet altogether from the solar system into interstellar space.) A comet's content is changed each time it passes near the sun—part of its mass forming the tail, which eventually diffuses into space.

A comet may also split into two or more parts during a perihelion passage, or when passing close to one of the major planets. Heavy tides formed at such close passage are primarily responsible for the splitting.

Roche's limit (see Sec. 15.27) indicates that a comet passing within 90 million miles of the sun, or 9 million miles from Jupiter, or 2 million miles from the earth, should disintegrate as a result of the tides produced in it.

The theoretical predictions are verified by observation. The 1947 XIV comet (the fourteenth comet in 1947) passed within 10 million miles of the sun and was split in two.

Even if the comet does not split, its lifetime is limited to a few hundred perihelion passages. Toward the end, the comet has lost all the gases that could have been violatilized from it; the remaining debris continues along its normal orbit, colliding occasionally with the earth's atmosphere to produce meteoric showers.

New comets, however, are continuously being injected from the gigantic comet cloud to provide us once in a lifetime with the unforgettably brilliant spectacle.

PART II: METEOROIDS

16.5 INTRODUCTION

Meteoroids are tiny solid objects (mostly the size of sand particles) traversing space, many along orbits also occupied by comets.

A study of their locations and motions indicates that meteoroids are remnants of comets that have lost a great deal of their mass on successive passages near the sun, the gravitational attraction of the remaining mass being too weak to keep the particles together. Soon after the demise of the comet, the particles form a closely packed group, well described as a "flying gravel pile"; such a group is known as a **Swarm**. With time, there is a great deal of scattering both along the elliptical orbit and sideways; an elongated pile of such particles, which may extend all around the orbit, is known as a **Stream**. Compact swarms or streams produce the **Meteoric Showers** (see Sec. 16.6) that can be observed on certain nights of the year, while dispersed streams are responsible for the sporadic meteors that can be seen any dark clear night.

The earth, moving along its orbit, is continuously colliding with many of these scat-

tered solid particles, the vast majority of which do not survive the clash. Upon entering the earth's atmosphere at a fairly great speed (typically, 20 miles per second), these meteoroids are incinerated by the white heat produced by the compression of the air in front of them and by the friction between the air and their surfaces. Meteoroids are first visible from the earth at heights of 60 to 90 miles; most vanish at heights of 30 to 50 miles.

The light phenomenon which results from a meteoroid's entry into the earth's atmosphere is called a **Meteor, or Shooting Star.** The light seen by the observer is due to collision between atoms knocked off the meteoroids and atoms of hot air.

The volume occupied by these colliding atoms is in form of a tube, whose length is the length of the streak and whose cross section is a circle having a diameter of 10 or more feet.

Shooting stars are extremely common. On a clear night five or more per hour can be seen from any single point on earth. The number all over the earth's surface on a given night is estimated to be more than 20 million. The number of fainter meteors that can be seen only with the aid of a telescope is thought to be between 5 and 10 thousand million per night.

The dust resulting from the incineration of a meteoroid settles slowly toward the earth, increasing the mass of our planet daily by hundreds of tons.

Occasionally, a large meteoroid collides with the earth's atmosphere and survives, in part, the tremendous heat engendered in its passage. Such a survivor is called a **Meteorite.** Meteorites can be seen on exhibit in various museums, many of them several feet in each dimension. Meteorites follow counterclockwise orbits of low inclination. This, as well as other data, suggests that they were once members of the planetoid population and not remnants of comets (as the other meteoroids are which do not survive the impact with earth's atmosphere).

Twice, to our knowledge, the earth was hit by truly gigantic meteorites—one, on June 30, 1908, weighed 40,000 tons. Luckily, it fell in a deserted spot in central Siberia, causing no deaths but doing immense damage to forestland.

The other gigantic meteorite left its imprint in the desert of northeast Arizona, near Canyon Diablo. The crater formed by the impact is nearly 4,000 feet across and is surrounded by a rim which stands about 140 feet above the surface of the surrounding limestone plain; the bottom of the crater is nearly 600 feet below the rim. Geological estimates based on a study of the rocks within the crater indicate that the collision between that meteorite and the earth occurred about thirty or forty thousand years ago.

There are in the 1970s thirty known meteorite craters on the earth and many more geological formations that may have been created by impacts of meteorites. These include the 35-miles-wide Manicouagan crater in Quebec, Canada.

NOTE: The earth most likely has been hit by many more meteorites than the moon. The forces of erosion on earth, however, have erased the signs of all craters except the few that have been recently made.

16.6 FREQUENCY

The frequency of observable meteors varies with: (A) the time of day; (B) the season of the year; and (C) primarily, whether the earth collides with some stray meteoroids or with a stream or swarm of meteoroids that still follow the elongated elliptical orbit usually of an extinct comet.

A. Frequency is greatest in the hours after midnight. On the average, twice as many meteors can be seen in the hours between midnight and sunrise than in a similar interval before midnight, since during the former period, the observer is on the front side of the earth as it moves along its orbit, and sees both meteors that are overtaken by the earth and those that are met head on. See Fig. 16.6a.

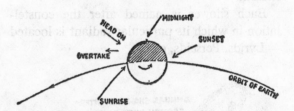

FIG. 16.6a. Frequency of meteors after midnight. Nearly twice as many meteors can be seen in any region of the sky after midnight, as compared to before midnight. Between midnight and sunrise a terrestrial observer is "riding" on the front part of the earth and can see both "head on" and "overtaken" collisions between meteors and the earth's atmosphere.

B. There is also a seasonal variation. Because of the inclination of the earth's equator to its orbit, the frequency of meteors is greatest, for observers in northern latitudes, in the fall.

C. Enormous increase in the number of meteors occurs when the earth goes through a swarm or a stream, at which time their number may be in the thousands per hour in any small region, as compared to the few that are normally seen per hour. **A large number of visible meteors is called a Meteoric Shower.**

Naturally, meteoric showers are much more spectacular when the earth goes through a swarm than when the earth goes through a stream, in which the particles are distributed throughout the orbit.

On the other hand, passages through streams are much more frequent than passages through swarms. The former occurs annually when the earth, moving in its own orbit, crosses the orbit of the stream. See Fig. 16.6b. For a meteoric shower due to a swarm to occur, both the earth and the swarm must be at the point of intersection at the same time. See Fig. 16.6c. For some swarms, this occurs once in 33 years; for others, at various intervals.

The meteors in a shower move in parallel paths. Because of perspective, these paths appear to an observer to converge at a point on the celestial sphere. This point is known as the radiant.

Each shower is named after the constellation in which its particular radiant is located —Lyrids, Perseids, etc.

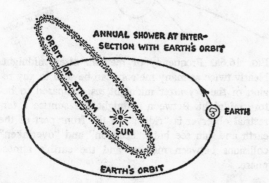

FIG. 16.6b. Meteoric showers due to a stream. These showers are annual events. They can be seen each time the earth is close to the stream of meteoroids.

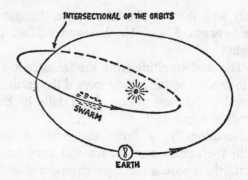

FIG. 16.6c. Meteoric showers due to a swarm. These showers are much more spectacular. They occur every time that the earth and the swarm are simultaneously at the point of intersection of their orbits. For some swarms this may be once every few hundred years.

Several of the principal meteoric showers and the associated comets are listed in Table 16.6.

16.7　METEORITES

Recoverable meteorites can be grouped into three distinct classes according to their composition:

A. **Siderites, or Iron Meteorites.** These consist of iron, and 5 to 15 per cent nickel. The two metals usually form an alloy. Quite often, a small percentage of cobalt and minute quantities of other elements are to be found in siderites.

B. **Aerolites, or Stony Meteorites.** These largely resemble terrestrial stones, although they are usually denser than the earthly variety.

Table 16.6
METEORIC SHOWERS

Name	Date	Comet	Period of Comet	Remarks
Lyrids	April 20–21	1861 I	415 years	A few every year.
Aquarids	May 2–6	Halley's	76.6 years	A few every year.
Perseids	August 2–22	1862 III	120 years	Many every year.
Orionids	October 16–26	Halley's	76.6 years	Many every year.
Leonids	November 14–18	Tempel's	33.3 years	Swift meteorites.
Geminids	December 10–16	?	?	Dependable showers.

C. Siderolites, or Stony Iron Meteorites. These meteorites usually consist of iron-nickel spongelike frames containing stony material in the interstices. The metals and the stones are mixed in about equal proportion.

A chemical analysis of meteorites reveals that nearly all the elements occur in them. In order of abundance they are iron, oxygen, and silicon. This mix is quite similar to that in the earth's crust: oxygen, silicon, aluminum, and iron.

16.8 HOW TO IDENTIFY METEORITES

A. Siderites. The iron meteorites or siderites are the easiest to identify. Siderites usually have a glossy, brownish appearance when discovered, due in part to the fusion which the metal underwent while in the air and in part to normal rusting on the ground.

To obtain final proof of the meteoritic ori-gin of a siderite, the following procedure may be followed: (1) cut off a piece of the meteorite; (2) polish the freshly exposed surface; (3) etch the polished surface with diluted nitric acid.

The etching brings out a crystalline design that is characteristic of iron meteorites.

B. Aerolites. The stony type of meteorite greatly resembles terrestrial rocks and is therefore much more difficult to identify. Two aids often used to identify aerolites involve the following procedures:

(1) Pulverize a small piece of the suspected stone. If the powder contains glistening flakes of metallic material (nickel, in particular), it is fairly safe to assume that the stone came from outer space.

(2) Put a small section under a microscope. If small round particles (called chondri) are embedded in the bulk of the specimen, you can be quite sure that the specimen has an extraterrestrial origin.

CHAPTER 17

ARTIFICIAL EARTH SATELLITES

An **artificial earth satellite** is a man-made object revolving about the earth in a circular or nearly circular (elliptical) orbit. The first such satellite, called Sputnik I, was launched by the U.S.S.R. on October 4, 1957. Sputnik I was a sphere that weighed 184 pounds and had a diameter of 23 inches. It circled the earth in an elliptical orbit with a perigee of 155 miles and an apogee of 580 miles, completing a trip around the earth in 96 minutes. During its lifetime, from the time of its launching until it disintegrated into the atmosphere, Sputnik I traveled 37 million miles.

To launch a satellite, it is necessary (1) to raise it to the proper height above sea level; (2) to orient it in the proper direction; (3) to give it the proper speed.

The satellite must be elevated several hundred miles so as to minimize the effect of atmospheric friction on its orbital motion.

It must be given a velocity perpendicular (90°) to the earth's radius if a circular orbit is desired. If an elliptical orbit is desired, the satellite must be given a velocity slightly different from perpendicular. The satellite must also be placed in the proper angle with the meridian. The proper angle is a compromise between making the best use of the "built-in" velocity caused by the earth's rotation about its axis and the best range of latitudes on the earth's surface for observation of the satellite.

To use most advantageously the velocity caused by the earth's rotation on its axis, the satellite should be launched at the equator and pointed in an easterly direction, where this "built-in" velocity is at a maximum, about 1,000 miles per hour. Any object at the equator has this velocity relative to space by virtue of the earth's completing one rotation (circumference 24,000 miles) in 24 hours. Such a satellite could only be seen by observers located at or near the equator. The satellite would only provide information about the 0° latitude.

To be seen by all terrestrial observers as well as to provide the maximum supply of information, a satellite should be set in a north-south direction. This would, however, negate the use of the "built-in" velocity.

The proper horizontal velocity is between 18,000 and 25,000 miles per hour or between 5 and 7 miles per second. Five miles per second is for very small orbits and 7 miles per second is for very large ones. If the horizontal velocity was less than 5 miles per second, the satellite would not go into orbit but would fall back to the earth. If the velocity was more than 7 miles per second, the object would not go into orbit around the earth but would escape from the earth's gravitational field.

The three tasks involved in launching a satellite are usually combined. The satellite is usually put into orbit by a multistage rocket. The primary purpose of the initial stage is to get the satellite through the thick part of the atmosphere, following the shortest route (i.e., straight up) and obtaining the optimum velocity (to minimize the effect of friction). The other stages turn the satellite toward the horizontal and bring its velocity up to the desired speed.

Before take-off, each stage is properly loaded with the correct amount of fuel. Each stage is discarded as soon as its mission is accomplished.

A typical rocket used to launch a satellite may consist of three stages and a nose cone. See Fig. 17.1a. The nose cone is put on the satellite to streamline it.

Once placed in an orbit, a satellite will continue there indefinitely, as the forces acting on a satellite cancel out, leaving a net force of zero.

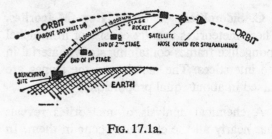

FIG. 17.1a.

Well above the earth's surface, there are only two forces acting on a satellite; these forces are:

A. Force of Gravity.

$$F_{grav.} = 6.7 \times 10^{-8} \frac{Mm}{r^2}$$

where M is the mass of the earth, m the mass of the satellite, and r the distance between the center of the earth and the center of the satellite. This force exerts a pull on the satellite, tending to bring it toward the earth.

B. The centrifugal force $F = \frac{mv^2}{r}$, where m is the mass of the satellite, v is the velocity along its orbit, and r is the distance of the satellite to the center of the orbit. This is a repelling force tending to increase the distance between the satellite and the earth.

For a proper value of velocity, these two forces are equal in magnitude and opposite in direction. Hence they cancel out one another. A satellite with the proper speed will thus continue to move in its orbit, there being no force to remove it from its established path.

Within the earth's atmosphere, the friction between the atmosphere and the satellite upsets the equilibrium between the gravitational and centrifugal force. The force due to friction slows down the forward speed of the satellite and starts the following chain of events:

A. The decrease in speed causes a decrease in centrifugal force.

B. The gravity force, being larger than the centrifugal force, causes the satellite to

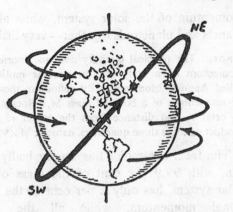

FIG. 17.1b. Motion of the satellite, The heavy line forms a hoop along which the satellite moves.

come closer and closer to the surface of the earth, following a spiral path.

C. The force of friction may create enough heat to burn the satellite before it reaches the ground, or the satellite may actually reach the ground the way large meteoroids often do.

The best time to visually observe a satellite is either at dawn or at dusk. At these times, the sun is below the horizon, the observer is in the region of darkness, while the satellite, several hundred miles up, is receiving and reflecting light from the sun.

The orbit followed by the satellite is fixed, except for some minor perturbations, in space while the earth inside that orbit is rotating once every 24 hours. See Fig. 17.1b.

Thus an observer in New York may view the satellite traveling from southwest to northeast, and 12 hours later he may see the same satellite in another part of its orbit moving from northwest to southeast.

A great deal of knowledge about outer space has been acquired with the aid of satellites. Some of those that have been placed in orbit are designed to perform specific functions. These satellites include:

A. **Communication satellites.** Some of these carry electronic equipment to receive, amplify and re-transmit signal messages.

B. **Weather satellites.** These report cloud cover, data on storms, paths of ocean currents.

C. **Earth-resources technology satellites.** These are used to increase our knowledge of the resources of the earth.

D. **Military satellites.**

CHAPTER 18

THE ORIGIN OF THE SOLAR SYSTEM

18.1 INTRODUCTION

It is now generally believed that the members of the solar system belong to three generations. The sun is the only first generation member, born about 5 billion years ago. The planets, planetoids and most of the other units of the system came into being at a slightly later date, and form the second generation. Satellites—the third generation—are the offspring of the planets, of still more recent date. It is also generally assumed that the masses of all these bodies were derived from matter originally belonging to the sun.

Several hypotheses attempt to explain the manner in which the planets, for instance, were created. Chief among these are:

A. The centrifugal-force hypothesis.
B. The tidal hypothesis.
C. The collision hypothesis.
D. The double-star encounter hypothesis.
E. The turbulence hypothesis.
F. The protoplanet hypothesis.

18.2 THE CENTRIFUGAL-FORCE HYPOTHESIS

The **Centrifugal-Force Hypothesis** is usually referred to as the **Nebular Theory of Laplace,** after the great French mathematician and astronomer Pierre Simon Laplace (1749–1827), who first proposed it in 1796. According to this theory, the sun was once a slowly rotating vast disk-shaped mass of hot gas, extending well beyond the orbit of Pluto, the outermost planet. The birth of the planets resulted from the following chain of events:

A. The gas cooled.

B. As a result it contracted, the radius of the disk becoming smaller.

C. The decrease in radius caused an increase in rotational velocity, thus increasing the centrifugal force.

D. When the centrifugal force, acting on the outermost regions of the sun, exceeded in value the force of attraction, a ring was separated from the main body of the sun.

E. The gaseous ring gradually condensed into a sphere which became one of the planets.

The sun continued to cool, and this process repeated itself to produce the other planets.

Criticism of the Laplace Theory. While, at first glance, the theory seems reasonable, further thought shows it to be completely untenable, as it is inconsistent with several fundamental principles of mechanics. Two of these inconsistencies are:

a. It can be shown that the rings, after being separated from the sun, could not coalesce to form a single body, nor even a few bodies. Instead, physical theory shows that most of the material in these rings would evaporate, molecule by molecule, into space; the remainder, due to tidal effects from the sun on the ring, would become a multitude of gravel-sized, or smaller, particles.

b. It can be shown that planets thus created should rotate and revolve much more slowly than they actually do (or that the sun should rotate much faster). Otherwise stated, the sun should possess most of the angular momentum of the solar system, while all the planets and planetoids together—very little.

NOTE: The physical quantity used to describe the momentum of a body due to circular motion, is called **Angular Momentum.** By definition, the angular momentum of a body of mass M, velocity along its orbit v, and distance from the center r, is the product of these three quantities, namely, $M \times v \times r$.

The facts contradict this theory badly: the sun, with 99.9 per cent of the mass of the solar system, has only 2 per cent of the rotational momentum, while all the other members of the solar system combined have .1 per cent of the mass, but 98 per cent of the angular momentum.

Thus, according to theory the nebula, while cooling, should concentrate and retain the major portion of this angular momentum in its central mass (the sun), and endow the departing rings with only a minute fraction of this rotational inertia—the fact is, however, that the sun possesses only 2 per cent of the momentum.

18.3 THE TIDAL AND THE COLLISION HYPOTHESES

The **Tidal Hypothesis,** also known as the **Encounter Hypothesis,** maintains that the planets were created as a result of enormous tides raised on the sun by a passing star. The dense gases drawn out of the sun were also endowed with a sideward motion in the direction in which the passing star was moving. Part of the matter thus raised would very likely follow the star; another part would presumably return to the surface of the sun. Still another would be acted upon with a centrifugal force large enough to overcome gravitational attraction and would form the several planets. This hypothesis, suggested by Forrest R. Moulton and Thomas C. Chamberlin of the University of Chicago in 1900, was originally known as the planetesimal theory, the term "planetesimal" meaning "little planet." This diminutive suggests that the immediate results of the tidal action was only small planets; these grew in size by picking up neighboring scattered material to form the system of the nine known planets.

The **Collision Hypothesis** differs from the tidal hypothesis in that it assumes that the encounter between the sun and the visiting star took the form of an actual collision.

Criticism. Computations, based on fundamental formulas of Physics, show that neither hypothesis is acceptable. Again the primary difficulty has to do with the observed distribution of angular momenta, namely, that the sun has only 2 per cent, while the planets have close to 98 per cent of the rotational momentum. Professor Henry Norris Russell of Princeton University concluded that under no reasonable assumption relating to an encounter could as much as 10 per cent of the known angular momentum per ton of planet be possible. Also the probability of a collision is extremely rare. Computations indicate that no more than ten collisions have taken place among the 100 billion stars in our galaxy in the last 5 billion years.

18.4   THE DOUBLE-STAR ENCOUNTER HYPOTHESIS

The **Double-Star Encounter Hypothesis**, introduced by the English astronomer R. A. Lyttleton, has the enormous advantage over the preceding ones in that it does not contradict the observed facts of angular momentum. Lyttleton's hypothesis supposes that the sun was originally a double star, and that a passing star collided with the sun's companion. The events that followed this collision, which may have lasted about an hour, were:

A. The colliding stars (the intruder and the companion of the sun), after the rebound, drew out a ribbon of material, large enough to produce all the planets, satellites, etc.

B. The two stars (like billiard balls after a collision) proceeded along their courses, carrying away the parts of their "ribbon" that were under immediate influence of their respective gravitational fields.

C. The various members of the solar system came into being from the central part of that withdrawn matter; the angular momentum of the matter in this central part could conceivably correspond to the observed values.

Criticism. Computations show that 94 per cent of the ribbon would be taken along by the two colliding stars, while the 6 per cent of the central portion would follow the intruder and the sun's companion for some time before returning to the sole influence of the sun. The probability that planets would be formed from this 6 per cent of the matter is extremely slight. It is infinitely more likely that tidal effects from the intruder and the companion tore this part of the ribbon into shreds that eventually were scattered into neighboring space.

18.5   THE TURBULENCE HYPOTHESIS

One of the most promising hypotheses, the **Turbulence Hypothesis,** is the work of the contemporary German physicist Carl Friedrich von Weizsäcker. The point of departure of his hypothesis, published in 1945, is similar to that of Laplace. Von Weizsäcker's theory assumes that at one time in its development, the sun was surrounded by a slowly rotating disk-shaped cloud of gas. The diameter of the disk was of the order of magnitude of the diameter of the present solar system, and the temperature at various distances from the central sun corresponded to the temperatures now prevalent on the nine planets located at the same distances (e.g., the temperature of the gases in the disk at the distance of the earth is assumed to be equal to the earth's present temperature). The mass of the nebula is assumed to be 100 times larger than the combined masses of the planets, equal approximately to 10 per cent of the sun's mass; and consisting primarily (99 per cent) of hydrogen and helium and only 1 per cent of the heavier elements. The following chain of events presumably followed this initial state:

A. In 200 million years, the molecules of hydrogen and helium were dissipated into space, diminishing the mass of the gases from the original 10 per cent to the present value of slightly more than .1 per cent of the sun's mass, but leaving the angular momentum of the nebula basically unchanged, thus accounting for its present large value.

B. In those 200 million years, due to the differences in speed between parts of the nebula close to the sun (great speeds), and those farther from it (small speeds), turbulence cells were formed. The matter in each cell moved in a clockwise direction, while the cells themselves (see Figure 18.5) moved counterclockwise. The planets, according to this hypothesis, formed in the dead-end region between the cells. These regions, due to the conflicting currents at its boundaries, are most active in accretion of material from the neighboring cells, and are thus instrumental in building up great quantities of matter rotating in a counterclockwise direction. Five such equidistant quantities eventually join in the formation of the planet at the given distance.

Criticism. Much that we know about the

Fig. 18.5. The turbulence hypothesis. Due to differences in speed in the various parts of the nebular turbulence cells were formed. Five such cells are shown at the outer boundary, as are five neighboring cells. Each one of these cells spins in a clockwise direction, while the center of the cells proceeds in a counterclockwise direction about the sun.

Large masses of matter formed in the regions between the cells; several of these are shown shaded in the diagram. According to Von Weizsäcker's theory, these lumps eventually formed the planet at that particular distance from the sun.

solar system can be explained on the basis of Von Weizsäcker's hypothesis. Many questions, however, still remain unanswered.

The hypothesis explains, for example:

(a) the fact that the planets, as well as the planetoids, revolve in nearly a common plane;

(b) the fact that the sun's equatorial plane nearly coincides with the orbital planes of the planets;

(c) the fact that the planets possess nearly all of the angular momentum of the whole system; and

(d) the fact that the spacing of the planets follows a regular pattern, as described in Bode's law for planetary distances.

The number of questions that are still unanswered are many. Among these are:

1. How did the droplets and particles form the lumps?
2. By what process did the several lumps unite to form a single planet?
3. Why does Uranus rotate about an axis that is almost perpendicular to the axis of its orbital plane?
4. Why do a few of the satellites move in retrograde motion?

18.6 THE PROTOPLANET HYPOTHESIS

The **Protoplanet Hypothesis,** proposed in 1950 by the Dutch-born American astronomer G. P. Kuiper modifies several parts of the nebular theory of Laplace.

According to this hypothesis:

A. The large sphere of gas and dust, under the influence of gravitational and centrifugal forces, became a fast-rotating disk. Ninety-five per cent of the original material settled near the center of the disk (this material soon to become the young, cool sun), the other 5 per cent remained in the disk (soon to become protoplanets of the solar system).

B. Turbulence was the rule in the disk, and concentration of matter formed in various parts of it, only to be dissolved soon after formation. At one time or another, though, a concentration of matter did form in which the gravitational attraction was strong enough to overcome the disruptive forces of the turbulence. Such a concentration grew rapidly in size and mass by adding neighboring matter to itself, eventually becoming a protoplanet (i.e., a large fragment of gas and dust destined to become a planet). The other protoplanets were similarly formed at various distances from the sun. The protoplanets close to the sun accumulated little mass, since most of the material at that distance was already picked up by the sun. Protoplanets far from the sun, too, did not grow much in size, since they formed at the outskirts of the disk where the quantity of material was small.

C. The young, cool sun continued to shrink and warm up. Eventually, about 5 billion years ago, the core became hot enough to trigger the hydrogen into helium fusion, and the sun began to emit radiation as well as solar wind at full power. The radiation and the solar wind (1) swept out of all the material between the protoplanets in the system, and (2) heated the protoplanets, thus causing a great deal of their mass to escape into interstellar space.

In this sweeping-out process the earth lost 99.9 per cent (!) of its protoplanetic mass (the mass lost was mainly hydrogen and helium). The protoplanet Jupiter, too, lost nearly all its mass (95 per cent) in the process of changing to the planet Jupiter.

18.7 THE FORMATION OF SATELLITES

In a process similar to their own formation, protoplanets under the influence of gravitational and centrifugal forces became flattened disks in which concentrations of matter (protosatellites) formed.

NOTES: 1. Mercury and Venus do not have satellites because their slow rotation did not permit sufficient material to spill out to form these bodies.

2. It seems highly likely that the earth's satellite, the moon, was once an autonomous protoplanet. One of the arguments for this theory is the fact that the moon's orbit is nearly in the same plane as the other planets, rather than in the plane of the earth's equator.

3. The Kuiper theory also gives an explanation for the dozen satellites that do not move in the near-circular coplanar orbits pursued by the majority. The theory assumes that these satellites were originally formed far away from the mother protoplanet, and when the latter lost a major part of its mass, the following chain of events took place:

a. The gravitational hold of the planet vanished and those satellites came under the influence of the gravitational field of the sun, i.e., the satellites became planets.

b. After few or many revolutions about the sun, these bodies were captured again by the vast atmospheres of the planet, now moving in an orbit totally different from the original.

4. Because the planet Pluto differs from its neighbors (smaller size, slow rotation, unusually high inclination, unusually high eccentricity of orbit), there is good reason to think that it at one time was a satellite of Neptune.

18.8 THE FORMATION OF PLANETOIDS

The origin of planetoids is explained as follows:

The massive proto-Jupiter having acquired most of the material in the space between Mars and itself, the remainder was barely sufficient to form a handful of small bodies. One or more pairs of these small objects later collided to form many of the planetoids and meteorites known today.

18.9 THE FORMATION OF COMETS

The protoplanet hypothesis assumes that the comets were formed in a ring close to the rim of the flattened disk of gas and dust. One by one, or several at a time, under the influence of the gravitational force of Pluto, comets underwent major changes in their orbits. In due course, the comets found themselves occupying an enormous volume of space, centered on the sun and extending to a distance of 100,000 astronomical units.

It is now assumed that there are more than a 1,000 billion (maybe even 1 million billion) comets in that space, their total mass amounting to several hundred earth masses.

It is also assumed that, from time to time, a

passing star perturbs a comet and starts it out on the trip that will eventually bring it close to the sun and then become an object for astronomical observations.

18.10 THE FUTURE OF THE SOLAR SYSTEM

To the best of our knowledge, the major changes in the solar system will be due to the aging of the sun.

The sun is now in its maturity (see Sec. 9.7), deriving its energy from the thermonuclear process, i.e., from the reaction that changes hydrogen into helium. This age will probably go on for another several (five or more) billions of years.

Next, the sun will start on its way to become a red-giant star (see Sec. 9.8). At that time:

A. The sun will grow bigger, possibly engulfing the orbit of Mercury or maybe even the orbit of Venus.
B. The sun will cool at its surface and appear redder.
C. The sun will increase by a factor of maybe a 100 the amount of radiation emitted toward the earth.

On our earth, as a result of all this:

a. The oceans will boil away.
b. The molecules composing the atmosphere will acquire enough velocity to escape into space.

c. The earth will take on all the aspects of a charred cinder.

NOTE: The nearest place for human climatic comfort at that time will probably be the planet Saturn.

The red-giant period for the sun is likely to last several hundred million years and will be followed by the transition to a white dwarf (see Sec. 9.10), that is:

A. The sun will grow smaller (eventually smaller than the size of the planet earth).
B. The sun will change color to blue or white.
C. The sun will decrease in brightness by a factor of $\frac{1}{10,000}$ of its present value.
D. The sun will appear to a hypothetical terrestrial observer as a point of light (and not as a disk).

On the earth, as a consequence of that:

a. Temperatures will drop drastically, eventually approaching absolute zero.
b. Darkness will be the rule 24 hours a day.
c. The stars will still be in the sky (among them one particularly bright one—our sun). The planets will be invisible, a very pale moon will go through its phases, and from time to time a comet will be seen not too far from the particularly bright star.

All of this—the too-hot period and the too-cold period—is billions of years away.

A period that can be well used to advance ethical, moral, and scientific values on the planet now occupied by man.

APPENDIX

HOME-BUILT TELESCOPES

INTRODUCTION

Excellent telescopes are being designed and constructed by an evergrowing number of amateur astronomers, using rather simple "ingredients" and a great deal of devotion and "elbow grease."

Some homemade telescopes are of simple

construction; others approach in complexity instruments produced in professional shops. In all cases, many decisions have to be made in the course of production.

The very first decision that has to be made is whether to build a refractor (the objective-a lens) or a reflector (the objective-a mirror). The relative merits to be considered are:

A. For a Refractor

I. Of the two, the percentage of light transmitted to the eyepiece by a lens objective is slightly higher—a lens of 5-inch clear diameter being the equal of a mirror of 5½-inch clear diameter.

II. Surveys of large portions of the sky are much more efficiently carried out with refractors. The field of a reflector is limited to a fraction of a degree.

III. Upkeep is small for any telescope; it is slightly less for a refractor. The aluminum coating on the mirror deteriorates and has to be renewed every few years. A refractor does not deteriorate with time; its adjustments, once made, are permanent.

B. For a Reflector

1. A mirror is perfectly achromatic, while a lens, even when corrected, has a residual color defect.

2. To reduce the residual color defect to a tolerable minimum, the ratio $\dfrac{\text{focal length}}{\text{diameter}}$ of the objective lens has to be large,* say 15 or 20; while in the case of a mirror objective, chromatic aberration is nonexistent and the focal length is usually designed to be 3 or 4 or 5 times the size of the diameter. Small ratios imply short telescopic tubes which are easier to mount and easier to transport from place to place. Also, long focal ratio refractors are too slow for photographic work. Mirror objectives are much more efficient in photographing both individual objects and clusters of stars.

3. The probability of success is larger, especially for a beginner, with a reflector. A beginner is much more likely to construct a good concave mirror, which has to have the proper curvature only on one side, than a good achromatic lens with exact curvatures on four surfaces, two of which have to fit together.

4. Cost, too, is on the side of a reflector.

---

* The larger the ratio $\dfrac{\text{focal length}}{\text{diameter}}$ in a lens, the less objectionable is its color aberration. The focal length of an achromatic objective with tolerable color aberration is given to fair accuracy by the formula $f=5d^2$, where f is the focal length in inches and d is the diameter in inches.

The expense connected with a reflector is usually less than 50 per cent of the cost of a refractor of similar size objective.

Having weighed all these factors, most amateur astronomers decide on a reflector. Detailed instructions for both follow.

HOMEMADE REFRACTOR

An astronomical refractor consists of an objective lens, housed in the front part of the objective tube; and an eyepiece housed at the rear end of the mounting. See Fig. A1.

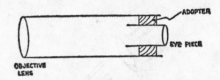

FIG. A1. An astronomical refractor. The front lens points toward the object and is known as the objective or objective lens. The eyepiece is used to magnify the (first) image produced by the objective. The diameter of the eyepiece mounting is usually smaller than the diameter of the objective tube: an adapter made of wood or other material is used to fill the gap.

A. The Objective Lens

A beginner would do well to acquire a ready-made objective and forego the desire to produce one himself. Good assortments of perfect or nearly perfect war surplus large-diameter, achromatic, large f-number, and coated lenses are available at reasonable prices and should be used in the first attempt to design a refractor.

Such a lens, 3¼-inch diameter, achromatic, coated, 40 inches focal length, and an f-number equal to 12.3 will be used as an example in what follows. General formulas will be given which can be used with other objective lenses.

The meanings of the various terms are given elsewhere in the book and are briefly summarized here.

Achromatic usually means that the lens consists of two components cemented together to form a unit, free of most color defect (see Sec. 5.5).

Coated usually means that the surfaces of the lens have been covered with a coating of magnesium fluoride to eliminate reflection of light at these surfaces. This coating is extremely thin; its thickness equals a quarter of a wavelength of yellow-green light (see Sec. 5.12).

Focal length means the distance between the center of the lens and the focus. This distance can easily be checked by placing the lens perpendicularly to solar rays, finding on a screen the focus, and measuring the distance F. See Fig. A2; see also Sec. 5.3.

Fɪɢ. A2. Focal length F is the distance between the center of the lens and the focus. It is usually stated either in inches or in millimeters.

f-Number, also known as **focal ratio,** is simply the ratio between the focal length and the diameter of the lens. In the example under consideration, the f ratio is $\frac{40}{3\frac{1}{4}} = 12.3$. This ratio is of particular importance in photographic work. Small values of ratio correspond to great photographic speeds; large values correspond to slow speed, i.e., require large exposure times.

B. Tubing for Objective

Cardboard tubing, the kind used for mailing charts and calendars, is quite satisfactory. Aluminum tubing is better. The inside of the tube should be well covered with flat black lacquer.

Aluminum tubing with inside diameter of 3.281 inches and an outside diameter of 3.406 inches, will exactly accommodate a 3¼-inch-diameter lens.

The length of the objective tube should be larger by an inch than the focal length of the objective. A piece of tubing 41 inches long will serve for a f=40-inch lens.

C. Mounting of Objective in Tubing

There are many ways to attach the objective to the tubing; the goal always is to produce a firm attachment, without covering much of the lens surface (the "clear" diameter of the lens should be as close as possible to its "real" diameter).

An aluminum tubing mounting can be made from two narrow (say ¼ inch) rings, from which small segments are cut (see Fig.

Fɪɢ. A3. One of the two narrow rings with small segments missing that are used to mount the objective in the tube.

A3), so that the remainder will just fit inside the objective tubing. The rings may be attached to the tubing with two or three small machine screws. See Fig. A4.

Fɪɢ. A4. The rings minus the segment just fit inside the tubing (only one ring is shown here). The lens is placed between the two rings.

D. The Eyepiece

The three (**Huygenian, Kellner,** and **Orthoscopic**) common types of eyepieces were described in Secs. 5.9, 5.10, and 5.11. These descriptions, with particular attention to the merits of each type, should be carefully reviewed before acquiring this part of the telescope. Let us assume that a Kellner ½-inch focal length, coated, 40° apparent field of view eyepiece has been selected for the 3¼-inch-diameter objective; the eyepiece is mounted in a piece of tubing, the outside diameter of which is 1¼ inches.

E. Calculations

Given the optical data about the objective, and the optical data of the eyepiece, many of the properties of their combination (i.e., the telescope) can be computed:

1. Magnification=$\dfrac{\text{focal length of objective}}{\text{focal length of eyepiece}}$

For the objective and eyepiece on hand,

$$\text{Magnification}=\frac{40}{\frac{1}{2}}=80 \text{ times.}$$

2. True field of view=

$$\frac{\text{apparent field of view of eyepiece}}{\text{magnification}}$$

In the example being worked out, the apparent field of view of the eyepiece is 40°, the magnification is 80X. Hence,

$$\text{true field of view}=\frac{40}{80}=\frac{1}{2}°.$$

This answer implies that half a degree (about the size of the angular diameter of the moon) of the sky is seen through a telescope made of this objective and eyepiece. See Fig. A5.

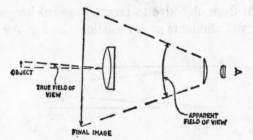

Fig. A5. Apparent field of view is the angle subtended at the eye by the final image. True field of view is the angle subtended by the object at the eye.

3. Resolving power of telescope:

$$\text{Resolving power}=\frac{5}{\text{diameter of objective}}.$$

A telescope having a 3¼-inch objective has a resolving power of

$$\frac{5}{3\frac{1}{4}}=1.5 \text{ seconds of angle;}$$

that is, two stars at an angular distance of 1.5 seconds of angle will be seen as two distinct points of light. See Fig. A6.

Fig. A6. Resolving power is the smallest angle that two distant objects may subtend and still be seen as two distinct units.

4. Size of exit pupil
Exit pupil is, by definition, the diameter of the cylindrical beam of light emerging from the eyepiece.
This diameter should never be larger than the diameter of the pupil of the human eye (say ⅙ of an inch) or smaller than, say say 1/64th of an inch. The value of the exit pupil is computed from the formula:

$$\text{Exit pupil}=\frac{\text{diameter of objective}}{\text{magnification}}.$$

For a 3¼-inch-diameter lens and a magnification of 80 times, the exit pupil is equal to:

$$\frac{3\frac{1}{4}}{80}=\frac{13}{320}=\frac{26}{640}=\frac{2.6}{64}\text{inches.}$$

This value is well within the limits prescribed for the diameter. See Fig. A7.

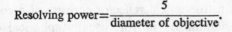

Fig. A7. Exit pupil is the diameter of the cylinder of light leaving the eyepiece.

5. Radius of image produced by objective.
The size of the first image, i.e., the image produced by the objective alone, depends on (a) the true field of view, and (b) the

focal length of the objective. The formula is:

Radius of image=
$$\frac{\text{true field of view} \times \text{focal length of objective}}{57.3}$$

The 57.3 in the denominator is a conversion factor from angles in degrees to angles in terms of radians. For an objective lens of 40 inch focal length and ½ degree of angle field of view, the radius of the first image is:

$$\frac{.5 \times 40}{57.3} = \frac{20}{57.3} = .35 \text{ inch.}$$

F. Mounting of the Eyepiece

The outside diameter of eyepiece mountings (standardized to 1¼ inches in diameter) is usually materially smaller than the inner diameter of the draw tube; and an adapter has to be used between the mounting and the tube. Such an adapter, in the form of a hollow cylinder, may be made of wood or any other convenient material. The outside radius of the hollow cylinder would have to fit inside the objective tube (say 3¼ inches in diameter); the inner radius would have to accommodate the 1¼-inch eyepiece mounting. The adapter should not be too thick, so as not to interfere with the light going from objective to eyepiece.

It is important to make sure that when the eyepiece mounting is fully inserted, the field lens (the lens in the eyepiece close to the objective) is close to the focus of the objective, and that the mounting can be pulled out half an inch or so without becoming detached from the objective tubing. The focus of the eyepiece is just a little ahead of the field lens.

G. Layout

In the case of a 3¼-inch objective and the ½-inch Kellner eyepiece, the simplest arrangement would be as shown in Figure A8.

H. Image Stop and Glare Stop

An image stop is placed in the focal plane of the objective in order to cut out weak edge rays and thus obtain a sharp well-defined

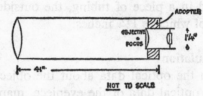

FIG. A8. Layout of telescope. The focus of the eyepiece is just ahead of the field lens, the ½-inch being measured from the center of the eyepiece.

image. The stop consists of a round disk of blackened cardboard or other convenient material, with a central hole of radius equal to the radius of the image formed by the objective. In the case of the 3¼-inch lens, this radius was computed (see E Calculations above) to be equal to .35 inches.

Two or three glare stops are often inserted in the objective tube to eliminate stray radiation which enters the telescope from outside the field of view. These, too, are round disks, with a central hole, usually made of the same material as the image stop.

The stops are placed so that they divide the distance between the objective and first image in equal parts. The size of the hole is determined from a drawing showing (to scale) the objective, the first image, and two lines (such as AC and BD) joining the ends of same.

A typical stop placed at a distance of 13 inches from the objective should have a diameter KL; this would permit the full cone of light from objective to proceed toward image, but will eliminate stray radiation. See Fig. A9.

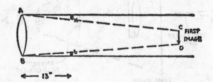

FIG. A9. Diameter of stop. A stop at the distance of 13 inches would have a diameter of KL, K and L being points on the lines AC and BD that include the full cone of light proceeding from the objective to the image.

HOMEMADE REFLECTOR

An astronomical reflector consists of a concave aluminized mirror, usually spherical or paraboloidal in shape, mounted at the bottom of an open tube, a plane mirror (known as a flat or as a diagonal), and an eyepiece. See Fig. A10.

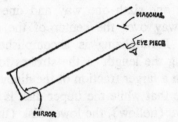

FIG. A10. A reflector consists of concave mirror, a diagonal (flat mirror) or a prism, and an eyepiece.

Light from the object under study passes down the tube to the mirror, which reflects it back up to form the first image (the action of the mirror in the reflector is thus similar to the action of the objective lens in the refractor). The small plane mirror intercepts the reflected rays just before their focal plane and diverts them at right angles toward the side of the upper end of the tube. The first image formed by these rays is viewed by the eyepiece located in this upper tube. See Fig. A11.

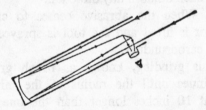

FIG. A11. Path of light in a reflector. Rays of light from object pass down the tube to concave mirror, the first image (the action of the mirror in the reflected rays are intercepted before image was formed) by plane mirror and diverted toward the side of the tube. The image formed there is magnified by the eyepiece.

Eyepieces have been described earlier in this book (see Chapter 5); the same types can be used for both reflectors and refractors.

It is assumed that both the eyepiece and the diagonal will be acquired ready-made.

The following description will deal primarily with the grinding, polishing, and testing of the mirror.

MIRROR GRINDING

Ready-made mirrors of various sizes and perfections are now available in the stores. But there is no substitute for the satisfaction of having a mirror of one's own making.

The starting point is extremely simple—two glass disks (blanks): one for the mirror, one for the "tool"; a supply of a few kinds of abrasives used in glass grinding; the final result may very well be a mirror that excels in definition and perfection the best obtainable in the stores.

The mirror disk is usually made of pyrex glass; its thickness is approximately equal to one sixth the diameter. The sides of the blank are usually tapered, one surface having a slightly larger diameter than the other (the larger surface is to be ground to the proper curvature of the mirror).

For example, let the larger surface of the mirror disk be 6 inches in diameter (this is now the most popular size, many thousands of these were made in recent years). Let the desired focal length of the finished product be 48 inches.

The tool is usually ordinary plate glass of the same diameter as the mirror and of thickness equal to or slightly less than the mirror blank.

The first abrasive used in the grinding process is usually carborundum #80. Carborundum, a synthetic abrasive consisting of silicon carbide, is considerably harder than emery and many times more efficient. The 80 indicates that it just goes through a mesh having 80 strands per inch. The second abrasive is usually carborundum #220; this is followed by three or four successively thinner abrasives to complete the grinding process.

The working setup resembles a sandwich. The plate-glass blank is on the bottom; water and carborundum powder are in the middle; and the pyrex blank is on top. See Fig. A12.

The steps involved are as follows:

A. The tool is fastened to the working platform, usually a barrel, with the aid of a

FIG. A12. The working setup. The plate-glass flat cylinder is on the bottom; the pyrex blank to be ground is on the top; the abrasive is in between.

wooden base. The glass is warmed; one side of it is covered with turpentine. Melted pitch is poured on the wooden base and then the wet face of the blank is pressed tightly against the pitch-covered wood. See Fig. A13.

FIG. A13. The tool is glued (pitch is used) to the wooden base. The wooden base is bolted firmly to the top of the barrel.

B. A handle is attached to the pyrex disk. To do this, the back of the mirror is warmed, the center of it is wet with turpentine, upon which warm pitch is poured, and the handle is then firmly pressed on. See Fig. A14.

FIG. A14. A handle is attached, with the aid of pitch, to the pyrex blank.

C. The abrasive is introduced. Carborundum ✕80 is sprayed on the tool; the face of the mirror is dipped in water and the grinding begins.

D. Three motions are followed simultaneously during the grinding. (1) A to-and-fro motion (center over center) of the pyrex disk over the tool; (2) rotation of the pyrex blank about its own center; and (3) slow walk of worker around the barrel, so as to cover the whole circumference of the stationary tool.

The first of these three motions is the all-important one. The length of the stroke determines the shape of the mirror. To produce a spherical shape (usually a perfect spherical

shape is produced first; the parabolic correction is added later) the length of the stroke should be about one third the diameter of the disk, that is, the center of the top blank is moved one sixth one way and one sixth the other way over the center of the stationary blank. Parabolizing is accomplished by increasing the length of the strokes to one half or even a larger fraction of the diameter.

Note that while the upper disk is becoming concave (hollow), the lower disk (the tool) is becoming convex. This is due partly to the increased pressure between the disks, when only part of them are in contact. See Fig. A15.

FIG. A15. The pyrex disk becomes concave as the tool becomes convex.

Note that in this overhang position the pressure between the disks is larger than in the normal sandwich position.

Note also that both surfaces become spherical in shape; spherical surfaces remain in continuous contact at every point when moved over each other in any direction.

E. When the abrasive ceases to cut, the mirror is lifted and the tool is sprayed anew with carborundum.

This grinding, known as rough grinding, continues until the radius of the mirror is about 10 inches longer than the one aimed for. In the example under study, the aim is a 96-inch radius (or 48-inch focus; the radius of the mirror is twice its focal length). The rough grinding will continue until the radius is about 106 inches; the excess will be taken care of by the next grinding stage.

A quick determination of the radius of the mirror is obtained by:

1. placing the mirror in a vertical position,
2. placing the eye on level with center, and
3. holding in one hand a candle, moving it back and forth at right angles to the axis of the mirror and noting the direction of motion of the candle's reflection in the mirror.

If the reflection moves in the same direction as the candle, the eye is closer to the mirror than its center of curvature. If the reflection moves the opposite way from that of the candle, the eye is farther from the mirror than its center of curvature.

By moving the eye closer to or farther from the mirror, its center of curvature can be ascertained within an accuracy of several inches.

F. The fine grinding brings the radius to within ½ or ¼ inch of its ultimate radius; the process of polishing usually shortens the radius of the curve by ¼ or ½ inch.

Carborundum ✕220 is used in the first stage of this fine grinding. Care should be taken to remove, by thorough washing and rinsing, every last trace of the carborundum ✕80 that was used in the rough grinding process.

Usually seven or eight charges of the ✕220 are sufficient for this stage. Each charge (known as a "wet," because the carborundum has water added to it) lasts about 5 minutes before it ceases to cut; this whole stage of fine grinding takes about 40 minutes.

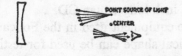

Fig. A16. Setup for Foucault test. Light from the point source is reflected by the mirror (only the beginning and the end of the path of light is shown) toward the eye.

G. The fine grinding process is then repeated by three or four successively thinner abrasives (say, abrasive numbers 320, 400, and 600), care again being taken to remove the coarse abrasive before the finer one is applied. Again six "wets" (charges) are usually sufficient for each stage.

H. Testing the spherical shape of the mirror is the next job.

There are several tests to ascertain whether the mirror has a perfectly spherical shape—the best known of these we owe to the Frenchman Foucault (of the Foucault pendulum experiment-fame).

The equipment for the test consists of a point source of light; (a small hole in a metal chimney containing an electric light usually serves as the pinhole); and a knife edge.

The point source of light is placed several inches to one side of the center; the eye is placed an equal distance on the opposite side. See Fig. A16.

If the curvature of the mirror is spherical, then

1. The light reflected by the mirror will meet at *one* point.
2. A knife edge "cutting" that point will cause the mirror:
   a. to darken *evenly* all over;
   b. look flat.
3. A slight movement of the knife edge across that point will cause no moving shadow in the mirror. See Fig. A17.

Fig. A17. Test for spherical shape. If the face of the mirror is perfectly spherical all the reflected rays will meet at one point. A knife edge placed at that point will block these rays from the eye. The mirror seen in the light of starry radiation will appear evenly dark. (Only the end of the paths of the light is shown.)

If the mirror is not spherical, none of these characteristics will be present, e.g., slight movements of the knife edge at right angles to the axis of the mirror will cause its shadow to move one way across the mirror's face.

I. The polishing of the mirror can be done with either fine optical rouge (Fe_2O_3), Cerium oxide (CeO_2), or Barnesite (a mixture of several rare earth oxides). Cerium oxide is two to three times as efficient as rouge. Of the three, Barnesite probably yields the superior polish.

To arrange for the polishing:

1. Cover the tool with a layer of pitch.
2. Cut out channels, usually of a V cross-section. These serve as reservoirs for the liquid

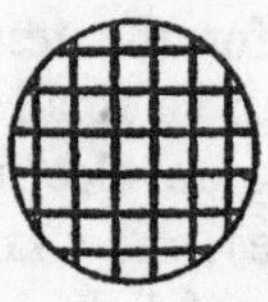

FIG. A18. Polishing setup. The tool is covered with a layer of pitch in which channels are cut.

mixture of water and polishing agent. See Fig. A18.

The polishing consists of moving the mirror over the pitch-covered tool with a ⅓ diameter stroke center over center, and should be continued until all the pits (which may be seen through a magnifying glass) are removed from the mirror. The rotational motions used in grinding (rotation of the mirror and walking about the tool) are used in polishing as well.

J. The job of changing the spherical into a paraboloidal shape is known as "figuring." It will be recalled that paraboloidal shape is superior to spherical as it converges all the paraxial (parallel to axis) rays entering the telescope to meet in a single point (the focus).

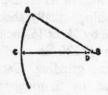

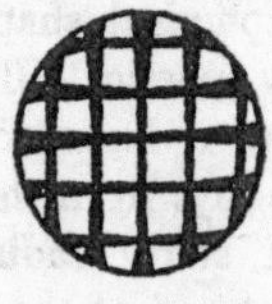

FIG. A19. View of the polishing tool, when used for figuring. The facets (the squares) are smaller near the perimeter; hence less polish abrasion takes place there. The central part of the mirror becomes more curved than the outlying zones, typical of the paraboloidal shape.

One of the ways to figure a spherical mirror is known as "parabolizing by graduating facets." In this method, the channels are widened progressively from center to edge, thus decreasing the area of the facets and the resulting rate of polish abrasion. The center of

the mirror is thus deepened faster than its edges; the cross section acquires the curvature typical of a parabola. See Fig. A19.

A perfect cross section is obtained when the radius of the peripheral zones, such as AB, is longer than the radius at the axis, CD, by an amount $\frac{R}{r^2}$, where r is the radius of the face of the mirror and R is the average radius of the curvature. See Fig. A20.

FIG. A20. A parabola is more curved at its center than at the edges, hence the radius CD is smaller than the radius AB.

In the example under consideration, the radius is 3 inches and the radius of curvature is approximately 96 inches (twice the focal length of 48 inches); hence, AB should be longer by $\frac{3^2}{96} = \frac{9}{96} = .09$ inch, or approximately .1 inch longer than CD.

K. The equipment used in the Foucault test for spherical shape can be used for testing the paraboloidal shape of the mirror. This testing consists basically in measuring the two radii AB and CD; the polishing continues until such time as the difference in length between AB and CD is equal to $\frac{r^2}{R}$. When AB is measured, the central part of the mirror is covered with non-reflecting material, the light being reflected toward the eye from the peripheral zones only. When CD is measured, the peripheral zones are made non-reflecting.

L. The aluminizing of the mirror has to be performed under vacuum and is best done in shops specializing in that kind of work.

GLOSSARY

Absolute Magnitude. The magnitude that would be assigned to a star if it were placed at a distance of 10 parsecs from the observer. Stars closer to us than that distance would appear fainter. Stars farther from the solar system would appear brighter.

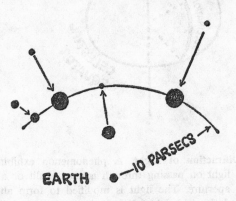

Achromatic Lens. A lens that transmits white light without dispersing it into a color spectrum. It usually consists of two component parts, cemented together to form one unit.

Albedo. Percentage of light reflected by a body, such as a planet, of total amount of light falling on it.

Altitude. Angular distance between the horizon and a given object, measured along a vertical circle.

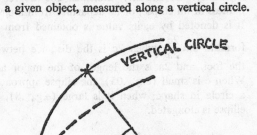

Annular Eclipse. An eclipse of the central portion of the solar disk; an outer ring shows.

Aphelion. The point on planet's orbit farthest from the sun.

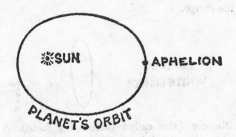

Apogee. Point on the moon's orbit farthest from the earth.

Apollo. The name assigned to the U.S. project, whose mission was to land men on the moon. Also the name of the vehicles used. Apollo 11 landed Neil Armstrong and Edwin Aldrin on the moon on July 20, 1969.

Artificial Satellite. A man-made object placed into an orbit about the earth or about another celestial body such as the sun or the moon.

Astronomical Unit. The average distance between the earth and the sun 93 million miles or, more exactly, 92,955,700.

Aurora. A diffused glow of light in the form of curtains, or bands, seen at high latitudes (70° N or 70° S). The glow is due to the interaction between the solar wind and particles in the earth's atmosphere. The aurora in the northern hemisphere is known as the Aurora Borealis, or northern lights; in the southern hemisphere it is known as the Aurora Australis, or southern lights.

Binary Star. Two close stars held together by a gravitational force and revolving like a dumbbell about a common center of gravity. The center is closer to the more massive star.

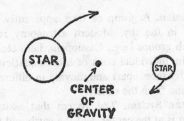

Cassini's Division. The empty space that separates the outer rings of Saturn from the bright inner rings.

Celestial Sphere. An imaginary sphere of infinite radius surrounding the earth and serving as a screen against which all celestial objects are seen.

Cepheid. A star the brightness of which varies periodically because of pulsations.

Chromatic Aberration (also called **Color Defect**). Blurring of image due to the separation of colors by a lens. A point of white light in the object appears as a complete spectrum of colored points in the image.

Collimator (also called **Collimating Lens**). A lens whose function it is to make rays of light parallel.

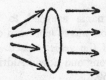

Colure, equinoctial (also called **Prime Hour Circle**). The hour circle that goes through the first point of Aries. The hour angles (same as longitude on earth) are measured from the equinoctial colure.

Conjunction. Apparent line-up of sun, earth, and a planet. Inferior conjunction is when the planet is between the earth and the sun.

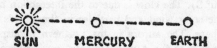

Superior conjunction is when the planet is on the opposite side of the sun.

Constellation. A group of stars apparently close together in the sky. Modern astronomy recognizes 88 such groups (e.g., Cassiopeia, Leo, etc.). Actually, the individual stars of a constellation may be great distances apart and moving in different directions one from the other.

Copernican System. The system that assumes that the sun is at the center, and the earth and the other planets move around it.

Culmination. The position of a celestial body when it is on the meridian. A star is said to be at its "upper culmination" when it has reached its highest point for the day.

Declination. Angular distance of an object from the celestial equator, measured in degrees, minutes and seconds. Analogous to latitude in geography.

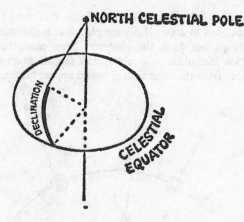

Diffraction of Light. A phenomenon exhibited by light on passing through a narrow slit or a small aperture. The light is modified to form alternate dark and bright fringes.

Discrete Source. A small area in the sky—almost a point—from which very intense electromagnetic waves of radio frequency reach the earth. These points were formerly called radio stars.

Doppler Effect. Change in frequency of light due to relative motion between observer and source of light.

Eccentricity. Eccentricity indicates the degree of flatness of an ellipse, or its departure from a circle. It is denoted by e; its value is obtained from the formula $e = \frac{2c}{2a}$, when 2c is the distance between the foci, and 2a is the length of the major axis. When e is small (e.g., .05), the ellipse approaches a circle in shape; when it is large (e.g., .8), the ellipse is elongated.

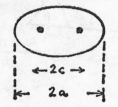

Eclipse

  A. *Solar.* The sun's light is cut off by the moon's interposition between the sun and the earth.

  B. *Lunar.* The moon darkens because the earth intercepts the sunlight on its way to the moon.

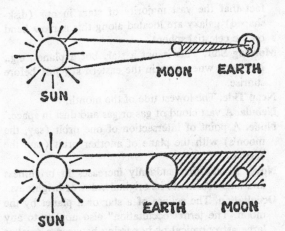

Ecliptic. Two equivalent definitions are possible.

A. The great circle on the celestial sphere formed by the intersection of that sphere with the plane of the earth's orbit.

B. The path described on the celestial sphere by the sun during its apparent annual motion around the earth.

Elongation. Angular distance from the sun, measured in degrees, minutes and seconds of angle.

Ephemeris. A book of tables showing computed daily positions of heavenly objects.

Equinox. One of the points of intersection between the ecliptic and the celestial equator. When the sun is at one of these two points, the length of day and night are equal everywhere on the earth. The sun is at these points every year on or about March 21 (vernal) and September 23 (autumnal).

Evening Star. This is not a star, but a planet, especially Mercury or Venus when seen in the western sky just after sunset.

Extragalactic. Beyond our galaxy.

Faculae. Areas on the surface of the sun that appear brighter by comparison to surrounding regions.

Flyby. A research mission in which the satellite collects data while passing close to the object of research.

Galaxy. A large community of stars in space, such as the Milky Way (our galaxy), to which the sun belongs. Galaxies contain billions of stars. Many are shaped in the form of a spiral.

Gemini. The name given to the U.S. program, as well as to the vehicles, designed to prepare man for landing on the moon. Gemini 3 to Gemini 12 (1965–66) carried crews of two astronauts each. The program included space walks, rendezvous with other spacecraft, as well as docking techniques.

Granules. The smallest visible units on the sun's surface. Granules or granulations have diameters hundreds of miles long. They change in size and in structure continuously.

Heliocentric Parallax. The apparent motion of nearby stars seen against the background of far away stars. The apparent motion is actually due to the revolution of the earth around the sun.

Helmholtz Contraction. The theory that the energy of the light emitted by a star is derived from the gravitational potential energy (i.e., contraction) of the star.

Hertzsprung-Russell Diagram. A diagram showing a scatter distribution of stars according to luminosity and temperature. The scatter distribution is related to the various ages of the stars.

Hour Angle. This is analogous to longitude in geography: an angle between the local celestial meridian and the hour circle of a given object in the sky, measured westward from the meridian. It may be given in units of time (hours, minutes and seconds); 1 hour=15 degrees of angle. Hour angles are easily visualized as either arcs along the celestial equator, or angles at the celestial poles.

Hour Circle. This is similar to meridian in geography: a great circle passing through the two celestial poles.

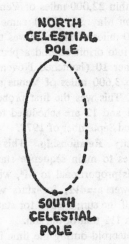

Hubble's Constant. The ratio of the velocity of recession to the distance of a galaxy. This ratio is 100 km/sec for every 1 million parsecs.

Infrared Radiation. Invisible radiation of wavelength slightly longer than red light.

Ionosphere. Several layers of ionized air high in the atmosphere. The ionosphere plays an important part in reflecting radio waves.

Libration. Apparent "rocking" or "nodding" of moon or the planet Mercury. Due to this oscillation, some of the usually hidden sides are exhibited to the terrestrial observer.

Light Year. The distance that light travels in a year.

Luminosity. The ratio of the total light emitted by a celestial object to the total light emitted by the sun. Also, the total energy emitted by a star, per second.

Lunar Module. The term for the vehicles that carried two men, in the Apollo project, from the command modules to the surface of the moon and back.

Magellanic Clouds. These are not clouds; they are galaxies. Two relatively nearby galaxies visible from the southern hemisphere, of irregular shape, named after Magellan, the Portuguese explorer who first described them.

Magnitude (also called **Apparent Magnitude**). A number indicating the apparent brightness of a star. Bright stars are designated by small numbers (magnitude 1, say) while dim stars are designated by large numbers (e.g., magnitude 15).

Main Sequence. A band in the scatter Hertzsprung-Russell diagram. It includes more than 80 per cent of all stars. The energy emitted by these stars is obtained from thermonuclear reactions in the core of the stars.

Mariner. The name given to a U.S. series of space probes designed to obtain data from Venus, Mercury, and Mars. On December 14, 1962, Mariner 2 passed within 22,000 miles of Venus. Mariner 9 (launched on May 30, 1971) came within a distance of 900 miles of Mars. It was the first spacecraft to go into oribit around a planet other than earth. Mariner 10 (launched November 3, 1973) came within 3,600 miles of Venus and 450 miles of Mercury. This was the first probe of Mercury. Mariners 11 and 12 are scheduled to be launched in August and September of 1977.

Mass-Luminosity Relationship. This relationship, which applies to main sequence stars, states that luminosity is proportional to M^a, where M=mass and the power a=4½, for stars whose mass is less than half the sun; a=3½ for stars whose mass is more than 1½ that of the sun.

Meteor. A meteoroid during the time it is giving off light. Also called a shooting star.

Meteorite. A meteoroid that survived, because of its size, collision with the earth's atmosphere and reached the earth's surface. Meteorites can be seen on exhibit in many natural history museums.

Meteoroid. A tiny solid object, usually the size of a sand particle, which the earth encounters in its orbit around the sun.

Micrometeorite. A fine dust particle floating in space, too small to be seen with unaided eye and too small to become incandescent during its passage through the atmosphere.

Milky Way. A luminous band across the sky, of which our galaxy is part. The light is due to the fact that the vast majority of stars in our (disk-shaped) galaxy are located along this narrow band on the celestial sphere.

Morning Star. This is not a star, but a planet, e.g., Mercury, when seen in the eastern sky just before sunrise.

Neap Tide. The lowest tide of the month.

Nebula. A vast cloud of gas or gas and dust in space.

Node. A point of intersection of one orbit (say, the moon's) with the plane of another orbit (say, the earth's).

Nova. A star that suddenly increases in brightness and later returns to its original value of brightness.

Occultation. The eclipse of a star or a planet by the moon. The term "occultation" also applies to any large astronomical body passing between a smaller body and the observer.

Parallax. Apparent shift of position of an object with respect to its background due to a shift in position of the observer. An observer at A sees the star in region a of the sky. An observer at B sees the same star in region b.

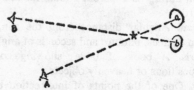

Parsec. A unit of stellar distance. It is the distance BD in the triangle ABD.
One parsec is equal to 19.2 million million miles.

Penumbra. The outer and lighter part of a shadow cast by a planet or satellite, as in regions A and B.

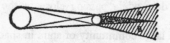

Perigee. The point in orbit of, say, the moon nearest the earth (point A).

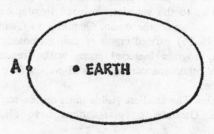

Perihelion. The point in orbit of a planet or a comet nearest the sun (point A).

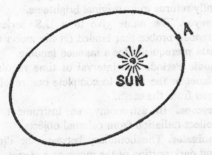

Photosphere. The visible surface of the sun or star. Below it is the interior of the sun; above it, the atmosphere.

Pioneer. The name given to the first series of U.S. unmanned space-probe vehicles. They were instrumental in developing launching and guiding techniques for the Mariner, Lunar Orbiter, Ranger, and Surveyor series.

Planet. One of the nine bodies revolving about the sun in almost circular orbits. Planets are made visible to us by reflected sunlight. It is reasonable to assume that many stars have planets revolving about them.

Planetary Nebula. A nebula resembling a planet in shape.

Planetoid (also called **Asteroid**). A small irregularly shaped solid body revolving about the sun. Also considered to be a minor planet.

Plasma. An ionized gas.

Poles, Celestial. Points of intersection of extensions of earth's axis and the celestial sphere.

Precession. The slow change in direction of the earth's axis due to the gravitational pull of the moon on the bulge at the earth's equator. The slow change in the axis causes the westward motion of the equinoxes among the constellations.

Proper Motion of Star. The angular velocity (in seconds of angle per year) of a star in a direction perpendicular to the line of sight of a terrestrial observer.

Protostar. The portion of a nebula that is about to become a star.

Pulsar. A neutron star emitting pulsed radio signals. The first pulsar was discovered in 1967. Its pulse lasts ⅓ of a second and repeats with great regularity every 1⅓ second.

Pulsating Stars. Stars that periodically vary in brightness because of periodic changes in volume.

Quadrature. An elongation of 90° east or west of the sun.

Quasar. The popular name for quasi-stellar object. These are extremely luminous objects (the most luminous known) at enormous distances (the most distant object known), which generate incredible amounts of energy. The true nature of quasars is still under study.

Radial Velocity of Star. The velocity (in miles or kilometers per second) in line of sight of a terrestrial observer.

Radiant Point of Meteors. A point in the sky from which meteors seem to come.

Radio Astronomy. The branch of astronomy that deals with the radio waves emitted by various celestial bodies, as well as the theory of their emission.

Radio Star. See **Discrete Source.**

Radio Telescope. An instrument used for examination of celestial objects by means of the radio waves emitted by these objects.

Radio Window. The transparency of the atmosphere to radio waves that range between .25 cm and 30 m in length.

Ranger. The name given to a series of nine U.S. lunar probe vehicles, designed to transmit photographs before crashlanding on the moon. More than 17,000 photographs were obtained from the Rangers, the closest one taken .2 seconds before impact.

Red Giant. A member of the giant sequence in the Hertzsprung-Russell diagram. They have radii fifteen to thirty times larger than the radius of sun and luminosities a hundred times that of the sun.

Red Shift. The shift of all spectral lines toward longer wavelengths observed in all galaxies. Galactic red shift is due to the expansion of the universe. Gravitational red shift is due to the high value of the mass of the emitter.

Refraction. A change in direction of light on entering a different medium (such as glass).

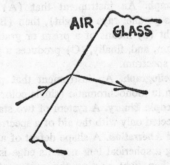

Resolving Power of Telescope. The power to separate two close points into two distinct units.

Retrograde Motion. Apparent backward (westward) motion of a planet, through a starfield.

Reversing Layer. The lowest of the three solar atmospheric layers; it is responsible for most of the dark lines in the solar spectrum.

Right Ascension. The angular distance from the prime meridian to a celestial body measured eastward along the celestial equator from 0° to 360°, or from 0 to 24 hours. Analogous to longitude in geography.

Rocket. A tube designed to move through space that derives its thrust by ejecting hot, expanding gases —called a jet—that have been generated in its motor. The rocket contains within itself all the material needed for the production of the jet.

Saros. The interval (about 18⅓ years) between two successive lunar or solar eclipses of the same series.

Satellite. A celestial body revolving about one of the planets; e.g., the moon. Also any small body that revolves about a larger body, man-made or otherwise.

Sedimentary Rocks. Rocks formed by precipitation from water or any other solution.

Service Module. That part of the vehicle in the Apollo and other programs that contains the power, supplies, and fuel.

Sidereal Period. The interval of time required by a planet to make one revolution (as seen from one of the fixed stars) about the sun.

Solar Constant. The quantity of radiant solar heat, 1.94 calories per minute, received per square centimeter of the earth's surface.

Solar Wind. The material, mainly protons and electrons, streaming out from the sun into space. The sun loses normally millions of tons per second of its mass because of this wind.

Solstice. The point of maximum declination of the earth on the ecliptic. The solstices are halfway between the equinoctial points. In the northern hemisphere, the summer solstice occurs when the sun is farthest north from the equator; the winter solstice, when the sun is farthest south.

Space Probe. An unmanned vehicle that is sent into space to obtain scientific data.

Spectrograph. An instrument that (A) collimates (makes parallel rays of light), then (B) disperses the light (by means of a prism or grating) into a spectrum, and, finally, (C) produces a photograph of the spectrum.

Spectroheliograph. An instrument that photographs the sun in monochromatic (single color) light.

Spectroscopic Binary. A system of two stars that can be detected only with the aid of a spectroscope.

Spherical Aberration. A shape defect of a lens. Light passing a spherical lens near its edge is converged more than light passing the center of the same lens, which causes the image to blur.

Spiral Nebula. A galaxy of stars (*not* a nebula) in the form of a spiral.

Star. A large globe of intensely hot gas, shining by its own light (e.g., the sun).

Sunspots. Dark (by contrast with the surroundings) patches that appear from time to time on the photosphere of the sun.

Supernova. A star that quite suddenly increases, perhaps a million times, in brightness. It is similar to a nova, but its increase is vastly greater. It never fully returns to its original brightness.

Surveyor. The name give to a U.S. series of unmanned probes that landed on the moon to obtain data prerequisite for a manned landing.

Synodic Period. The interval of time required by a planet or the moon to complete one revolution, as seen from the earth.

Telescope. In astronomy, an instrument used to collect radiation from celestial objects.

Terminator. The boundary between the illuminated and dark portion of the moon or a planet.

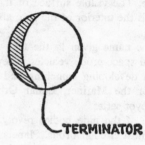

Transit. The motion of a small body (e.g., Mercury) across the face of a larger body (e.g., the sun).

Tropical Year. The ordinary year. The year used in everyday life.

Umbra. The dark shadow cast by a planet or a satellite.

Universal Time. Greenwich time. The mean solar time at the 0° meridian passing through Greenwich, England. Used as a world standard.

Van Allen Radiation Belts. Two doughnut-shaped regions surrounding the earth in which high-energy particles are trapped.

Velocity of Escape. The velocity that an object must acquire in order to escape from the gravitational pull exerted upon it by another body. The velocity of escape at the earth's surface is 7 miles per second. Any terrestrial body that can reach this velocity will permanently leave the earth.

Venera. The name given a U.S.S.R. series of space probes made to collect data about Venus.

White Dwarf. A white star of low luminosity, small size, and extremely high density.

Zeeman Effect. A change in wavelength of emitted light when the source of light is placed in a magnetic field.

Zenith. The point on the celestial sphere directly overhead.

Zodiac. A band of the celestial sphere, 8° wide, on each side of the ecliptic. The zodiac is divided lengthwise into twelve equal sections; each 30° section is popularly identified by a "sign of the zodiac." The signs are named for the constellations that were located in them at the time of Hipparchus more than 2,000 years ago. The sun, moon, and planets appear to "travel" within this belt. The sun passes through three signs each season of the year, e.g., during spring the sun passes through Aries, Taurus, and Gemini.

INDEX